MW00659395

EVIDENCE

FIFTH EDITION

STEVEN L. EMANUEL

Founder and Editor-in-Chief, the *CrunchTime* series,
Emanuel Law Outlines, and *Emanuel Bar Review*

Harvard Law School, J.D. 1976
Member, NY, CT, MD and VA bars

The *CrunchTime*® Series

Wolters Kluwer
Law & Business

Published by Wolters Kluwer Law & Business in New York.

Wolters Kluwer Law & Business serves customers worldwide with CCH, Aspen Publishers, and Kluwer Law International products. (www.wolterskluwerlb.com)

To contact Customer Service, e-mail customer.service@wolterskluwer.com, call 1-800-234-1660, fax 1-800-901-9075, or mail correspondence to:

Wolters Kluwer Law & Business
Attn: Order Department
PO Box 990
Frederick, MD 21705

Printed in the United States of America.

6 7 8 9 0

ISBN 978-1-4548-2489-3

About Wolters Kluwer Law & Business

Wolters Kluwer Law & Business is a leading global provider of intelligent information and digital solutions for legal and business professionals in key specialty areas, and respected educational resources for professors and law students. Wolters Kluwer Law & Business connects legal and business professionals as well as those in the education market with timely, specialized authoritative content and information-enabled solutions to support success through productivity, accuracy and mobility.

Serving customers worldwide, Wolters Kluwer Law & Business products include those under the Aspen Publishers, CCH, Kluwer Law International, Loislaw, Best Case, ftwilliam.com and MediRegs family of products.

CCH products have been a trusted resource since 1913, and are highly regarded resources for legal, securities, antitrust and trade regulation, government contracting, banking, pension, payroll, employment and labor, and healthcare reimbursement and compliance professionals.

Aspen Publishers products provide essential information to attorneys, business professionals and law students. Written by preeminent authorities, the product line offers analytical and practical information in a range of specialty practice areas from securities law and intellectual property to mergers and acquisitions and pension/benefits. Aspen's trusted legal education resources provide professors and students with high-quality, up-to-date and effective resources for successful instruction and study in all areas of the law.

Kluwer Law International products provide the global business community with reliable international legal information in English. Legal practitioners, corporate counsel and business executives around the world rely on Kluwer Law journals, looseleafs, books, and electronic products for comprehensive information in many areas of international legal practice.

Loislaw is a comprehensive online legal research product providing legal content to law firm practitioners of various specializations. Loislaw provides attorneys with the ability to quickly and efficiently find the necessary legal information they need, when and where they need it, by facilitating access to primary law as well as state-specific law, records, forms and treatises.

Best Case Solutions is the leading bankruptcy software product to the bankruptcy industry. It provides software and workflow tools to flawlessly streamline petition preparation and the electronic filing process, while timely incorporating ever-changing court requirements.

ftwilliam.com offers employee benefits professionals the highest quality plan documents (retirement, welfare and non-qualified) and government forms (5500/PBGC, 1099 and IRS) software at highly competitive prices.

MediRegs products provide integrated health care compliance content and software solutions for professionals in healthcare, higher education and life sciences, including professionals in accounting, law and consulting.

Wolters Kluwer Law & Business, a division of Wolters Kluwer, is headquartered in New York. Wolters Kluwer is a market-leading global information services company focused on professionals.

TABLE OF CONTENTS

Preface

Thank you for buying this book.

The *CrunchTime* Series is intended for people who want Emanuel quality, but don't have the time or money to buy and use the full-length *Emanuel Law Outline* on a subject. We've designed the Series to be used in the last few weeks (or even less) before your final exams.

This book includes the following features, some of which have been extracted from the corresponding *Emanuel Law Outline*:

- ***Flow Charts*** — We've reduced most principles of *Evidence* to a series of Flow Charts written by Professor David Faigman. We think these will be especially useful on open-book exams. A summary list of all the Flow Charts is printed on p. 2, with a more detailed list at the bottom of p. 4.
- ***Capsule Summary*** — This is a 105-page summary of the subject. We've carefully crafted it to cover the things you're most likely to be asked on an exam. The Capsule Summary starts on p. 27, following the Flow Charts.
- ***Exam Tips*** — We've compiled these by reviewing dozens of actual essay and multiple-choice questions asked in past law-school and bar exams, and extracting the issues and "tricks" that surface most often on exams. The Exam Tips start on p. 137.
- ***Short-Answer Questions and Answers*** — These questions are generally in a Yes/No format, with a "mini-essay" explaining each one. They've been adapted from our *Law in a Flash* Series. The questions start on p. 215, and the answers on p. 237.
- ***Multiple-Choice Questions and Answers*** — These are in a Multistate-Bar-Exam style, and are adapted from *The Finz Multistate Method,* also published by Wolters Kluwer Law & Business. The questions start on p. 267, and the answers on p. 281.

We hope you find this book helpful and instructive.

Steve Emanuel
Larchmont, NY
March 2013

FLOW CHARTS

SUMMARY OF CONTENTS
for
FLOW CHARTS

Note: For a more detailed Table of Contents to the Flow Charts, see page 4.

Evidence Flow Charts

By Professor David L. Faigman

University of California, Hastings College of the Law

Preface by Professor Faigman

These flow charts of the Federal Rules of Evidence are designed to provide a helpful guide for those who find themselves lost in the seemingly seamless web of the Federal Rules. One of the most difficult tasks confronting users of the Federal Rules involves integrating the details of individual rules into the greater structure of the Code. These charts meet that difficulty, endeavoring to make plain the details within particular Rules and, moreover, to illustrate the connections between certain Rules.

The flow charts are couched almost entirely in the language of the Rules. This format avoids the appearance that the charts constitute a delphic oracle for evidentiary queries. Contrary to their appearance, perhaps, the flow charts do not provide "answers" to the countless inquiries that might arise under the Rules. Instead, they arrange the questions that the user must scrutinize in order to reach satisfactory answers.

In the first instance, the flow charts provide a detailed rendering of the most often studied Rules. All of the Rules, to varying degrees, contain multiple components that can sometimes be quite confusing. Hence, the charts offer step-by-step guidance through the details within particular Rules.

Of greater importance, the flow charts also offer a schematic of the relations between certain Rules. Many perceive the subject of Evidence as a series of discrete areas, such as hearsay, character, expert testimony and so on, without appreciating how they relate to one another. The Rules, however, were intended to provide a comprehensive scheme to resolve questions of admissibility. Evidence does not come neatly divided into discrete packages, labeled "hearsay," "character," or some other designation. A single item of evidence might raise an assortment of evidence problems spanning the spectrum of the Rules. The real challenge comes from the difficulty in recognizing the range of possible objections posed by a particular form of evidence.

The flow charts provide an elementary attempt to illustrate some of the more important connections between particular Rules. Of course, the innumerable interactions among the many Federal Rules could never be fully captured in a set of flow charts. The charts, therefore, provide only a rough and rather incomplete guide to the Rules and cannot substitute for the personal exploration of the terrain necessary to fully understand its complexity. The flow charts are merely a beginning point; it is the user who must invest the time before meaningful discovery can occur.

Figure 1
An Overview of the Rules of Evidence

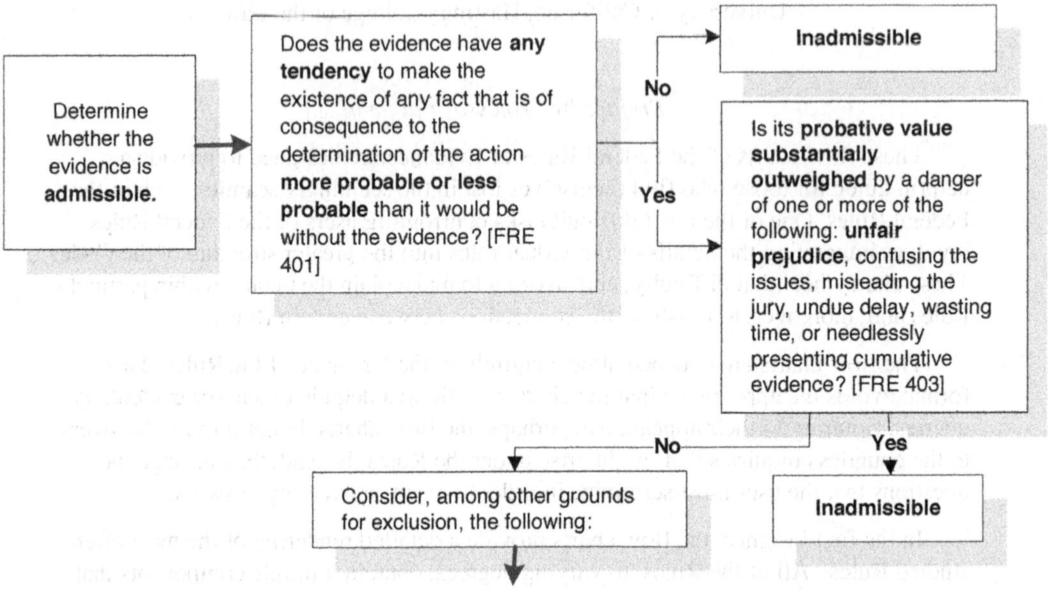

Figure 2

Judicial Notice of Adjudicative Facts

Rule 201

Does the matter concern an **adjudicative fact**[1] that is not subject to reasonable dispute in that it either:
(1) is **generally known** within the trial court's territorial jurisdiction; or
(2) can be accurately and readily **determined** from **sources whose accuracy cannot reasonably be questioned?**
[FRE 201(a) & (b)]

Yes

The Court **may take judicial notice.** Judicial notice may be taken **at any stage** of the proceeding [FRE 201{F)]; a court has discretion to take judicial notice **whether requested or not** [FRE 201(c)]; and a court **must** take judicial notice if requested by a party and supplied with the necessary information [FRE 201(d)].

No

The Court **may not take judicial notice**; consider general rules relating to the admissibility of evidence to prove the fact.

Note: A party is entitled upon timely request to an **opportunity to be heard** as to the propriety of taking judicial notice and the tenor of the matter noticed. In the absence of prior notification, the request may be made after judicial notice has been taken.

Is the proceeding in which judicial notice has been taken a **criminal proceeding**?

Yes

The court must instruct the jury that it **may or may not accept** the noticed fact as conclusive. [FRE 201(g)]

No

The court must instruct the jury to accept as **conclusive** any fact judicially noticed. [FRE 201(g)]

Footnotes:

1. Adjudicative facts are facts that relate to the specific case and typically involve the who, what, where, when and how questions of adjudication. Adjudicative facts are usefully contrasted with "legislative facts," which are fact questions that are relevant to resolving policy questions or interpretations of law. Whereas adjudicative facts are case-specific, legislative facts typically transcend a particular dispute.

Figure 3
Character Evidence

Character Evidence Generally; Methods of Proving Character; Habit
Rules 404, 405, 406

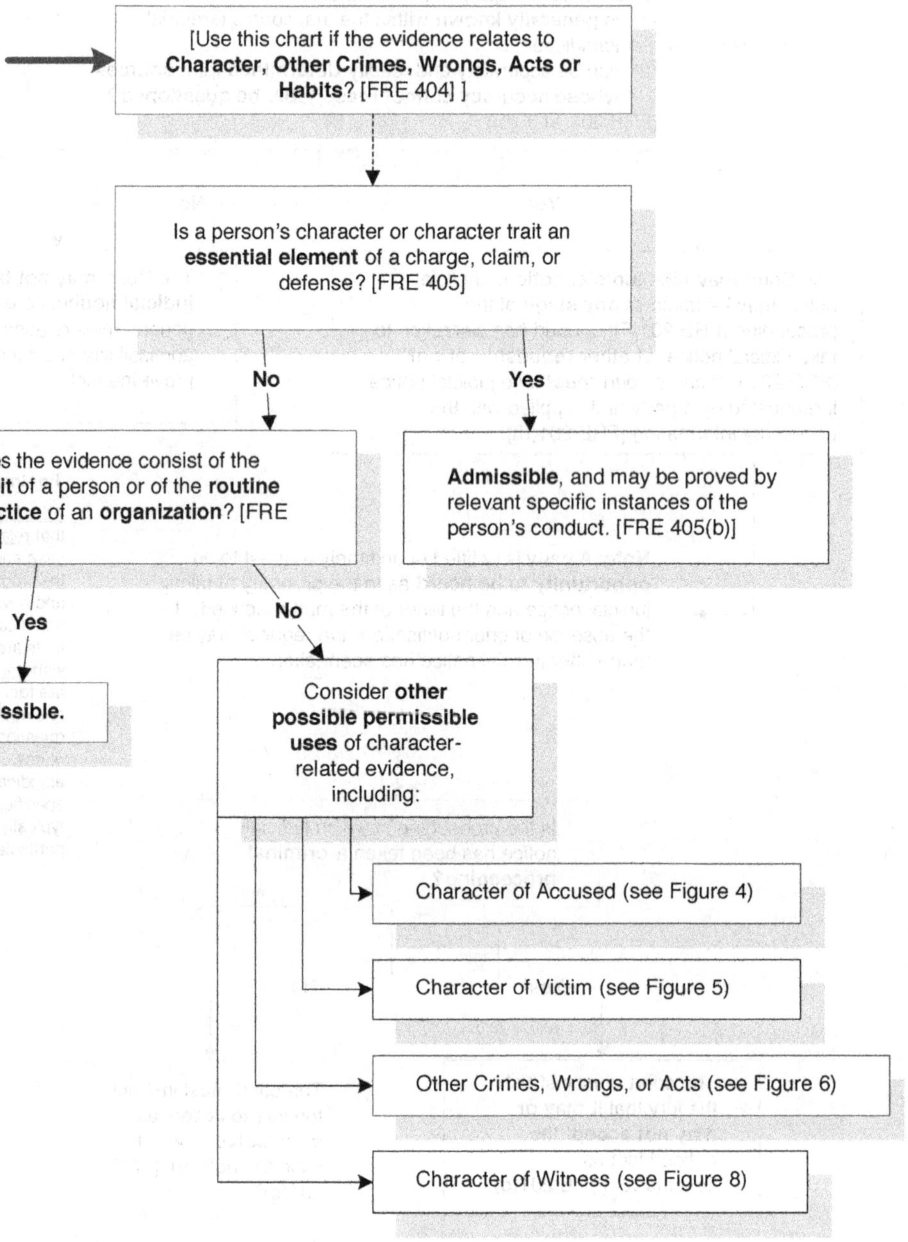

Figure 4
Character Evidence

Character of the Accused; Methods of Proving Character
Rules 404(a)(2), 405(a)

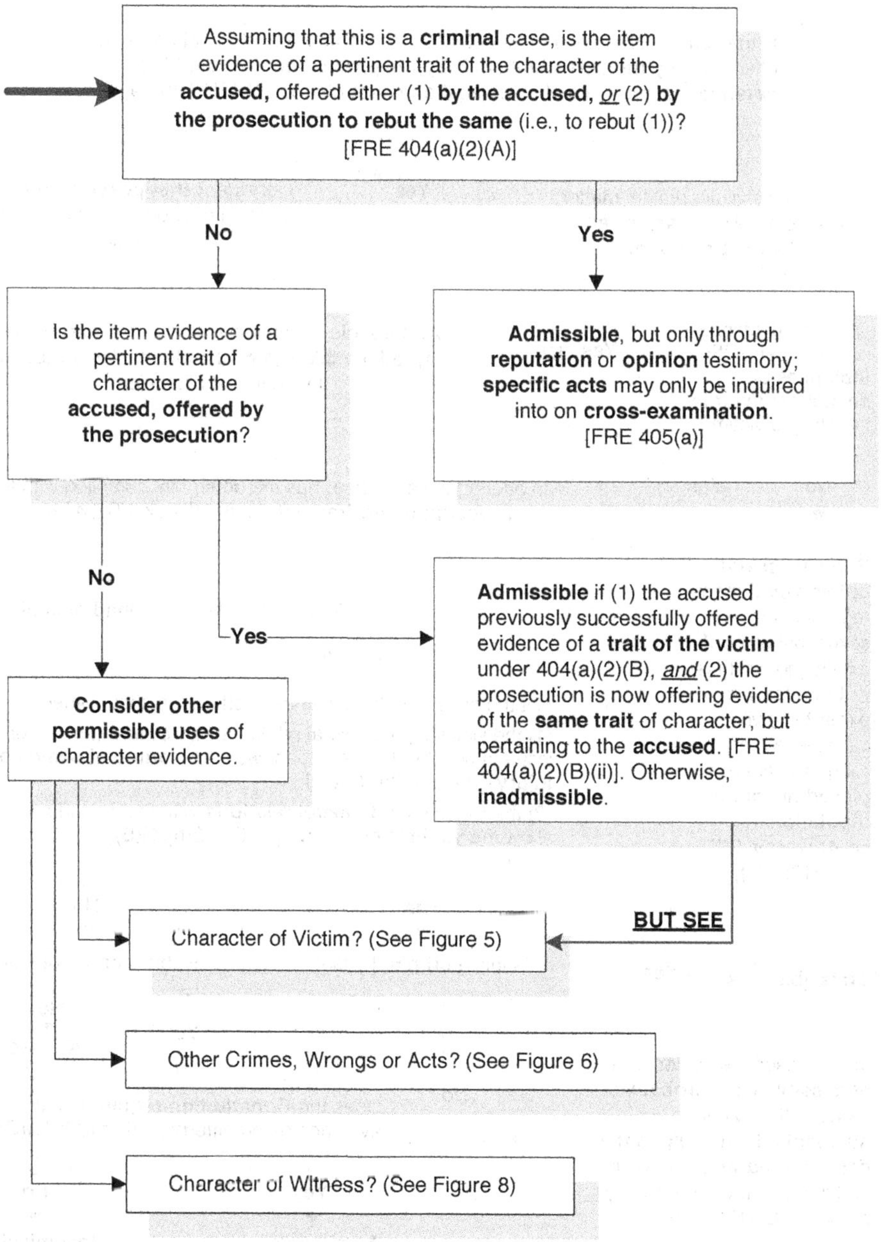

Figure 5
Character Evidence

Character of the Victim; Sex Offense Cases
Rules 404(a)(2), 412

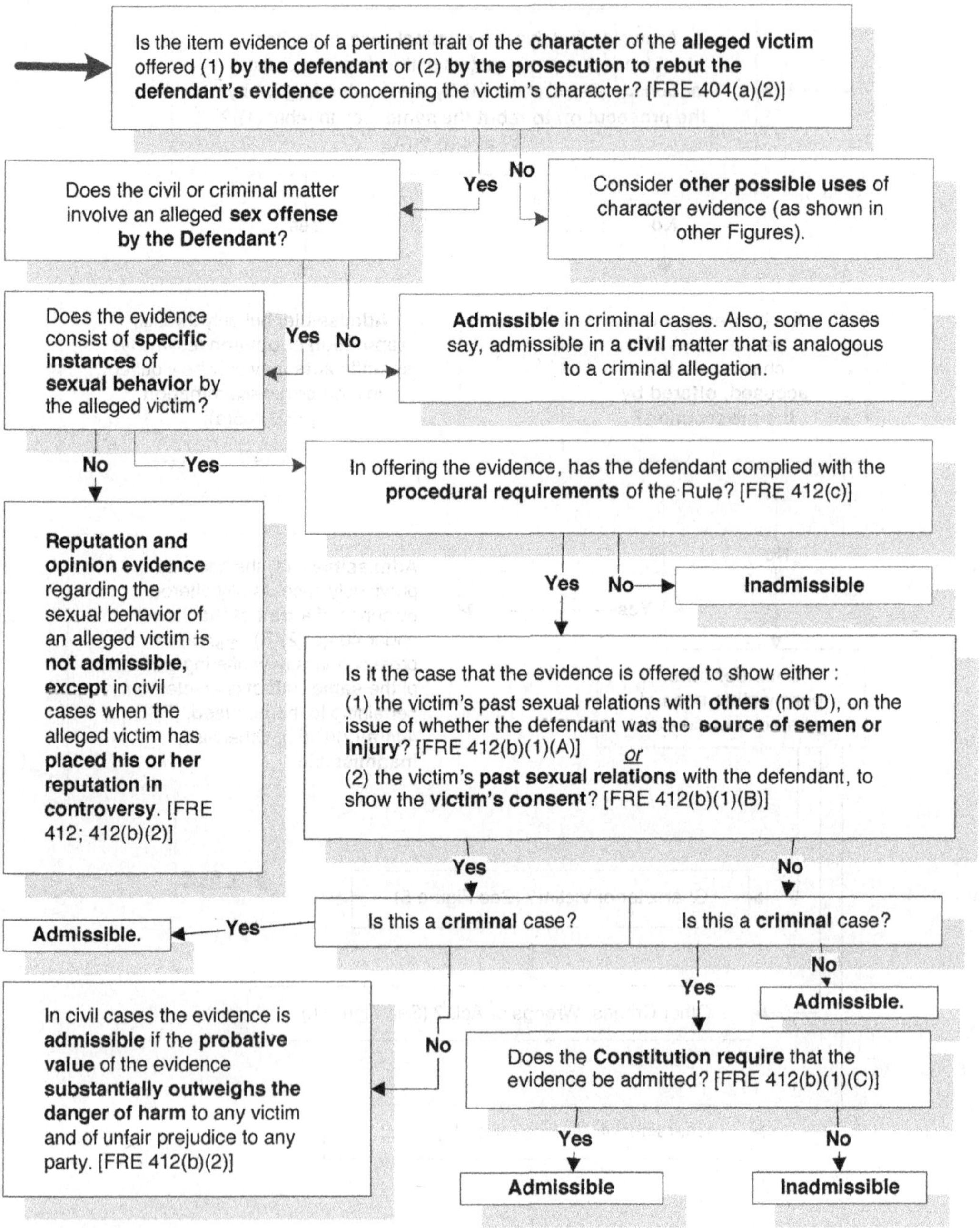

Figure 6
Character Evidence

Other Crimes, Wrongs, or Acts; Similar Crimes in Sexual Assault and Child-Molestation Cases
Rules 104(b), 403, 404(b), 413, 414, 415

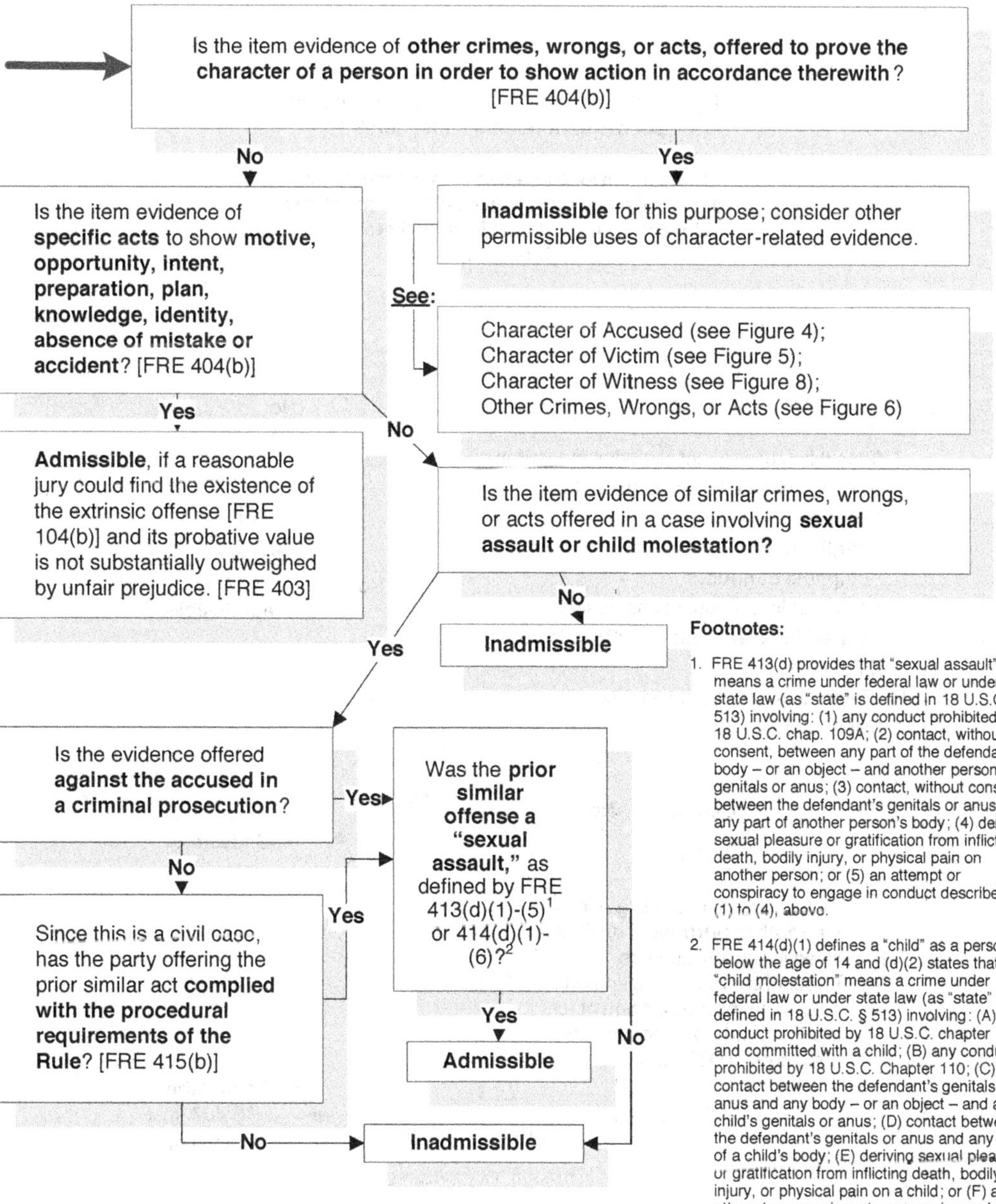

Footnotes:

1. FRE 413(d) provides that "sexual assault" means a crime under federal law or under state law (as "state" is defined in 18 U.S.C. § 513) involving: (1) any conduct prohibited by 18 U.S.C. chap. 109A; (2) contact, without consent, between any part of the defendant's body – or an object – and another person's genitals or anus; (3) contact, without consent, between the defendant's genitals or anus and any part of another person's body; (4) deriving sexual pleasure or gratification from inflicting death, bodily injury, or physical pain on another person; or (5) an attempt or conspiracy to engage in conduct described in (1) to (4), above.

2. FRE 414(d)(1) defines a "child" as a person below the age of 14 and (d)(2) states that "child molestation" means a crime under federal law or under state law (as "state" is defined in 18 U.S.C. § 513) involving: (A) any conduct prohibited by 18 U.S.C. chapter 109A and committed with a child; (B) any conduct prohibited by 18 U.S.C. Chapter 110; (C) contact between the defendant's genitals or anus and any body – or an object – and a child's genitals or anus; (D) contact between the defendant's genitals or anus and any part of a child's body; (E) deriving sexual pleasure or gratification from inflicting death, bodily injury, or physical pain on a child; or (F) an attempt or conspiracy to engage in conduct described in (A) to (E) above.

Figure 7
Character Evidence

Subsequent Remedial Measures
Rule 407

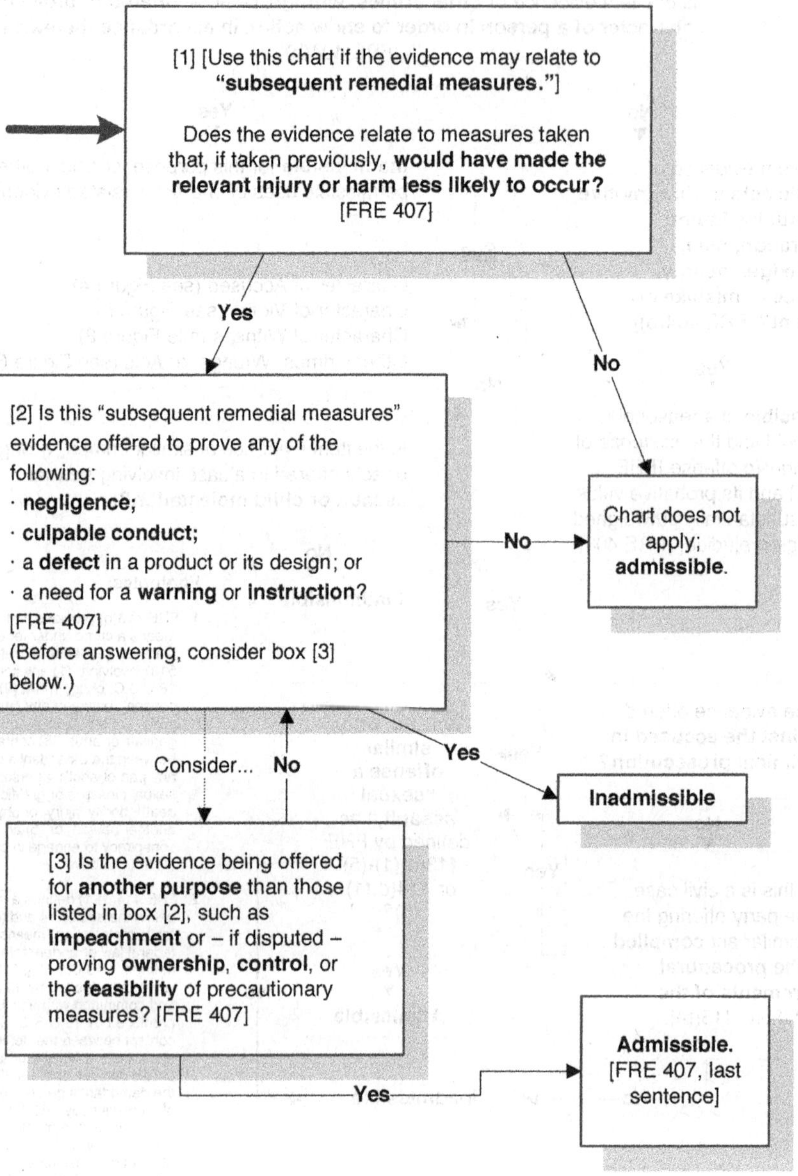

Figure 8
Character and Impeachment

Evidence of Character and Conduct of Witness; Impeachment by Conviction of Crime
Rules 403, 608, 609

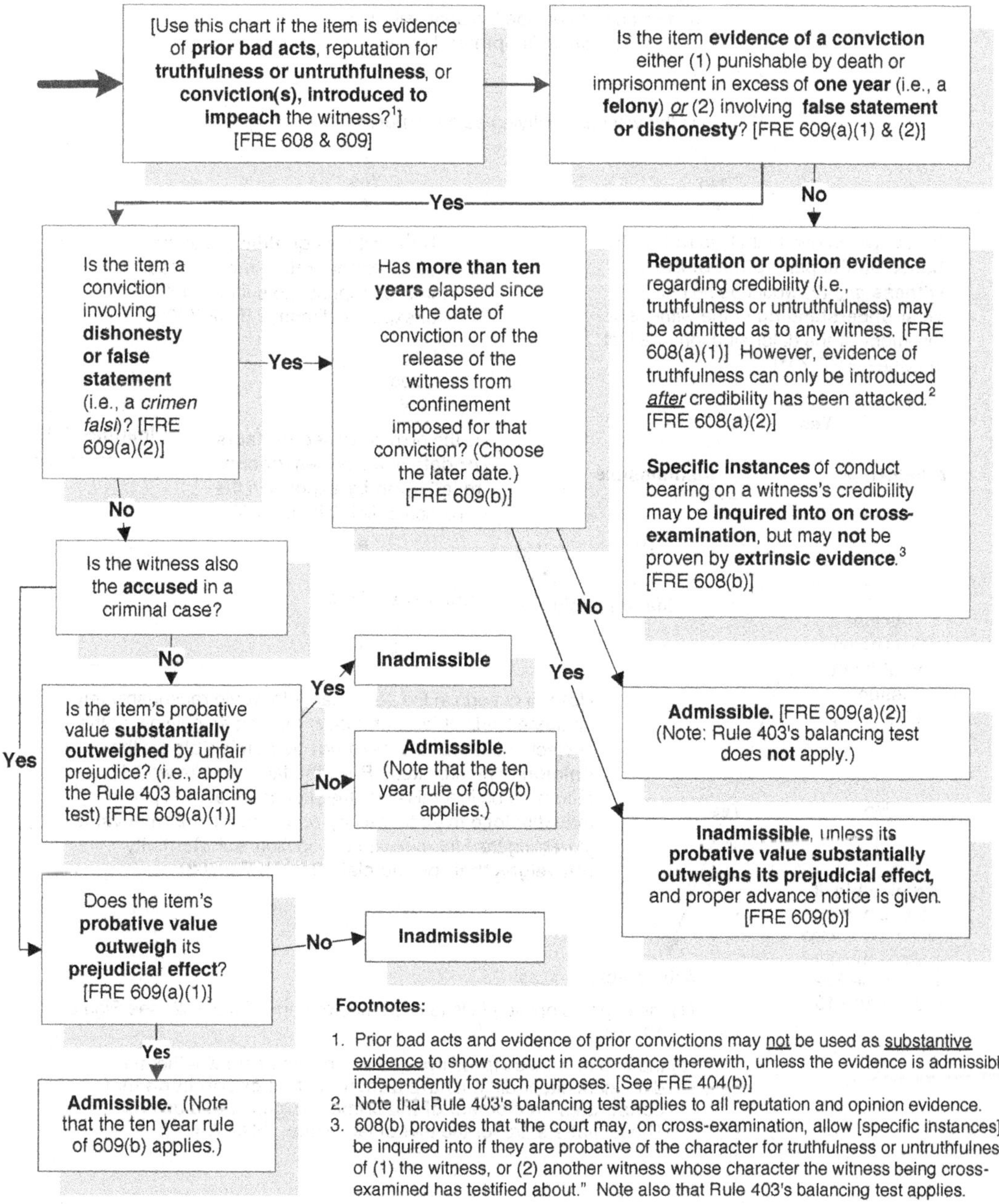

Footnotes:

1. Prior bad acts and evidence of prior convictions may <u>not</u> be used as <u>substantive evidence</u> to show conduct in accordance therewith, unless the evidence is admissible independently for such purposes. [See FRE 404(b)]
2. Note that Rule 403's balancing test applies to all reputation and opinion evidence.
3. 608(b) provides that "the court may, on cross-examination, allow [specific instances] to be inquired into if they are probative of the character for truthfulness or untruthfulness of (1) the witness, or (2) another witness whose character the witness being cross-examined has testified about." Note also that Rule 403's balancing test applies.

Figure 9
Opinion and Expert Testimony

Opinion Testimony by Lay & Expert Witnesses; Bases of Opinion Testimony by Experts; Opinion on Ultimate Issue
Rules 701, 702, 703, 704

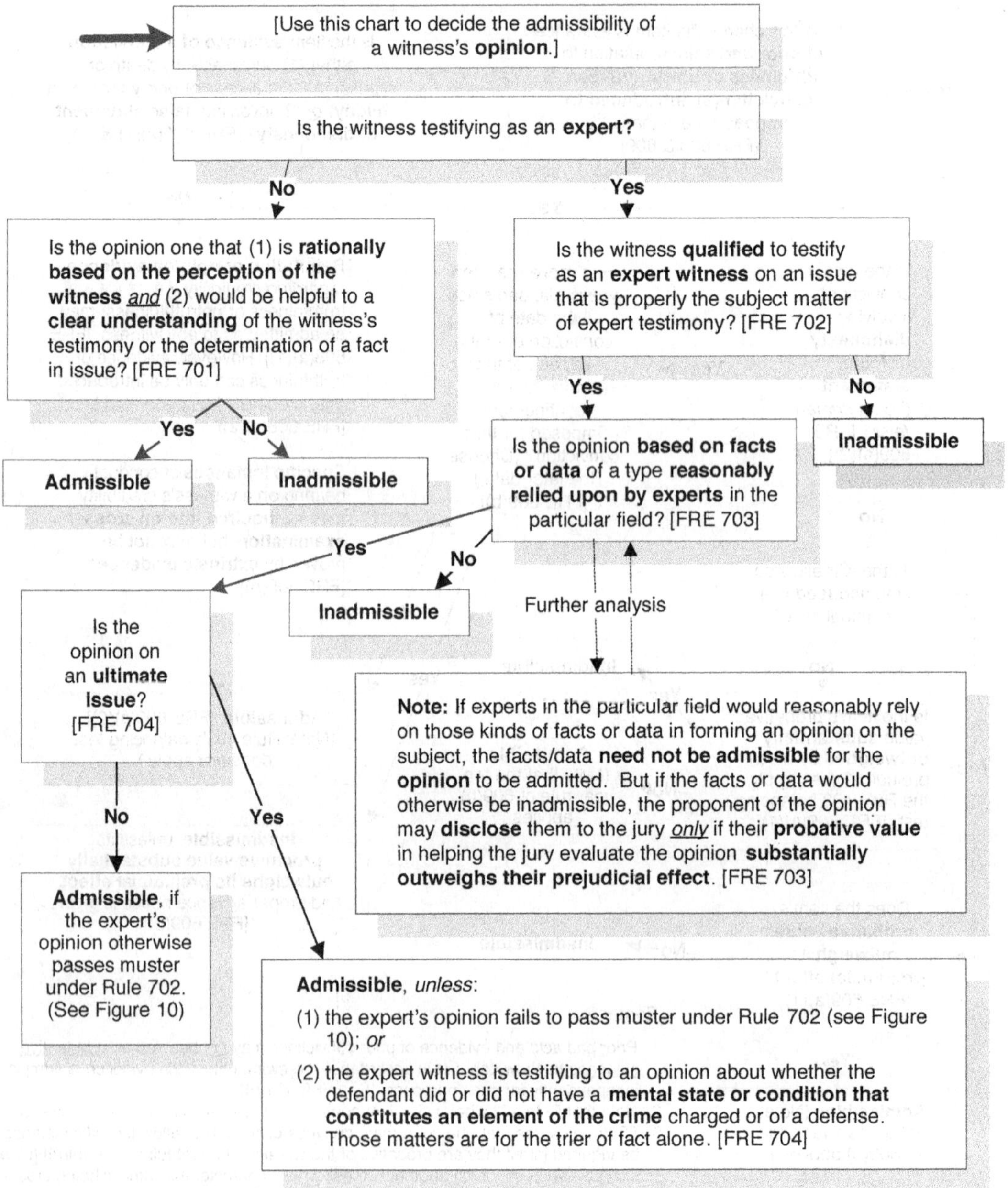

Figure 10
Opinion and Expert Testimony

Testimony by Expert Witnesses
Rules 104(a), 702

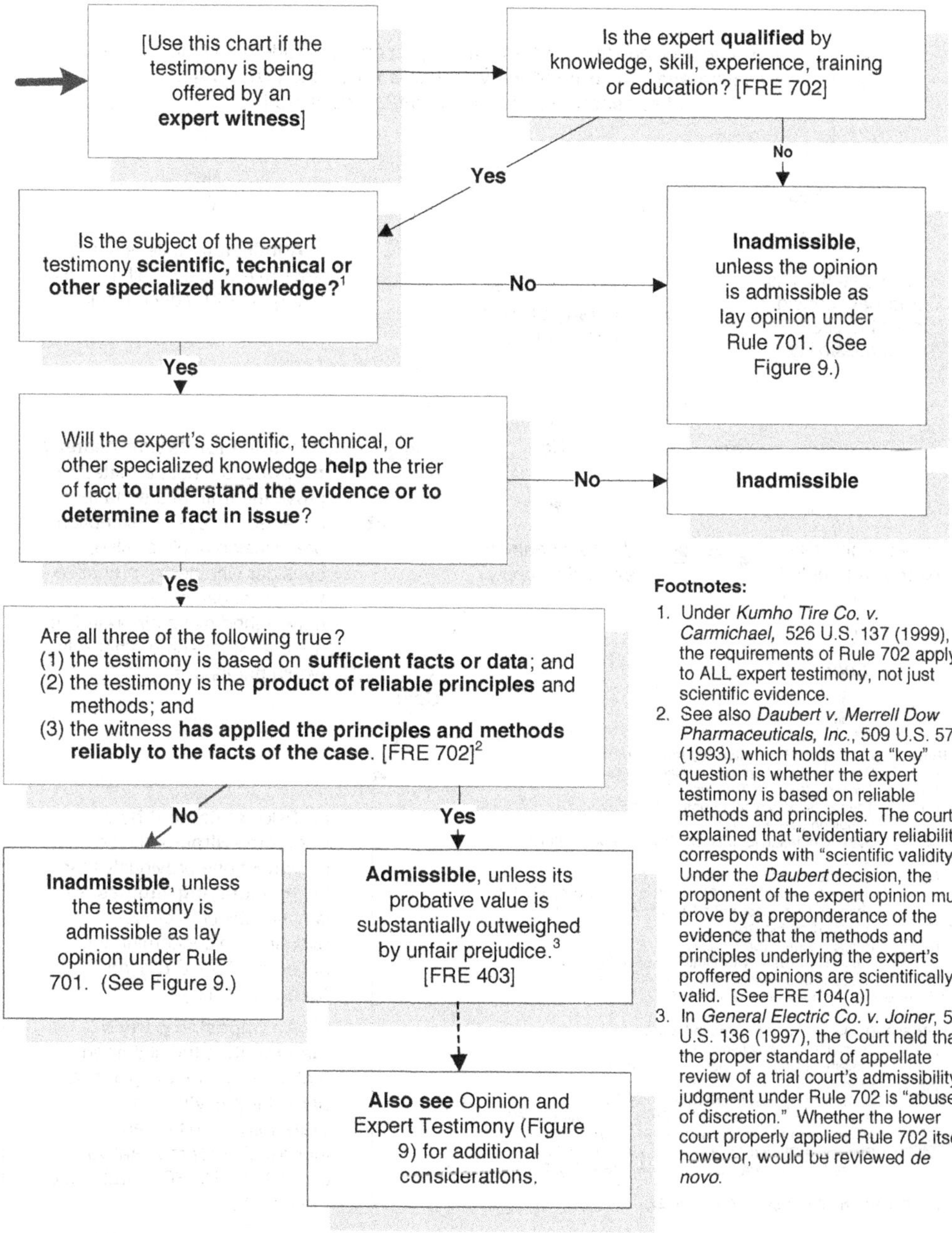

Footnotes:

1. Under *Kumho Tire Co. v. Carmichael,* 526 U.S. 137 (1999), the requirements of Rule 702 apply to ALL expert testimony, not just scientific evidence.
2. See also *Daubert v. Merrell Dow Pharmaceuticals, Inc.*, 509 U.S. 579 (1993), which holds that a "key" question is whether the expert testimony is based on reliable methods and principles. The court explained that "evidentiary reliability" corresponds with "scientific validity." Under the *Daubert* decision, the proponent of the expert opinion must prove by a preponderance of the evidence that the methods and principles underlying the expert's proffered opinions are scientifically valid. [See FRE 104(a)]
3. In *General Electric Co. v. Joiner*, 522 U.S. 136 (1997), the Court held that the proper standard of appellate review of a trial court's admissibility judgment under Rule 702 is "abuse of discretion." Whether the lower court properly applied Rule 702 itself, however, would be reviewed *de novo*.

Figure 11
Hearsay Evidence

Hearsay Generally
Rules 801, 802, 803, 804

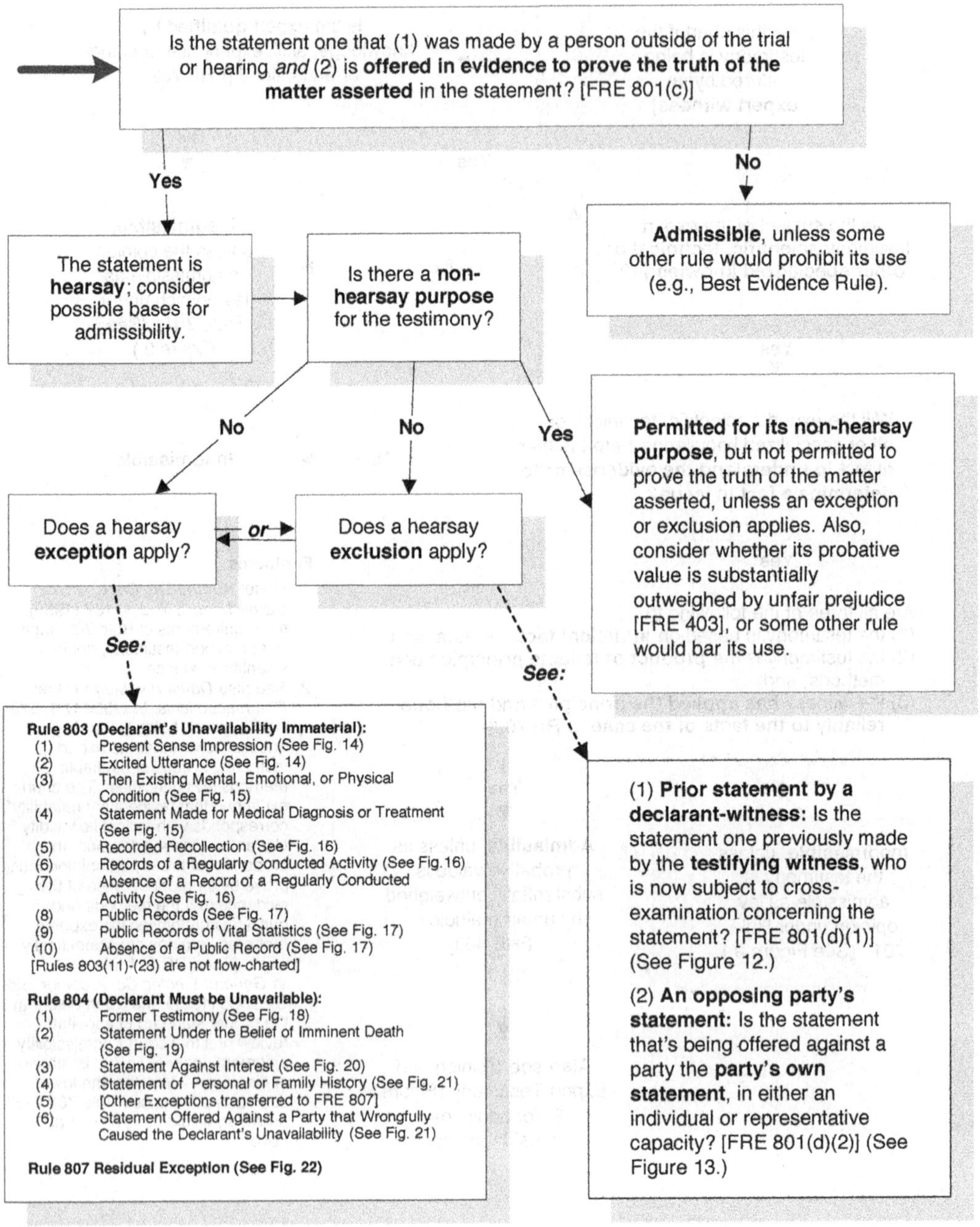

Figure 12
Hearsay Exclusions and Impeachment

Prior Statements of a Witness: Impeachment Use and Hearsay Exclusion
Rules 613, 801(d)(1)

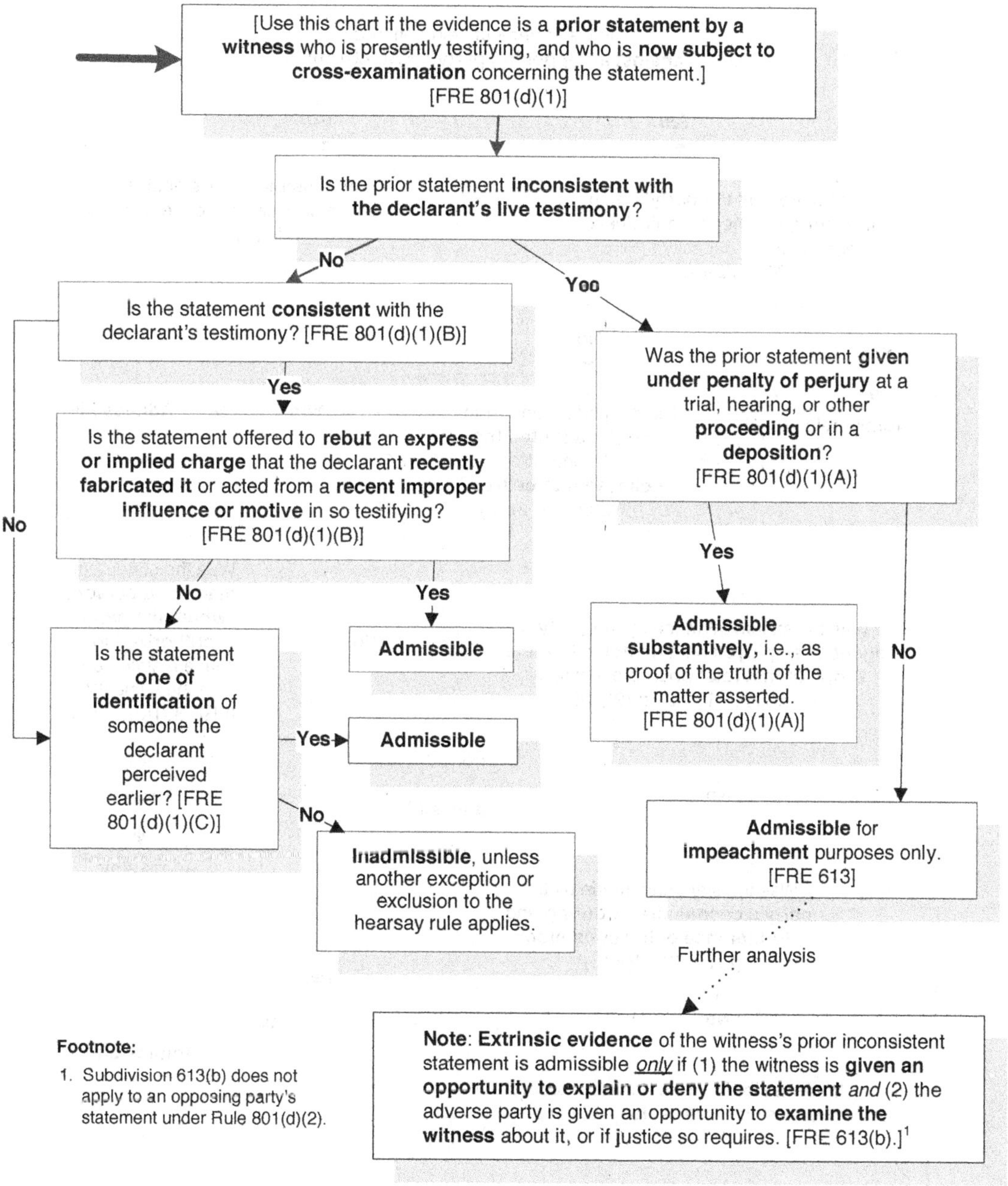

Footnote:

1. Subdivision 613(b) does not apply to an opposing party's statement under Rule 801(d)(2).

Figure 13
Hearsay Exclusions

Admissions by a Party-Opponent
Rule 801(d)(2)

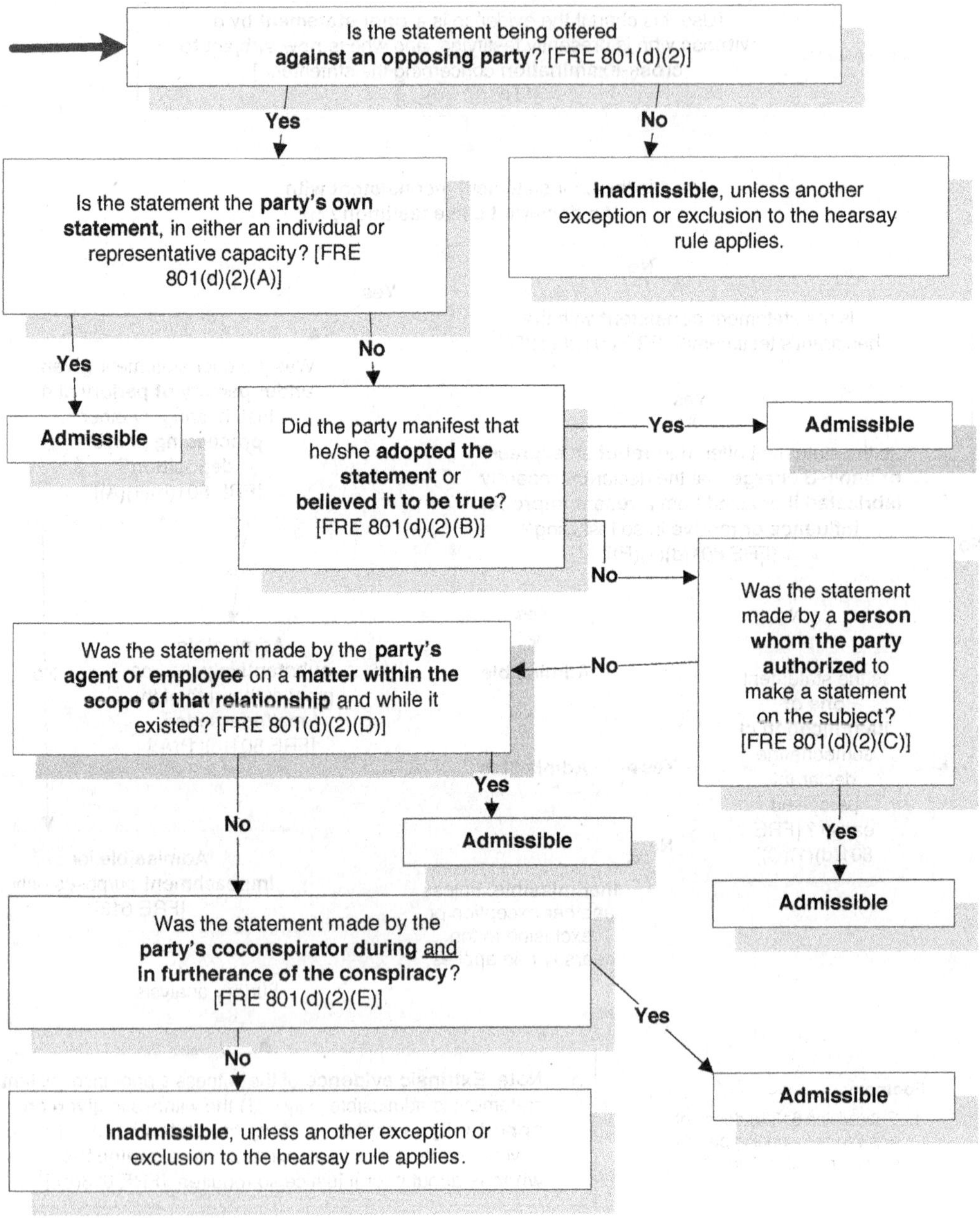

Figure 14
Hearsay Exceptions

Present Sense Impressions; Excited Utterances

Rules 803(1), 803(2)

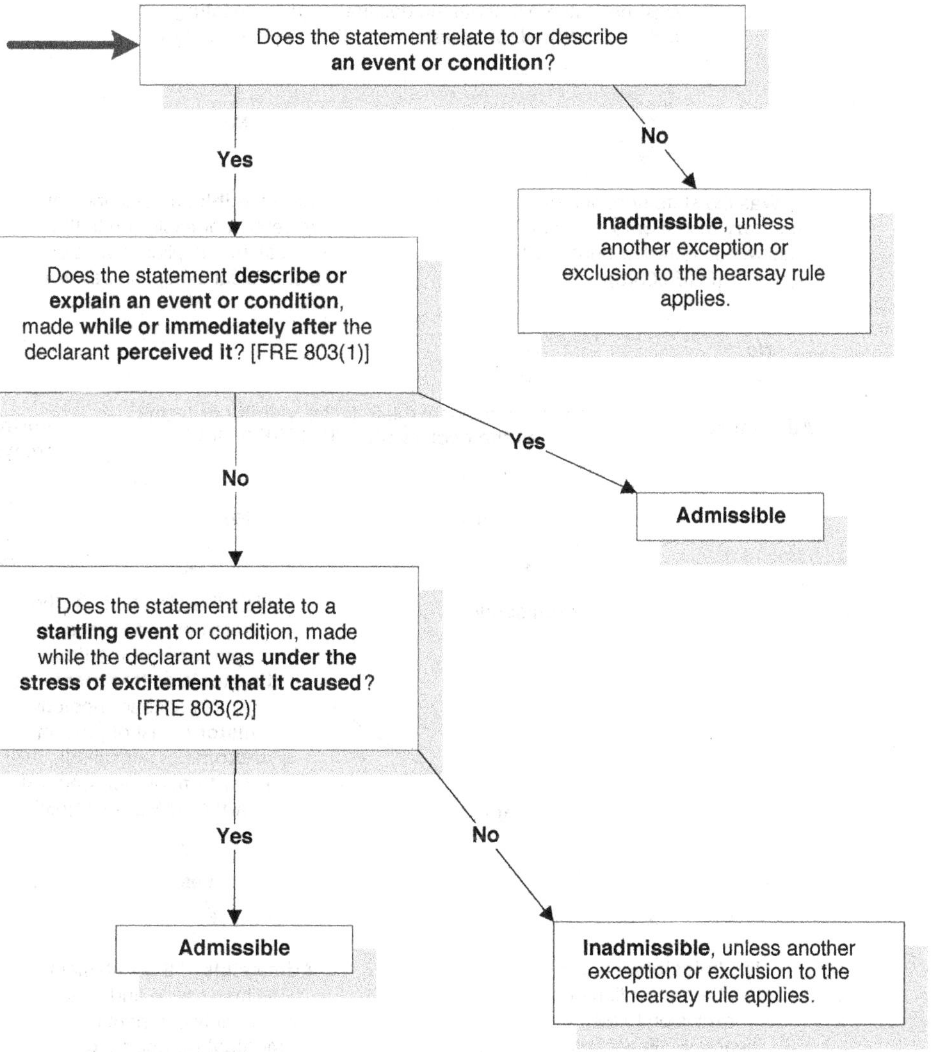

Figure 15
Hearsay Exceptions

Then-Existing Mental, Emotional or Physical Condition; Statement Made for Medical Diagnosis or Treatment
Rules 803(3), 803(4)

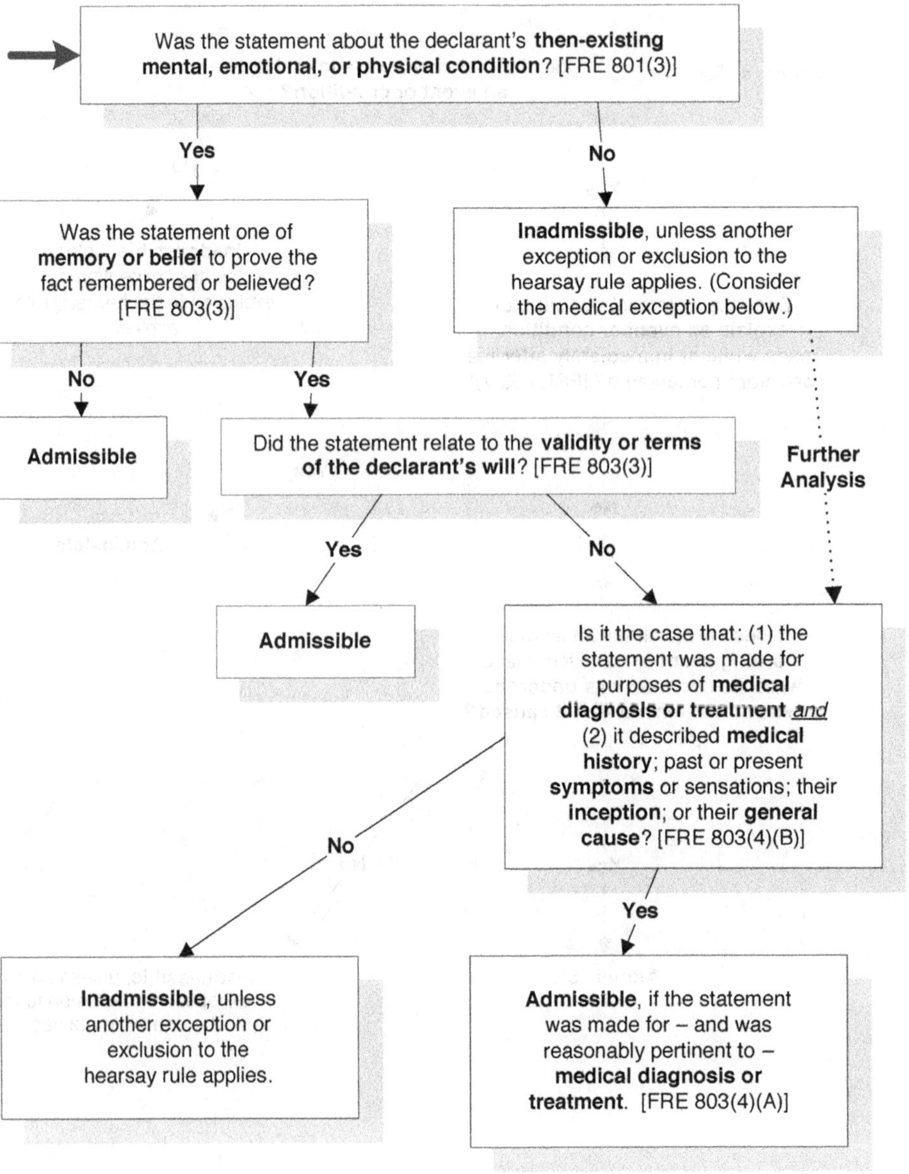

Figure 16
Hearsay Exceptions

Writing to Refresh Memory; Recorded Recollection; Records of Regularly-Conducted Activity; Absence of Records

Rules 612, 803(5), 803(6), 803(7)

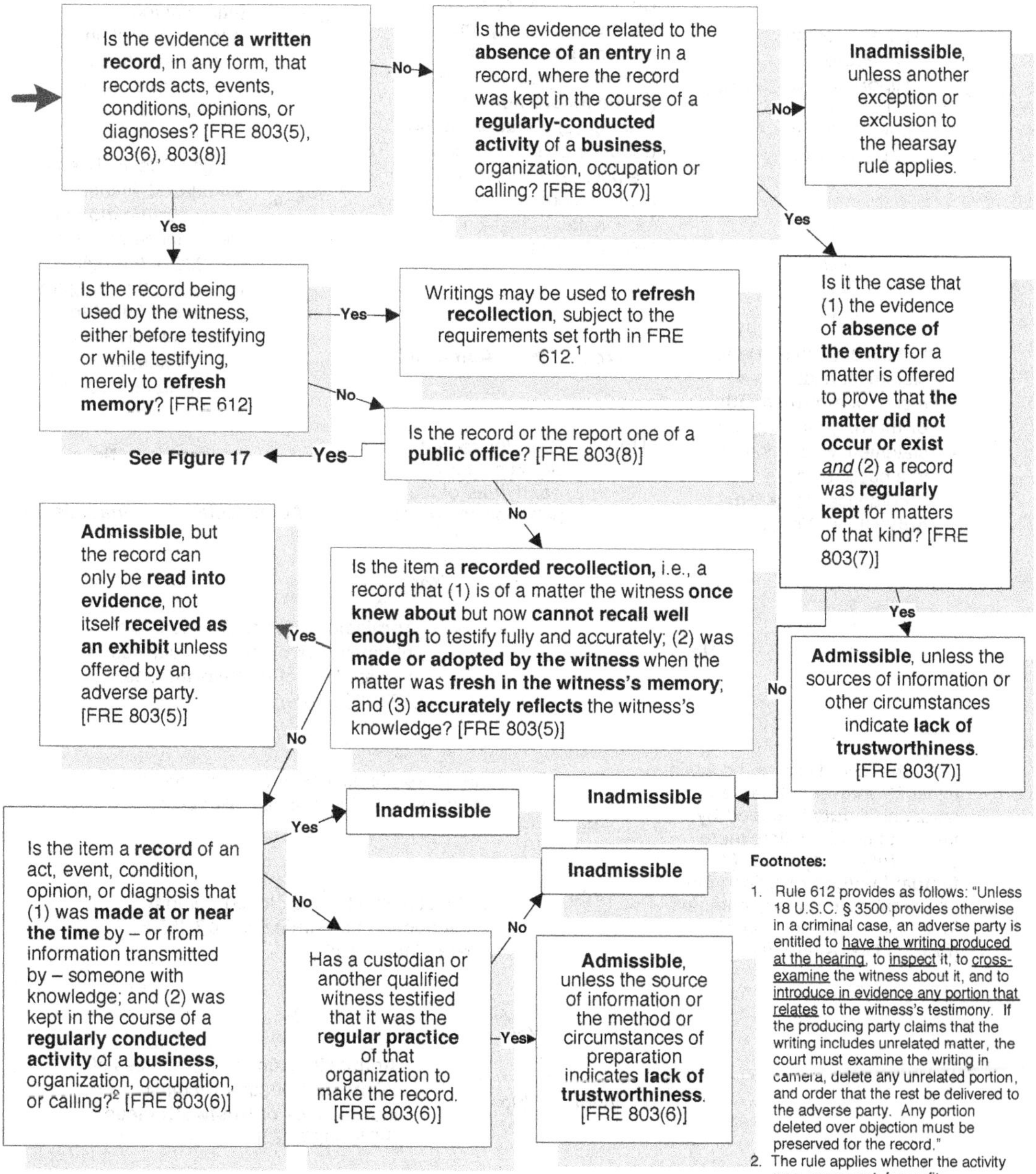

Footnotes:

1. Rule 612 provides as follows: "Unless 18 U.S.C. § 3500 provides otherwise in a criminal case, an adverse party is entitled to have the writing produced at the hearing, to inspect it, to cross-examine the witness about it, and to introduce in evidence any portion that relates to the witness's testimony. If the producing party claims that the writing includes unrelated matter, the court must examine the writing in camera, delete any unrelated portion, and order that the rest be delivered to the adverse party. Any portion deleted over objection must be preserved for the record."
2. The rule applies whether the activity was, or was not, for profit.

Figure 17
Hearsay Exceptions

Public Records; Records of Vital Statistics; Absence of Public Record
Rules 803(8), 803(9), 803(10)

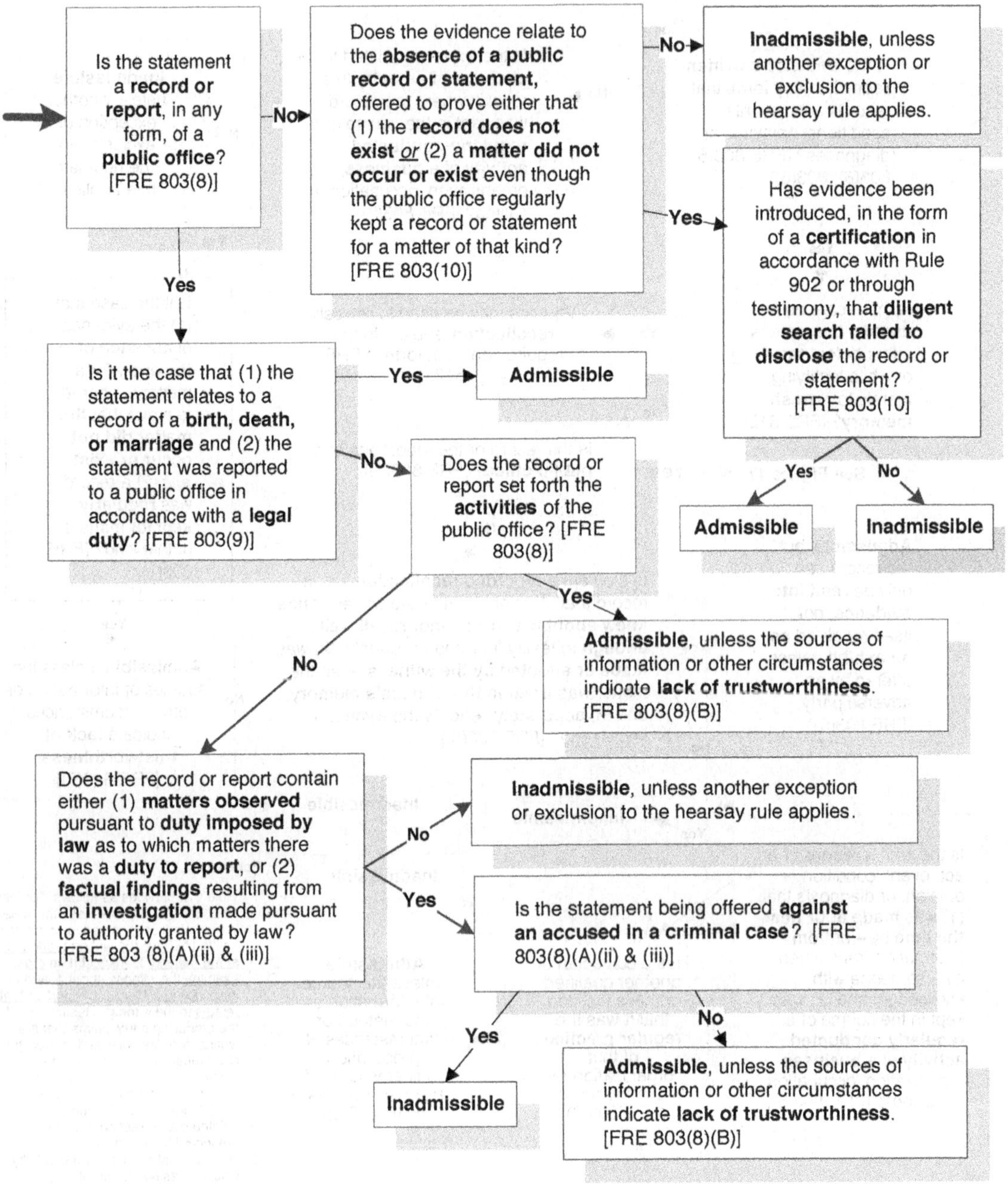

Figure 18
Hearsay Exceptions

Former Testimony
Rules 804(a), 804(b)(1)

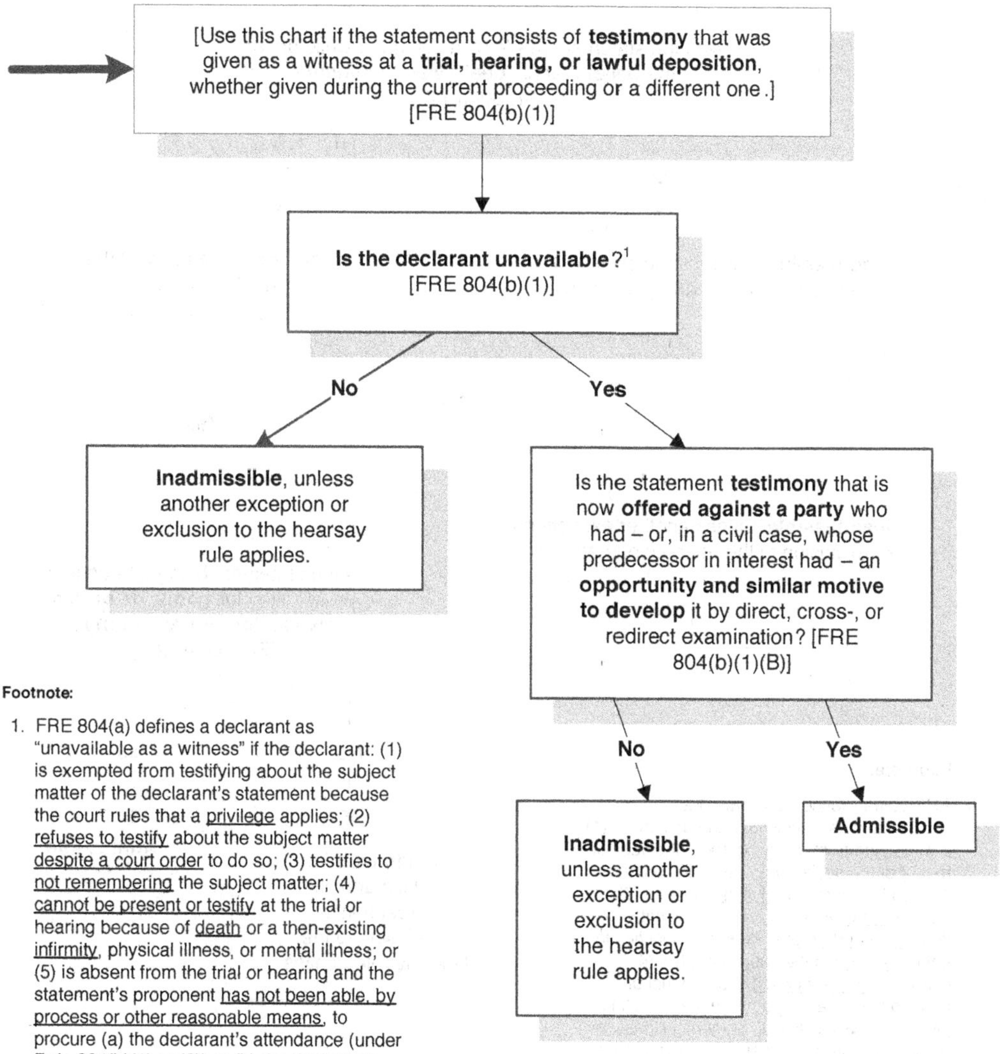

Footnote:

1. FRE 804(a) defines a declarant as "unavailable as a witness" if the declarant: (1) is exempted from testifying about the subject matter of the declarant's statement because the court rules that a privilege applies; (2) refuses to testify about the subject matter despite a court order to do so; (3) testifies to not remembering the subject matter; (4) cannot be present or testify at the trial or hearing because of death or a then-existing infirmity, physical illness, or mental illness; or (5) is absent from the trial or hearing and the statement's proponent has not been able, by process or other reasonable means, to procure (a) the declarant's attendance (under Rule 804(b)(1) or (6)) or (b) the declarant's attendance or testimony (under Rule 804(b)(2), (3) or (4)).

Figure 19
Hearsay Exceptions

Statement under Belief of Imminent Death
Rules 804(a), 804(b)(2)

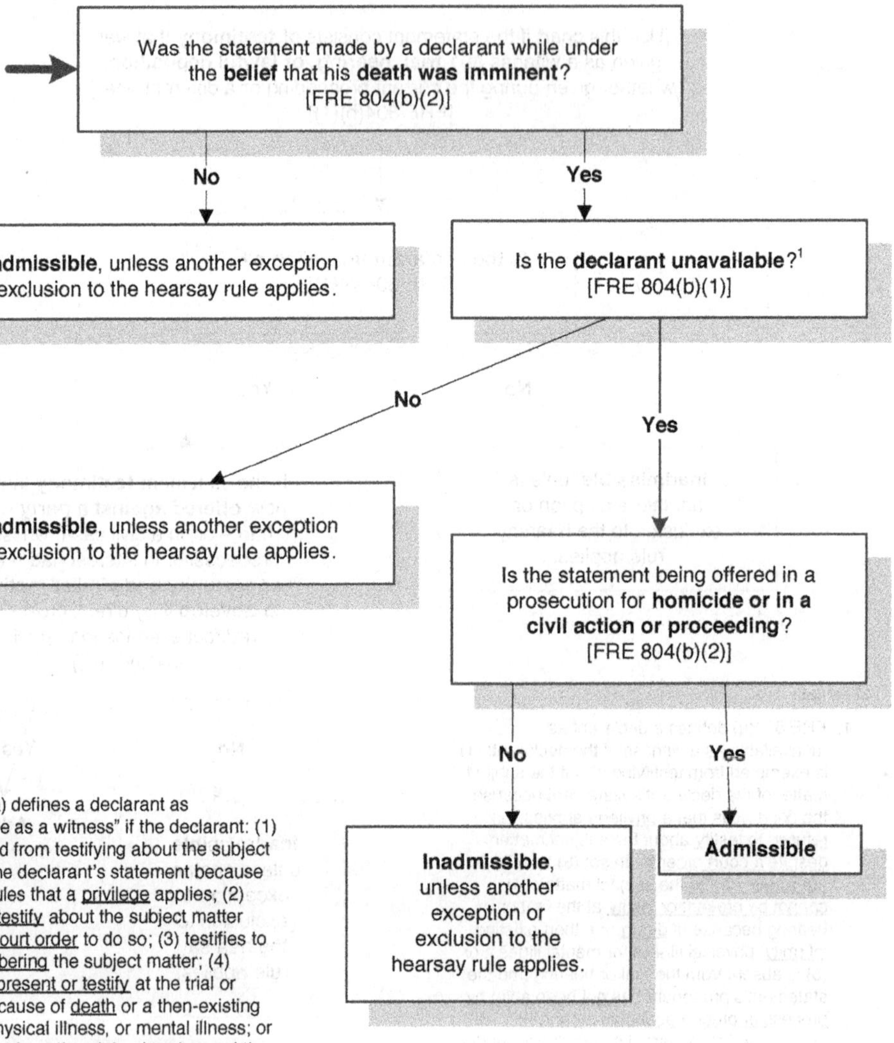

Footnote:

1. FRE 804(a) defines a declarant as "unavailable as a witness" if the declarant: (1) is exempted from testifying about the subject matter of the declarant's statement because the court rules that a privilege applies; (2) refuses to testify about the subject matter despite a court order to do so; (3) testifies to not remembering the subject matter; (4) cannot be present or testify at the trial or hearing because of death or a then-existing infirmity, physical illness, or mental illness; or (5) is absent from the trial or hearing and the statement's proponent has not been able, by process or other reasonable means, to procure (a) the declarant's attendance (under Rule 804(b)(1) or (6)) or (b) the declarant's attendance or testimony (under Rule 804(b)(2), (3) or (4)).

Figure 20
Hearsay Exceptions

Statement Against Interest
Rules 804(a), 804(b)(3)

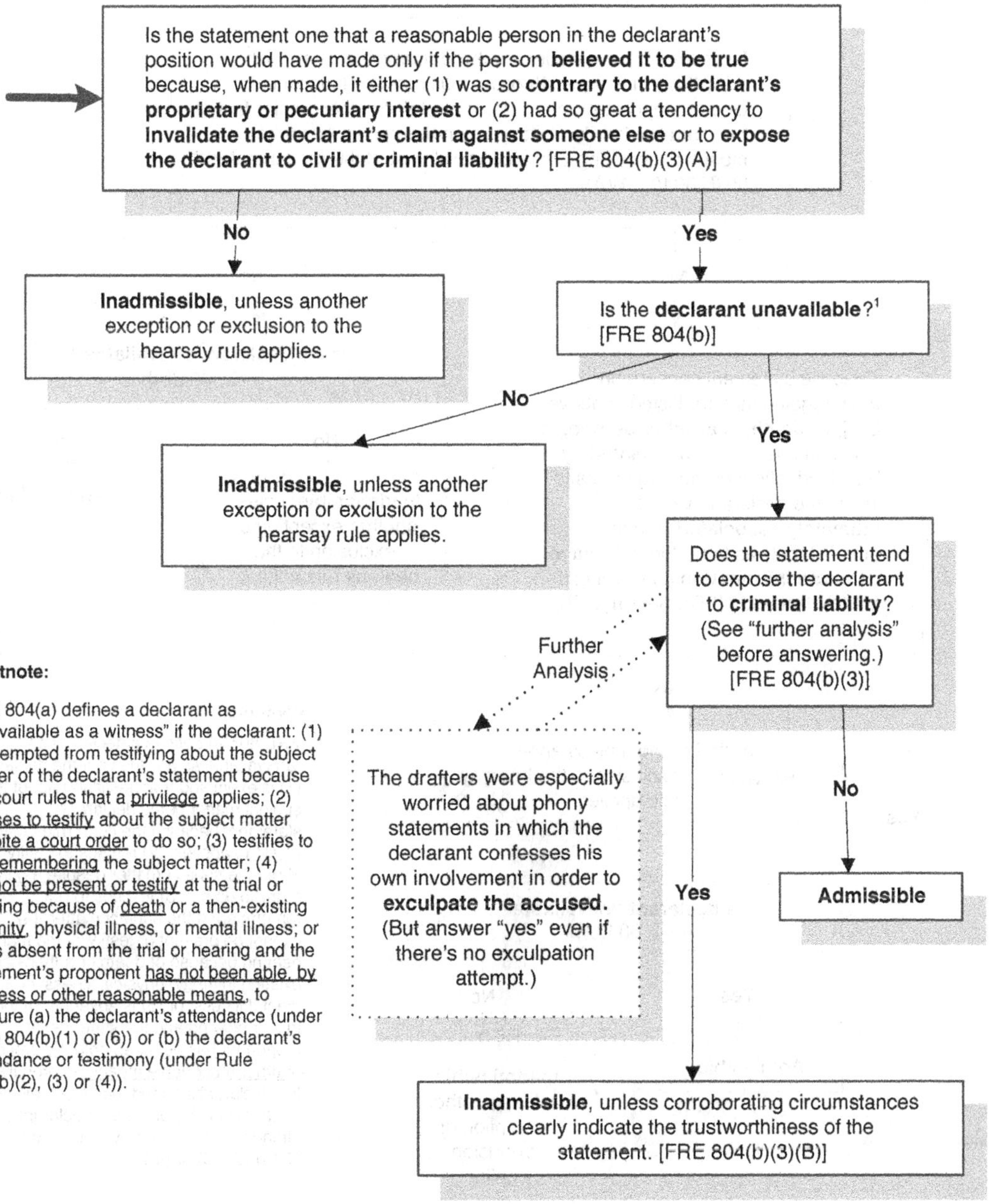

Footnote:

1. FRE 804(a) defines a declarant as "unavailable as a witness" if the declarant: (1) is exempted from testifying about the subject matter of the declarant's statement because the court rules that a privilege applies; (2) refuses to testify about the subject matter despite a court order to do so; (3) testifies to not remembering the subject matter; (4) cannot be present or testify at the trial or hearing because of death or a then-existing infirmity, physical illness, or mental illness; or (5) is absent from the trial or hearing and the statement's proponent has not been able, by process or other reasonable means, to procure (a) the declarant's attendance (under Rule 804(b)(1) or (6)) or (b) the declarant's attendance or testimony (under Rule 804(b)(2), (3) or (4)).

Figure 21
Hearsay Exceptions

Statement of Personal or Family History
Rules 804(a), 804(b)(4)

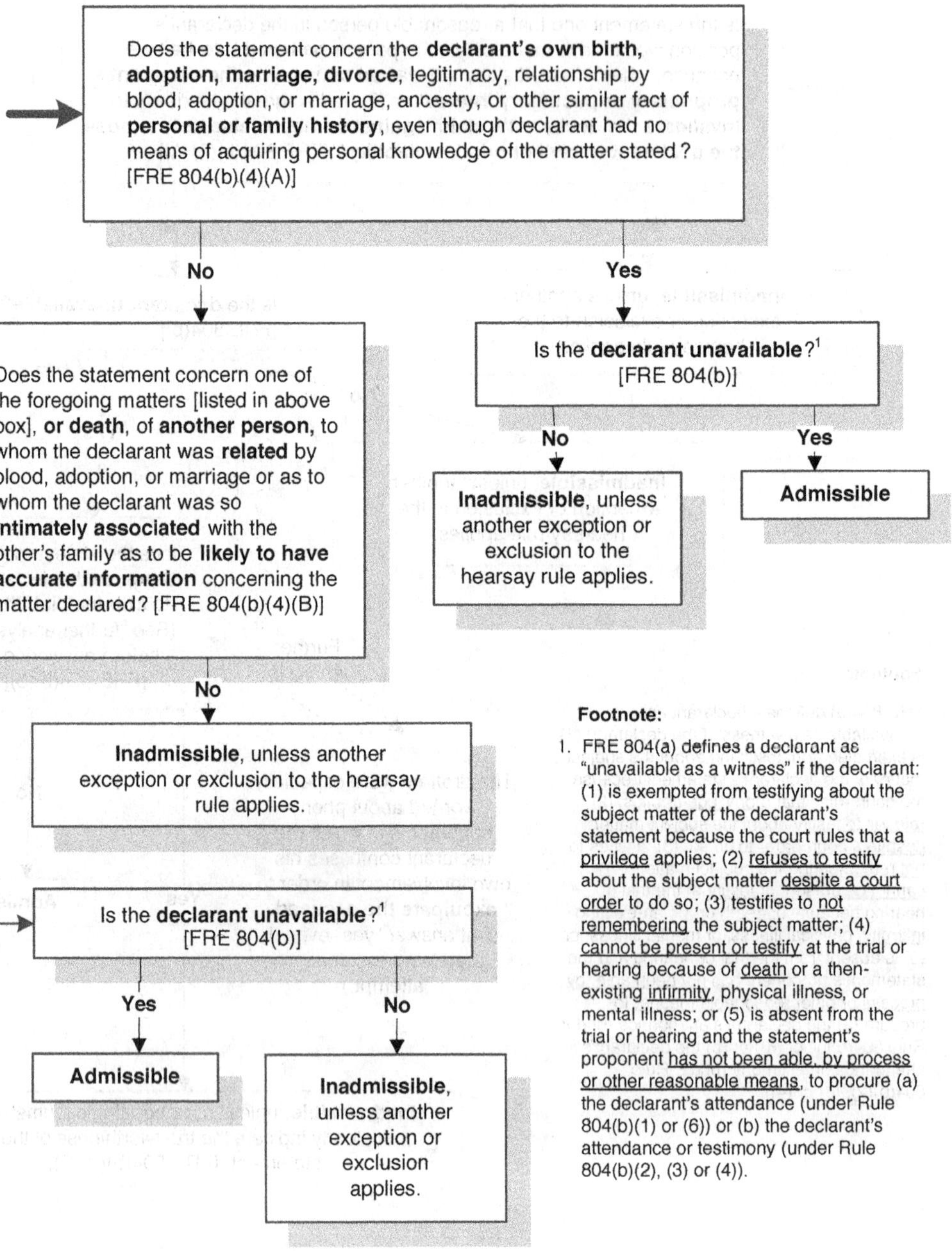

Footnote:

1. FRE 804(a) defines a declarant as "unavailable as a witness" if the declarant: (1) is exempted from testifying about the subject matter of the declarant's statement because the court rules that a privilege applies; (2) refuses to testify about the subject matter despite a court order to do so; (3) testifies to not remembering the subject matter; (4) cannot be present or testify at the trial or hearing because of death or a then-existing infirmity, physical illness, or mental illness; or (5) is absent from the trial or hearing and the statement's proponent has not been able, by process or other reasonable means, to procure (a) the declarant's attendance (under Rule 804(b)(1) or (6)) or (b) the declarant's attendance or testimony (under Rule 804(b)(2), (3) or (4)).

Figure 22

Hearsay Exceptions

The Residual ("Catchall") Exception

Rules 804(a), 804(b)(2)

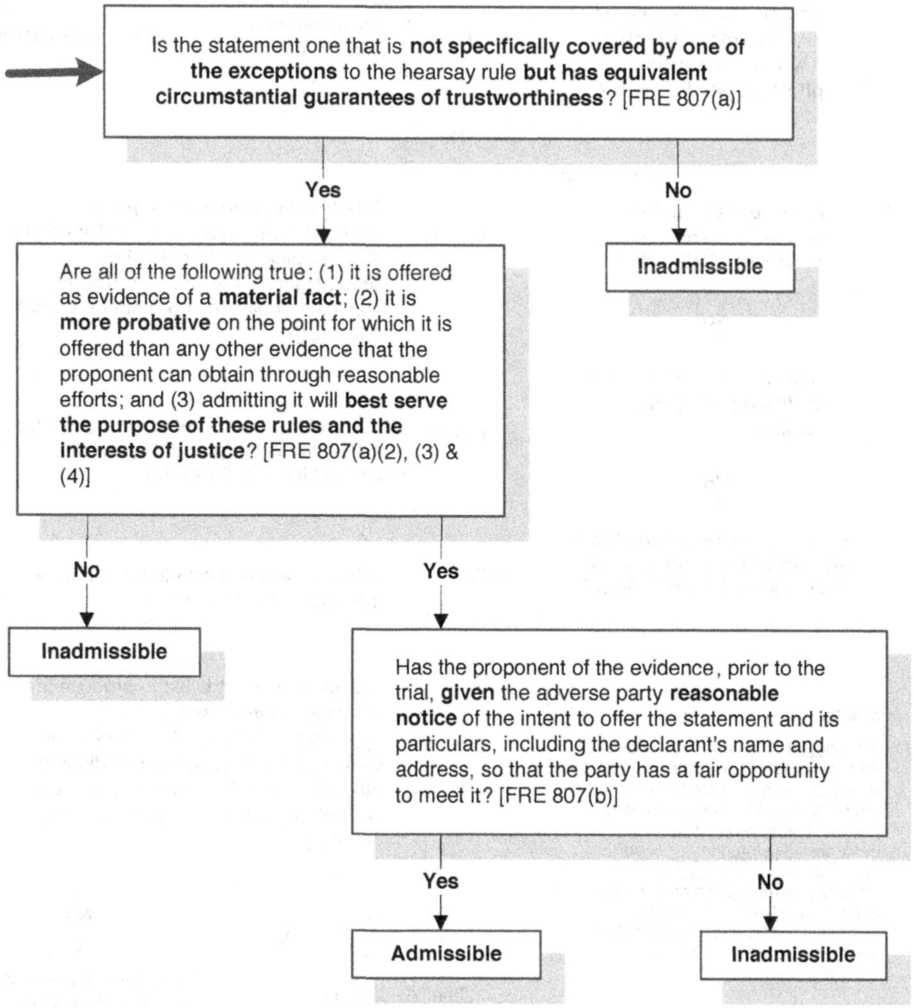

Figure 23
Contents of Writings, Recordings and Photographs

Best Evidence Rule
Rules 1001, 1002, 1003, 1004

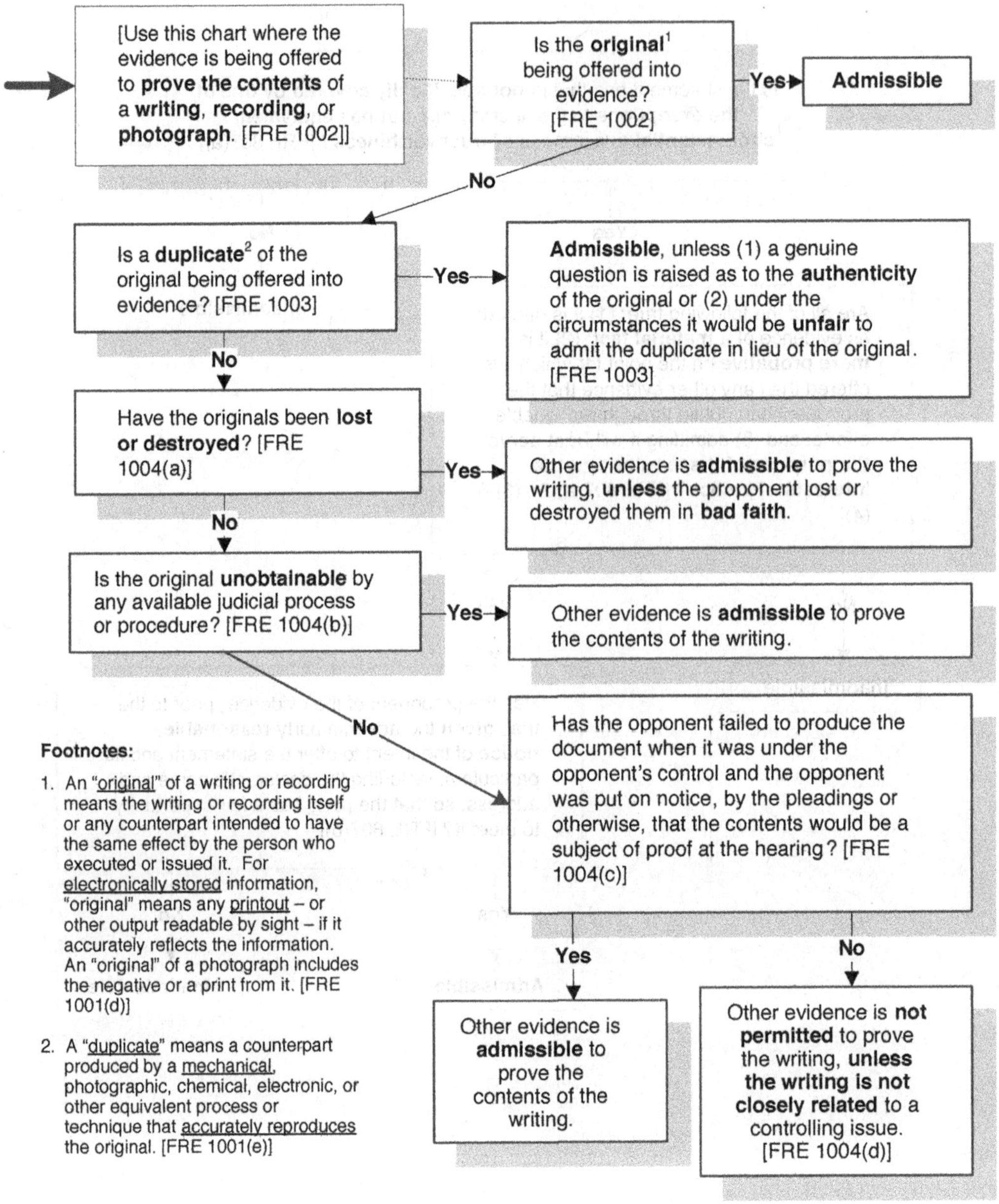

Footnotes:

1. An "original" of a writing or recording means the writing or recording itself or any counterpart intended to have the same effect by the person who executed or issued it. For electronically stored information, "original" means any printout – or other output readable by sight – if it accurately reflects the information. An "original" of a photograph includes the negative or a print from it. [FRE 1001(d)]

2. A "duplicate" means a counterpart produced by a mechanical, photographic, chemical, electronic, or other equivalent process or technique that accurately reproduces the original. [FRE 1001(e)]

CAPSULE SUMMARY

TABLE OF CONTENTS OF CAPSULE SUMMARY

CAPSULE SUMMARY

CHAPTER 1

BASIC CONCEPTS

I. FIRST PRINCIPLES

A. Roles of judge and jury: In cases tried to a jury, the judge and the jury divide the responsibility of dealing with the evidence:

1. **Judge's role:** The role of the *judge* is to determine ***whether the evidence is admissible***.

2. **Role of the jury:** Once the judge has decided to admit the evidence, the jury's role is to determine what ***weight*** the evidence should be given. For instance, it is up to the jury to judge the ***credibility*** of a witness, and the jury may choose to completely disregard admissible testimony because it believes the witness who is giving that testimony is mistaken or lying.

B. The Federal Rules: The ***Federal Rules of Evidence*** apply to ***all trials in federal courts,*** whether civil or criminal, and whether to a judge or a jury. See FRE 101.

1. **Adoption by states:** The Federal Rules of Evidence have also been adopted, in one form or another, by ***over four-fifths of the states***.

2. **2011 Restyling:** The language of the Federal Rules was extensively revised in 2011. This ***"restyling"*** project was done to make the rules more easily understood and to make style and terminology consistent. The restyling was not intended to change any actual evidence-ruling result.

II. ORGANIZATION OF THE TRIAL

A. Flow of the case: In the usual case, the plaintiff's case is presented first, followed by the defendant's. The typical case flows as follows:

1. **Opening statement:** The plaintiff (or, in a criminal case, the prosecutor) makes his ***opening statement*** first. Then, the defendant may make his opening statement (though many courts allow him to reserve his opening statement until the end of the plaintiff/prosecutor's case).

2. **Plaintiff's case:** Then, the plaintiff (or prosecutor) puts on his ***case in chief.*** That is, he presents the witnesses, as well as documents and other tangible evidence, to establish the facts needed for him to prevail.

3. **Defendant's case:** After the plaintiff or prosecutor "rests" his case, it is the defendant's turn. The defendant presents witnesses and documents to disprove the elements of the plaintiff's case and/or to establish ***affirmative defenses***.

4. **Plaintiff's rebuttal:** After the defendant rests, the plaintiff or prosecutor gets another turn at bat. This is called the plaintiff's ***rebuttal*** — the plaintiff may present additional witnesses, recall former witnesses, or present new exhibits, but ***only to rebut the defendant's evidence***, not to buttress his own case in chief.

5. **Defendant's rejoinder:** Likewise, after the plaintiff's rebuttal, the defendant has a ***rejoinder*** — here, he may only rebut evidence brought out in the plaintiff's rebuttal.

6. **Closing arguments:** After both parties have presented all of their evidence, the two sides make ***closing arguments***. Usually, the plaintiff (or prosecutor) goes first, the defendant goes second, and the plaintiff/prosecutor gets a last chance to rebut the defendant's closing remarks.

7. **Instructions:** Finally, the judge gives ***instructions*** to the jury, in which he explains to them the applicable law. In some jurisdictions, he may also comment upon, or summarize, the evidence.

B. Examination of witnesses: Here are the steps by which witnesses are examined.

1. **Four stages:** The examination of a given witness proceeds through up to four stages:

   a. **Direct:** First, the party who has called a witness engages in the ***direct examination.***

   b. **Cross-examination:** After the side that called the witness has finished the direct examination, the other side has the chance to ***cross-examine*** the witness.

   c. **Re-direct:** The calling side then has an opportunity to conduct ***re-direct*** examination of the witness. Re-direct is generally limited to rebutting points made on cross-examination.

   d. **Re-cross:** Finally, the cross-examining side gets a brief opportunity to conduct ***re-cross***. This is limited to rebutting the effect of re-direct.

2. **Sequestration of witnesses:** If a witness were permitted to observe the testimony of other witnesses for the same side, he would be able to ***tailor*** his testimony (perhaps by ***perjury***) so that it matched this other testimony. To prevent this, judges have, and often use, the power to ***exclude all other witnesses*** from the courtroom while one witness is testifying. This is known as the power to ***"sequester"*** witnesses.

   a. **Federal Rule:** The trial judge's right to sequester witnesses is codified in FRE 615, which says: "At a party's request, the court ***must order witnesses excluded*** so that they ***cannot hear other witnesses' testimony.*** Or the court may do so on its own."

      i. **Mandatory at party's request:** So under FRE 615, ***any party*** has the ***absolute right*** to require the judge to exclude all witnesses (other than witnesses covered by the above exceptions) from hearing other witnesses' testimony. In other words, once a party makes the request for sequestration, the ***judge does not have discretion to deny the request.***

III. COMPETENCY OF WITNESSES

A. Meaning: A witness is said to be ***"competent"*** if she possesses the qualifications necessary to give testimony.

B. Modern approach: Witnesses are ***presumed competent.***

1. **Federal Rules:** Under the Federal Rules, witnesses (other than the judge and the jury in the particular case) will be incompetent to testify ***only for two reasons***:

   [1] **Lack of personal knowledge:** First, as a general matter a witness may not testify to a matter unless she has ***personal knowledge*** of the matter. FRE 602. Thus if a witness describes a particular event, her testimony will be stricken if it turns out that she did not personally observe that event, and instead heard about it from someone else.

   [2] **Oath:** Second, if the witness will not solemnly ***promise to tell the truth***, the court will not hear his testimony.

   See FRE 603.

   a. **Mental incapacity or immaturity:** Thus under the federal approach, even a witness who is quite ***insane***, or very ***young***, will not be prevented from testifying if the trial judge is convinced that he has relevant first-hand knowledge and understands the obligation to tell the truth. Similarly, even if the witness was ***intoxicated*** or under the ***influence of drugs*** when he witnessed an event, he will be permitted, under the federal approach, to testify about it.

IV. KINDS OF EVIDENCE

A. Direct versus circumstantial

1. **Direct evidence:** Direct evidence is evidence which, if believed, automatically resolves the issue.

   Example: W says, "I saw D strangle V." This is direct evidence on whether D strangled V.

2. **Circumstantial:** Circumstantial evidence is evidence which, even if believed, does not resolve the issue unless ***additional reasoning*** is used.

   Example: W says, "I saw D running from the place where V's body was found, and I found a stocking in D's pocket." This is only circumstantial evidence of whether D strangled V.

3. **Probative value:** The probative value of direct evidence is not necessarily higher than circumstantial evidence, but it will sometimes be more readily admitted by the judge.

B. Testimonial versus real and demonstrative:

1. **Testimonial:** Testimonial evidence arises when W makes assertions in court. The fact-finder must rely on W's interpretation of W's sensory data, W's memory, etc.

2. **Real and demonstrative:** Real evidence is a thing involved in the underlying event (e.g., a weapon, document, or other tangible item). Demonstrative evidence is a tangible item that illustrates some material proposition (e.g., a map, chart, summary). The fact-finder may interpret either real or demonstrative evidence by use of its own senses, without intervening sensing and interpreting by a witness.

V. CONDITIONS FOR ADMITTING EVIDENCE

A. Relevant: Only ***relevant*** evidence may be admitted. (FRE 402)

1. **Definition:** Evidence is "relevant" if "(a) it has any tendency to make a fact ***more or less probable*** than it would be without the evidence; and (b) the fact is of consequence in determining the action." (FRE 401)

    a. **"Brick is not wall":** The piece of evidence need not make a material fact more probable than not; it must merely increase the probability (even by a small amount) that the material fact is so. "A brick is not a wall," and the piece of evidence merely has to be one brick in the wall establishing a particular fact.

2. **Exclusion under FRE 403:** Even relevant evidence may be ***excluded*** if its ***probative value*** is ***substantially outweighed*** by the danger of:

    [1] ***unfair prejudice***;

    [2] ***confusion*** of the issues;

    [3] ***misleading*** of the jury; or

    [4] considerations of ***undue delay***, ***waste of time***, or needless presentation of ***cumulative evidence***.

    See FRE ***403***. This ***balancing test*** imposed by FRE 403 gives the trial judge a lot of ***discretion*** about what evidence to allow.

B. Offering testimonial evidence

1. **Lay (i.e., non-expert) witness:**

    a. W must take an ***oath***, i.e., solemnly promise to testify truthfully. (FRE 603)

    b. W must testify from ***personal knowledge***. (FRE 602)

    c. W must preferably state ***facts*** rather than ***opinions***. But under FRE 701, W *may* give an opinion if it is: (1) rationally based on his own perceptions; (2) helpful to the fact-finder ; and (3) not based on scientific, technical or other specialized knowledge.

    d. W must be ***competent*** (see p. 33).

2. **Experts:** The same rules apply to ***experts*** as to lay witnesses, except:

    a. **Broader scope:** The expert (W) may give an opinion ***under*** broader circumstances than a non-expert. The opinion is admissible if:

    ❑ the opinion relates to "scientific, technical or other ***specialized knowl-***

edge";

- ❑ the opinion will assist the trier to "***understand the evidence*** or determine a fact in issue"; and
- ❑ the testimony is based on ***sufficient facts or data*** and is the product of "***reliable*** principles and methods," and W has ***applied*** those principles and methods ***reliably*** to the ***facts of the case***.

See FRE 702.

b. No personal knowledge required: The expert's opinion need not be based on his personal knowledge — it may be based on information supplied by others. At common law, this is usually done by the hypothetical question. Under Federal Rules, it may be done either by the hypothetical or by out-of-court statements made to the expert (even inadmissible evidence); FRE 703. Under FRE 705, facts relied on by the expert need not be disclosed except under cross-examination or as required by court.

c. Qualification: The expert may be qualified by reason of "knowledge, skill, experience, training, or otherwise" (FRE 702), so formal academic training is not necessary.

3. Ultimate issues: At common law, opinions on "***ultimate***" issues are usually barred. But under FRE 704, even such opinions are allowed (except when they relate to the mental state of a criminal defendant).

C. Offering real and demonstrative evidence: See p. 110 of this Capsule Summary.

D. Making and responding to objections:

1. Making objections:

a. Not automatic: Evidence will not be excluded unless the opponent makes an ***objection***. FRE 103(a)(1).

b. Timely: The objection must be ***timely*** (usually before the witness can answer the question). FRE 103(a)(1).

c. Specific: The objection must be ***specific*** enough to explain to the trial judge and the appeals court the basis for it. *Id.*

d. Taking of exceptions: At common law, the opponent whose objection is denied must ***"take exception"*** in order to preserve the objection for appeal. In most states today, and under the Federal Rules, exceptions are no longer necessary.

2. Responding to objection: If the judge sustains objection, the proponent must usually make an ***"offer of proof"*** in order to preserve his right to argue on appeal that the evidence should have been admitted. That is, proponent must make it clear to the court (either by the lawyer's own explanation of what the evidence would be, or by questions and answers to the witness outside the jury's presence) what the evidence would be. FRE 103(a)(2).

CHAPTER 2

CIRCUMSTANTIAL PROOF: SPECIAL PROBLEMS

I. RELEVANT EVIDENCE SOMETIMES EXCLUDED

A. Possible exclusion: Normally, all relevant evidence is admissible. (FRE 402) But even relevant evidence may be excluded if its probative value is "***substantially outweighed*** by a danger of one or more of the following: ***unfair prejudice***, confusing the issues, misleading the jury," etc. (FRE 403) Special rules govern certain types of circumstantial evidence which have been found over the years to be so misleading or so prejudicial that they should be categorically excluded without a case-by-case balancing of probative value against prejudice.

II. CHARACTER EVIDENCE

A. General rule: Evidence of a person's character or character trait is, in general, ***not admissible*** to prove that "on a ***particular occasion*** the person ***acted in accordance*** with the character or trait." FRE 404(a)(1).

> **Example:** In a civil suit from an auto accident, P cannot show that D has the general character trait of carelessness, or even that D is a generally careless driver, to suggest that D probably acted carelessly in the particular accident under litigation.

B. Character in issue:

1. **Essential element:** A person's general character, or his particular character trait, is admissible if it is an ***essential element*** of the case.

   > **Example:** P says that D has libeled him by calling him a liar. D may introduce evidence of P's character for untruthfulness, since that character trait is an essential element of D's defense that his statement was true.

   a. **Illustrations:** True "character in issue" situations are rare. Civilly, ***negligent entrustment*** (D gave dangerous instrumentality, like a car, to one he should have known was of careless or otherwise bad character) and ***defamation*** (above example) are the most common. Criminally, ***entrapment*** (prosecution rebuts by showing D was "predisposed" to commit the crime) is the only instance.

2. **Types of evidence:** When character is directly in issue, all three types of character evidence (specific acts, W's opinion, or the subject's reputation) are admissible.

C. Circumstantial evidence in civil cases: In civil cases, circumstantial evidence of character is generally inadmissible.

1. **Quasi-criminal acts:** A few courts allow one who is charged in a civil case with conduct that would also be a crime to rebut this charge by presenting circumstantial evidence of his good character. But most courts, and the Federal Rules, do not.

D. Other-crimes (and "bad acts") evidence in criminal cases:

1. **General rule:** The prosecutor may ***not*** introduce evidence of ***other crimes*** committed by D for the purpose of proving that because D is a person of criminal character, he probably committed the crime with which he is charged. Nor may the prosecutor show D's prior ***"bad acts"*** that didn't lead to convictions for this purpose.

   a. **FRE:** See FRE 404(b)(1): "Evidence of a ***crime, wrong, or other act*** is not admissible to ***prove a person's character*** in order to show that on ***a particular occasion the person acted in accordance with the character."***

2. **Proof of elements:** But other crimes or bad acts by D may be admitted if this is done not to show D's general criminal disposition, but to establish circumstantially ***some element of the crime charged.*** See FRE 404(b): other crimes, wrongs or acts "may be admissible for ***another purpose***, such as ***proving motive, opportunity, intent, preparation, plan, knowledge, identity, absence of mistake, or lack of accident.***"

   Here are some common elements that may be circumstantially proved by other crimes that D has committed:

   a. **Signature:** If the perpetrator's ***identity*** is in doubt, proof that D has committed prior crimes that are so similar in method that they constitute his ***"signature,"*** and thus identify him as the perpetrator of the crime charged, may be proved. This is often described as proof of ***"modus operandi"*** or "m.o."

   Example: D is on trial for robbing a convenience store after midnight while wearing a mask similar to the very distinctive one worn in the movie "Clockwork Orange." The prosecution shows the jury a surveillance tape in which the masked robber can be seen wearing such a mask. D testifies that he wasn't the robber, and that the man in the tape must be someone else. The prosecution asks D, "Isn't it true that you were convicted two years ago of robbing another convenience store while wearing a 'Clockwork Orange' mask?" (It's true that D was so convicted.)

   The question is proper — the evidence of D's conviction is available not only to impeach him, but as substantive proof that he robbed the other store wearing such a mask. That's because the other crime is so similar to the present one that it tends to prove D's identity as the masked robber on the present occasion. Therefore, the evidence of the conviction is non-character other-crimes evidence offered for "another purpose, such as proving ... identity[.]" FRE 404(b).

   b. **Intent:** Other crimes may be used to prove that D had the particular ***intent*** required for the crime charged. Generally, this is done to rebut D's contention that he did the act charged ***innocently*** or ***unknowingly***.

   Example: D, a mail carrier, is charged with stealing a coin from the mails. The prosecution is allowed to show that D also unlawfully possessed credit cards taken from the mails, in order to rebut D's argument that the coin accidentally fell out of an envelope and he planned to return it.

c. **Motive:** Other crimes may be used to establish the defendant's ***motive*** for the crime charged.

Example: D, a nurse, is charged with stealing Demerol from the hospital where she works. The prosecution may show that D is a Demerol addict, to show that she had a motive to steal the drug. [*U.S. v. Cunningham*].

d. **Identity:** Other crimes may be used to show that D was really the perpetrator, if he disputes this. For instance, the prosecution may be allowed to show that D committed other crimes, and that the other crimes and the crime charged are part of a ***common plan or scheme***.

Example: D is charged with embezzling from his employer; he claims that someone else did the embezzling. The prosecution will be allowed to show that D embezzled from three prior employers, since this demonstrates that D was probably acting as part of a general scheme to steal from each of his employers.

3. **Other aspects of other-crimes evidence:**

a. **No conviction:** The other crimes need ***not*** have led to a ***conviction***. Many state courts require that the evidence of the defendant's guilt of the other crime be "clear and convincing" or "substantial." But in federal courts, it does not even have to be by a preponderance of the evidence.

b. **Acquittal:** The fact that the defendant was ***acquitted*** of the other crime will be a factor in determining whether there is "substantial" evidence of his guilt (in courts requiring this). But most courts will probably not automatically exclude the evidence of the other crime merely because of the acquittal.

Example: D is charged with murdering her child. Evidence that four of her other children died of unnatural causes will probably be allowed because of its strong tendency to prove that the death currently charged was not accidental, even though D was acquitted of similar charges as to the first death, when no cumulative evidence was available.

c. **Balancing:** Even where other crimes by D circumstantially establish an element of the present charge, the judge must still balance probative value against prejudice, and must exclude if the latter substantially outweighs the former. (FRE 403.)

d. **Use by D:** It's ordinarily the prosecution that uses the proof of D's prior crime or bad act to show some element of the present crime. But *D*, too, may show someone's past crimes or bad acts, to suggest that ***it's that other person***, not D, who did the present crime.

E. **Evidence of criminal defendant's good character:**

1. **Allowed:** Evidence by a criminal defendant that he has a ***good character*** — or a particular favorable character trait — is ***allowed*** by all courts, assuming that the trait is pertinent.

Example: D is charged with murder. He will be allowed to show that he has the general character of being law-abiding. He will also be permitted to show the narrower trait of being peaceable, since that trait is relevant to the crime charged.

2. **Method of proof:**

   a. **Common law:** At common law, proof of good character must be made by ***reputation*** evidence only (not by the character witness's opinion, or by proof of specific acts showing good character).

   b. **Federal:** FRE 405(a) allows not only reputation evidence but also the character witness's own ***opinion*** as to D's good character. (But not even the Federal Rules allow proof of ***specific incidents*** showing D's good character.)

3. **Relevance:** The trait on which the defendant is offering good-character evidence must be ***relevant (or "pertinent") to the crime charged***.

   Example: D is charged with beating V almost to death in a barroom brawl. D (without ever taking the stand) presents a witness, Wit, who expresses the opinion that D is a truthful person.

   Even though FRE 404(a)(1) allows an accused to offer favorable character evidence about himself, Wit's testimony would be excluded because it is not "pertinent" to any issue in the case. That is, to the extent that any character trait of D is an issue, it would be the trait of peaceableness, *not truthfulness*.

4. **Rebuttal by prosecution:** If D puts on proof of his good character, the prosecution may ***rebut*** this evidence:

   a. **Own witnesses:** The prosecution may do this by putting on its own witnesses to say that D's character is bad.

   b. **Cross-examination:** The prosecution may cross-examine D's character witness to show that D's character is not really good. The prosecutor may even do this by asking the witness about ***specific instances*** of bad conduct by D, provided that: (i) the prosecutor has a ***good faith basis*** for believing that D really committed the specific bad act; and (ii) the specific bad act is ***relevant*** to the ***specific character trait*** testified to by the witness (so if W testified that D was honest, the prosecutor could not ask about specific bad acts showing D's character for violence). Even an arrest that did not lead to a conviction may be brought up in cross-examination, if relevant to the character trait in question.

   c. **No extrinsic evidence:** The prosecutor's ability to show specific bad acts is limited to cross-examination. He may not put on extrinsic evidence (e.g., other witnesses) to prove that the specific acts took place, if the character witness denied that they did. Conversely, the defendant may not put on other witnesses to show that the specific act referred to by the prosecutor on cross-examination never took place.

F. **Character of victim:**

1. **V's violent character:** The defendant in a homicide or assault case who claims that the victim was the first aggressor, may in all courts introduce evidence that the ***victim*** had a ***violent character.*** This is true even if D cannot show that he was aware of the victim's violent character at the time of the assault or murder. This character evidence must generally be in the form of reputation or opinion evidence; most states (and the Federal Rules) prohibit evidence of ***specific past acts*** of violence by the victim.

2. **Federal Rules:** FRE 404(a)(2)(B) allows the defendant to show not only proof of a murder or assault victim's violent character, but *any* "evidence of an alleged victim's ***pertinent trait***[.]" (But this is very limited in sexual assault cases, discussed below.)

3. **Rebuttal by prosecution:** Once the defendant introduces evidence of the victim's character for violence, the prosecution may then ***rebut*** this evidence by showing the victim's ***peaceable*** character. The Federal Rules expand this right of rebuttal; in a homicide case, if the defendant claims that the victim was the first aggressor (even though the defendant does not put in proof of the victim's general character for violence), the prosecution may put in evidence of the victim's peaceful character. FRE 404(a)(2)(C).

4. **Rape:** At common law, the defendant in a ***rape or sexual assault*** case could usually show the victim's character for ***unchastity***, to show that the victim ***consented*** on this particular occasion. But nearly all states have now enacted ***rape shield statutes*** to restrict evidence of the victim's past sexual conduct.

   a. **FRE:** The FRE's rape shield provision, Rule 412, completely disallows reputation or opinion evidence concerning the victim's past sexual behavior. FRE 412 also prohibits evidence of specific acts concerning the victim's past sexual behavior in most situations; for instance, D is never allowed to offer evidence of V's past sexual behavior with ***persons other than himself*** if offered on the issue of whether there was consent.

      i. **Civil:** FRE 412 also applies to certain ***civil*** suits. For instance, if P sues for ***sexual harassment***, D usually can't show that P was known to be promiscuous with others or dressed seductively, and thus indicated her willingness to accept sexual advances at work.

G. **Prosecution's evidence of criminal defendant's bad character:** If a criminal defendant uses FRE 404(a)(2)(B) to put on evidence of that V has a particular bad character trait, the prosecution is then automatically entitled to put on evidence that the ***defendant has that same bad character trait.*** See FRE 404(a)(2)(B)(ii).

1. **Evidence of D's violent character:** Most commonly, the way this happens is that D, charged with a crime of violence against V, uses FRE 404(a)(2) to put on evidence that ***V had or has a violent character*** (to show that V, not D, probably started the violence). The prosecution will then be entitled to show that ***D, too, had a violent disposition.***

   a. **Not applicable if D uses source other than 404(a)(2):** But this special rule applies only where D's evidence about V's violent disposition is admitted under FRE ***404(a)(2)(B),*** not where D relies on ***some other evidentiary theory*** for the evidence of V's violent tendencies.

Example: D is charged with murdering V by stabbing him during a barroom brawl. D defends on the grounds of self-defense, and shows that before the altercation, he knew that V had a reputation for often drawing a knife without warning. D testifies that this reputation was on his mind when he drew his own knife first. Since D is offering the evidence about V's violent reputation not under FRE 404(a)(2)(B) (i.e., not as a way of showing that V had a generally violent disposition, making it more likely that V started the fight), but rather as a way of supporting his self-defense claim (i.e., that he reasonably feared for his life), the prosecution will not be able to show that D, too, has a previously-demonstrated propensity for violence.

III. METHODS OF PROVING CHARACTER: REPUTATION, OPINION AND PROOF OF SPECIFIC ACTS

A. FRE: Whenever proof of a character trait is allowed, the FRE let that proof be by either ***reputation*** or ***opinion*** testimony. FRE 405(a).

1. **D's good-character evidence:** So D in a criminal case can show his own good character by W's testimony that D has a good reputation for, say, honesty or non-violence, or by testimony that in W's opinion, D possesses these favorable character traits. (But D ***can't*** show ***specific instances*** of his own good character.)

   a. **Rebuttal:** If D makes this showing (thus "opening the door"), the prosecution may ***rebut*** by reputation or opinion evidence of D's poor character. Also, the prosecution may use ***specific acts evidence*** during its ***cross*** of D's good-character witnesses.

   Example: Prosecution can ask D's character witness, "Would it change your opinion of D's peaceful nature to know that he started three fights at the Tavern on the Green in the last year alone?"

   i. **Good-faith basis for specific-act question:** Before the cross examiner asks about a specific act during cross, she must have a ***"good faith basis"*** for believing that the specific act really occurred.

   Example: In the above example, the prosecutor must have a good-faith basis for believing that the barroom fights really occurred.

   ii. **No extrinsic acts:** Also, the prosecution can't use ***extrinsic evidence*** of the specific acts — it may merely ask the defense's good-character witness about them.

   Example: In the above barroom-fights example, if D's witness W said, "I don't believe those fights ever happened, and if they did they weren't started by D," the prosecution can't prove otherwise. The prosecution must "take the answer of the witness." So, for instance, the prosecution can't put on testimony by W2 to say, "D was involved in two barroom fights that I personally witnessed."

2. **Character of victim:** Similarly, D can show the character of the victim by use of reputation or opinion evidence.

   Example: In murder case where D claims self-defense, D can put on W to testify, "In my opinion, V was always the kind of guy who liked to start fights."

   a. **Rebuttal:** Again, the prosecution in rebuttal can not only use reputation or opinion, but can also refer to specific acts on cross.

3. **Proof for "other purposes":** Where a party (usually the prosecution) is using D's prior crimes or bad acts for some "other purpose" (e.g., identity, knowledge, etc.), this proof can be by "specific acts."

   Example: If D is charged with robbing the 2nd Nat'l Bank with a blue ski mask and yellow raincoat, and D denies that he's the one who did it, prosecution can show that on June 21, D robbed the 1st Nat'l Bank wearing this distinctive garb, because it's so unusual as to amount to a "signature."

IV. PAST SEXUAL ASSAULT OR CHILD MOLESTATION BY D

A. **FRE allows:** Under FRE 413, if D is accused of a sexual assault, evidence that D has ***committed a sexual assault in the past*** is ***admissible***, and may be considered on any relevant matter.

   Example: If D's charged with raping V, prosecution may show that 20 years ago, D raped someone else. Prosecution may also argue, "The fact that D raped before means he's extra likely to have committed the present rape."

   1. **Child molestations; civil suits:** Similar rules (FRE 414 and 415) allow: (i) proof that D previously ***molested a child*** to be introduced in his present molestation trial, and (ii) proof of D's prior sexual assaults or child molestations to be introduced in ***civil*** proceedings where P claims D sexually assaulted or molested P.

V. HABIT AND CUSTOM

A. **Generally allowable:** Evidence of a person's ***habit*** is admissible in most courts (and the FRE) to show that he ***followed this habit on a particular occasion***. "Habits" are thus to be distinguished from "character traits" (generally disallowed as circumstantial evidence that the character trait was followed on a particular occasion).

   1. **Three factors:** There are three main factors courts look to in deciding whether something is a "habit" or merely a trait of character:

      a. **Specificity:** The more *specific* the behavior, the more likely it is to be deemed a habit.

      Example: If V is killed when his car is hit on the railroad tracks, his estate will be allowed to show that he had almost always stopped and looked before crossing those tracks every day — this conduct will be a "habit," because it is very specific. But V's general "carefulness" will be found to be a character trait, not a habit, and will thus not be admissible to show that he probably behaved carefully at the time of the fatal crossing.

b. **Regularity:** The more ***"regular"*** the behavior, the more likely to be a habit. "Regularity" means "ratio of reaction to situations." (So something that X does 95% of the time she's in a particular situation is more likely to be a habit than something X does 55% of the time in that situation.)

c. **Unreflective behavior:** The more ***"unreflective"*** or ***"semi-automatic"*** the behavior, the more likely it is to be a habit.

Examples: Using a left-hand turn signal is probably a habit because it's semi-automatic; going to temple for the Sabbath each Friday night is probably not a habit, because it requires conscious thought and volition.

B. Federal Rules: FRE 406 follows the majority rule, by providing that "[e]vidence of a person's habit or an organization's routine practice may be admitted to prove that on a particular occasion the person or organization acted in accordance with the habit or routine practice."

C. Business practices: All courts allow evidence of the ***routine practice*** of an ***organization***, to show that that practice was followed on a particular occasion.

Example: A business may prove that a particular letter was mailed by showing that it was the organization's routine practice to mail all letters placed in any worker's "outgoing mail" box, and that the letter in question was placed in such a box.

VI. SIMILAR HAPPENINGS

A. General rule: Evidence that similar happenings have occurred in the past (offered to prove that the event in question really happened) is generally ***allowed***. However, the proponent must show that there is ***substantial similarity*** between the past similar happening and the event under litigation.

1. **Accidents and injuries:** Thus evidence of past similar injuries or accidents will often be admitted to show that the same kind of mishap occurred in the present case, or to show that the defendant was negligent in not fixing the problem after the prior mishaps. But the plaintiff will have to show that the conditions were the same in the prior and present situations.

2. **Past safety:** Conversely, the defendant will usually be allowed to show due care or the absence of a defect, by showing that there have ***not*** been similar accidents in the past. However, D must show that: (1) ***conditions were the same*** in the past as when the accident occurred; and (2) had there been any injuries in the past, they would have been ***reported*** to D.

VII. SUBSEQUENT REMEDIAL MEASURES

A. General rule: Courts generally ***do not allow*** evidence that a party has merely taken ***subsequent remedial measures***, when offered to show that the party was negligent, or was conscious of being at fault.

Example: P trips on D's sidewalk; P may not show that just after the fall, D repaved the sidewalk and thus conceded the sidewalk's dangerousness.

1. **Federal Rules:** FRE 407 follows this rule: subsequent remedial measures may not be admitted to prove negligence or culpable conduct in connection with an event.

B. Other purposes: But subsequent remedial measures may be shown to prove elements other than culpability or negligence. For instance, such measures may be used to rebut the defendant's claim that there was no safer way to handle the situation. Or, if the defendant claims that he did not own or control property involved in an accident, the fact that he subsequently repaired the property may be shown to rebut this assertion.

C. Product liability: The FRE ***apply*** the no-subsequent-remedial-measures rule to ***product-liability*** cases, just as they apply it to negligence cases. FRE 407 says that subsequent-measures evidence is not admissible to prove "negligence; culpable conduct; a ***defect in a product or its design***; or a need for a ***warning or instruction***."

Example: P, the owner of a single-engine plane made by D, crashes in the plane when it runs out of fuel because water has gotten into the fuel tanks. P sues D on a products liability defective-design theory. P's theory is that a defective design of the fuel tanks allowed condensation to form inside the tank. In support of this theory, P offers evidence that shortly after this and two other similar accidents, D redesigned the fuel tanks to make such condensation less likely. Under FRE 407, this evidence will not be admissible.

VIII. LIABILITY INSURANCE

A. General rule: Evidence that person carried or did not carry ***liability insurance*** is ***never*** admissible on the issue of whether he acted negligently. See FRE 411. (But evidence of the existence or non-existence of liability insurance is admissible for purposes other than proving negligence. For instance, the fact that W, a witness for D in a tort suit, works for D's liability insurance company, could be admitted to show bias on W's part.)

IX. SETTLEMENTS AND PLEA BARGAINS

A. Settlements: The fact that a party has offered to ***settle*** a claim may ***not*** be admitted on the issue of the claim's validity. See FRE 408.

1. **Collateral admissions of fact:** ***Admissions of fact*** made during the course of settlement negotiations are generally admissible at common law, but not admissible under FRE 408.

Example: "I was drunk when I ran over you, so I'll pay you $5,000 in damages," would be admissible at common law to prove D's drunkenness, but not admissible under FRE 408.

2. **Other purposes:** But settlement offers may be admissible to prove issues other than liability.

   Example: If W testifies on behalf of D in a civil suit, the fact that W received money from D in settlement for a related claim may be admitted to show that W is biased in favor of D and against P.

B. **Guilty pleas:**

1. **Defendant's offer to plead:** The fact that the defendant has offered to ***plead guilty*** (and the offer has been rejected by the prosecutor) may ***not*** be shown to prove that D is guilty or is conscious of his guilt. FRE 410(4) excludes not only the offer to plead guilty but any other ***statement*** made in the course of plea discussions with the prosecutor, from being used against the defendant.

2. **Withdrawn plea:** Similarly, the fact that D made a guilty plea and then later ***withdrew it*** may not be admitted against D in the ultimate trial.

3. **Later civil case:** The plea offer or withdrawn plea, and the accompanying factual admissions, are also not admissible in any ***later civil case***. FRE 410(4).

C. **Offer to pay medical expenses:** The fact that a party has paid the ***medical expenses*** of an injured person is not admissible to show that party's liability for the accident that caused the injury. See FRE 409. But only the fact of payment, not related admissions of fact, are excluded.

   Example: D says to P, "I'm paying your medical expenses because if I hadn't been drunk that night, I wouldn't have hit you." This may be admitted to show D's drunkenness but not to show that D paid the expenses.

CHAPTER 3

EXAMINATION AND IMPEACHMENT OF WITNESSES

I. FLOW OF EXAMINATION

A. **Four stages:** The examination of a witness goes through up to four stages:

1. **Direct:** First, the party who called the witness engages in the ***direct*** examination.

2. **Cross:** After the calling side has finished the direct exam, the other side may ***cross-examine*** the witness.

3. **Re-direct:** The calling side then has the opportunity to conduct ***re-direct*** examination.

4. **Re-cross:** Finally, the cross-examining side gets a brief opportunity to conduct ***re-cross***.

II. DIRECT EXAMINATION

A. **Leading questions:** Generally, the examiner ***may not ask leading questions*** on direct.

1. **Definition:** A leading question is one that ***suggests to the witness the answer desired by the questioner***.

   Example: Auto negligence suit by P against D. Question by P's lawyer to P: "Was D driving faster than the speed limit at the time he hit you?" This is leading, since it suggests that the questioner desires a "yes" answer.

2. **Hostile witness:** Leading questions are allowed on direct if the witness is ***"hostile."*** The ***opposing party*** will almost always be deemed hostile; so will a witness who is shown to be biased against the calling side, as well as a witness whose demeanor on the stand shows hostility to the calling side.

B. Jurors as witnesses: Unsuccessful litigants would often like to be able to ***impeach*** a jury verdict by offering ***testimony of a juror*** as to statements ***made or heard during deliberations***. But the common law and the Federal Rules generally ***prohibit admission*** of juror testimony to impeach a jury verdict. See FRE 606(b).

III. CROSS-EXAMINATION

A. Leading questions: Leading questions are usually ***permitted*** during cross-examination. (FRE 611(c))

1. **Exception:** But if the witness is biased in favor of the cross-examiner (e.g., one party is called by the other and then "cross"-examined by his own lawyer), leading questions are not allowed.

B. Scope: The majority (and federal) rule is that cross is ***limited*** to the ***matters testified to on the direct examination***. (FRE 611(b))

C. Credibility: The witness's ***credibility*** may always be attacked on cross-examination.

IV. RE-DIRECT AND RE-CROSS

A. Re-direct: Re-direct is limited to those aspects of the witness's testimony that were ***first brought out during cross***.

B. Re-cross: Similarly, re-cross is limited to matters newly brought up on the re-direct.

V. REFRESHING RECOLLECTION AND OTHER TECHNIQUES

A. Refreshing recollection: If the witness's memory on a subject is hazy, ***any item*** (picture, document, weapon, etc.) may be ***shown to the witness*** to refresh his recollection. This is the technique of ***"present recollection refreshed."***

1. **Not necessarily admissible:** The item need ***not*** be ***admissible***. For instance, it can consist of ***inadmissible hearsay***. Furthermore, the item ***does not become admissible*** by virtue of being used for refreshment.

   Example: D is charged with bank robbery. The prosecution offers testimony by Officer, who investigated the crime. While testifying, Officer consults notes prepared by him during the course of his investigation. D's lawyer objects on the grounds that the notes haven't been introduced into evidence, that the notes *can't* be introduced because they are hearsay not within any exception, and that Officer should therefore be barred from testifying in reliance on their contents.

As long as the court is satisfied that Officer is testifying from his own now-refreshed recollection, the fact that the notes haven't been introduced into evidence (and can't be, because of hearsay problems) is irrelevant. And once Officer has consulted the notes, they don't thereby become evidence.

2. **Abuse:** If the item shown to the witness is a ***document***, and the trial judge concludes that the witness is really ***reading the document on the stand*** instead of testifying from his now-refreshed recollection, he may order the testimony stricken.

3. **Cross-examination:** The cross-examiner may ***examine*** the document or other item shown to the witness, and ***use*** any part of the document during cross-examination. Further, the cross-examiner may ***introduce into evidence*** any parts of the document that relate to the witness's testimony.

4. **Documents seen before trial:** If a document has been consulted by the witness ***before he took the stand***, the Federal Rules give the trial court ***discretion*** to order that the document be ***shown to the other side***, "if the court decides that ***justice [so] requires***[.]" (FRE 612(a)(2)).

B. **Argumentative and misleading questions:** A question will be stricken if it is either ***argumentative*** or ***misleading***.

1. **Argumentative:** An ***argumentative*** question is one which tries to get the witness to agree with counsel's interpretation of the evidence. It is more common on cross than on direct, and usually has an element of badgering the witness.

2. **Misleading:** A ***misleading*** question is one that assumes as true a fact that is either ***not in evidence*** or is in dispute. It usually has a "trick" aspect.

Example: "When did you stop beating your wife," will be misleading if there is no or disputed evidence of wife-beating, since any answer by W will be an implicit admission that he has beaten her.

VI. EXAMINATION BY COURT

A. **General rule:** The trial judge may call his own witnesses, and may question any witness (whether called by the judge or by a party). (FRE 614(a) and (b))

VII. IMPEACHMENT — GENERALLY

A. **Five types:** There are five main ways of ***impeaching*** a witness, i.e., of destroying the witness's credibility:

[1] by attacking W's ***general character*** (e.g., by showing past crimes, past bad acts, or bad reputation);

[2] by showing a ***prior inconsistent statement*** by W;

[3] by showing that W is ***biased***;

[4] by showing that W has a ***sensory or mental defect***; and

[5] by *other evidence* (e.g., a second witness's testimony) that ***contradicts*** W's testimony.

B. Impeaching one's own witness:

1. **Common law:** At common law, ***a party may not impeach his own witness***. That is, impeachment is generally ***not allowed on direct examination***.

   a. **Exceptions:** But this common-law rule has several exceptions. Impeachment on direct is allowed if: (1) W's unfavorable testimony comes as a genuine surprise to the direct examiner (who may then show prior inconsistent statements by W); or (2) W is an adverse party or a hostile witness.

2. **Modern and Federal Rule:** Many states, and the Federal Rules, have now completely ***abandoned*** the common law rule prohibiting impeachment of one's own witness. See, e.g., FRE 607: "Any party, including the party that called the witness, may attack the witness's credibility." Also, a criminal defendant may have the right under the Sixth Amendment's Confrontation Clause to impeach a witness he has called.

VIII. IMPEACHMENT BY PRIOR CRIMINAL CONVICTION

A. Common-law rule: At common law, two types of prior convictions may be used to impeach W's credibility:

1. *Any felony* conviction;

2. A ***misdemeanor*** conviction, but only if the crime involved ***dishonesty*** or a ***false statement***.

B. Federal Rule: The Federal Rules make it slightly harder to use prior convictions to impeach the witness. Under FRE 609(a):

1. ***Crimen falsi:*** If the crime included as an element ***dishonesty or false statement*** ("*crimen falsi*"), ***it may always be used to impeach W,*** regardless of whether it was a misdemeanor or a felony, and regardless of the degree of prejudice to W (who will usually be the defendant in a criminal proceeding).

   a. **Judge has no discretion to exclude:** Once it's established that the conviction is for a *crimen falsi*, the judge does ***not*** even have ***discretion*** to exclude it under FRE 403, which normally allows exclusion of evidence whose probative value is substantially outweighed by the danger of unfair prejudice. So no matter how prejudicial to the opponent the evidence is, and no matter how tiny its probative value, the judge must let it come in.

   b. **Catalog of *crimen falsi*:** Here is a partial catalog of crimes that ***are*** generally considered to be *crimen falsi*:

      - ❑ ***Perjury*** or ***subornation of perjury***;
      - ❑ ***False statement***;
      - ❑ ***Criminal fraud***;

- ❑ ***Embezzlement***;
- ❑ Taking property by ***false pretenses***;
- ❑ ***Counterfeiting***;
- ❑ ***Forgery***; and
- ❑ ***Filing false tax returns***, or failing to file returns at all. (Not all courts agree on the latter.)

Example of *crimen falsi* analysis: D is charged with possession of marijuana, found on the front seat of a car in which D was a passenger when stopped. The prosecution calls the owner of the car, who testifies that the marijuana was not his. D's lawyer now asks the owner, "Isn't it true that three years ago, you were convicted of misdemeanor perjury charges?" The owner denies this, at which point D's lawyer offers into evidence proof of such a conviction.

The question and proof of conviction are admissible. That's because ***perjury is always a crimen falsi***, i.e., a crime the conviction of which "required proving — or the witness's admitting — a dishonest act or false statement." (609(a)(2)). Therefore, the conviction is admissible (1) even though it was a misdemeanor rather than a felony (i.e., "regardless of the punishment," in the language of 609(a)(2)), and (2) regardless of the relationship between its prejudicial impact and its probative value.

c. **Not *crimen falsi*:** Other crimes just as clearly fall on the ***non-****crimen falsi* side of the line. These are crimes that are defined in such a way that deception is not one of the elements. Most crimes of ***violence*** (***murder***, ***rape***, ***assault and battery***, for instance), as well as a number of non-violent crimes (***drug offenses***; ***prostitution***; driving while intoxicated; resisting arrest) are not *crimen falsi,* since dishonesty or false statement is not an element of those crimes.

   i. **Other theft crimes:** ***Theft*** crimes other than false pretenses and embezzlement are ***not*** *crimen falsi*. So ***shoplifting, robbery*** and ***receiving stolen goods*** aren't *crimen falsi* under the FRE.

d. **Don't look to underlying facts:** Under FRE 609(a), the court may ***not*** treat a crime as *crimen falsi* ***unless it is defined so as to require proof of dishonesty or false statement*** — it's not enough that the defendant ***actually behaved in a deceitful way***.

   Example: D sees V on the street, lures her into a secluded alleyway by falsely telling her he has a message for her from her husband, and then robs her. Since robbery is not defined to include dishonesty or false statement as an element of the crime, D's robbery conviction is not a *crimen falsi* under FRE 609(a) even though D committed this particular crime in a deceitful manner.

2. **Non-*crimen-falsi* felony used against criminal D:** If the crime was a ***felony*** not involving dishonesty or false statement, and the witness is the ***defendant in a criminal case***, the crime may be used only "if the probative value of the evidence ***outweighs*** its prejudicial effect to [the] defendant." So criminal defendants get a

slight degree of ***extra protection*** against having their non-*crimen-falsi* convictions used against them.

a. **Witnesses other than an accused:** By contrast, where the witness being impeached by a non-*crimen-falsi* felony conviction is ***not*** a criminal defendant (i.e., she's a prosecution witness, a witness for a criminal defendant, or any witness in a civil case), the witness gets no special protection against impeachment. Instead, FRE 403 applies, allowing a prior conviction to be excluded only if the person *opposing* its introduction bears the burden of showing that the conviction's probative value is "substantially outweighed by a danger of ... unfair prejudice[.]"

3. **Other misdemeanors:** If the crime was a ***misdemeanor not involving dishonesty or false statement***, it may ***not*** be used for impeachment under any circumstances.

4. **Old convictions:** If ***more than 10 years*** have elapsed from both the conviction and the prison term for that conviction, the conviction may not be used for impeachment unless the court determines that there are "specific facts and circumstances" that make the probative value of the conviction substantially outweigh its prejudicial effect. FRE 609(b)(1). This makes it much harder to get more-than-10-year-old convictions into evidence.

5. ***In limine*** **motions:** D may, before taking the stand, ask the trial court to rule *in limine* whether a particular conviction will be allowed to impeach him. If the ruling goes against D, D can then elect not to take the stand. (But if he doesn't take the stand, the *in limine* ruling will not be reviewed on appeal, at least in federal courts.)

6. **Ineligible convictions:** Certain types of convictions are excluded by special rules: If W was ***pardoned***, based on a finding of ***innocence***, the conviction may never be used. (If the pardon was because W was rehabilitated, it may be used for impeachment only if W has been convicted of a subsequent felony.) A ***"juvenile adjudication"*** of D may not be used to impeach him. FRE 609(c), (d).

IX. IMPEACHMENT BY PRIOR BAD ACTS

A. Common law:

1. **Generally allowed:** Most common-law courts allow the cross-examiner to bring out the fact that the witness has committed ***prior bad acts***, even though these have not led to a criminal conviction. (E.g., "Isn't it true that you lied on your job application by falsely stating that you had never used drugs?")

a. **Questions about arrests:** Most courts say that the witness can't be asked whether he's been ***arrested*** for a particular act — the question must be, "Did you commit thus-and-such an act?" not "Did you get arrested for thus-and-such an act?"

2. **No extrinsic evidence:** The prior bad acts ***must*** be introduced solely through the cross-examination, ***not*** through ***extrinsic evidence.*** (*Example:* If W denies having

lied on a job application, the cross-examiner cannot call a different witness to prove that the lie occurred.)

3. **Good-faith basis:** Before the prosecutor may ask a witness about a prior specific bad act, he must have a ***good faith basis*** for believing that the witness really committed the act.

B. Federal Rule: The Federal Rules basically follow the common-law approach to prior bad act impeachment. (FRE 608(b))

1. **Probative of truthfulness:** However, only prior bad acts that are ***probative of truthfulness*** may be asked about.

   Example: A prior act of lying on a job application or embezzling from an employer could be asked about, but the fact that W killed his wife and was never tried could not be, because this act does not make it more likely than it would otherwise be that W is now lying.

2. **No extrinsic evidence:** As at common law, any prior bad act must be shown only through cross-examination, not through extrinsic evidence.

3. **Discretion of court:** All questions about prior bad acts are in the ***discretion of the court***. The extent to which the questioner has a good faith basis for believing W really committed the act will, of course, be one factor the court normally considers.

X. IMPEACHMENT BY OPINION AND REPUTATION REGARDING CHARACTER

A. Common law:

1. **Allowed at common law:** Common law allows W1's credibility to be impeached by testimony from W2 that W1 has a ***bad reputation for truthfulness***.

2. **Opening issue:** As soon as a criminal defendant takes the stand, he opens himself up to this kind of evidence, even if he does not affirmatively state that he is a truthful person.

3. **Opinions:** W2 must say that W1 has a bad reputation for truthfulness; W2 may not state his own ***opinion*** that W1 is untruthful. Nor may W2 describe ***specific instances*** of conduct by W1 that led to his bad reputation for truthfulness.

4. **General bad character:** W2 must talk only about W1's reputation for truthfulness, not W1's reputation for general bad character.

B. Federal Rules: FRE 608(a) basically follows the common law, except that W2 may state his ***opinion*** that W1 is a liar (as well as stating that W1 has a reputation for being a liar). Here, too, no specific instances of untruthfulness by W1 are allowed.

XI. IMPEACHMENT BY PRIOR INCONSISTENT STATEMENT

A. General rule: W's credibility may generally be impeached by showing that he has made a ***prior inconsistent statement.***

B. Foundation: But before W's prior inconsistent statement may be admitted to impeach him, a ***foundation*** must be laid.

1. **Common law:** At common law, the foundation requirement is rigid: W must be told the substance of the alleged statement, the time, the place, and the person to whom it was made. He must then be given a chance to deny having made the statement, or to explain away the inconsistency. Only after all this may the prior inconsistent statement be introduced into evidence.

2. **Federal Rule:** The Federal Rules liberalize the foundation requirement: W must still be given a chance to explain or deny the prior inconsistent statement, but this opportunity does not have to be given to him until ***after*** the statement has been proved (e.g., by testimony from W2 that W1 made the prior inconsistent statement). For more about this, see Paragraph (C), "Extrinsic evidence," below.

3. **Writing:** If the prior inconsistent statement is ***written***, the common-law rule is that the writing must be shown to the witness before it is admitted. But FRE 613(a) relaxes this requirement, too: the examiner may first get W to deny having made the prior statement, and then admit it into evidence.

C. Extrinsic evidence: Special rules limit the questioner's ability to prove that W made a prior inconsistent statement by ***"extrinsic"*** evidence, i.e., by evidence other than W's admitting that he did so (e.g., testimony by W2 or admission of a copy of W's prior written statement).

1. **Federal Rule:** The Federal Rules make it ***easier*** than the common law did for a questioner to prove by extrinsic evidence that a witness made a prior inconsistent statement. But the FRE still impose important limits on this process. FRE 613(b) says that such extrinsic proof can only be made where ***two requirements*** are satisfied:

   [1] The witness who made the prior inconsistent statement must be ***"given an opportunity to explain or deny"*** it; and

   [2] The ***opposite party*** (the proponent of the testimony of the witness being impeached by the prior inconsistent statement) must be given "an ***opportunity to examine*** the witness [who made the inconsistent statement] about it."

   (But both of these requirements may be dispensed with if "justice so requires.")

   These two requirements mean that, as a practical matter, ***if the principal witness*** (call her W1) ***is to be impeached by a prior inconsistent statement***, the impeacher will have to be sure that ***after the extrinsic evidence is presented***, ***W1 remains physically available*** to "explain or deny" it and to be interrogated about the statement by W1's proponent.

   Example: W testifies in an auto accident case, "D was travelling over 70 mph." W is excused by P, and leaves the country. D presents testimony by Officer that when Officer interviewed W two days after the accident, W said "D wasn't going more than 60 mph."

Since W is no longer available to explain or deny making this statement, or to be interrogated about the alleged statement by P's counsel, FRE 613(b) prevents Officer's testimony.

a. No specific rule about extrinsic evidence on collateral matter: What if the prior inconsistent statement concerns a ***"collateral matter"*** (i.e., a matter that is not probative on any material issue in the case)?

i. Common law: At common law, there was an outright ***prohibition*** on extrinsic proof of prior inconsistent statements dealing with collateral matters.

ii. No specific Federal Rule on collateral matters: The Federal Rules do not expressly say whether this collateral-matters rule is maintained. But the effective answer is ***yes***. You'll remember that the trial judge has discretion, under FRE 403, to exclude any evidence whose probative value is "substantially outweighed by a danger of ... confusing the issues, or undue delay [or] wasting time[.]" Since extrinsic evidence that a witness made a prior inconsistent statement on a collateral matter will tend to cause confusion, delay and waste of time, the judge will often ***be justified in excluding*** the extrinsic evidence under 403.

Example: In an car-accident case, P calls W, who saw D's car collide with P's at a stoplight. W testifies at length about what he saw. Towards the end of his testimony, he mentions, "While D was talking to the responding police officer after the accident, I noticed that D was wearing tennis sneakers." D's lawyer cross-examines W extensively, during which he asks W, "Didn't you tell your neighbor N the day after the accident that D was wearing running shoes, not tennis sneakers?" W denies having made such a statement. D's lawyer now calls N as a rebuttal witness, to testify, "The day after the accident, W told me that when D was talking to the policeman right after the accident, W noticed that D was wearing running shoes."

N's testimony about W's prior inconsistent statement (1) is extrinsic evidence (i.e., not out of the mouth of W); and (2) concerns a collateral matter (since whether D's shoes were tennis sneakers or running shoes is not a material issue in the case). Therefore, the trial judge has authority — which she will likely exercise — to exclude W's testimony under Rule 403 on the grounds that its small probative value (its tendency to show that W is not a reliable witness) is substantially outweighed by the danger of confusing the jury, delaying the trial or wasting time.

XII. IMPEACHMENT FOR BIAS

A. Generally allowed: All courts allow proof that the witness is ***biased.*** W may be shown to be biased in favor of a party (e.g., W and P are friends or relatives), or biased against a party (e.g., W and D were once involved in litigation). W's ***interest in the***

outcome may be also shown as a form of bias (e.g., if W is an expert, the fact that he is being paid a fee for his testimony is generally allowed as showing that he has an interest in having the case decided in favor of the party retaining him).

B. Extrinsic evidence: Bias may be shown by use of ***extrinsic evidence***. However, most courts require a foundation before extrinsic evidence may be used for this purpose: the examiner must ask W about the alleged bias, and only if W denies it may the extrinsic evidence (e.g., testimony by another person that W is biased) be presented.

XIII. IMPEACHMENT BY SENSORY OR MENTAL DEFECT

A. Generally allowed: W may be impeached by showing that his capacity to ***observe***, ***remember***, or ***narrate*** events correctly has been impaired.

Example: W may be shown to have such poor eyesight that he couldn't have seen what he claims to have seen.

B. Alcohol and drugs:

1. **Use during event:** W may be impeached by showing that he was ***drunk*** or ***high on drugs*** at the time of the events he claims to have witnessed.
2. **Addiction:** Courts are split on whether W may be shown to be a ***habitual*** or addicted user of alcohol and drugs — many courts will not allow this if there is no showing that W was drunk or high at the time of the events in question.

XIV. IMPEACHMENT BY CONTRADICTION; THE "COLLATERAL ISSUE" RULE

A. Showing of contradiction allowed: W1 may be impeached by presenting W2, who contradicts W1 on some point.

Example: W1 says that perpetrator of robbery had red hair; defense can put on W2 to testify that robber had brown hair — this not only is evidence of a material fact, but also impeaches W1.

B. Collateral issue rule: However, the right to put on a second witness to impeach the first by contradicting him, is limited by the ***"collateral issue"*** rule, at least at common law. By this rule, certain types of testimony by W2 are deemed to be of such collateral interest to the case that they will not be allowed if their sole purpose is to contradict W1.

1. **Disallowed:** Thus, W2 may not testify as to: (1) prior bad acts by W1 that did not lead to a conviction; (2) prior inconsistent statements made by W1 that do not relate to a material fact in the case; or (3) things said by W1 in his testimony which according to W2 are not true, unless these facts are material to the case.
2. **Allowed:** On the other hand, testimony by W2 will not be deemed to be collateral, and will thus be allowed, as to the following subjects: (1) prior criminal convictions by W1; (2) W1's bad character for truthfulness; (3) W1's bias; or (4)

W1's sensory or mental defect that prevents W1 from observing, remembering or narrating events correctly.

3. **Federal Rule:** The Federal Rules do not contain any explicit "collateral issue" rule. However, the trial judge can apply the policies behind the rule by using FRE 403's balancing test (evidence excludable where its probative value is substantially outweighed by confusion, prejudice, or waste of time).

XV. RELIGIOUS BELIEFS

A. **General rule:** Most courts do not allow W to be impeached by a showing that he does not believe in God. Impeachment based on religious beliefs is also barred by FRE 610.

XVI. REHABILITATING IMPEACHED WITNESS

A. **No bolstering:** A lawyer may not offer evidence ***supporting his witness's credibility***, unless that credibility has first been ***attacked*** by the other side. This is known as the rule against ***"bolstering one's witness"***. (*Example:* On direct, W tells a story favorable to P. P's lawyer will not be permitted to bring out on direct the fact that prior to the trial, W told the same story to the police — W's credibility has not yet been attacked, so it may not be bolstered by a showing that W made a prior consistent statement.)

1. **Prior identification:** However, the "no bolstering" rule does not apply where W has made a prior out-of-court ***identification*** — most courts allow this to be brought out as part of the direct examination of W.

2. **Prompt complaint:** Similarly, in ***rape*** cases most courts allow the victim to in effect bolster her own testimony by stating that she made a ***prompt complaint*** to the police immediately following the crime.

B. **Rehabilitation:** Apart from these exceptions, W's credibility may be supported only to rehabilitate it, i.e., only to repair the damage done by the ***other side's attack*** on that credibility.

1. **Meet attack:** The rehabilitating evidence must ***"meet the attack."*** That is, it must support W's credibility in the same respect as that in which the credibility has been attacked by the other side.

   Example: P attacks W as being biased because he is D's son. D may rehabilitate W's credibility by showing evidence of non-bias. But D may not rehabilitate W by showing W's good reputation for truthfulness, or W's prior out-of-court statements that are consistent with his trial testimony — D's attempts at rehabilitation do not respond directly to the charge of bias.

2. **Good character:** If W's credibility is attacked by evidence tending to show that he is generally untruthful, the proponent may show that W has a good character for truthfulness. Thus evidence of W's ***good character for truthfulness*** may be used to rebut evidence that: (1) W has a ***bad reputation*** for truthfulness; (2) that W2 has a ***bad opinion*** of W's truthfulness; (3) that W has been ***convicted*** of a crime; or (4) that W has committed a ***prior bad act***; and perhaps (5) that W has

been subjected to a slashing ***cross-examination*** by the opponent, implying or stating that W is a ***liar***.

a. **Attack on present testimony:** But if the attack on W has merely been to show that his testimony in the present case is inaccurate, W's credibility may not be rehabilitated by a showing of his general good character for truthfulness. Thus good character evidence will not be allowed to rebut evidence that: (1) W is ***biased*** because he is related to the other party; (2) W has given ***erroneous testimony*** in this case, perhaps through honest mistake.

b. **Prior inconsistent statement:** If W has been attacked by a showing that he made a ***prior inconsistent statement***, the courts are split. Most treat this as an implicit attack on W's general credibility, and thus allow him to be rehabilitated by a showing of good general character for truthfulness.

3. **Prior consistent statement:** The fact that W has made a ***prior consistent statement*** (i.e., an out-of-court statement that matches his trial testimony) may be used only to rebut an express or implied charge that W's trial testimony is a ***recent fabrication*** or the product of ***improper influence or motive***. This is the common-law rule, and is also carried out by FRE 801(d)(1)(B).

a. **Attack on general character:** Thus if W is attacked by showing his ***prior criminal convictions***, ***prior bad acts***, or his general ***bad reputation*** for veracity, his credibility may ***not*** be rehabilitated by a showing that he made prior consistent statements.

b. **Prior inconsistent statement:** The opponent's showing that W has made a prior ***inconsistent*** statement will not, by itself, entitle the proponent to show that W has also made a prior consistent statement. The proponent must demonstrate that the adversary's use of the prior inconsistent statement amounts to an express or implied claim that W has recently made up his trial testimony, or is lying because of improper influence or ulterior motives. (Thus if the showing of the prior inconsistent statement can reasonably be interpreted as suggesting that W is merely honestly mistaken, W cannot be rehabilitated by the prior consistent statement.)

c. **Before motive arose:** The proponent who wants to use a prior consistent statement must show that the prior statement was made ***before*** the alleged motive to fabricate or improper influence arose. This rule applies both at common-law and under FRE 801(d)(1)(B). [*Tome v. U.S.*]

XVII. SPECIAL TECHNIQUES FOR DEVELOPING OR EVALUATING TESTIMONY

A. **Psychiatric testimony:** The trial judge has discretion to allow psychiatric expert testimony to show that W's accuracy is doubtful because of some mental illness or defect. For instance, the judge might appoint a psychiatrist to give expert testimony as to whether V's mental illness may have caused her to imagine a rape, or to have falsified the surrounding details. But judges will generally order a party or witness to undergo psychiatric examination for purposes of evaluating credibility only if there are ***compelling reasons*** to do so.

B. Hypnosis and truth serum:

1. **Statement made under influence:** Statements made under the influence of hypnosis or truth serum are almost always ***rejected.***

2. **Testimony at trial:** Live testimony by W about an event, his recall of which has been refreshed through hypnosis or truth serum, is also usually ***rejected.*** But a minority of courts allow hypnosis-influenced testimony if stringent safeguards have been followed (e.g., a video tape was made of the hypnosis session).

   a. **Criminal defendant's right to testify:** Where the hypnotized witness is a ***criminal defendant***, the court's right to reject hypnotically-refreshed testimony is limited by the defendant's constitutional right to ***testify in his own defense***. [*Rock v. Arkansas*]

C. Lie detectors:

1. **General rule:** Nearly all courts ***reject*** lie detector evidence when offered on the issue of whether the statements made by the subject during the test are true. (However, *Daubert v. Merrell Dow*, holding that scientifically valid techniques can't be excluded from federal trials just because they're not "generally accepted," may now be changing this blanket rule.)

2. **Stipulation:** A substantial minority of courts allow lie detector results where both parties have ***stipulated*** before the test that the results may be admitted.

CHAPTER 4

HEARSAY

I. DEFINITION

A. Simple definition: Hearsay is ***"a statement or assertive conduct that was made or occurred out of court and is offered in court to prove the truth of the matter asserted."***

Example: V says, "D tried to poison me last night." This is hearsay if offered to show that D really tried to kill V last night, since it is an out-of-court statement offered to prove the truth of the matter asserted.

1. **Writing:** Hearsay may be ***written*** as well as oral.

   Example: A letter written by V to her mother, "D tried to kill me last night," would be hearsay if offered to prove that D really did this, just as would V's oral statement to her mother to the same effect.

B. Four dangers: The use of hearsay testimony presents four main dangers: (1) ***ambiguity***; (2) ***insincerity***; (3) ***incorrect memory***; and (4) ***inaccurate perception***. All of these relate to the fact that the person making the out-of-court statement (the declarant) is not available for cross-examination.

C. Triangle: In terms of the "testimonial triangle" in Fig. C-1 (see next page), O's statement will only be hearsay if the trier of fact is asked to travel from point A to point B to point C (i.e., the fact-finder must be asked to determine that the declarant truly held

Figure C-1

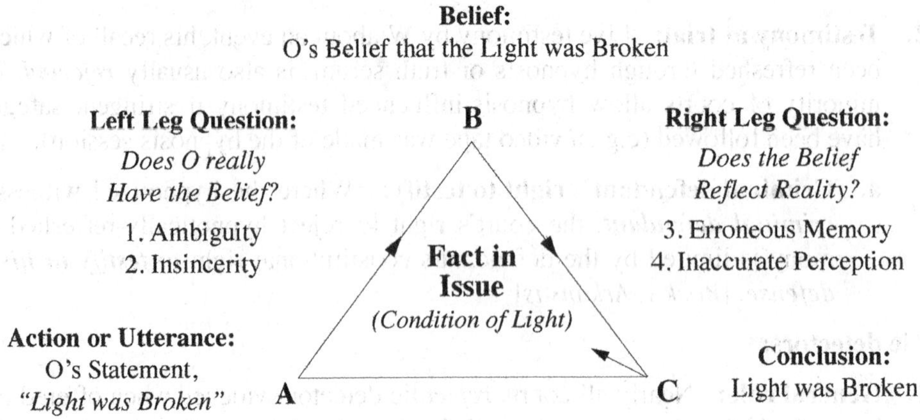

the belief which his declaration suggests he held — point B — and also that declarant's belief accurately reflects reality — point C).

Example: O is prosecuted for robbery; he claims that he was captured and forced to take part in the robbery. He offers a note he wrote to his wife during the captivity, "If I don't take part in the robbery, they'll kill me." The fact-finder is asked to travel from point A to point B (i.e., to determine whether O really believed his statement), but not to travel from point B to point C (i.e., to determine whether O's belief accorded with reality). Since the fact-finder is not asked to travel all the way around the triangle, O's statement is not hearsay.

II. SPECIAL ISSUES

A. "Out of court" statement: An out-of-court statement is any statement except one made "by a witness during the trial while testifying before the trier of fact." Therefore, the following will be out-of-court statements (and thus might be hearsay):

1. Any oral or written statement by someone other than the at-trial witness; and

2. A prior statement by the at-trial witness, where the prior statement was not made in the present trial before the trier of fact. Therefore, W's prior statement made in a ***deposition*** or at an ***earlier trial***, or even W's statement made in the judge's chambers during the present trial, are all "out of court" and so may be hearsay.

B. "Truth of matter asserted": Here are some uses to which a statement may be put that do ***not*** constitute offering the statement for the "truth of the matter asserted":

1. **Verbal acts:** The statement is a ***"verbal act,"*** i.e., an operative fact that gives rise to legal consequences.

Example: O says to W (a vice officer), "If you pay me $25 I will have sex with you." If O is prosecuted for solicitation, her statement will not be hearsay because it is not offered to show its truth (that O would really have had sex with W had he paid her $25); rather, the crime of solicitation is defined so as to make an offer to have sex for money an act with legal consequences.

a. **Verbal parts of act:** Similarly, a ***"verbal part of the act"***, i.e., words that accompany an ambiguous physical act, is not offered for truth and thus is not hearsay.

Example: O gives X money, saying, "This will repay you for the money you lent me last year." If offered by X in defense of a bribery charge, this will be non-hearsay because the words that accompanied the payment give the payment its particular legal effect — loan repayment.

2. **Effect on hearer/reader:** A statement offered to show its effect on the ***listener*** or ***reader*** will generally not be hearsay. Thus if a statement is offered to show that the listener or reader was ***put on notice***, had certain ***knowledge***, had a certain ***emotion***, or behaved ***reasonably*** or unreasonably, this will not be hearsay.

Example: Malpractice suit against D, a hospital, for having hired X as a doctor. P offers written statements by two other hospitals refusing to allow X on their staffs because he was incompetent. If P shows that D saw the letters before admitting X to the staff, this will not be hearsay — the letters are not being offered to prove the truth of the matters asserted (that X was really incompetent), merely to show that a reasonable person in D's position would have doubted X's competence.

3. **Declarant's state of mind:** Statements introduced to show the ***state of mind*** of the ***declarant*** are not offered for the "truth of the matter asserted" and thus are not hearsay.

a. **Knowledge:** Thus a statement offered to show the declarant's ***knowledge*** is not hearsay.

Example: D says to X, "I need to get my brakes checked because they haven't been working well." In a negligence suit by P against D, that statement is not hearsay, because it is not offered to show that the brakes really were defective, merely that D had knowledge that the brakes might be defective.

b. **Other mental state:** Statements offered to show the declarant's ***sanity*** or ***emotion*** (e.g., fear) are similarly not offered for truth and thus are not hearsay. (Also, there is an exception for "statements evidencing states of mind.")

4. **Reputation:** Statements about a person's ***reputation*** may not be hearsay.

Example: Libel action; W testifies at trial, "O told me that P has a reputation for thievery." If offered to show that O's statement caused this false reputation of P, this will not be hearsay — it is not offered to prove that P is really a thief, merely to prove that P has been given a false reputation for thievery.

5. **Impeachment:** If W makes a statement at trial, use of a prior inconsistent statement made out of court by W will not be hearsay when used to ***impeach*** W's present testimony — what is being shown is not that the prior out-of-court statement was truthful, but that the conflict between the two statements raises questions about W's credibility.

C. **"Statement" and conduct:** The hearsay rule applies only to "statements." An oral or written assertion is obviously a statement. But certain types of ***conduct*** may also be statements:

1. **Assertive conduct:** ***Assertive conduct*** is treated as if it were a "statement," so that it can be hearsay.

   Example: O pulls D's mug shot out of a collection of photos; since by this act O intends to assert, "That's the perpetrator," this act will be hearsay if offered on the issue of whether D was the perpetrator.

2. **Silence:** A person's ***silence*** will be treated as a "statement," and thus possibly hearsay, only if it is ***intended*** by the person as an assertion.

   a. **Absence of complaints:** The fact that one or more people have ***not made complaints*** about a situation will ***not*** usually be treated as the equivalent of a statement by them that there is nothing to complain about. Therefore, absence of prior complaints can usually be admitted without hearsay problems.

   b. **Silence in face of accusation:** But a person's silence in the face of an ***accusation against him***, where the silence is offered to show that the accusation was true, usually will be held to be intended as an assertion, and thus hearsay. (But the hearsay exception for admissions will usually apply anyway.)

3. **Non-assertive conduct:** Conduct that is ***not intended as an assertion*** will ***never*** be hearsay, under the modern and Federal Rules. (This reverses the earlier common-law rule of *Wright v. Doe*.)

   a. **Non-assertive verbal conduct:** Even a verbal statement will not be hearsay if it is not intended as an assertion.

   Example: D is charged with running a bookmaking operation out of his premises. W testifies that he answered D's phone, and the caller on the other end said, "Secretariat to place in the third." Caller's statement will not be hearsay, because even though it was verbal, the caller did not intend to assert, "I am talking to a betting parlor," or anything else.

   b. **Non-verbal conduct:** Similarly, non-verbal conduct that is not intended as an assertion will not give rise to hearsay.

   Example: O, while walking down the street, suddenly puts up his umbrella. If this act is introduced to show that it was raining, it will not be hearsay — O was not intending to assert to anyone, "It's raining."

4. **Assertions not offered to prove truth of matter asserted:** If an assertion is offered to prove another assertion that is ***implied by*** (or can be inferred from) the former, there is a hearsay problem only if the person making the assertion was ***thinking about the proposition now sought to be proved***.

   Example: O writes to T, "Cousin, the weather is wonderful in America and you would like it here." This assertion would not be hearsay if offered to establish that O thought T was sane, since it is unlikely that O was consciously thinking to himself when he wrote this letter, "T is sane." On the other hand, if O wrote to T, "As of your last letter, you seemed to be of sound mind," this would be hearsay even if offered as circumstantial proof that at some later date, T was still sane — O was thinking about the very issue now sought to be proved, T's sanity.

D. Multiple hearsay: If one out-of-court declaration quotes or paraphrases another out-of-court declaration, there is a problem of ***"multiple hearsay."*** The evidence is inadmissible if ***any*** of the declarations is hearsay not falling within an exception.

Example: W, an investigator, writes a report saying, "D told me that at the time of the crash, he was travelling at 65 mph." If this report is offered by P to show that D was indeed travelling at 65 mph, there are two levels of hearsay: D's original oral statement and W's out-of-court written paraphrase of it. But each would probably fall within an exception — D's original statement as an admission, and W's report under the business records rule. Therefore, the report could come into evidence.

CHAPTER 5

HEARSAY EXCEPTIONS

I. ADMISSIONS

A. General rule: "Admissions" receive an exceptions from the hearsay rule. That is, ***a party's words or acts may be offered as evidence against him,*** even though these would be inadmissible hearsay if said or done by someone other than a party. (Under the Federal Rules, an admission is simply not hearsay at all. See FRE 801(d)(2). At common law, admissions are hearsay, but receive an exception.)

1. **Distinguished from declaration against interest:** Be sure to distinguish admissions from declarations against interest. Unlike a declaration against interest, an admission need not be against the declarant's interest at the time it is made; thus even a statement that seems neutral or self-serving at the time it is made may be introduced against the party who made it.

2. **Opinion:** An admission is admissible even though it contains an ***opinion*** or a ***conclusion of law***, and even though it is not based on the maker's ***first-hand knowledge.*** Thus it can be admitted more easily even than the same statement when made at trial.

B. Personal admissions: One type of admission is a ***party's own statement***, offered against him ("personal admission").

1. **Pleadings:** Statements a party makes in his ***pleadings*** are treated as personal admissions for most purposes, and are thus admissible.

2. **Conduct as admission:** A party's conduct, even if it is intended as an assertion (and thus is hearsay under the modern rule) will be admissible under the exception for admissions.

Example: Proof of D's attempt to conceal V's body would be admissible as an admission by D of his guilt, even if the court decided that this was assertive conduct.

C. Adoptive: Under common law and the Federal Rules, a party may be deemed to have ***adopted*** another person's statement, in which case the statement will be admissible as an admission by the former party.

1. **"Real and knowing" test:** If a party is claimed to have adopted another's statement and the adoption is merely ***implied***, the test is: whether, taking into account all circumstances, the party's conduct or silence justifies the conclusion that he ***knowingly agreed*** with the other person's statement.

2. **Silence:** Often, the party's ***silence*** in the face of the other person's statement will, under the circumstances, indicate that the party agrees with the statement. If so, he will be held to have made an adoptive admission, which will thus be admissible.

   Example: While D flashes a large wad of bills, X, his girlfriend, says to W, "D got that money as his piece of the National Bank job last week." D's silence in the face of this statement will probably be found by the court to show D's knowing agreement with X's statement, since otherwise, D would have denied the statement. Therefore, the statement will be admissible against D as an adoptive admission.

   a. **Criminal cases:** In criminal cases, D's failure to respond to accusations made by the police while D is in ***custody*** will not be admissible against him as adoptive admissions, because this would violate the spirit of *Miranda*. But silence in the face of accusations made outside of police custody, or silence to accusations made by non-police, may be admitted against the criminal defendant under the adoptive-admission theory.

   b. **Writing:** A party's silence in the face of a ***writing*** will similarly be an adoptive admission, if the party can reasonably be expected to have objected were the writing untrue.

      Example: D receives a bill from a creditor, reciting certain sums owed for specified work. If D does not respond, his silence in the face of the bill will be treated as an adoptive admission by him of the truth of the bill's contents.

D. Representative admission: Even if a party did not make (or even learn of) another person's admission, that admission may be admissible against the party because he ***authorized it*** in some way. This is a "representative" or "vicarious" admission.

1. **Explicit authorization:** This may occur because the party ***explicitly*** authorized another person to speak for him.

   Example: Transport Co. authorizes any employee who is involved in an accident to make a statement to the police. A statement made by Employee arising out of such an accident will be admissible against Transport, because it was explicitly authorized.

   a. **Statements to principal:** Even if the principal authorizes the agent only to make the report ***to the principal,*** the modern and federal approach is to treat this as an adoptive admission. Thus, an employee's accident investigation report, given only to the employee's boss, would nonetheless be admissible against the boss.

2. **Vicarious:** Even if an agent is not explicitly authorized to make statements, statements he makes arising from a ***transaction within his authority*** will, under the modern view, be deemed to be authorized admissions by the principal. These are called ***"vicarious"*** admissions.

   a. **Common law:** At common law, this was not so: only "authorized" admissions, not "vicarious" ones, would be admissible against the principal.

   b. **Modern and Federal Rule:** But the modern and Federal Rule recognizes vicarious admissions. See, e.g., FRE 801(d)(2)(D), admitting a statement offered against a party if made "by the party's ***agent or employee*** on a ***matter within the scope of that relationship*** and ***while it existed***[.]"

   Example: Truck Driver makes an accident statement to the police. Even if Employer, the company for which Driver works, never authorized him to make accident reports, under the modern/federal rule Driver's statement will be admissible against Employer because it relates to matters — driving and accidents — that were within Driver's employment.

      i. **How to prove:** The proponent of the admission may ***use the statement itself as one item of evidence*** to show that the agent was acting within the scope of his agency or employment relationship when the declaration was made. But the statement ***cannot be the sole item of evidence*** demonstrating this point. FRE 801(d)2), last sent.

      Example: Same facts as above example. Suppose that in Driver's accident statement to the police, he says, "I was making a delivery for Employer at the time of the accident." When the trial judge determines whether Driver was acting on behalf of Employer at the time of the accident, the judge can consider, as one piece of evidence, the fact that in the statement at issue, Driver confirmed that he was acting on Employer's business. But there must be some additional evidence, beyond the statement, that Driver really was on company business at the time of the accident.

E. Co-conspirators:

1. **General rule:** There is an important hearsay exception for statements by ***co-conspirators***: a statement by one co-conspirator is admissible against other members of the ***same conspiracy***, so long as the statement is made: (1) ***during the course*** of the conspiracy; and (2) in ***furtherance*** of the conspiracy. See FRE 801(d)(2)(E).

   Example: A says to X, "Don't you want to join B and me in robbing the First National Bank next Thursday?" This statement may be used against B in a prosecution for the robbery of that bank that took place on that date, since the statement was made by a member of the same conspiracy, made while the conspiracy was taking place, and made for the purpose of furthering its aims by recruitment.

2. **"During course of":** The requirement that the statement take place "during the course of" the conspiracy means that:

a. **After end:** Statements made ***after the conspiracy has ended*** are admissible only against the declarant, not against the other members. Thus, if the conspiracy is broken up by the ***arrest*** of A and B (the only members of the conspiracy), anything B says to the police will not be admissible against A, since the arrest has terminated the conspiracy.

b. **Conspirator leaves:** If A leaves the conspiracy, but B and C continue the conspiracy without him, statements made by B and C after A leaves may not be admitted against A. (But the converse is not true: statements made by A to the authorities after he has left the conspiracy might be admissible against B and C, since their conspiratorial activities are still continuing at the time of A's statement.)

c. **Statements before:** Statements made by early conspirators ***before*** a later entry joins are admissible against the latter — when a conspirator enters an ongoing conspiracy, he is held to have adopted the earlier statements of fellow co-conspirators, so these are admissible against him.

3. **In furtherance:** The "in furtherance" requirement means that a statement should be admitted against a co-conspirator only if it was made for the purpose of advancing the conspiracy's objectives.

   a. **Weakly applied:** But this requirement is often not taken seriously. Thus, confessions by a co-conspirator, narratives of past events, or statements by the declarant blaming a crime on his co-conspirators rather than himself, are all frequently admitted under the exception even though, strictly speaking, they don't seem to meet the "in furtherance" requirement since they don't advance the conspiracy's objectives.

4. **No need to charge conspiracy:** Statements by one co-conspirator against another may be admitted under the exception ***even if no conspiracy crime is formally charged.***

5. **Procedure:** It is the judge who decides whether a conspiracy has been shown, so that the exception applies. He reaches this decision as follows:

   a. **Preponderance:** He need only find that a conspiracy exists by a ***preponderance of the evidence***, not "beyond a reasonable doubt."

   b. **Statements:** In determining whether a conspiracy exists by a preponderance, he may ***consider the alleged statement itself.***

      i. **May not be sole proof of conspiracy:** But the contents of the statement ***may not be the sole proof*** that the conspiracy existed (or that the defendant and the declarant were members). FRE 801(d)(2), final sent. In other words, there must be ***some independent evidence*** that the conspiracy existed.

II. AVAILABILITY IMMATERIAL — GENERALLY

A. **List of exceptions:** Four major hearsay exceptions apply even where the declarant is ***available*** to give courtroom testimony:

1. ***Spontaneous, excited,*** or ***contemporaneous utterances*** (including statements about ***physical or mental condition***);
2. ***Past recollection recorded***;
3. ***Business records***; and
4. ***Public records*** and ***reports***.

III. SPONTANEOUS, EXCITED, OR CONTEMPORANEOUS UTTERANCES (INCLUDING STATEMENTS ABOUT THEN-EXISTING PHYSICAL OR MENTAL CONDITION)

A. Statements of physical condition: There is a hearsay exception for statements by a person about his then-existing ***physical condition***.

1. **Statement to lay person:** If the statement is made to a lay person, it is covered by the exception only if it relates to the declarant's ***present*** bodily condition or symptoms. Usually, it will relate to pain.

   Example: X says to W, "I'm feeling terrible chest pains." W can testify about this statement even if it is offered for the purpose of showing that X did indeed suffer chest pains.

2. **To treating doctor:** For statements made by a person about his bodily condition, when made to a ***physician*** who is ***treating*** him, the exception is broader:

   a. **Past symptoms:** The statement may be about ***past*** pain or past symptoms.

   b. **Cause:** The statement may include references to the ***cause*** of the bodily condition (though statements about whose ***fault*** the condition is will generally not be allowed; thus W's statement that he was hit by a car will qualify, but his statement that the car was driven through a red light would not).

   c. **Statement by friend or relative:** A statement made ***by a third person*** (e.g., a friend or relative of the patient) is also covered, if made to help the patient get treatment.

   d. **Non-M.D.:** Under FRE 803(4), statements made for purposes of getting medical treatment that are made to a ***nurse***, ambulance driver, hospital admitting clerk, or other third person involved in the health-care process, are covered by the exception.

   e. **Non-treating physician:** If the statement is made to a doctor who is not furnishing ***treatment***, but who is consulted so that he can testify about the patient's condition at trial, the statement is covered by the federal exception (but not by the common-law exception).

B. Declaration of mental condition: There is a hearsay exception for statements by a person concerning his ***present mental or emotional state***.

1. **State of mind directly in issue:** The exception is often used where a declarant's state of mind is directly in issue.

Example: P sues D for alienating the affections of W, who is P's wife. W's statement to P, "I don't like you anymore," if offered to show that W does not like P anymore — an element of P's *prima facie* case — comes within the exception.

a. **Presently existing:** The statement must relate to the declarant's ***presently existing*** state of mind.

   Example: "I hate my husband," is acceptable to show the declarant now hates her husband. But, "Yesterday I was really furious at my husband," is not admissible, because it relates to a prior mental or emotional state, rather than the declarant's present one.

b. **Surrounding circumstances:** If statement of present mental state includes a reference to surrounding circumstances, the entire statement will normally be admitted, but with a limiting instruction.

   Example: "I hate my husband because he's an adulterer." The whole statement will be admitted under the exception, if offered to prove that the declarant hated her husband at the time of the statement; the jury will be instructed that it may not use the statement as proof that the husband was an adulterer.

2. **Proof of subsequent event:** The exception also applies where a declaration of present mental state (especially present ***intent***) is offered not because the mental state itself is in issue, but because that mental state is circumstantial evidence that a ***subsequent event*** actually took place.

   Example: O says, "I plan to go to Crooked Creek." This statement of present intent is admissible to show that O probably subsequently went to Crooked Creek. [*Mutual Life Ins. v. Hillmon.*]

   a. **Intent coupled with recital of past acts:** If the statement is mainly an expression of ***intent to do a future act,*** the fact that it contains a brief recital about some past, relevant, fact will not cause the statement to be excluded. This is especially true where the declarant explains a ***past motive*** for his contemplated action.

      Example: O says to W, "D has asked for some bribe money. I'm going to send it to him in Bridgeport." Most courts would probably allow in the entire statement, since it is mainly a statement of intent offered to show that the intended act — delivering the money — eventually took place, and the reference to the past act is merely by way of explaining the intended act.

   b. **Cooperation of other:** If the statement of present intent concerns an act which requires the ***cooperation*** of a third person, most courts will allow the statement to be used as circumstantial evidence that the declarant did the contemplated act with the third person's cooperation. However, in this situation, courts usually require that there be ***independent evidence*** either that declarant really did the intended act, or that the third person actually participated.

      Example: V says, "I'm going to buy drugs from D in the parking lot." This statement of present intent will be admissible to show that V probably did meet D in the parking lot, but only if there is some independent evidence —

other than the statement — either that D really went to the parking lot or that V did. [*U.S. v. Pheaster.*]

3. **Statements of memory or belief:** The "state of mind" exception does ***not*** apply to statements of ***memory*** or belief about ***past actions or events***, when offered to prove that the past action or event took place. Thus FRE 803(3) excludes "a statement of memory or belief to prove the fact remembered or believed. . . ."

   Example: O says, "I believe that my husband has poisoned me." Even though this is a statement of present belief, it is not admissible under the "state of mind" exception to prove that the husband really did poison O, since it is offered to prove the fact believed. [*Shepard v. U.S.*]

   a. **Execution of will:** A declarant's statement relating to his ***will*** is covered by the "state of mind" exception, even though the statement may be one of memory or belief offered to prove the fact remembered or believed. See FRE 803(3), making the hearsay exception applicable to a statement of memory or belief that "relates to the validity or terms of the declarant's will."

      Example: O says, "I changed my will yesterday to disinherit my no-good husband." If offered in a will contest to show that O intended to disinherit her husband, this statement will be admissible even though it is a statement of memory offered to prove the truth of the fact remembered.

C. **Excited utterance:** There is a hearsay exception for certain statements made under the influence of a ***startling event***; this is called the ***"excited utterance"*** exception.

1. **Requirements:** Under the Federal Rules and most courts, there are two requirements for the exception: (1) the statement must relate to a ***startling event*** or condition; and (2) the statement must have been made while the declarant was still ***under the stress*** of excitement caused by the event or condition. See FRE 803(2).

2. **Time factor:** In determining whether the declarant was still under the influence of the startling event, the ***time*** that has passed between the event and the statement is of paramount importance. Usually, statements made during the exciting event or within half an hour afterward are admitted, statements made more than an hour later are not, and statements between a half hour and an hour are decided based on the surrounding circumstances.

3. **Reflection:** Since the rationale behind the exception is that statements made by a declarant who does not have the ***opportunity to reflect*** should be admitted as unusually reliable, facts showing that the declarant really did reflect will cause the exception not to apply. Thus if the statement is very self-serving, or is in response to a detailed question, the court is likely to find that the declarant reflected (rather than speaking spontaneously), so that the exception should not apply.

4. **Reference to startling event:** Some courts insist that the excited utterance explain or refer to the startling event. But this is not required by the Federal Rules or other courts.

   Example: Truck Driver, after getting in an accident, says, "Hurry up, I've got to get to my next customer." If offered to prove that Driver was on business on behalf of his employer, some courts would reject the statement because it does not refer to the startling event — the accident — but the Federal Rules and other state courts would admit the statement anyway.

D. Present sense impression: Many courts, and the Federal Rules, today recognize an exception for "present sense impressions," even where the declarant is not excited. Thus FRE 803(1) gives an exception for a statement "describing or explaining an event or condition, made while or immediately after the declarant perceived it."

Example: O sees a car speed by in the opposite direction, and says, "If the driver keeps up that rate of speed, he'll surely crash." In courts recognizing the exception for present sense impressions, this statement would be admissible to show that the car was traveling fast. [*Houston Oxygen Co. v. Davis.*]

1. **Immediacy:** In contrast to the excited-utterance exception, the present-sense-impression exception applies only if ***virtually no time passes*** between the event being perceived and the declarant's statement about it.

2. **Must describe or explain:** The present sense impression must ***describe or explain*** the event that the declarant has perceived (in contrast to the usual rule for excited utterances).

IV. PAST RECOLLECTION RECORDED

A. Four requirements: A ***written*** record of an event, made shortly after the event has occurred, will be admissible under the hearsay exception for ***"past recollection recorded,"*** if four requirements are met (FRE 803(5)):

1. **First-hand knowledge:** The memorandum must relate to matters of which the sponsoring witness once had ***first-hand knowledge***.

   Example: W writes down an inventory. If he says at trial that some of the information in the inventory was known only to his assistant who supplied the information, not to W, the memorandum will not be admissible under the past recollection recorded requirement unless the assistant is also available to testify.

2. **Made when fresh in memory:** The record must have been made when the matter was ***fresh in the witness's memory***. Under the Federal Rules, even a record made several days after the events in question might be held to satisfy this requirement if there was evidence that the person doing the recording would still have had a clear memory of it.

3. **Impaired recollection:** A sponsoring witness's memory of the event recorded must now be ***impaired*** — if he can clearly remember the events, he must testify from memory rather than have the document admitted. Under the Federal Rules, he must merely have ***some*** impairment of his memory (it must be the case that he "now cannot recall ***well enough to testify fully and accurately***," FRE 803(5)(A)), in contrast to the common law requirement that he lack ***any*** present memory of the event.

4. **Accurate when written:** The sponsoring witness at the trial must testify that the record was ***accurate*** when it was made. (But the sponsoring witness does not have to be the person who made the record; thus if X made the record, it may be spon-

sored by W, X's assistant, who can testify that after the record was made, W checked it and determined it to be accurate.)

a. **Multi-party problem:** If A knows the facts and B records them, both A and B will probably have to testify at the trial for the record to be admissible: A will testify that the facts he told B were ones that he, A, knew to be accurate; then B will testify that he accurately recorded what A told him.

B. Status as exhibit: Under the Federal Rules, the record may merely be ***read*** to the jury; it cannot be taken into the jury room as an exhibit, unlike other forms of real or demonstrative evidence — the theory is that the record is in lieu of testimony, so it should not be given greater weight than testimony by being taken to the jury room. FRE 803(5), last sentence. But the record is ***evidence.*** (This makes the past recollection recorded different from a document used to jog the witness's memory under the present recollection refreshed exception — the latter is not evidence, but is merely an aid to stimulate testimony.)

V. BUSINESS RECORDS (A/K/A "RECORDS OF REGULARLY CONDUCTED ACTIVITY")

A. General/Federal Rule: Nearly all states recognize a hearsay exception for certain types of ***business records***. The Federal provision (FRE 803(6)) is typical.

The 803(6) provision is formally called the exception for ***"records of regularly conducted activity,"*** because it is not limited to for-profit businesses. But it's commonly referred to as the business records exception. Under the exception, a record is admissible if four conditions are satisfied:

[1] **Regular business activity:** The record was kept in the course of a ***"regularly conducted business activity";***

[2] **Routine of the business:** It was the ***"regular practice"*** of that business activity to keep the record (i.e., the keeping of the record was part of the consistent ***routine*** of the business);

[3] **Personal knowledge:** The record was made by, or from information supplied by, a person with ***personal knowledge*** of the matter recorded and who had a ***business duty to disclose*** that knowledge; and

[4] **Timeliness:** The entry was made ***"at or near the time"*** of the matter recorded.

Example: The shipping department of Store records every shipment sent out to a customer. Store's ledger showing a shipment made to D will be admissible under FRE 803(6) if Store establishes that: (1) Store conducts a regular business activity (e.g., it doesn't just open up a couple of days a year); (2) Store regularly kept a written record of every shipment that went out; (3) the person who wrote the ledger entries did so either from his personal knowledge that a given shipment had gone out, or by being told that this had happened by a person with direct knowledge and a business duty to disclose that knowledge; and (4) the ledger entries were made shortly after each shipment actually went out.

B. "Business" defined: "Business" is defined ***broadly*** under modern statutes. Thus, FRE 803(6) applies to "organizations" (e.g., schools, churches, and hospitals), even though these are not necessarily profit-making entities. It also applies to any "occupation" or "calling."

1. **Non-profit-making:** So 803(6) applies to ***schools, churches, hospitals,*** and ***members of the clergy***, even though these would not necessarily be called "business" in ordinary speech, and are not necessarily profit-making entities.

C. **Person supplying info:** The person who originally supplies the information that goes in to the record must satisfy two requirements: (1) he must have first-hand knowledge of the fact he reports; and (2) he must do his reporting ***while having a business duty to make the report***. The latter requirement means that if the source of the information is not an employee of the business that keeps the record, the exception may not apply — thus statements by ***witnesses to an accident***, even if made to a police officer or other person with a business duty to compile a report, will ***not*** be admissible. [*Johnson v. Lutz.*]

1. **Other exception covering source of info:** But if the third-party information (from a source who is not an employee of the business that keeps the record) falls within ***some other hearsay exception***, then by a ***two-step process*** the ***entire report*** may nonetheless be admissible.

Example: P accuses her employer D, a business, of sexual harassment, because P's boss X made advances to her. D hires Security Co., a private-investigation firm, to investigate P's claim; D tells all its employees to cooperate with the investigation. Security Co. interviews W, who works for D; W tells Security Co., "Yes, I saw X make advances to P at the office." Security Co. prepares a report which repeats W's statement. At trial, P now seeks to introduce the report as evidence that W saw X make advances to P.

The business-records exception won't by itself be enough to get the whole report into evidence, because W (the source of the information) didn't work for Security Co. (the business keeping the record, i.e., the report). But since W was an employee of D at the time he made the statement to Security Co., and did so as part of his job (which included cooperating with the investigation), W's statement will be admissible against D as an agent's admission, admissible against the principal. So the "outer layer" (the report) is admissible as a business record, and the "inner layer" (W's statement to Security Co.) is admissible as an admission by an agent. [Cf. *Norcon v. Kotowski*]

D. **"Regular course of business":** Although the proponent must show that the report was made in the "regular course of business," even reports of a sort that are rarely made may qualify. For instance, if a business makes a practice of making a record of any ***accident*** that occurs during the transaction of business, the "regular course of business" requirement will be satisfied even though accidents happen rarely. (But the rareness with which a certain type of record is kept may suggest that the particular record is untrustworthy, violating a different requirement, discussed below.)

E. **Opinion:** The modern trend is to accept even ***opinions*** contained in the report, if these would be admissible when given as part of live testimony. Thus, if the person supplying the report or making the record is an expert, his statement (e.g., "Patient seems to be suffering from schizophrenia") will be admitted if he would be permitted to make the same statement at trial. FRE 803(6) even allows lay opinions to be admitted, assuming there is no grounds for doubting their trustworthiness.

F. Untrustworthy: If the surrounding circumstances make the record seem ***untrustworthy***, the court should exclude it. For instance, if the facts indicate that the business that made record had a strong motive to create a ***self-serving*** record, the court may exclude it.

Example: After a train crash, Railroad conducts an internal investigation, and makes a report absolving the engineer. Railroad's strong incentive to cover-up so as to avoid liability may cause the court to exclude the report for untrustworthiness.

G. Absence of entry: If a regularly kept business record would otherwise qualify, it may usually be admitted to show that a particular entry is ***absent***, if such an entry would normally have been made had a particular event occurred. FRE 803(7).

Example: Merchant keeps regular records of every payment by a customer. If the issue is whether Customer has paid a particular bill, Merchant may admit its records to show that no indication that Customer paid this particular bill was ever placed on its records.

H. Oral reports: Most courts hold that the record must be ***in writing***.

Example: Foreman reports to Boss that Employee has hurt his hand on a machine. Even if making such an oral report is part of Foreman's job, Boss will not be permitted to testify that Foreman made the report, because the report was not in writing.

I. Proving the record: The business record is not "self admitting." Instead, a ***sponsoring witness*** must normally be called, who can testify that the requirements of the business-records statute were satisfied. Typically, this will be someone who knows enough about the record-keeping routine of the business to testify that the records were appropriately kept in the particular instance (even if this witness did not make or observe the particular entry in question).

1. **Certification as alternative:** However, FRE 803(6) (together with FRE 902(11)) gives an alternative method for a business record to be admitted, a method that does not need a "live" sponsoring witness. Instead, the proponent can supply a written ***"certification,"*** by a person who would be qualified to be a live sponsoring witness. As long as the certification document describes how the record meets the requirements for a business record, the hearsay rule does not bar the document, and no live sponsoring testimony is needed.

J. Special situations: Here are two recurring situations where the business records exception is often applied:

1. **Hospital records:** ***Hospital records*** are often introduced to prove the truth of statements contained in them. Even statements contained in the record that are not declarations of symptoms (e.g., "Patient said he was hit by a truck") will be admitted if part of the record. But totally extraneous matter (e.g., "Patient says that the car that hit him ran a red light") will not be admitted.

a. **Patient under no duty:** If the information comes from the patient, it will not normally satisfy the requirement that the person supplying the information must have been working for the business (in this case, for the hospital). However, the hospital record can usually be admitted for the limited purpose of showing that the patient made a particular statement; then, some other exception may apply to allow the patient's statement to be offered for the truth of the matter asserted. For instance, if the patient is the plaintiff, the defendant will be able to introduce the statement against him because it is an admission; similarly, if the patient is reporting his current symptoms or other bodily condition, the "statement of present physical condition" exception will apply.

2. **Computer print-out:** Computer print-outs will often be admissible to prove the truth of matters stated in the print-out. However, the proponent must show that: (1) the print-out comes from data that was entered into the system relatively promptly; and (2) the procedures by which the data was entered, the program written, the report prepared, etc., are all reasonably reliable.

VI. PUBLIC RECORDS AND REPORTS

A. **Common-law rule:** At common law, there is an exception for admission of a ***written report or record*** of a ***public official*** if: (1) the official has ***first-hand knowledge*** of the facts reported; and (2) the official had a ***duty*** to make the record or report.

B. **Federal Rule:** The federal public records and reports exception is even broader. FRE 803(8) admits three different types of public records and reports:

1. **Agency's own activities:** Subsection (A)(i) allows admission of a government agency's records of its ***own activities***, if offered to show that those activities occurred.

   Example: P sues the FBI for invading his privacy; he could introduce the agency's own surveillance records to prove that the agency tapped his phone.

2. **Matters observed under duty:** Subsection (A)(ii) makes the written records of ***observations*** made by public officials admissible if: (1) the observation was made ***in the line of duty***; and (2) the official had a ***duty to report*** those observations.

   Example: An IRS agent does a field audit of Smith's tax return at Smith's house. If Smith claims a deduction for "home office," and the agent finds no evidence of one, his written report to his superior can be introduced in a later civil suit on the issue of whether Smith had a home office. But the agent's observation that Smith possessed cocaine would not be admissible, since the agent had no duty to report non-tax related matters.

3. **Investigative reports:** Subsection (A)(iii) allows the admission of ***"factual findings"*** resulting from ***investigations***, except when used against a criminal defendant.

   Example: Following an accident, the police send an accident investigator, who writes a report that concludes that the crash was caused when the vehicle traveling east-west went through a stop light. This report would be admissible in a civil suit arising out of the crash.

C. Criminal cases: Use of FRE 803(8) in criminal cases raises special issues:

1. **No use of (A)(ii) and (iii):** Subsections (A)(ii) and (iii) may ***not*** be used against the ***defendant in a criminal case.*** Thus a police officer's written report stating that he has seen D commit a robbery, or a detective's report concluding that a previously unsolved crime has probably been committed by D, could not be admitted against D in his trial. (Probably each of these reports, however, could be used ***by*** D against the government in the criminal trial.)

2. **"Law enforcement personnel":** Subsection (A)(ii) does not apply in criminal cases to matters "observed by ***law-enforcement personnel.***"

   a. **Laboratory technicians:** An important issue is whether ***laboratory technicians*** who work for law enforcement agencies doing substance analysis, are to be treated as "law enforcement personnel" whose out-of-court descriptions of tests they've made are therefore excluded.

      i. **Not admissible:** The answer is almost certainly ***yes***, as the result of a comment the Supreme Court made in a 2009 state-law case, *Melendez-Diaz v. Massachusetts* (also discussed *infra*, p. 89).

         [1] **Cocaine test results:** The issue in *Melendez-Diaz* was whether the defendant's ***Confrontation Clause rights*** were violated by the prosecution's introduction against him of a ***laboratory test report*** showing that the tested substance was cocaine; the prosecution did not make the writer of the report available for cross examination. In the course of deciding that the defendant's Confrontation Clause rights had been violated, the majority indicated that FRE 803(8)(B)'s ban on the hearsay use of "matters observed by police officers and other law enforcement personnel" will be read to apply to ***test reports prepared by technicians affiliated with law enforcement.***

3. **Use of other exceptions:** It is not clear whether a report that would otherwise come within subsection (A)(ii) or (iii), and that is excluded under those provisions because it is used against a criminal defendant, may nonetheless be admitted under ***some other*** exception, e.g., the business records exception.

   a. **Minority view:** Some courts have flatly rejected all such evidence.

      Example: The prosecution offers a substance analysis report prepared by a chemist working for the government, to prove that substance taken from D was heroin. *Held*, even though this is a "regularly kept record" by an organization, and thus would otherwise have qualified under the business records exception, it must be disallowed because it falls within the explicit exclusion of what is now 803(8)(A)(ii). [*U.S. v. Oates*]

   b. **Majority view:** But probably most courts under the FRE *would* allow a report of direct observations or investigations to be admitted against D, at least where the maker of the report is ***produced in court*** and is subject to cross-examination.

Example: If the government chemist in the above example were produced as a witness, a court applying the FRE would probably admit his report concluding that the substance taken from D was heroin.

D. Other issues: Other issues arise in both a civil and criminal context:

1. **Evaluations:** Subsection (A)(iii) refers to the "factual findings" in investigative reports. But so long as an investigative report includes factual findings, other ***"evaluative"*** parts of the report — ***opinions, evaluations*** and ***conclusions*** — may ***also*** be admitted. [*Beech Aircraft Corp. v. Rainey*]

   Example: The government, after investigating the crash of a Navy plane, produces a report containing numerous factual findings. The report then says that "the most probable cause of the accident was pilot error." This statement may be admitted, even though it is an "opinion" or "conclusion." [*Beech Aircraft*]

2. **Multiple hearsay:** A government report must be carefully scrutinized for ***multiple hearsay*** problems.

   a. **Report by one government agent to another:** If government employee A tells facts to employee B, who writes them up into a government report, A's statements will be admissible if A had a duty to give the report to B.

   Example: Officer Jones witnesses a car accident, and later says to Officer Smith, "I saw the green Plymouth run a red light and cause the accident." Smith includes this statement in a report on the accident. The entire report, including Jones' quoted statement, will be admissible under 803(8)(A)(ii), because Jones had a duty to furnish the information to Smith, and Smith's report was otherwise covered as a "report of matters observed."

   b. **Statement by one without duty to talk:** But if information is supplied by one who does ***not*** work for the government and does not have a duty to give the report, the resulting written report may not include the quoted statement, unless the quoted statement independently falls within some exception.

   Example: Bystander tells Officer Jones, "I saw the blue car jump the light and cause the accident." Jones' report will be generally admissible as an investigative report under subsection (A)(iii), but Bystander's statement will have to be removed, because he did not observe the accident pursuant to any duty, or have any duty to make a report.

3. **Trustworthiness:** If the "source of the information [or] other circumstances indicate a lack of ***trustworthiness***," the judge must keep the report out of evidence. FRE 803(8)(B). This is probably the case with respect to reports falling under any of the three subsections.

   Example: Evidence that the public official who prepared a report had been bribed, or was motivated by ulterior motives, would cause it to be excluded for lack of trustworthiness.

VII. MISCELLANEOUS "AVAILABILITY IMMATERIAL" EXCEPTIONS

A. **Learned writings and commercial publications:** A learned writing (e.g., a ***scientific treatise*** or article) may be admitted for the truth of the matter asserted, under FRE 803(18). (The common law allowed such learned works to be used only for impeachment of the other side's expert witness.)

1. **Use on direct:** The application may come in as part of a party's ***direct*** case, if a favorable expert testifies that the treatise is authoritative.

2. **Cross-examination:** The publication can be used as part of the ***cross-examination*** of the other side's expert, even if the expert refuses to admit that the publication is authoritative. (But the cross-examiner must establish the authoritativeness of the publication by some other means, such as another witness.)

3. **Expert must be on the stand:** Whether it is introduced as part of the direct or cross-examination, the publication may only be introduced if there is an ***expert on the stand*** who can help the jury interpret its meaning.

4. **Commercial publications:** The Federal Rules recognize a similar exception for ***commercial publications*** that are commonly relied upon by business people. See FRE 803(17), allowing admission of "market quotations, lists, directories, or other published compilations that are generally relied on by the public or by persons in particular occupations."

B. **Ancient documents:**

1. **Common law:** The common law makes it easy to admit ***"ancient documents."*** A document will be presumed to be authentic if it is: (1) at least 30 years old; (2) unsuspicious in appearance; and (3) shown to have come from a place of custody natural for such a writing. However, in most courts this is merely a rule of authentication, not an exception to the hearsay rule, so the statements contained in it may not be shown for their truth. But some courts do treat it as a hearsay exception.

   a. **Ancient deeds:** ***All*** courts allow statements contained in an ancient ***deed*** to be shown for their truth. Thus a statement in a will, "O purchased this property from X in 1872," could everywhere be used to show that O really did purchase the property in 1872, if the above three requirements are satisfied.

2. **Federal Rules:** The Federal Rules explicitly make the ancient documents rule a hearsay exception. The document need merely have been in existence ***20*** years (not the 30 required at common law). The proponent must prove that the document is "authentic" (i.e., that it is at least 20 years old and meets the "no suspicion" and "likely place of custody" requirements). See FRE 901(b)(8).

   a. **Newer title documents:** A separate federal hearsay exception exists for less-than-20-year-old documents that relate to ***title to property***. See FRE 803(15).

   Example: A 10-year-old deed recites, "O sold this property to X in 2003." This will be admissible to prove that O did indeed sell the property to X in 2003.

C. Reputation: There is a hearsay exception for several types of ***reputation*** evidence:

1. **Birth, marriage, etc.:** There is an exception for a person's reputation within his family regarding some aspect of ***birth, marriage***, or ***relationship.*** (*Example:* Reputation within the family that *A* is *B*'s son, offered to prove that *A* really is *B*'s son.) FRE 803(19) extends this to cover a reputation among one's ***business*** colleagues or one's reputation in a ***community***, concerning some fact of the person's personal or family history.

2. **General historical facts:** There is an exception for proof of ***facts of general history*** and for proof of land boundaries. See FRE 803(20).

   Example: To prove that there was an earthquake in San Francisco in 1906, a party could call a historian who would testify that in Northern California, it is commonly believed or remembered that there was an earthquake in that year.

3. **Reputation for character:** There is an exception for proof that a person had a particular ***reputation*** for character.

   Example: W may testify that P has a reputation in his hometown for being a liar, if offered by D to prove that P really is a liar and that therefore D did not commit libel by calling him one.

D. Miscellaneous:

1. **Vital statistics, marriage certificates:** Statements of fact contained in public records have an exception.

   Examples:

   ❑ A report that X died on a certain day, offered to prove that fact.

   ❑ A statement in a marriage certificate that X married Y on a certain day, offered to prove that fact.)

2. **Absence of public record:** There is an exception for the fact that a certain record is ***absent*** from the public records, offered to prove that fact.

   Example: Testimony that a search of the IRS's records does not disclose D's 1985 tax return, offered to prove that D did not file a return that year.

3. **Previous felony conviction:** Proof that X is guilty of a particular ***crime*** may be made by showing that X was convicted of that crime. (But the fact that X was convicted of a misdemeanor may not be used in a subsequent case to prove that he did the act charged.)

VIII. UNAVAILABILITY REQUIRED — GENERALLY

A. Five exceptions: Under the FRE, there are five hearsay exceptions that require that the declarant be unavailable to testify at trial:

1. **Prior proceeding:** ***Testimony*** given in a ***prior proceeding***;

2. **Dying declarations:** Statements made while the declarant believed his death was impending so-called ***"dying declarations"***);

3. **Against interest:** Statements which were ***against the declarant's interest*** when made;

4. **Pedigree:** Statements concerning either the declarant's or his relatives' ***personal*** or family history (so-called statements of "pedigree"); and

5. **Forfeiture by wrongdoing:** Statements offered against a party that has engaged in (or acquiesced in) ***wrongdoing*** that was intended to, and did, ***procure the unavailability*** of the declarant as a witness. (The party is deemed to have ***forfeited*** his right to object on hearsay grounds.)

   See FRE 804(b).

B. Meaning of "unavailable":

1. **Federal:** FRE 804(a) defines five situations in which the declarant will be deemed to be unavailable:

   a. He is ***privileged*** against testifying about the subject matter of his out-of-court statement;

   b. He ***refuses*** to testify despite a court order;

   c. He testifies that he ***cannot remember*** the statement's subject matter;

   d. He cannot be present to testify because of ***death***, or physical or mental ***illness***; or

   e. He is absent, and the proponent of his statement has been unable to procure his attendance (or his deposition) by ***process*** or other reasonable means (e.g., persuasion).

   f. **Proponent's fault:** But none of the above reasons will make the declarant "unavailable" if his unavailability occurred because the ***proponent "procured or wrongfully caused"*** the declarant's unavailablity "in order to ***prevent the declarant from attending or testifying.***" FRE 804(a), last sentence.

2. **States follow:** Most states recognize the first four exceptions. But with respect to the fifth, absence from the jurisdiction, most courts automatically treat the declarant as being "unavailable" if he is outside the jurisdiction — they don't require the proponent to make non-subpoena efforts (e.g., persuasion or the taking of a deposition) to procure his attendance or testimony.

3. **Constitutional problems:** If the hearsay exception is one traditionally requiring unavailability, a criminal defendant's Sixth Amendment ***Confrontation Clause*** rights may be violated if the court admits the out-of-court statement without a showing that the declarant really was unavailable.

   a. **"Unavailable" defined:** For this purpose, a witness will be deemed sufficiently "unavailable" (and the use of his out-of-court declaration will not violate his Sixth Amendment right) if the state shows both:

      [1] that the witness is ***beyond that state's own process***; and

      [2] that either the government made a ***good faith effort*** to get the witness to attend by means other than process, or such efforts would have been ***very***

unlikely to succeed.

b. **D purposely causes unavailability to evade testimony:** But where the defendant ***caused*** the declarant's unavailability ***for the purpose of avoiding the declarant's trial testimony***, then the defendant will be deemed to have ***forfeited*** his right to invoke the Confrontation Clause. [*Giles v. California*].

IX. FORMER TESTIMONY

A. **General rule:** There is a hearsay exception for ***former testimony*** — that is, testimony given in an ***earlier proceeding*** — if the witness is unavailable for trial. FRE 804(b)(1), which basically follows the common law, imposes these requirements:

1. **Hearing or deposition:** The testimony was given either at a ***hearing*** in the same or earlier action, or in a ***deposition*** in the same or different proceeding;

2. **Party present:** The party against whom the testimony is now offered was ***present*** at the earlier testimony (or, in a civil case, that party's "predecessor in interest" was present); and

3. **Opportunity to cross-examine:** The party against whom the testimony is offered had the ***opportunity*** and ***similar motive*** to develop the testimony. Usually, this opportunity will have been the chance to ***cross-examine***, but it may have been a chance to expand the testimony by ***direct*** or redirect examination.

   Example 1: P sues D for negligence. At a deposition in which D is present, P asks questions to X, a witness to the accident. Because D has had the chance to cross-examine X during the deposition, X's deposition answers may be introduced against D in the eventual suit, if X is unavailable to testify at trial (even if D did not use his right to cross-examine X at the deposition).

   Example 2: W gives testimony unfavorable to D before a grand jury while D is not present. At D's eventual criminal trial, this testimony cannot be introduced against D even if W is now unavailable, because D had no opportunity to cross-examine (but some courts might apply the residual or "catch all" exception, discussed below).

B. **Meaning of "hearing" and "proceeding":** "Hearing" and "proceeding" seem to include any official inquiry in which ***sworn testimony*** is taken. So a ***prior trial***, a ***preliminary hearing*** in a criminal case, a ***grand jury*** hearing, and a ***deposition***, all qualify.

1. **Not covered:** But ***affidavits***, and ***statements*** (written or oral) made to ***law enforcement officials during investigations***, ***aren't*** covered because they're not truly hearings or proceedings.

C. **Identity of issues:** There must be enough overlap between the issues existing at the time of the prior hearing or deposition, and the issues existing at the present trial, that the above opportunity for cross-examination was a meaningful substitute for cross-examination in the present case. At common law, there must be "substantial identity" between issues; under the Federal Rules, the opponent must have had a ***"similar motive"*** in the earlier situation.

1. **Different contexts:** This requirement can be satisfied even though the earlier and present proceedings are quite different contexts. (*Examples:* Testimony given at a ***preliminary hearing*** can be used at a later criminal trial, even though the issues are not absolutely "identical" in the two situations. Similarly, testimony given at a criminal trial can be admitted at a later civil proceeding, even though the issues and burdens of proof are not identical.)

D. **Identity of parties:** The ***proponent*** of the former testimony need ***not*** have been a party to the taking of the former testimony. Only the ***opponent*** must have been present.

1. **Similar party in interest:** Furthermore, even if the opponent was not present, under the Federal Rule the testimony can be used so long as the present opponent's "predecessor in interest" was present, if the case is a civil case. This probably means merely that a person with a very similar motive must have been present. (But in criminal cases, there is no "predecessor in interest" provision. Thus a statement may not be offered against a criminal defendant who was not present, even if another person — e.g., a co-defendant — was present at the prior proceeding and had a highly similar motive to cross-examine.)

X. DYING DECLARATIONS

A. **General rule:** There is an exception for ***"dying declarations."*** The common law version is narrow: a declarant's statement, while believing that his death is imminent, concerning the cause or circumstances of his impending death, is admissible in a subsequent homicide prosecution concerning that death. FRE 804(b)(2) loosens several of these restrictions.

B. **Requirements in detail:**

1. **Awareness of imminent death:** The declarant must, at the time he made his statement, have been aware of his impending death. It is not enough that he knows he is seriously ill or wounded, or that he will probably die — at common law he must have ***lost all hope*** of recovery. (Under the Federal Rule, he must speak "while ***believing*** [his] ***death*** to be ***imminent.***")

2. **Actual death:** At common law, the declarant ***must in fact be dead*** by the time the evidence is offered. But this is not required under the Federal Rule (though the declarant must of course be unavailable, since this is one of the "unavailability required" exceptions).

3. **Homicide:** At common law, the declaration may be used ***only in a homicide case.*** Thus it may not be used in civil cases, or in criminal cases not charging homicide (e.g., a case in which D is charged with rape alone, even though V died after the rape). Under the Federal Rules, dying declarations are usable in civil suits and homicide cases, but not in non-homicide criminal cases.

4. **Declarant is victim:** At common law, declaration may be offered only in a trial for the killing of the ***declarant***, not the killing of someone else.

Example: D has probably murdered both H and W. He is prosecuted for the murder of H only. At common law, the prosecution cannot introduce W's dying declaration, "D did this to H and me." But the Federal Rules drop this requirement.

5. **Relating to circumstances of killing:** Both at common law and under the Federal Rules, the declaration must relate to the ***causes or circumstances of the killing.***

   Example: Declarant, while dying, says, "X and I have been enemies for years." The exception probably does not apply, since it does not relate directly to the causes or circumstances of declarant's death. But, "X has been stalking me for two days," would satisfy this test.

6. **For accused:** The statement may be admitted ***on behalf of*** the accused (though usually, it is admitted *against* him).

XI. DECLARATIONS AGAINST INTEREST

A. Generally: There is a hearsay exception for declarations which, at the time they are made, are ***so against the declarant's interest that it is unlikely that they would have been made if they were not true.***

1. **Common law:** At common law, there are three main requirements for the exception:

   a. The declaration must have been against the declarant's ***pecuniary or*** proprietary interest (not his penal interest) when made;

   b. The declarant must now be ***unavailable***; and

   c. The declarant must have had first-hand knowledge of the facts asserted in the declaration.

2. **Federal Rule:** FRE 804(b)(3) follows this approach, except that declarations against ***penal interest*** are also admissible (except uncorroborated statements exculpating the accused).

B. Meaning of "against interest":

1. **When made:** The declaration must have been made against the declarant's interest ***at the time it was made.*** The fact that later developments have turned what was an innocent-seeming statement into one that now harms some interest of the declarant is ***not*** enough to satisfy this requirement.

2. **Pecuniary interest:** At common law, only statements against the declarant's pecuniary or proprietary interest qualify.

   a. **Property:** Thus, a statement limiting the declarant's ***property*** rights, or a creditor's statement that a debt has been paid, will qualify. Modern cases also allow a statement subjecting the declarant to possible ***tort liability*** to qualify.

3. **Penal interest:**

   a. **Common law:** At common law, statements against the declarant's ***penal*** interest — that is, statements tending to subject him to ***criminal*** liability — do *not* qualify. (This is due mainly to fears that people will falsely confess, or falsely claim to have heard others confess, in order to exculpate the defendant.)

b. **Federal approach:** The Federal Rules treat statements against penal interest as ***qualifying.*** However, a statement against penal interest that exposes the declarant to criminal liability (e.g., one that's offered to exculpate the accused by implicating the declarant instead as the purpetrator) is not admissible unless it is "supported by ***corroborating circumstances*** that clearly indicate its ***trustworthiness***[.]"

Example: D is charged with burglary. W offers to testify that while in jail, he heard X, another inmate, confess to having done this burglary alone. Because both W and X are felons whose word is somewhat doubtful, this testimony will be allowed only if there is independent evidence that X may well have done the burglary — e.g., he was out of prison at the time, and is known to have performed other, similar burglaries.

4. **Collateral statements:** If statement includes a disserving part but also a self-serving part, the court will try to excise the self-serving part. If the statement has both a disserving and a neutral part, the court will probably let in the whole statement.

Example: "It was Joe and I that pulled off that bank job," will be admissible against Joe, even though the part of the statement referring to Joe was not directly against the declarant's interest.

a. **Neutral or self-serving statements not allowed as collateral:** But a ***neutral*** or ***self-serving*** declaration ***won't*** be allowed in merely because it's part of the same broader statement that includes against-interest declarations — ***each individual declaration*** must be scrutinized to see if it's against interest.

Example: W, in custody for a particular crime, says, "I participated in a small way." W then goes on to describe D's participation in detail, and says that D was the ringleader. The description of D's participation won't be allowed in as against-interest, because that description isn't specifically against W's interest. [*Williamson v. U.S.*]

C. **Constitutional issues:**

1. **Use by prosecution:** When the prosecution tries to introduce a third party's declaration to inculpate the accused, the Sixth Amendment ***Confrontation Clause*** rights of the accused may help him keep the statement out. For instance, a statement exposing the declarant to criminal liability, given while the declarant is under ***police interrogation***, will always be excluded from being used against the accused, if the declarant doesn't take the stand (and undergo cross on behalf of the accused) at the accused's trial. [*Crawford v. Washington*]

Example: X is arrested on suspicion of burglary. While under interrogation, he confesses to the burglary, and says he did it with D. At D's burglary trial (X hasn't been tried yet), the prosecution puts X on the stand. X pleads the Fifth. The prosecution now offers X's confession, to show that D did the crime with X. Even though the confession was against X's interest, the Confrontation Clause prohibits its being used against D, because X is unavailable for cross on behalf of D.

2. **Use by accused:** Where it is the accused who seeks to ***exculpate*** himself by use of third person's declaration against interest, the accused may be able to rely on the Due Process Clause and the Sixth Amendment right to compulsory process to get the statement into evidence.

   Example: D tries to show that X has confessed to the crime that D is charged with. If there are some solid facts corroborating X's confession, and X is unavailable to testify, D probably has a due process or compulsory process right to have X's out-of-court confession introduced.

XII. STATEMENTS OF PEDIGREE

A. General rule: There is a hearsay exception for statements of ***"pedigree,"*** i.e., statements about a person's birth, death, marriage, genealogy, or other fact of personal or family history. Here are the requirements at common law and under the Federal Rules:

1. **Declarant unavailable:** The declarant must be unavailable to testify;

2. **Person or relative:** At common law, the declarant must be either the person whose history the statement concerns, or a ***relative*** of the person whom the statement concerns. Under FRE 804(b)(4), it will also suffice if the declarant is so "intimately associated" with the family of the person the statement concerns that "the declarant's information is likely to be accurate."

   Example: O is the servant for X's family during X's entire lifetime. If O tells W, "X is the illegitimate son of Y," under the federal but not the common-law approach, W will be permitted to repeat the statement in court, even though O was not a member of the family.

3. **Before controversy:** The statement must have been made before the ***present controversy arose***, under the common-law approach. (But this requirement is completely dropped by the Federal Rules.)

4. **No motive to falsify:** The declarant must not have had any ***apparent motive*** to falsify.

XIII. FORFEITURE BY WRONGDOING

A. The problem generally: A criminal defendant will often have an incentive to attempt to keep a witness from testifying against him at trial. A defendant might do this by ***intimidating*** the witness, ***bribing*** him, or even ***murdering*** him. However, in many instances the witness will previously have made an out-of-court declaration (e.g., a statement to the police, "D did it.").

B. FRE 804(b)(6)'s solution: To remove the incentive for witness-tampering, FRE 804(b)(6) now gives a hearsay exception for "[a] statement offered against a party that ***wrongfully caused*** — or ***acquiesced in wrongfully causing*** — the ***declarant's unavailability*** as a witness, and did so ***intending*** that result."

Example: W is arrested at an airport when large quantities of cocaine are discovered on his person. While under arrest, he tells DEA agents, "I was doing this smuggling for D [a drug kingpin], who promised to pay me $1,000 when the drugs got through." D is then arrested and charged with conspiracy to import narcotics. D learns of W's statements, and wants to make sure that W does not testify at D's (or W's own) trial. D therefore tells W that if W testifies at D's trial he will be killed. W is frightened, and refuses to testify.

Under 804(b)(6), the government will be able to introduce at D's trial W's original out-of-court statement to the agents that D was W's boss. This is true even though the statement does not fall under any other hearsay exception. D has, through his threats, "***wrongfully caused*** ... [W's] ***unavailability*** as a witness, and did so ***intending*** that result."

1. **Common scenarios:** The out-of-court statements to which 804(b)(6) is often applied include:

   - ❑ Statements made by W while under ***police interrogation*** (as in the above example);
   - ❑ Statements made by W in a ***grand jury proceeding*** or preliminary hearing;
   - ❑ Statements made by W in ***W's own criminal trial***, or in a criminal trial of some third person.

2. **No reliability requirement:** Rule 804(b)(6) does not contain any requirement that the out-of-court declaration be ***reliable*** in order to be admitted. This makes the exception much easier to use than, say, the residual exception of FRE 807 (which requires "circumstantial guarantees of trustworthiness" equal to those required by the standard 803 and 804 exceptions).

   Example: A suspect, W, is being interrogated by the police for a particular robbery. W admits to some involvement, but says that the robbery was masterminded by someone else, D. W's statements implicating D are probably not especially trustworthy, given W's strong incentive to get rid of the blame by putting it on someone else. Therefore, W's statements are unlikely to make it into evidence under the residual exception.

   But now suppose that the prosecution can show that D threatened W so that W refused to testify at D's trial even under a grant of immunity. Here, W's prior statement under police interrogation is exempt from the hearsay rule, no matter how untrustworthy the statement appears to be.

XIV. PRIOR STATEMENTS OF AVAILABLE WITNESS

A. Common-law rules: At common law, it is very difficult to make use of ***prior statements*** by a person who is a ***witness*** at the current trial:

1. **Prior inconsistent statement:** The trial witness's prior ***inconsistent*** statement is inadmissible hearsay at common law. (However, the prior inconsistent statement may used to ***impeach*** the witness at the present trial.)

2. **Prior consistent statement:** Similarly, the trial witness's prior ***consistent*** statement is not substantively admissible at common law. (But if the witness is accused of having recently fabricated his trial testimony, or of having been improperly influenced or motivated, the prior consistent statement may be used for the non-substantive purpose of rehabilitating his credibility.)

3. **Prior identification:** Proof that the trial witness has previously made an ***eyewitness identification*** is technically hearsay, but many common-law courts allow it as substantive evidence if it seems to have probative value.

   Example: D is charged with robbing V. Many common-law courts would allow trial testimony by W, a police officer, that shortly after the episode, V pointed to D in a police lineup and said, "That's the one who robbed me."

B. Federal Rule on prior inconsistent statements:

1. **General rule:** FRE 801(d)(1) makes certain prior ***inconsistent*** statements of the trial witness substantively admissible (i.e., not hearsay). If the defendant testifies at trial and is ***subject to cross-examination*** concerning his prior statement, that statement is admissible if it is "inconsistent with the declarant's [trial] testimony and was given ***under penalty of perjury*** [i.e., under oath] at a ***trial, hearing,*** or ***other proceeding*** or in a ***deposition***[.]"

   a. **Proceeding:** In other words, only statements given under oath as part of a formal proceeding (generally a trial, preliminary hearing, or deposition) may be substantively introduced if the witness's trial testimony differs. An ***informal oral*** statement previously made by the witness will ***not*** be substantively admissible.

      Example: In an accident case, W testifies at trial on behalf of P, "D went through the red light." D cannot introduce for substantive purposes a previous statement by W to her husband H, "The light was green when D went through it." But if W had made that same statement during the course of a deposition under oath, or during testimony at a prior trial, it could be substantively admitted in the present trial.

2. **Cross-examination not required:** This Federal Rule allows the prior inconsistent statement into evidence even when there was ***no cross-examination***, or even any ***opportunity*** for cross-examination.

   Example: W testifies in favor of D at a criminal trial. The prosecution may substantively introduce W's prior inconsistent grand jury testimony, even though D and his lawyer were not present and had no opportunity to cross-examine W at that grand jury session — the theory is that D has the opportunity to cross-examine W *now*.

C. Federal Rule on prior consistent statements: If the prior statement is ***consistent*** with the witness's trial testimony, it is substantively admissible, but only if it is "offered to rebut an express or implied charge that the declarant ***recently fabricated it*** or acted from a ***recent improper influence*** or motive in so testifying[.]" FRE 801(d)(1)(B).

Example: W, a witness to a robbery, testifies at trial that the robber was not D. The prosecutor asserts in cross-examination that D has recently intimidated W and gotten him to change his story. D's lawyer may substantively introduce a statement made long ago by W at a grand jury, in which W told the same story.

D. Federal Rule on prior identifications: A statement that "***identifies*** a person as someone the declarant ***perceived earlier***" is substantively admissible, if the declarant testifies at the trial and is available for cross-examination. FRE 801(d)(1)(C).

1. **No oath or proceeding:** Unlike a prior inconsistent statement, a statement of identification is substantively admissible under this provision even though it was ***not made under oath*** or at a formal ***proceeding***.

   Example: V, a robbery victim, is walking down the street the day after the robbery when she spots D. She says to H, who is with her, "That's the robber." H will be permitted to repeat this statement at D's trial, even though W's statement was not made under oath or at a proceeding.

XV. RESIDUAL ("CATCH ALL") EXCEPTION

A. Federal Rule generally: Modern courts now tend to admit hearsay evidence that does not fall within any well-defined exclusion, if it is highly reliable and badly needed in the particular case. The Federal Rules codify this ***residual*** or ***"catch all"*** exception in FRE 807. FRE 807 imposes five requirements:

1. **Circumstantial guarantees of trustworthiness:** The statement must have ***"circumstantial guarantees of trustworthiness"*** that are equivalent to those inherent in the other, more specific, federal hearsay exceptions. (Factors the courts consider are summarized below.)
2. **Material fact:** The statement must be offered as evidence of a ***material fact***.
3. **More probative:** The statement must be ***"more probative"*** on the point for which it is offered than any other evidence which is available through reasonable efforts.

   Example: If the declarant can give equally probative live testimony, or if there is some other witness who can give the same evidence as that contained in the out-of-court declaration, the catch all exception does not apply.
4. **Interests of justice:** Use of the evidence must be consistent with "the general purposes of [the Federal] Rules and the interests of justice."
5. **Notice:** The proponent of the evidence must give the adversary ***"reasonable notice*** of the intent to offer the statement" so that the adversary has "a fair opportunity to meet [the statement]." The notice must include the "***particulars***" of the statement, including the declarant's name and address. (But federal courts often disregard the precise languagc of this requirement, and allow use of evidence without a pre-trial notice if the need for the evidence does not become apparent until the trial starts; the court will usually give a continuance to the opponent in order to let him prepare to meet the evidence.)

Example 1: W has given detailed, credible, and important *grand jury testimony*, and is not available to testify at a civil trial. The residual exception will probably apply. (The "former testimony" exception of 804(b)(1) does not apply to this testimony, because the opponent did not have the opportunity to cross-examine.)

Example 2: X took contemporaneous *hand-written notes* of an event he witnessed, but is not available to testify at a civil trial. If the notes seem to be reliable, and there is no equally probative or better testimony available, the notes will be admitted under the residual exception. (The document cannot constitute Past Recollection Recorded, under FRE 803(5), because the author is by hypothesis not available as a witness to authenticate it.)

Example 3: W, D's building superintendent, orally tells P not to use a particular safety measure because it will inconvenience W's pets. P is injured. W is not available as a trial witness, and P has no other way to rebut D's claim that P was contributorily negligent. Assuming that there is some corroboration of W's alleged statement (e.g., some independent proof that the safety measure would indeed have inconvenienced W's pets), the court will probably apply the residual exception.

B. Circumstantial guarantees of trustworthiness: In determining whether the statement has "equivalent circumstantial guarantees of trustworthiness" (requirement 1 above), the court is likely to consider these factors, among others:

[1] Oath: Whether the declaration was ***under oath.*** (If so, it is more reliable.)

[2] Time lapse: How much ***time elapsed*** between the event and the statement. (The longer the time lapse, the less reliable the statement.)

[3] Motive: The declarant's *motive* for telling the truth. (The stronger the motive to tell the truth, the more reliable.) (*Example:* D1, who is been arrested on a criminal charge, tells a grand jury that the crime was committed by D2, and that D1 was just a bystander. Because D1 had a strong motive to exculpate himself by incriminating another, his statement will probably be viewed as unreliable.)

[4] First-hand knowledge: Whether the declarant had *first-hand knowledge* of what he said. (If he merely repeated what someone else said, this makes the statement less reliable.)

[5] Written vs. oral: Whether the statement is *written* or oral. (Written statements, whether written by the declarant or transcribed stenographically as in a confession to police, are presumed to be more reliable than oral statements.)

[6] Recanted statement: Whether the declarant has subsequently ***recanted*** his statement. (A statement that has subsequently been recanted is less reliable.)

C. "Near miss": When a particular fact pattern comes very close to matching the requirements for a recognized hearsay exception, but just misses, a few courts refuse to apply the residual exception. But most courts are willing to apply the residual exception in this ***"near miss"*** situation, if the other requirements are met.

D. Grand jury testimony: Prior to 2004, the most common use of the residual exception was to allow ***grand jury testimony*** to be used against a criminal defendant when the testifier isn't available to testify at trial. But the 2004 decision in *Crawford v. Washington* means that because of the ***Confrontation Clause*** of the Sixth Amendment, grand jury testimony can't be used against a criminal defendant (other than the testifier, that is) unless the testifier takes the stand and is available for cross examination.

Example: W witnesses a fatal shooting of V. W tells a grand jury looking into the shooting, "I saw the shooter, and it was D." At D's later trial, W can't be found (he's moved out of state, with no forwarding address). Since W is not available to be cross-examined by D's lawyer at trial, and since D didn't have the opportunity to cross-examine W at the time of the grand jury, W's grand-jury testimony can't be used against D on account of D's Sixth Amendment right to be confronted with witnesses against him. And that's true even if the trial court is convinced that the grand-jury testimony has circumstantial guarantees of trustworthiness, and that it meets all the other requirements for the residual exception.

CHAPTER 6

CONFRONTATION AND COMPULSORY PROCESS

I. INTRODUCTION

A. Confrontation Clause: The Confrontation Clause of the Sixth Amendment guarantees a criminal defendant the right "to be confronted with the witnesses against him." This Clause gives a criminal defendant the right to keep out of evidence certain out-of-court declarations, where the declarant is not available to be cross-examined in court.

B. Compulsory process: The Sixth Amendment's Compulsory Process Clause gives the criminal defendant the right "to have compulsory process for obtaining Witnesses in his favor." This Clause may allow the defendant to ***gain admission*** of otherwise-inadmissible evidence. For instance, this Clause may give the defendant the right to introduce an out-of-court declaration (e.g., a confession to the crime by someone else) that would otherwise be excluded under traditional hearsay principles.

II. CONFRONTATION CLAUSE

A. First thing to decide: When you analyze hearsay evidence used against a criminal defendant to see whether it violates the Confrontation Clause rights of the accused, you must first decide whether the out-of-court statement at issue is ***"testimonial."*** That's because the testimonial/nontestimonial distinction makes a huge difference in how or whether the Confrontation Clause applies. [*Crawford v. Washington*; *Davis v. Washington; Michigan v. Bryant*]

1. **Summary of rule:** In brief, here's why the testimonial/non-testimonial distinction is key:

❑ an out-of-court ***testimonial*** statement by W ***can't be admitted*** in a criminal case against D unless W is ***made available for cross-examination*** at D's trial (or was subject to cross by D at the time W made the statement), but

- ❑ an out-of-court ***non-testimonial*** statement by W *can* be admitted against D ***without any Confrontation Clause problem*** even if W is never made available for cross by D.

2. What is "testimonial": Here's an overview of when a statement will be considered ***"testimonial"***:

a. Rough definition: The rough meaning of "testimonial" is "bearing testimony." The idea is that the declarant has some idea that the statement will be or may be ***used in a serious legal proceeding***, such as a ***criminal investigation.*** So a ***casual offhand remark*** to a friend or acquaintance who happens to be standing near the declarant would typically *not* be testimonial.

In the case of a ***police interrogation,*** a testimonial statement is one where "the primary purpose of the interrogation is to ***establish or prove past events potentially relevant to later criminal prosecution."*** [*Davis v. Washington*]

b. Listing of "testimonial" statements: At a minimum, the following types of statements ***will*** be considered testimonial under *Crawford* and *Davis v. Washington*:

- ❑ ***prior testimony*** at a ***preliminary hearing***;
- ❑ ***prior testimony*** before a ***grand jury***;
- ❑ testimony at a ***former trial*** (whether of the present defendant or of someone else);
- ❑ an ***affidavit*** issued as part of a law-enforcement proceeding;
- ❑ statements made in ***forensic laboratory reports*** created to help solve or prosecute a crime; and
- ❑ perhaps most significantly, ***statements made during the course of police interrogations,*** including interviews by police at ***crime scenes,*** as long as the focus of the interrogation is on investigating a completed crime, not on managing an ongoing emergency.

  Example: The police get a report that a domestic disturbance is occurring at V's house. They show up, and determine that sometime previously, V may have been attacked by her husband D, but that there is no present danger. An officer asks V, "What happened?", and V answers, "My husband John attacked me." V's statement is "testimonial" (made as part of an investigation into a completed crime rather than in response to a present emergency); therefore, as we'll see below it can't be introduced against D unless V is available for cross-examination. [Cf. the "Hammon" portion of *Davis v. Washington*]

c. Presence of ongoing emergency: The presence of an ***ongoing emergency*** makes it much more likely that a statement made during an interrogation will be found to be ***non-testimonial.***

i. **Consider both declarant and interrogator:** What counts is the "primary purpose of the ***interrogation***," and the statements and actions of ***both*** the declarant ***and the interrogators*** are to be considered in determining the "investigation's" purpose. So if the police interrogators believe they're dealing with an ongoing emergency, apparently that can be enough to override a lack of evidence about what the *declarant* intended.

Example: Police, responding to a dispatch call, find V lying on the ground in great pain from a gunshot wound to the abdomen. The police ask V a number of questions, including "Who shot you?" and "Where did it happen?" V answers that "Rick shot me through the back door of his house," which is a few miles away. After about 10 minutes of such questioning by multiple officers, EMT workers arrive and take V to the hospital, where he dies. In prosecuting "Rick" (D), the government offers V's statement that D was the shooter. D's counsel objects that since V can't be cross-examined, use of his statement violates D's Confrontation Clause rights.

Held (by a 5-4 Supreme Court vote), the statement was properly admitted, because it was not testimonial. The issue is whether the primary purpose of "the interrogation" was testimonial, and that issue requires considering the intent of both the declarant and the interrogators. Here, V was in such pain that he probably had no primary intent of any sort. And the primary purpose of the police questioning was to "allow the police to '***assess the situation***, the ***threat to their own safety***, and possible danger to the potential victim' ... and ***to the public***[.]" Since the primary purpose was to deal with the ongoing emergency, the admission of V's statements did not violate D's Confrontation Clause rights. [*Michigan v. Bryant*]

ii. **Consider the level of formality:** The degree of ***formality*** in the encounter is another significant factor in the emergency/non-emergency decision. The presence of formality suggests the ***absence of an emergency.*** By contrast, if the encounter is very ***informal,*** that's an indication that the interrogation is focused on ***resolving an emergency***, not gathering facts to be used in a prosecution.

Example: In *Bryant*, *supra*, the questioning occurred "in an ***exposed, public area*** ... and in a ***disorganized fashion***," helping to make apparent that it was focused on an ongoing emergency. By contrast, the formal station-house interrogation in *Crawford* made that interrogation more likely to be found devoted to finding facts for an ultimate prosecution, not for dealing with any emergency.

iii. **Lab reports by law-enforcement personnel:** ***Laboratory reports*** by created by or for ***law enforcement*** personnel ***are "testimonial."*** Therefore, these reports cannot be introduced unless the ***person who produced them is made available*** for cross-examination at trial. [*Melendez-Diaz v. Massachusetts* (2009)]

Example: D is charged with cocaine trafficking under state law. To prove that the substance seized by the police from D is cocaine, the prosecution offers into evidence (as allowed by an unusual state law) "certificates of analysis" stating that the tests conducted by the state police lab on the substance confirm that it's cocaine. The analysts who prepared the certificates sign them and have them notarized. The prosecution does not make the analysts themselves available at trial.

Held (5-4), the certificates ***are "testimonial statements"*** under *Crawford* and *Davis*. Therefore, the analysts who prepared them were "witnesses" for Confrontation Clause purposes. Since the prosecution did not produce the analysts for cross-examination at trial and didn't show that they were unavailable, admission of the certificates violated D's Confrontation Clause rights. [*Melendez-Diaz, supra*].

Note: For a discussion of *whose* testimony must be given live in the case of a laboratory report, see *infra*, p. 91.

d. Non-testimonial statements: The following types of statements are probably ***not*** "testimonial," because the circumstances surrounding them don't suggest that the statement will be used in a later proceeding:

- ❑ statements by a ***co-conspirator*** during the course of the conspiracy, and in furtherance of it;
- ❑ ***excited utterances***, spoken to a friend or relative who happens to be nearby, or spoken to a ***911*** operator under emergency conditions;

  Example: V phones a 911 line, and tells the operator, "My boyfriend is attacking me." The operator, in order to do a records search to find out whether the boyfriend is likely to be dangerous to police officers, asks, "What's your boyfriend's name?" V answers, "His name is John Smith." Because this statement, although made in response to official interrogation, was made under emergency circumstances (rather than as part of an investigation into a completed crime), it is non-testimonial (and therefore may be admitted against Simth in a criminal trial without Confrontation Clause review.) [Cf. the "Davis" portion of *Davis v. Washington*.]
- ❑ ***present sense impressions,*** spoken to a friend or relative who happens to be nearby;
- ❑ ***state-of-mind*** statements, spoken to a friend or relative who happens to be nearby.

B. Rule for testimonial statements: If the statement ***is "testimonial,"*** *Crawford v. Washington* imposes a bright-line rule: the statement ***may not be admitted against the accused unless the declarant is made available for cross-examination by the accused,*** either at the ***time of the statement, or at the time of the accused's trial.***

1. Three important scenarios: There are three especially important scenarios in which the bright-line rule of *Crawford* is likely to apply: (1) statements made ***during police interrogations;*** (2) ***grand jury testimony***; and (3) statements made in ***forensic or laboratory reports***.

a. Police interrogations: The situation in which the *Crawford* rule probably applies most often is where W is ***interrogated by the police***, perhaps while under suspicion of some sort of criminality, and W implicates D. If W doesn't testify at D's trial, W's statement can't be used against D (unless somehow D had a prior opportunity to cross-examine W about the statement).

Example: X is questioned by the police about the fatal shooting of V. X says, "I didn't shoot V, but I did lend my gun to D knowing that D wanted to shoot V, and I then watched as D did the shooting." At D's murder trial, X pleads the Fifth Amendment. The prosecution then offers (as a declaration against interest) testimony by Ollie, the police detective who interviewed X, about what X said concerning the shooting.

Because X's statement during interrogation is "testimonial," it can't come in against D unless X is made available for cross by D. Since X has pleaded the Fifth, he's deemed not available for cross. Therefore, the Confrontation Clause blocks X's statement from being used against D.

i. **Crime-scene interview:** Statements made by W under police interrogation at a ***crime scene*** will be testimonial even if W is not under suspicion, as long as the police's focus is on asking the questions is to find out "what happened" (with a view towards "solving the case") rather than to deal with a present emergency.

Example: In the domestic-disturbance example on p. 88 (V says that her husband D attacked her earlier), V's statement is testimonial, even though V was never under suspicion and even though the possible crime had occurred fairly recently. That's because the police were in an investigative "what happened?" mode rather than in a "solve the pending emergency" mode. Therefore, if V doesn't take the stand to testify in D's trial, an officer may not testify, "V told me that her husband attacked her." [Cf. the "Hammon" portion of *Davis v. Washington*.]

b. **Grand jury testimony:** Another important instance in which the rule of *Crawford* will lead to the declaration's being kept out is where the declaration is made in ***grand jury testimony***, and the declarant refuses to testify at D's later trial.

Example: Same basic fact pattern as above example in which X says he lent his gun to D. Now, however, assume that X makes his statement — "I didn't shoot V, but I did lend my gun to D knowing that D wanted to shoot V, and I then watched as D did the shooting" — not to the police, but to a grand jury. This, too, is obviously a "testimonial" statement. And, of course, D's lawyer doesn't have the opportunity to cross-examine X about it in front of the grand jury (since lawyers for the suspect never get the right to cross-examine grand jury witnesses). Then, suppose the prosecution wants to use this against D at his trial, under the hearsay exception for declarations against the speaker's (X's) interest. If X pleads the Fifth at D's trial instead of repeating the remark, his grand jury testimony inculpating D can't be used against D.

c. **Who must testify (forensic report situation):** In the case of a declaration in a ***forensic report*** (e.g., a report of a laboratory test), obviously the live testimony of the person who did the test and wrote the report will suffice. But what if that person is not available? Can someone ***other than the preparer*** of the report — a ***"surrogate witness"*** — testify in court and meet the demands of the Confrontation Clause? The answer is ***"no"*** — someone who ***worked on***, or at the very least ***observed or reviewed*** the test and the report — must testify. If the witness didn't observe or review the work or report, then her testimony won't suffice, even if she is familiar with the ***general methods used*** by the person who actually prepared the report. [*Bullcoming v. New Mexico* (2011)]

Example: In a police lab, X uses a gas chromatograph to test D's blood sample for its blood alcohol level, then writes the result ("blood alcohol level = .11%) in a report, which he signs and certifies as true. At trial, because X has recently been put on unpaid leave, the prosecution offers the report into evidence, supported by testimony by Y, X's co-worker at the lab. Y testifies about how a gas chromatograph works, but says she didn't watch X do the test, and can't answer questions about whether he made any mistakes, or about why he was put on unpaid leave.

Held (by 5-4 vote in the Supreme Court), Y's testimony did not satisfy D's Confrontation Clause rights. Only X's testimony could have sufficed, because had X been present, D's counsel "could have asked questions designed to reveal whether incompetence, evasiveness, or dishonesty accounted for [X's] removal from his workstation." [*Bullcoming*, *supra*.]

2. **Mere unused "opportunity" to cross-examine:** What if the accused merely has an ***"opportunity"*** to conduct such a cross-examination of the declarant at the time of the declaration, and ***does not take advantage*** of that opportunity? Here, it is less clear whether the declaration can be used at the accused's later trial without Confrontation Clause problems, if the declarant is unavailable at that trial. We simply don't know the answer yet.

   Example: Same basic fact pattern as prior two examples. Now, however, assume that X makes his statement — "I didn't shoot V, but I did lend my gun to D knowing that D wanted to shoot V, and I then watched as D did the shooting" — at a preliminary hearing into whether to charge D with the murder. D's lawyer chooses, for tactical reasons, not to cross-examine X. Then, at D's trial, X refuses to repeat the statement, pleading the Fifth. We don't yet know whether this unused opportunity on D's part to cross-examine W about the statement at the preliminary hearing is enough to strip D of his automatic right under *Crawford* to keep the statement out of the trial.

3. **What is "availability" for cross:** There are situations in which it's not perfectly clear whether the declarant (call him "W" for witness) is ***"available"*** for cross by the accused at trial. Here are some of the important availability scenarios:

   a. **W not found, or doesn't come to court:** If W ***cannot be located*** for a subpoena, or ***receives the subpoena but doesn't come to court***, W is clearly "unavailable." In that event, W's prior un-cross-examined testimonial statement can't be used against D. This is true even if the prosecution made all possible efforts to get W into court.

b. **W pleads privilege:** If W takes the stand at D's trial, but then ***refuses to testify*** about the statement and instead ***pleads a privilege*** (e.g., the ***Fifth Amendment***), W is unavailable.

c. **W can't remember or is evasive:** But if W takes the stand, and purports to answer questions, the fact that W is ***evasive***, or says he ***can't remember***, probably does ***not*** prevent W from being considered "available" for cross by D. And that's probably true even if W seems to be ***behaving in bad faith.***

C. Rules for nontestimonial statements: Next, let's look at the rules governing use of ***"non-testimonial"*** statements. The ***Confrontation Clause plays no role where a non-testimonial statement is concerned.*** Therefore, as a Confrontation Clause matter, the statement can come into evidence ***no matter*** whether it falls within a ***firmly-rooted hearsay exception***, and no matter whether the circumstances surrounding its making suggest that it is reliable. [*Crawford v. Washington*; *Davis v. Washington*]

Example: Suppose that X and W are old friends, who have committed various crimes together and who trust each other. One day, while the two are having a casual conversation, X says to W, "You know that murder of V last year — well, D and I were the doers." (X is not intending to supply "evidence" against D – he's just gossiping.) Later, in a prosecution of D for the murder, the prosecution would like to offer W's testimony about what X told him. X refuses to repeat the remark at D's trial, pleading the Fifth Amendment.

The remark is *non-testimonial* (since X was not speaking as part of a formal proceeding or a police investigation, and had no reason to believe that the remark would become part of a criminal proceeding). Therefore, under *Crawford* and *Davis*, this non-testimonial declaration ***doesn't get Confrontation Clause analysis at all***, and there is no constitutional barrier to its use against D in the form of W's live testimony about what X said to him.

D. D's forfeiture of rights by making the witness unavailable: Suppose the defendant ***causes the declarant to be unavailable***, for instance by ***killing*** her. This will cause the defendant to be deemed to have ***forfeited*** his Confrontation Clause right, but ***only if the defendant acted for the purpose of procuring the declarant's unavailability.*** [*Giles v. California* (2008)]

1. **Ordinary murder case:** So in an ordinary murder case – ordinary in the sense that D killed V for some purpose *other than* preventing V from testifying against D – the fact that D killed V will ***not*** be deemed to be a forfeiture by D of his Confrontation Clause rights. Therefore, the prosecution will still be blocked by the Confrontation Clause from introducing testimonial-type statements made by V before the murder (e.g., a statement by V to police investigators about a threat of violence D made to V three months previously).

2. **D acts to avoid V's testimony:** But if the prosecution can show that D procured the declarant's unavailability ***for the purpose of avoiding the declarant's trial testimony*** (e.g., by killing her), then D *will* be deemed to have forfeited his Confrontation Clause rights.

Example: D kills V to prevent V from testifying against him at D's upcoming trial for burglary. V's prior statements to the police about the burglary are admissible notwithstanding D's Confrontation Clause rights.

E. Confession implicating someone else, used during joint trial: Special problems arise when *A* and *B* are tried together, and *A*'s confession implicating himself and *B* is sought to be used by the prosecution. If the same jury hears *A*'s confession implicating *B* (and *A* doesn't take the stand), then *B*'s Confrontation Clause rights are violated even if the prosecution only purports to be offering the confession against *A*. That's true even if the judge warns the jury not to consider *A*'s confession as evidence against *B*. [*Bruton v. U.S.*]

1. The "two jury" technique: One way around this problem is to use ***two juries*** when co-conspirators are being tried. The trial court empanels a separate jury for each defendant. Then, D1 is allowed to withdraw his jury during presentation of evidence that D2 confessed and implicated D1. This saves the necessity of conducting two entirely separate trials.

III. COMPULSORY PROCESS

A. Generally: The Compulsory Process Clause gives the defendant the right to obtain and present all evidence helpful to his defense.

B. State rules restricting evidence: This means that a state evidence rule that restricts the defendant's ability to present exculpatory evidence may run afoul of his Compulsory Process rights.

1. Ban on accomplice's testimony: For instance, a statute providing that if A and B are charged as co-participants, A may not testify in B's defense, violates B's compulsory process rights.

2. Restrictive hearsay rule: Similarly, a state hearsay rule that prevents D from showing that someone else has made an out-of-court declaration confessing to the crime, may violate D's compulsory process rights. However, this will only happen if D convinces the court that the third person's alleged out-of-court confession is somewhat ***corroborated*** by surrounding circumstances. Thus if D offers X's out-of-court confession, but the prosecution shows that X was in jail at the time of the crime, D has no compulsory process right to present that confession.

C. "Arbitrary or disproportionate" standard: Rules excluding particular types of evidence will not violate an accused's Compulsory Process rights "so long as they are ***not 'arbitrary' or 'disproportionate*** to the purposes they are designed to serve.' " (Furthermore, this "arbitrary or disproportionate" standard will be violated only if the exclusion of evidence infringes upon a "weighty interest" of the accused.) [*U.S. v. Scheffer*]

Example: Rules prohibiting all parties (including criminal defendants) from introducing lie-detector evidence don't violate the accused's Compulsory Process rights. That's because polygraph evidence is of debatable reliability, so excluding it is not "arbitrary" or "disproportionate to the purpose" (ensuring reliability of evidence) that the rule of exclusion is designed to achieve. [*Scheffer*]

D. Equality principle: State rules that consistently *favor the prosecution* are especially likely to violate the Compulsory Process Clause.

Example: A state rule banning one accomplice from testifying on behalf of another, but not banning one accomplice from testifying against the other, favors the prosecution consistently, and therefore, violates the Compulsory Process Clause.

CHAPTER 7

PRIVILEGES

I. PRIVILEGES GENERALLY

A. Not constitutionally based: Most privileges are not constitutionally based. (The privilege against self-incrimination is the only exception.) Therefore, each state is free to establish whatever privileges it wishes and to define the contours of those privileges as it wishes.

1. **Federal:** There were a number of specific proposed federal rules of privilege. But these were never enacted. Instead, FRE 501 is the only Federal Rule dealing with privileges. It provides that normally, "[t]he common law — as interpreted by United States courts in the light of reason and experience — governs a claim of privilege[.]" That is, normally federal judges will decide what privileges to recognize based on ***prior federal case law*** and the court's ***own judgment.***

   a. **Diversity:** But in ***diversity*** cases, the existence and scope of a privilege will be decided by the law of the ***state*** whose substantive law is being followed.

2. **States:** The states vary greatly on what privileges they recognize. All recognize the husband-wife and attorney-client privileges, most by statute. All recognize a privilege for certain government information. Nearly all recognize some kind of physician-patient and clergyman-penitent privileges. Three other privileges are recognized only in a minority of states: journalist-source, parent-child, and accountant-client.

B. Proceedings where applicable: If a privilege not to disclose certain information exists, that privilege applies ***regardless of the proceeding***. That is, it will apply to protect the holder against disclosure in a trial, administrative hearing, deposition, or any other proceeding.

C. Who may assert: The privilege ***belongs*** to the ***person whose interest or relationship is intended to be fostered*** by that privilege. Therefore, he is the ***only one*** who may assert it.

Examples:

- ❑ The client is the one protected by the lawyer-client privilege, so it may be asserted only by him, or on his behalf, not by the lawyer on the lawyer's behalf.

- ❑ Similarly, the physician-patient privilege is meant to protect only the patient, so only he, not the doctor, may assert it.

D. Third person learns: Most privileges protect communications between two parties to a specified relationship. If a ***third party*** somehow learns of the conversation, the privilege may be found to have been ***waived***.

1. **Older, strict view:** The traditional view is very strict: if a third party somehow learns of the conversation, even if the original parties to it had no reason to anticipate this, the privilege will be held to be lost.

   Example: Telephone operator eavesdrops on a phone conversation between lawyer and client; the privilege is held to lost, and the operator may testify as to what she heard.

2. **Modern view:** But modern courts usually hold that the communication is protected even if intercepted, as long as the interception was not reasonably to be anticipated. (So the prior example would be decided differently today.) But if the party protected should ***reasonably have anticipated the interception***, he will not be protected.

   Example: Patient or client discloses a confidence to his doctor or lawyer in a crowded elevator; the risk of it being overheard is so great that if it is overheard, the privilege will be held waived.

II. THE ATTORNEY-CLIENT PRIVILEGE

A. Generally: The privilege is basically that a client has ***right not to disclose*** (and the right to prevent his lawyer from disclosing) ***any confidential communication between the two of them relating to the professional relationship***. The key elements are:

1. **Client:** The "client" can be a ***corporation*** as well as an individual.
2. **Belongs to client:** The privilege ***belongs to the client***, not to the lawyer or any third persons. The lawyer may assert it, but only if he is acting on behalf of the client in doing so.
3. **Professional relationship:** The privilege applies only to communications made for the purpose of facilitating the rendition of ***professional legal services***.
4. **Confidential:** The privilege applies only to communications which are intended to be ***"confidential."***
5. **Fact of employment or client's identity:** The fact that the lawyer-client relationship ***exists***, and the ***identity*** of the client, are normally ***not*** privileged. Only the substance of the confidences exchanged between them is generally privileged (though there are a couple of exceptions).
6. **Physical evidence:** Normally, the privilege does not permit the lawyer to conceal ***physical evidence*** or documents given to him by the client; the lawyer may not only have to turn over the physical evidence but describe how and where he got it.
7. **Crime or fraud exception:** The privilege does not apply where the confidence relates to the commission of a ***future crime or fraud***.

B. Professional relationship: The privilege applies only in the context of a professional lawyer-client relationship.

1. **No retainer:** The required relationship can exist even though the client does ***not pay a fee.***

   Example: Client receives a free initial consultation; the privilege applies even though, at the end of the consultation, either lawyer or client decides that the lawyer will not handle the case.

2. **Non-legal advice:** But the mere fact that the person giving the advice is a lawyer is not enough — the relationship must involve the giving of legal advice. Thus, if the lawyer gives ***business*** advice, ***friendly*** advice, political advice, etc., the privilege does not apply.

3. **Reasonable belief:** So long as the client ***reasonably believes*** that the person he is talking to is a lawyer, the privilege applies even though the other person is in fact not a lawyer. Similarly, the privilege applies if the person is a lawyer who is not, and is known to the client not to be, admitted to practice in the state where the advice is given.

C. Confidential communications: Only ***"confidential"*** communications are protected.

1. **Client-to-lawyer:** Disclosures by the ***client to the lawyer*** are protected if they are intended to be confidential.

   a. **Lawyer's observation:** However, if the lawyer makes an ***observation*** that third parties could also have made, this will not be a confidential communication.

      Example: Lawyer observes scratch marks on Client's face, in a meeting that takes place right after Client's wife has been found stabbed to death. Since anyone could have made this observation, it is not privileged, and Lawyer can be forced to testify at Client's trial about the scratches.

2. **Lawyer-to-client statements:** The privilege also applies to statements made ***by the lawyer*** to the client.

3. **Information involving third parties:**

   a. **Representative of lawyer:** If a ***third party*** is assisting the lawyer, he is treated as being a representative of the lawyer and communications involving him are treated the same way as if he were himself a lawyer.

      Example: Lawyer retains Private Detective to help investigate the case; statements made by Client to Detective, Lawyer to Detective, Detective to Client, Detective to Lawyer, are all privileged.

   b. **Not assisting lawyer:** But if a third person is ***not*** assisting the lawyer, there is ***no*** privilege for communications between that third person and the lawyer, even if these communications relate to the lawyer's providing of legal services.

      Example: Lawyer interviews Witness; statements made by Witness that incriminate Client are not privileged, because Witness is not working on behalf of Lawyer. However, if the only reason Lawyer knew to interview Witness is because Client told him to do so, the privilege might apply to Witness's statements.

4. **Waiver:** The attorney-client privilege can be ***waived***. Most importantly, if the client ***voluntarily discloses*** the communication — or consents to its being disclosed by someone else, such as her attorney — the disclosure will normally act as a waiver.

   a. **Presence of third persons:** One form of waiver-by-disclosure will occur when the client permits a ***third person to be present*** when the communication takes place, if that person's presence does not advance the legal representation.

      Example: If the communication takes place on a crowded elevator, where it is overheard by third persons, this setting will indicate that the client could not reasonably have expected confidentiality. Similarly, if the client, following the conference with the lawyer, tells a friend all about the conference, this is likely to be held to be an implied waiver of confidentiality.

   b. **Inadvertent disclosure:** Disclosures of privileged information sometimes occur ***inadvertently***. For instance, a litigant might produce a large batch of documents in ***discovery***, one of which (unbeknownst to the litigant) contains a privileged communication. Under standard attorney-client-privilege principles, that disclosure might be held to constitute a waiver of any later claim by the litigant that the document is privileged.

      i. **FRE 502 helps:** FRE 502 (added in 2008) tries to help people avoid losing the privilege on account of such inadvertent disclosures. 502 says that for purposes of federal-court litigation, an inadvertent disclosure does ***not*** operate as a waiver as long as the privilege-holder (i) took ***reasonable steps*** to ***prevent*** the disclosure before it happened, and then (ii) ***promptly took reasonable steps*** to ***rectify*** the error after it occurred. Rule 502(b), (c).

5. **Presence of third person:** The ***presence*** of a ***third person*** when the communication takes place, or its later ***disclosure*** to such a person, may as noted indicate that the communication was never intended to be "confidential." If so, it will be deemed waived. But if the third party's presence is reasonably ***helpful*** to the conference, that presence will ***not*** destroy the confidentiality.

   Example: Client's friend attends a meeting between Client and Lawyer, in order to help supply facts and to cope with Client's language difficulties. Since the friend's presence was helpful to the purpose of the meeting, that presence will not indicate a lack of intended confidentiality, and will therefore not cause Client to be deemed to have waived the privilege.

6. **Underlying facts:** It is only the ***communication*** that is privileged, not the underlying fact communicated.

D. **Fact of employment; client's identity:** Generally, the ***fact*** that the attorney has been hired, and the ***identity*** of the client, are ***not*** privileged.

Example: At a grand jury investigating local cocaine trafficking, L, a well known specialist in defending high-level cocaine importers, may be required to say whether he is representing X, one such importer.

1. **Exceptions:** Some courts have recognized one or both of the following exceptions to this general rule of non-privilege:

   a. **Anonymous restitution:** Some courts allow Lawyer to make anonymous restitution on behalf of Client.

   Example: Lawyer sends tax money to the IRS, without disclosing that it comes from Client — the purpose is to give Client a restitution defense if his taxes are ever audited. Some courts will allow Lawyer to refuse the IRS' demand to identify the Client.

   b. **"Missing link":** Most courts will allow the lawyer to keep the client's identity secret where so much other information is already public that disclosure of the client's identity would have the effect of disclosing a privileged communication, or violating the client's self-incrimination privilege.

   Example: X and Y are both suspected of murdering V. L represents X before a grand jury. A court might allow L to refuse to say whether Y is paying L's fee for representing X, on the theory that an affirmative answer might tend to incriminate Y.

E. **Physical evidence:** If the client turns over to the lawyer ***physical evidence***, the lawyer may generally not conceal this evidence or refuse to answer questions about whether he has it, on attorney-client privilege grounds.

1. **No ongoing fraud:** The most important rule concerning this problem is that the attorney-client privilege does not apply where the lawyer's assistance is sought to enable the client to ***commit a future crime or fraud***. Since all states prohibit the concealment or destruction of evidence in a pending proceeding, a lawyer who helps his client conceal or destroy evidence is a co-conspirator to a new crime, and the lawyer's assistance is thus not privileged. This is especially true where the evidence is contraband, stolen money, or a weapon or other instrument used to commit the crime.

2. **Destruction advice:** Similarly, the lawyer may not advise his client to destroy the evidence, and if he does so, the giving of that advice is not privileged.

3. **Lawyer's choices:** The lawyer may, however, simply return the evidence to the client with the advice not to conceal it; if the lawyer does this, he is probably privileged not to disclose the evidence's existence to the other side (usually the prosecution). Alternatively, he may take the evidence for a reasonable time for inspection or testing, and then return it to the client, without disclosing this fact to the other side. (But if the property is stolen, the lawyer must take steps to return it to his rightful owner. Similarly, if the lawyer believes that the client will destroy the evidence, he probably must turn it over to the other side, and is not privileged to keep silent about the evidence's existence.)

4. **Evidence of source:** If the other side (e.g., the prosecution) learns of particular physical evidence in the lawyer's possession, some courts hold that the lawyer is not privileged to refuse to say how he came into possession of it.

   Example: D is charged with murdering and robbing V. From prison, D tells L to inspect D's garbage can; L does so, and finds V's wallet, which he takes with him and puts in his safe. At trial, many courts would require L to testify about how he came into possession of the wallet, since otherwise the prosecution is unfairly impeded in its efforts to tie the wallet to D.

   a. **No custody:** But if the lawyer merely learns of an item's existence for his client, or inspects it and then gives it back to the client, the lawyer may not be required to say at trial how he learned about the item.

F. Corporations as clients:

1. **Corporations have privilege:** A ***corporation*** may possess the attorney-client privilege just as an individual may.

2. **Who may communicate:** Only communications made "on behalf" of the corporation's business are covered. But probably no matter how low level an employee is, if he is really acting in what he reasonably perceives to be the corporation's interests, communications made between him and the corporation's lawyer will be privileged as to the corporation.

3. **Must concern employment:** The mere fact that one party to the communication is an employee is not sufficient — the communication must ***relate to the employee's performance of corporate duties.***

   Example: Driver, who works for Bus Co., happens to see an accident involving one of the company's buses while he is off duty. Statements about the accident by Driver to Bus Co.'s lawyer are not privileged, because they do not relate to anything that happened while Driver was performing his corporate duties.

4. **Reports and routine communications:** The communication must be primarily for the purpose of obtaining legal services. Therefore, if the communication is a ***routine report*** generated in the ordinary course of the corporation's business, the privilege will not apply merely because the report happened to be received by one of the corporation's attorneys.

   Examples: Accident reports, personnel records, and financial documents probably won't be privileged even if circulated to the company's attorneys, because none of these is typically created for the primary purpose of obtaining legal services.

5. **Confidentiality:** The requirement of confidentiality means that only those communications that the corporation handles on a ***"need to know"*** basis will be privileged.

G. Exceptions: There are several situations where the privilege will be held not to apply even though the usual requirements are met:

1. **Crime or fraud:** As noted above, a communication relating to the carrying out of a future ***crime or wrong*** is not privileged.

Example: Client says to Lawyer, "If X and I were to rob the First National Bank, and X were then to get caught and give a confession implicating me, could the police use this confession against me?" If the robbery is later committed, the statement may be used against Client, since even though he was seeking legal services, he was doing so with reference to a future crime.

2. **Death of client:** In general, the privilege ***survives*** the ***death*** of the client. But there is a key exception: if the suit is a will contest or other case in which the issue is who receives the deceased client's property, the privilege does not apply.

   Example: In will contest, Son may call Lawyer to testify about Lawyer's conversations with Testator, in which Testator said that he wanted to provide for Son in his will.

3. **Attorney-client dispute:** The privilege does not apply to a ***dispute between lawyer and client*** concerning the services provided by lawyer.

   Examples: The privilege does not apply if Lawyer sues Client for a fee, or if Client sues Lawyer for malpractice.

4. **Joint clients:** The privilege may be inapplicable to a dispute between multiple clients who were originally on the same side of a transaction.

   a. **Same lawyer:** If two clients ***retain a single lawyer***, and a dispute later breaks out between the two, the privilege does not apply. This is true regardless of whether the other client was privy to the communication in question.

      Example: Driver is sued by Passenger for injuries from a car crash. Insurer, who insures Driver, hires Lawyer for the case. Driver makes confidential communications to Lawyer. Later, Driver and Insurer have a dispute about policy limits. In that dispute, Insurer may probably compel Lawyer to disclose otherwise-privileged statements between Driver and Lawyer.

   b. **Different lawyers:** But if two clients retain ***separate*** lawyers, and both lawyers and both clients meet together and discuss common legal issues, the privilege applies even in the event of a later dispute between clients.

H. Work product immunity: Separately from the attorney-client privilege, the doctrine of ***work product immunity*** prevents an attorney from being required to disclose certain information that he obtains ***while preparing for a lawsuit.***

1. **Qualified protection:** Generally, documents prepared in anticipation of litigation may be discovered by the other side only if the party seeking discovery shows that he has a ***substantial need*** for the materials, and that he cannot get the substantial equivalent by other means. This is a ***"qualified"*** immunity. Fed. R. Civ. Proc. 26(b)(3).

   Example: Client fills out a questionnaire about the facts of his injuries, to help Lawyer prepare the case for trial. Even if the questionnaire is not covered by the attorney-client privilege — perhaps because Client has disclosed it to a journalist — Lawyer can refuse to release it in response to a discovery request by the other side.

a. **Absolute immunity:** Documents that show a lawyer's "mental impressions, conclusions, opinions, or legal theories" concerning litigation are probably ***absolutely*** privileged, in the sense that no showing of need by the other side will be sufficient to overcome the work product immunity.

III. PHYSICIAN-PATIENT PRIVILEGE

A. **Generally:** All but 10 states have a statutory physician-patient privilege. These statutes usually apply to:

1. a ***confidential communication***;
2. made to a ***physician*** (including psychiatrist);
3. if made for the purpose of obtaining ***treatment***, or diagnosis looking toward treatment.

B. **Constitutional underpinning:** Some aspects of the privilege may be constitutionally compelled. At least one state court (California) has held that the "confidentiality of the psychotherapeutic session" falls within one of the "zones of privacy" created by the U.S. Constitution (though California has held that its statute, with exceptions for the patient-litigant situation, see below, is constitutional).

C. **Relationships covered:** All statutes that cover general physician-patient confidences also cover ***psychotherapist***-patient confidences. In fact, virtually all states (even ones that don't cover physician-patient confidences) protect psychotherapist-patient confidences.

1. **Psychologist:** Nearly all states cover ***psychologists*** (not just psychiatrists) within the psychotherapist-patient privilege.
2. **Consulted for litigation:** Consultations that take place concerning ***litigation*** rather than for purposes of treatment or diagnosis are ***not*** covered. For instance, examination by or disclosures to a court-appointed physician, or an expert witness consulted so that he can testify at trial, are not covered.

D. **Patient-litigant exception:** Nearly all statutes have some kind of exception for the ***"patient-litigant"*** situation, under which a patient-litigant who puts his ***medical condition in issue*** is deemed to have in effect waived the privilege.

Example: Car collision case; P sues D for a broken leg. P's doctor and hospital records, including notations of disclosures made by P to the doctor, will be admissible, because P has placed the nature and extent of his injuries in issue by seeking damages for them.

IV. THE PRIVILEGE AGAINST SELF-INCRIMINATION

A. **Generally:**

1. **Constitutional basis:** The privilege derives from the U.S. Constitution. The Fifth Amendment provides that "no person . . . shall be compelled in any criminal case to be a witness against himself. . . ."

a. **Applicable to states:** This provision is binding not only on the federal judicial system but also on the ***states***, by operation of the Fourteenth Amendment's Due Process Clause.

b. **Two types:** The privilege applies not only to criminal defendants, but also to any other person who is asked to give testimony that may incriminate him (e.g., witnesses in grand jury proceedings, congressional investigations, other people's criminal trials, etc.).

B. **Requirements:** The privilege applies only when four requirements are met: (1) it is asserted by an ***individual***; (2) the communication sought is ***testimonial***; (3) the communication is ***compulsory***; and (4) the communication might ***incriminate*** the witness.

1. **Individuals:** The requirement that the privilege be individual and "personal" means that:

a. **Another's privilege:** A person may not assert ***another's*** privilege.

Example: D is on trial for robbery. The prosecution puts on testimony by X, an unindicted co-conspirator, in which X says that he and D did the robbery together. D may not exclude this testimony by claiming that it violates X's privilege — since it is X who is testifying, only he may assert or waive the privilege.

b. **Business organization:** ***Business organizations*** do ***not*** have the privilege. Thus, neither ***corporations***, partnerships, nor labor unions may claim the privilege. (But a person doing business as a sole proprietorship may assert it — it is not the fact of doing business that removes the privilege, but rather the use of an "artificial organization.")

c. **Agent:** An employee or other ***agent*** of a business organization will usually have to produce and identify the organization's books and records on request, even though those books and records (or the fact that the agent has them) might incriminate him. But he will usually not have to do anything more if this would incriminate him (e.g., he usually will not have to state the whereabouts of corporate records that he does not possess).

2. **Testimonial:** Only ***"testimonial"*** activity is covered. Thus, the suspect may be required to furnish a blood sample, fingerprints, handwriting samples, or even to speak so that his voice may be compared with a previously recorded conversation. Also, a suspect may be required to appear in a lineup for identification.

3. **"Compulsory":** A communication must be ***"compulsory."*** The main importance of this requirement is that if a person ***voluntarily*** puts the information in ***written form***, the document is not privileged. (But the writer may have a privilege against ***producing*** the document for the government, as discussed below.)

4. **Incriminatory:** The response must have a ***tendency to incriminate*** the person. Thus if there are procedural reasons why no prosecution can take place (e.g., the statute of limitations has run, or the witness has been given immunity), the privilege does not apply. The fact that answering the question might subject the witness to ridicule or civil liability is not enough.

C. Proceedings where applicable: The privilege applies not only where asserted by a defendant in a criminal trial, but also by any witness in ***any kind of proceeding.*** Thus it may be asserted by witnesses to a grand jury investigation, to another person's criminal trial, to a civil proceeding, to pre-trial discovery proceedings (e.g., W's deposition is being taken), or to questioning by the police.

D. Procedure for invoking:

1. **Criminal defendant:** When the assertion is made by the defendant in a criminal trial, he may invoke the privilege merely by ***declining to testify.*** In that event, he does not have to take the stand at all, and cannot even be questioned.

2. **Non-defendant witness:** But if the privilege is being claimed by a ***witness*** (i.e., someone other than the defendant in a criminal trial), the procedure is different: the witness must ***take the stand***, be sworn, listen to the question, and then assert the privilege. In this event, it is the judge who decides whether the response might be incriminatory; but the person seeking the testimony bears an extremely heavy burden of proving that the response ***could not possibly*** incriminate W, a showing that can only rarely be made.

E. Waiver: A person who takes the stand and gives some testimony may be held to have ***waived*** the privilege with respect to further questions:

1. **Criminal defendant:** If a criminal defendant does take the stand, and testifies in his own defense, he has waived his privilege at least with respect to those questions that are ***necessary for an effective cross-examination***.

   Example: In a murder trial, D testifies that he was not anywhere near the scene of the crime. The prosecution would certainly be entitled to ask D where he was, and D could not assert the privilege in refusing to answer.

2. **Witness:** Since an ordinary witness must take the stand and listen to each question, a witness who answers non-incriminating questions will not be held to have waived the privilege with respect to later, incriminating, questions. However, if W makes a general and incriminatory statement about a matter, he must then answer ***follow-up questions eliciting the details***, at least where these details would not add significantly to the incrimination.

3. **Later proceedings:** If the defendant or witness does waive the privilege, this waiver is effective ***throughout the current proceedings***, but not for subsequent proceedings.

   Example: W's waiver during grand jury proceedings would not prevent him from asserting the privilege when called as a witness at a subsequent trial of X on an indictment returned by that same grand jury.

F. Documentary evidence: When a document is subpoenaed by the government, the person receiving the subpoena may have a fifth amendment right not to comply:

1. **Contents:** The ***contents*** of the subpoenaed document will practically never be protected by the Fifth Amendment: so long as the taxpayer was not originally compelled to create the document, its contents are not protected by the privilege.

2. **Act of producing:** But a person's act of ***producing*** the documents in response to a subpoena may implicitly incriminate him, in which case he probably has a Fifth Amendment privilege not to produce it. For instance, if there were no way that the government could obtain or authenticate a certain personal diary kept by D except through production of this diary by him, D might be allowed to plead the Fifth by arguing that his production would implicitly mean that he is stating: (1) that the diary exists; (2) that the diary was in his possession or control; and (3) that he believes that this is indeed the genuine diary the government is seeking. (But if the government can show that it has other ways of authenticating this diary, then the privilege will not apply.)

3. **"Required records" exception:** Even if a person is ***compelled*** to keep a certain type of record, he may not have a Fifth Amendment right to refuse to do so: the record keeper must turn the record over even though it might incriminate him, if: (1) the record is one that a party has customarily kept, (2) the law requiring the keeping of it is "essentially regulatory," and (3) the records are analogous to a "public document." This is the ***"required records"*** exception to the privilege against self-incrimination. (*Example:* Records of prices charged to customers, kept under a mandatory price control law, still have to be turned over because they are essentially regulatory.)

G. **Inference and comment:** When a criminal defendant pleads the Fifth, he gets two other procedural safeguards to extend the privilege's usefulness.

1. **"No comment" rule:** First, neither the judge nor the prosecution may ***comment adversely*** on D's failure to testify (e.g., by saying, "If D is really innocent, why hasn't he taken the stand to tell you that?")

2. **Instruction:** Second, D has an affirmative right to have the judge ***instruct the jury*** that they are not to draw any adverse inference from his failure to testify.

3. **Prior silence:** If the criminal defendant has remained silent at ***prior proceedings***, the judge and prosecutor may not comment if the silence was the result of clear exercise of a constitutional privilege:

   a. **Arrest:** Thus, if D was previously silent during ***custodial police interrogation***, the prosecutor and judge may not comment on this fact at D's later criminal trial.

   b. **Pre-arrest silence:** But if D remained silent ***before being arrested***, this fact may be comment on, since D was not exercising any formal Fifth Amendment privilege.

   Example: D pleads self-defense to a murder charge. The prosecution may comment upon the fact that for the two weeks between the killing and D's arrest, he did not go to the police to tell them his story.

4. **Civil suit:** If the suit is a ***civil*** one, either side may freely comment adversely on the other party's (or a witness's) failure to testify.

   Example: P sues D for causing a car accident; D fails to take the stand because he is afraid that if he does so, the fact that he was drunk will come out, and he may be prosecuted. P may nonetheless say to the jury, "If D wasn't driving drunk, why doesn't he take the stand and tell you that?"

H. Immunity: If W is given ***immunity*** from prosecution, he may not assert the privilege (since he has received the same benefit — freedom from having his testimony used against him — that the privilege is designed to provide).

1. **"Transactional" vs. "use" immunity:** There are two types of immunity: ***"transactional"*** and ***"use."*** Transactional protects the witness against any prosecution for the ***transaction*** about which he testifies. Use immunity is much narrower — it merely protects against the direct or indirect use of the ***testimony*** in a subsequent prosecution.

2. **Use immunity sufficient:** Use immunity is ***sufficient*** to nullify the witness's Fifth Amendment privilege. (But the prosecutor then bears a heavy burden of showing that he could not have used the testimony, even indirectly, in preparing for the subsequent case.)

3. **Defense witness immunity:** If a person could give testimony that a criminal defendant thinks would help exonerate him, but the witness refuses to testify without immunity, the defendant may attempt to have ***"defense witness immunity"*** conferred upon this witness. But the vast majority of courts have refused to grant such defense witness immunity.

V. THE MARITAL PRIVILEGES

A. Generally:

1. **Two privileges:** In most states, two distinct privileges protect the marital relationship:

   a. **Adverse testimony:** The ***adverse testimony*** privilege (sometimes called "spousal immunity") gives a spouse ***complete*** protection from adverse testimony by the other spouse.

   Example: H is on trial for murder; the adverse testimony privilege protects H from having W take the witness stand to testify against him, regardless of whether her testimony concerns anything he said.

   b. **Confidential communication:** The ***confidential communications*** privilege is narrower: it protects only against the disclosure of confidential communications made by one spouse to the other during the marriage.

   Example: H is on trial for murder. The confidential communications privilege protects H against having W disclose that H confessed to her, "I shot V," but does not protect him against having W describe to the jury how she witnessed H kill V.

2. **Distinctions:** Here are some of the practical differences between the two privileges:

   a. **Before marriage, or after marriage ends:** The adverse testimony privilege applies only if the parties are still married at the time of the trial, but applies to statements made before the marriage took place. Conversely, the confidential communications privilege covers only statements made during the marriage, but applies even if the parties are no longer married by the time of the trial.

b. **Civil vs. criminal:** The adverse testimony privilege is usually allowed only in criminal cases, but the confidential communications privilege is usually available in civil as well as criminal cases.

c. **Acts:** The adverse testimony privilege prevents the non-party spouse from testifying even as to ***acts*** committed by the spouse, but the confidential communications privilege does not (since it covers only "communications").

3. **State coverage:** Only a slight majority of states recognize the adverse testimony privilege, but virtually all recognize the confidential communications privilege. In ***federal*** courts, ***both*** privileges are recognized.

B. Adverse testimony privilege:

1. **Who holds:** Courts disagree about who holds the adverse testimony privilege:

   a. **Federal:** In federal cases, the privilege belongs only to the ***testifying spouse***, not the party spouse. Thus, D in a federal criminal trial may not block his spouse's testimony; only the witness-spouse may assert or waive the right.

   b. **States:** Of those states recognizing the adverse testimony privilege, a slight majority give the privilege to the party (i.e., the criminal defendant); the rest follow the federal approach of giving the privilege only to the witness-spouse.

2. **Criminal vs. civil:** Most jurisdictions (including the federal courts) grant the adverse testimony privilege only in ***criminal*** cases.

3. **Special marriage:** If D is worried about his girlfriend's being required to disclose something she has heard or seen, he may marry her the night before the trial, and thereby keep her off the stand using the adverse testimony privilege.

C. Confidential communications: Virtually every state recognizes the confidential communications privilege.

1. **Federal:** Federal courts apply this privilege on the basis of ***general federal common law***, since there is no federal rule granting it.

2. **Who holds:** In most states, ***either spouse*** may assert the privilege. (But a few states grant it only to the spouse who made the communication.)

3. **"Communication" required:** Only "communications" are privileged. Strictly speaking, an "act" that is not intended to convey information is not covered. (But some states have held that if an act is done in front of the spouse only because the actor trusts the spouse, the privilege should apply. Thus if H allows W to see his recently-fired shotgun before putting it away, the court might hold that this was the equivalent of a "communication" since it would not have happened had H not trusted W.)

4. **Marital status:** The parties to the communication must be married at the time of the communication. If so, the privilege applies even though they have gotten divorced by the time of the trial.

5. **Exceptions:** Here are some common exceptions to the confidential communications privilege:

   a. **Crime against other spouse:** Prosecution for crimes ***committed by one spouse against the other***, or against the ***children*** of either;

   b. **Suit between spouses:** Suits by ***one spouse against the other*** (e.g., a divorce suit);

   c. **Facilitating crime:** Communications made for the purpose of ***planning or committing a crime***.

   Example: H brings home loot from a robbery, and asks W to help him hide it. Since H is seeking W's help in committing an additional crime — possession of stolen goods — most courts would find the privilege inapplicable to H's request for assistance.

VI. MISCELLANEOUS PRIVILEGES

A. **Priest-penitent:** Virtually all states recognize a privilege for ***confidential communications*** made to a ***clergyman*** in his profession capacity as ***spiritual advisor***.

B. **Journalist's source:** Most states now recognize a privilege for a journalist's sources:

1. **Statutes:** A slight majority of states have enacted ***"shield laws"*** preventing a journalist from being compelled to testify about his confidential sources. All of these statutes at least protect the journalist from having to disclose the ***identity*** of his sources; some protect him against forced disclosure of his ***notes and records*** of information learned from the source.

2. **Constitutional argument:** Some state and lower-federal courts have recognized a ***First Amendment*** basis for the privilege in some situations.

   Example: If the information being sought is not very central to the case of the litigant who is seeking it, or can be gotten from other sources, the court may find that the journalist has a constitutional right not to supply it.

   a. **No Supreme Court rule:** But the Supreme Court has never found such a First Amendment privilege to exist, and in one major case, a four-justice plurality concluded that no such privilege exists. [*Branzburg v. Hayes*.]

3. **Conflict with defendant's rights:** If the journalist's statutory or constitutional privilege ***conflicts*** with a criminal defendant's Sixth Amendment right to ***compulsory process*** or ***confrontation***, the journalist's privilege will probably have to give way.

   Example: Reporter conducts a murder investigation, leading to charges against D; D's constitutional right to compulsory process outweighs Reporter's rights under the state shield provision, so Reporter is required to supply his notes on his investigation. *In re Farber.*

C. **Government information:** The government may have a privilege not to disclose ***information in its possession***:

1. **Military or diplomatic secrets:** The government has an ***absolute*** privilege not to disclose ***military*** or ***diplomatic*** secrets. No matter how badly a litigant needs such information, the government is privileged not to disclose it.

2. **Other government information:** Other types of government information receive merely a ***qualified*** privilege. That is, the privilege applies only where the harm to the public welfare from disclosure outweighs the litigant's need for the information.

   a. **Internal deliberations and policy making:** Thus internal government opinions, deliberations, and recommendations about policies are qualifiedly privileged. (But factual reports are not.)

   b. **Law enforcement investigatory files:** Similarly, ***investigatory files*** compiled by a law enforcement agency are qualifiedly privileged.

   Example: A criminal defendant has no general evidence-law right to force the government to turn over to him the files it has compiled in investigating and preparing the case against him, though criminal discovery rules may give him the right to certain items, such as witnesses' statements.

3. **Informers:** The government has a special privilege to decline to disclose the ***identity of informants*** who have given information about crimes.

   a. **I.D. only:** Usually, the government informant privilege protects only the ***identity*** of the informant, not the substance of the ***information*** that he gives to the government (unless that information would effectively reveal the informant's identity).

   b. **Qualified:** The privilege is only a ***qualified*** one. Thus if disclosure of the informant's I.D. is likely to materially help the criminal defendant in his defense, the government must disclose it or drop the case. Participants and eyewitnesses are usually held to be so central that their I.D.s must be disclosed; but a mere "tipster" is not, so his identity may usually be concealed. Anyone called as a ***witness*** by the prosecution must be identified.

4. **Consequences of upholding claim:** If the court upholds the government's claim of privilege, and the government is the plaintiff (as in a criminal prosecution or a civil suit brought by the government), the government must normally ***choose*** between releasing the information or ***dropping the case***.

D. **Trade secrets:** Some courts recognize a qualified privilege for ***trade secrets***; that is, special secrets which a business possesses that aid it in competing.

Examples:

- ❑ Information about a company's relative market position;
- ❑ Secret information about a device or process;
- ❑ Design information about a product.

If the judge does partly override the privilege because of a litigant's great need for the material, he may issue a ***protective order*** limiting the use to which the information may be put (e.g., by ordering that the litigant not disclose it to anyone else).

CHAPTER 8

REAL AND DEMONSTRATIVE EVIDENCE, INCLUDING WRITINGS

I. INTRODUCTION

A. "Real" vs. "demonstrative" evidence:

1. **"Real":** "Real" evidence is a tangible object that ***played some actual role*** in the matter that gave rise to the litigation.

   Example: A knife used in a fatal stabbing.

2. **"Demonstrative":** Demonstrative evidence is tangible evidence that merely ***illustrates*** a matter of importance in the litigation.

   Examples: Maps, diagrams, models, summaries, and other materials created especially for the litigation. For instance, if the prosecution cannot find actual knife used in stabbing, a newly-acquired knife believed to be similar to the one actually used may be presented as a model to help the jury understand.

3. **Significance of distinction:** The foundation requirements needed to authenticate the two types of evidence are different. See below.

II. AUTHENTICATION

A. Generally: All real and demonstrative evidence must be ***"authenticated"*** before it is admitted. That is, it must be shown to be ***"genuine."*** This means that the object must be established to be ***what its proponent claims it to be***. See FRE 901(a).

1. **Real evidence:** If the object is real evidence, authentication usually means showing that the object is ***the*** object that was involved in the underlying event (e.g., the actual knife used in the stabbing).

2. **Demonstrative:** If the evidence is demonstrative, authentication usually means showing that the object ***fairly represents or illustrates*** what it is claimed to represent or illustrate (e.g., proof that a diagram offered in evidence really shows the position of the parties and witnesses at the time of the murder).

B. Methods of authentication:

1. **Real evidence:** For real evidence, authentication generally is done in one of two ways:

   a. **Readily or uniquely identifiable:** If the item is ***readily*** or ***uniquely*** identifiable, it can be authenticated by showing that this is the case, and that the object is therefore the one that played the actual role.

   Example: "I found the knife at the stabbing, and marked it with my initials; the knife you have just shown me has my carved initials, so it must be the knife found at the murder scene."

b. **Chain of custody:** Otherwise, the item's ***"chain of custody"*** must be demonstrated. That is, every person who handled or possessed the object since it was first recognized as being relevant must explain what he did with it.

Example: Each person who handled the white powder taken from D must testify about how he got it, how he handled it during his custody, and whom he turned it over to.

2. **Demonstrative evidence:** If the evidence is demonstrative, authentication is done merely by showing that the object ***fairly represents*** some aspect of the case.

3. **Federal Rules:** The Federal Rules have a simple, basic principle of authentication that applies to all evidence (real, demonstrative, writings, and intangibles): the proponent must come up with evidence ***"sufficient to support a finding*** that the item is ***what the proponent claims it is***." FRE 901(a). (901(b) gives illustrations of proper authentication.)

4. **Judge's role:** The judge does not have to decide whether the proffered item ***is*** what its proponent claims it to be (the jury does this). But the judge does have to decide whether there is ***some evidence*** from which a jury could reasonably find that the item is what it is claimed to be.

C. **Authentication of writings and recordings:** Special rules exist for authenticating ***writings*** and other recorded communications:

1. **Authorship:** Usually, authentication of a writing consists of showing ***who its author is***.

2. **No presumption of authenticity:** A writing or other communication (just like any non-assertive evidence like a knife) carries ***no presumption of authenticity***. Instead, the proponent bears the ***burden*** of making an affirmative showing that the writing or communication is what it appears to be and what the proponent claims it to be.

a. **Signature:** Thus, a ***writing's own statement*** concerning its authorship (e.g., its ***signature***) is ***not*** enough — the proponent must make some independent showing that the signature was made by the person who the proponent claims made it.

3. **Direct testimony:** One way to authenticate a writing or communication is by ***direct testimony*** that the document is what its proponent claims.

Example: If proponent wants to show that X really signed the document, he may produce W to testify that W saw X sign it.

4. **Distinctive characteristics:** A writing's ***distinctive characteristics***, or the ***circumstances*** surrounding it, may suffice for authentication. See FRE 901(b)(4).

Example: The fact that a diary contains the logo of D Corp.; its entries match testimony previously given by X (D Corp.'s employee); it was produced by D Corp. during discovery; and it is similar to other diaries previously authenticated, all suffices to authenticate the diary as having been kept by X.

5. **Signature or handwriting:** A document's author can be established by showing that it was signed or written in the hand of a particular person. Even if no witness is available who saw the person do the signing or writing, the document may be authenticated by a witness who can identify the ***signature or handwriting*** as belonging to a particular person.

   a. **Expert:** If W, the person identifying the signature or handwriting, is a handwriting ***expert***, he may base his testimony based solely on handwriting specimens from X that he examined in preparation for his trial testimony. (But expert testimony on handwriting or signature-matching must meet the FRE 702 / *Daubert* requirements for ***scientific evidence***, designed to ensure that such evidence is scientifically reliable.)

   b. **Non-expert:** But if W, the authenticating witness, is ***not*** a handwriting expert, his testimony may not be based on comparisons and studies made directly for the litigation; instead, he must testify that he saw X's handwriting at some time before the litigation began, and that he recognizes the signature or handwriting in question to be that of X.

   c. **Exemplars:** Exemplars (specimens prepared by the person claimed to have written the document in question) may be shown to the jury, which is then invited to make its own conclusion about whether the exemplar and the questioned document were by the same person.

6. **Reply letters and telegrams:** A ***letter or telegram*** can sometimes be authenticated by the circumstantial fact that it appears to be a ***reply*** to a prior communication, and the prior communication is proved.

   Example: P proves that he wrote a letter to D on Jan. 1; a letter purporting to have been written by D to P on Jan. 15, that alludes to the contents of the earlier P-D letter, is authenticated by these circumstantial facts as indeed being a D-P letter.

7. **Phone conversation:** When the contents of a ***telephone conversation*** are sought to be proved, the proponent must authenticate the conversation by ***establishing the parties to it***.

   a. **Outgoing calls:** For ***outgoing*** calls (calls made ***by*** the sponsoring witness), the proponent can authenticate the call by showing that: (1) W made a call to the ***number assigned by the phone company*** to a particular person; and (2) the ***circumstances*** show that the person who talked on the other end was in fact the person the caller was trying to reach. FRE 901(b)(6).

      i. **Circumstances:** The "circumstances" showing that the person on the other end was the one the caller was trying to reach, include: (1) ***self-identification*** by the callee ("This is George you're speaking to"); or (2) the ***caller's identification*** of the callee's voice through prior familiarity.

      ii. **Call to business:** If the outgoing call is to a ***business***, FRE 901(b)(6)(B) says that authentication can be made by showing that the call was made to the listed number for the business and that the conversation "related to ***business*** [of a sort that would be] ***reasonably transacted over the telephone***."

b. **Incoming calls:** Where the call is an ***incoming*** one (i.e., the sponsoring witness is the ***recipient***), ***self-authentication by the caller is not enough***. There must be some additional evidence that the caller is who he said he was.

Example: W wants to testify that she received a call from X. It's not enough for W to testify, "I received a call from someone who said he was X." But if W adds, "I recognized the voice as belonging to X, from prior conversations with him," that *would* be enough to authenticate the call as having been from X.

8. **Attesting witnesses:** If a document is ***attested to*** or subscribed to by witnesses (e.g., a will), special rules sometimes apply:

a. **Common law:** At common law, at least one attesting witness must be called to testify (even if he does not authenticate the document) before non-attesting witnesses may authenticate it.

b. **Federal Rule:** But FRE 903 drops this requirement (except where the relevant state law imposes it).

9. **Ancient documents:**

a. **Common law:** At common law, a writing is automatically deemed authenticated as an ***"ancient document"*** if it: (1) is at least ***30 years old***; (2) is ***unsuspicious*** in appearance; and (3) has been found in a place of custody ***natural*** for such a document.

b. **Federal Rules:** FRE 901(b)(8) applies the same requirements as the common law (above) for ancient documents, except that: (1) the document needs to be only ***20*** years old; and (2) the rule covers not only "documents" but "data compilations" (e.g., a computer tape, and probably photos, X-rays, movies, and sound tapes as well).

c. **No guarantee of admissibility:** But keep in mind that a document that satisfies these requirements for the "ancient document" rule of authentication merely overcomes the authentication hurdle. The document still has to survive other obstacles (e.g., it must be not hearsay or fall within some exception; but there is also an ancient document exception to the hearsay rule; see *supra*, p. 75).

D. **Self-authentication:** A few types of documents are ***"self-authenticating,"*** because they are so likely to be what they seem, that no testimony or other evidence of their genuineness need be produced.

1. **State provisions:** Under most state statutes, the following are self-authenticating: (1) deeds and other instruments that are ***notarized***; (2) ***certified*** copies of ***public records*** (e.g., a certified copy of a death certificate); and (3) books of statutes which appear to be printed by a government body (e.g., a statute book appearing to be from a sister state or foreign country).

2. **Federal Rules:** FRE 902 recognizes the above three classes, and also adds: (1) all ***official publications*** (not just statutes); (2) ***newspapers*** or periodicals; and (3) ***labels, signs,*** or other inscriptions indicating "origin, ownership, or control" (e.g.,

a can of peas bearing the label "Green Giant Co." is self-authenticating as having been produced by Green Giant Co.).

E. Ways to avoid: Authentication is not necessary if:

1. **Admission:** The proponent has served on the opponent a written ***request for admission***, and the opponent has granted this.
2. **Stipulation:** The parties have jointly ***stipulated*** to the ***genuineness*** of a particular document or object.

III. THE "BEST EVIDENCE RULE" FOR RECORDED COMMUNICATIONS

A. Generally:

1. **Text of rule:** The common-law Best Evidence Rule (B.E.R.) provides that ***"in proving the terms of a writing, where the terms are material, the original writing must be produced unless it is shown to be unavailable for some reason other than the serious fault of the proponent."***
2. **Components:** The B.E.R. has three main components:
   a. **Original document:** The ***original document*** must be produced, rather than using a copy or oral testimony about the document;

   b. **Prove terms:** The Rule applies only where what is to be proved is the ***terms*** of a ***writing*** (or, under the modern approach, an equivalent recorded communication such as an audio tape of a conversation); and

   c. **Excuse:** The Rule does not apply if the original is ***unavailable*** because it has been destroyed, is in the possession of a third party, or cannot be conveniently obtained, and the unavailability is not due to the serious fault of the proponent.
3. **Not applicable to evidence generally:** The B.E.R. does ***not apply to evidence generally***, only to writings (or equivalent recorded communications).
4. **Federal Rule:** FRE 1002 gives the federal version of the B.E.R.: "An ***original writing, recording,*** or ***photograph*** is required in order to ***prove its content***[.]" The federal approach changes the common-law rule in two major ways:
   a. **Broadened coverage:** Not just writings, but also ***recordings*** and ***photographs*** are covered by the Federal Rule in contrast to the common-law rule.

   Examples: An audio tape of a conversation, or a computer tape of data, would be covered under the federal approach, so that if these items are available, they must be introduced instead of using oral testimony to describe their contents.

   b. **Duplicate:** But unlike the common law, the federal rules allow a ***duplicate*** (e.g., a photocopy) in lieu of the original unless the opponent raises a genuine question about authenticity or it would be unfair in the circumstances to allow the duplicate. FRE 1003.

B. What is a "writing" or other recorded communication:

1. **Short inscription:** An object that contains a short ***inscription*** (e.g., a pocket watch with words of affection engraved on it) might be held to be a "writing" covered by the B.E.R., depending on the surrounding circumstances (e.g., how important its precise, rather than approximate, content is to the litigation).

2. **Photographic evidence:** Under the modern and federal approach, a ***photograph*** or X-ray will be covered by the Rule, if offered to prove the contents of the item.

   Example: P, to prove that she has been injured, wants to prove that her X-rays show a spinal injury; the X-rays themselves must be used if available, rather than a radiologist's testimony about what the X-rays show.

3. **Sound recordings:** Similarly, if a party tries to prove the contents of a ***sound recording***, he must do so by presenting the actual recording rather than an oral or written account of what it provides.

C. Proving the contents: The B.E.R. only applies where what is sought to be proved are the "terms" or "contents" of the writing.

1. **Existence, execution, etc.:** Thus if all that is proved is that a writing ***exists***, was ***executed***, or was ***delivered***, the B.E.R. does not apply.

   Example: Prosecution of D for kidnapping; a prosecution witness, W, mentions that a ransom note was received but does not testify about the note's contents. Since this proof that the ransom note was delivered does not constitute proof of its terms, the note need not be produced in evidence. But if W goes on to give the details of what the note said, the note would have to be produced if available.

2. **Incidental record:** The fact that there happens to be a writing memorializing a transaction does not mean that the transaction can only be proved by the introduction of a writing. Here, the writing is treated as an ***incidental by-product*** of the transaction.

   Example: The earnings of a business can be proved by oral testimony, rather than by submitting the books and records, because those books and records are merely an incidental memorializing of the earnings.

   a. **Transcript:** A person's prior ***testimony*** can generally be proved by an oral account of a witness who heard the testimony, even if a ***transcript*** exists. The transcript is merely an incidental by-product of the testimony. (But a ***confession*** by a defendant to the crime charged must generally be proved by the transcript or recording.)

   b. **Photo:** If a photograph, X-ray, audio recording, video tape, etc., has been made of an object or event, live testimony about the object or event will generally be ***allowed*** in lieu of introducing the photograph, etc.

      Example: W may testify to seeing D shoot V, even though there happens to be a home movie showing the shooting. The movie is an incidental memorial of the event, so the event can be proved without the movie.

c. **Contract:** But if a document truly ***embodies*** a transaction, the document comes within the B.E.R. and must be produced if available.

Example: If two parties to an agreement have signed a formal written *contract*, that contract must be produced at the litigation, even though the parties could have bound themselves orally to the same terms; the contract embodies their arrangement, rather than merely being an incidental by-product of it.

D. Collateral writings: The ***"collateral writings"*** exception means that a document which has only a ***tangential connection*** to the litigation need not be produced, even though its contents are being proved. See FRE 1004(4) (original need not be produced if the writing, recording, etc., is "not closely related to a controlling issue").

E. Which is original: If one writing is derived from another, the earlier one is not necessarily the "writing itself" that must be produced. The proposition being proved may be such that the derivative writing is the one whose contents are being proved, in which case it is the original of that derivative writing that must be produced.

Example: D writes a handwritten letter to X possibly defaming P; D then hands the letter to his secretary, who retypes it and sends the typed version. At P's libel suit against D, it is the derivative typed version, not the handwritten version, which is the "original" that must be produced if available.

F. Reproductions:

1. **Common law:** At common law, no subsequently-created copy was the equivalent of the original. Therefore, if the B.E.R. applied, no copy (e.g., a handwritten version) could suffice.
2. **Modern statutes:** But today, most states have a statute by which regularly-kept ***photocopies*** of business and public records are admissible even if the original is available. Such statutes override the B.E.R.
3. **Federal:** The Federal Rules have a broad copying provision: copies produced by ***any reliable modern method*** (including photocopying) are "duplicates" that are ***presumptively admissible***. Such a duplicate is admissible even if the original is available, unless "a genuine question is raised about the original's authenticity or the circumstances make it unfair to admit the duplicate." FRE 1003; 1001(e).

   Examples: Photocopies, mimeograph copies, carbon copies, images scanned into a computer and then printed out, copies of an original video or audio tape made by re-recording, etc., would all qualify as "duplicates" under the federal approach. But any copies produced *manually*, whether by typing or handwriting, are *not* "duplicates" and therefore may not be used if the original is available.

G. Excuses for non-production: There are several types of ***"excuses"*** for non-production, which will allow the proponent to use derivative evidence (e.g., a manual copy or oral testimony) instead of the original:

1. **Loss or destruction:** If the proponent can show that the original has been ***destroyed*** or ***lost*** he may use a copy (unless the loss or destruction is due to the proponent's ***bad faith*** or serious fault).

2. **Inconvenience:** In some courts, ***extreme inconvenience*** of producing the original will suffice.

3. **Possession by third person:** If the original is in the ***possession of a third person***, and cannot be obtained by judicial efforts (e.g., a subpoena duces tecum), this will excuse non-production.

4. **Original in opponent's possession:** If the original is in the hands of the ***opponent***, or under the latter's control, and the proponent has ***notified him*** to produce it at the trial but the adversary has failed to do so, the proponent may use a copy instead. See FRE 1004(3).

H. Summaries: If original writings are so ***voluminous*** that they cannot conveniently be introduced into evidence and examined in court, most courts permit a ***summary*** to be introduced instead. FRE 1006.

1. **Sponsoring witness needed:** The summary must be ***sponsored*** by a ***witness*** (often an expert) who testifies that he has prepared or reviewed the underlying writings and the summary, and that the ***summary accurately reflects the underlying documents.***

2. **Documents become evidence:** When Rule 1006 is used, the ***underlying documents become evidence***, even though they are not individually presented in court.

3. **Absence of entries:** Testimony that one or more items ***have not been found*** in voluminous records, despite a diligent search by a person with access to the records, does ***not*** qualify under FRE 1006's summary-of-voluminous-records exception. So such testimony will have to come in under the exception in 803(7) for absence of regularly-kept records (*supra*, p. 71) or not at all.

I. Admission by adversary: An adversary's ***admission*** about the terms of a writing is sometimes usable in lieu of the writing itself, to prove the terms of the writing.

1. **Written:** A ***written*** admission or an admission under ***sworn testimony*** is always usable to prove the terms of the writing.

   Example: D writes to P, "Remember that I wrote you in December offering to buy your farm." This later letter is evidence that D made this statement in his December letter. Similarly, D's oral deposition testimony — "I wrote to P in December asking to buy his farm" — would suffice to prove that the December letter contained such an offer.

2. **Oral:** But courts are more reluctant to allow an ***unsworn oral*** admission by a party to be used by the other party to prove the terms of a writing. Thus FRE 1007 does ***not*** allow such proof of an unsworn oral admission.

J. Preferences among secondary evidence: If the original does not exist, courts are split as to whether the ***next best available*** evidence must be used.

1. **Majority rule:** Most American state courts ***do*** recognize "degrees of substantive evidence," and hold that where there is a choice between a written copy and oral testimony, the ***written copy must be used.***

2. Minority/Federal Rule: A minority of states (but also the ***Federal Rules***) hold that "there are no degrees of substantive evidence." Thus under FRE 1004, even if handwritten notes or a typed copy of a writing exist, a party may instead prove the terms of the writing by oral testimony.

K. Judge-jury allocation: The judge, not the jury, decides most questions relating to application of the B.E.R. Thus under FRE 1008, it is the judge who decides such questions as: (1) whether a particular item of evidence is an "original"; (2) whether the original has been lost or destroyed; and (3) whether the evidence relates to a "collateral matter."

IV. SPECIAL TYPES OF REAL AND DEMONSTRATIVE EVIDENCE

A. Pictorial evidence:

1. Authentication: There are now usually two ways to authenticate ***pictorial*** evidence (e.g., photographs, X-rays, movies, and video tapes):

a. Illustration of what W saw: First, the proponent puts on a sponsoring witness, W, who says that the picture illustrates what W saw.

Example: W testifies, "I observed the scene of the crime just as the police photographer was arriving, and this photograph accurately depicts the scene as it was at that moment."

b. "Silent witness" method: Alternatively, most courts allow a photograph to be verified not by the testimony of any witness who actually witnessed the scene or event portrayed, but rather from testimony about the ***reliability of the process*** by which the photo was produced. This is often used for X-rays and automatic picture-taking devices.

Example: W, an engineer for a company that makes bank surveillance photographic equipment, testifies, "Our machine reliably creates a photo with an image of a person doing a transaction at the teller's window on one side, and the document presented by that person to the teller on the other side. Therefore, this piece of film accurately shows that the person pictured presented the check pictured."

B. Computer print-outs:

1. Authentication: If a computer print-out is offered as evidence of the facts contained in the print-out (e.g., financial or numerical facts), the print-out must be authenticated. This is usually done by a witness who testifies that the methods used to put data into the computer, to program it, and to produce a print-out of the data, were all reliable.

2. Best Evidence Rule: Generally, a computer print-out can be used to prove the facts represented in the print-out without B.E.R. problems (the opponent can claim that the print-out is merely a "duplicate" of the original pre-computer paper documents, but he would then have the burden of showing that the print-out is not an accurate reproduction of the original paper record).

C. Maps, models, diagrams, etc.:

1. **Evidentiary status:** Courts will treat maps, models, diagrams, etc., as being ***incorporated into the witness's testimony***, so that they become evidence for purposes of trial and appeal.

D. Views: The judge may permit the jury to journey outside the courtroom to visit and observe a particular place, if this would help them understand an event. The excursion is called a ***"view."***

1. **Discretion:** The judge has ***broad discretion*** about whether to allow the jury to take a view.

2. **Presence of judge:** In civil cases, the judge need normally ***not be present.*** In criminal cases, most states have statutes requiring the judge to be present at the view.

3. **Defendant's right to be present:** A criminal defendant usually has a statutory right to be ***present*** at the view (and may have a constitutional Confrontation Clause right to be present).

4. **Evidentiary status:** Courts are split as to whether the view is ***evidence***, or merely an aid to the understanding of the evidence.

E. Experiments: An ***experiment*** conducted by a party may sometimes be admitted. If the experiment takes place out of court, its admissibility will depend mostly on whether the conditions are sufficiently ***similar*** between the experiment and the event that it is attempting to explain.

Example: Where P complains that his crash was caused by a defective transmission in a car produced by D, an experiment to see if the transmission breaks in a different car will be allowed only if both the test car and the conditions are shown to be highly similar to the original conditions.

CHAPTER 9

OPINIONS, EXPERTS, AND SCIENTIFIC EVIDENCE

I. FIRST-HAND KNOWLEDGE AND LAY OPINIONS

A. First-hand knowledge required: An ordinary (non-expert) witness must limit his testimony to facts of which he has first-hand knowledge.

1. **Distinguished from hearsay:** You must distinguish the "first-hand knowledge" requirement from the hearsay rule. If W's statement on its face makes it clear that W is merely repeating what someone else said, the objection is to hearsay; if W purports to be stating matters which he personally observed, but he is actually repeating statements by others, the objection is to lack of first-hand knowledge.

2. **Experts:** The rule requiring first-hand knowledge does not apply to experts. (See below.)

B. Lay opinions:

1. **Traditional view:** The traditional view is that a non-expert witness must state only facts, not "opinions."

   Example: If W observes D's driving behavior leading to a crash, W may not testify that D "drove very carelessly," but must instead give more specific testimony, e.g., D's estimated rate of speed, degree of attention, etc.

   a. **Exception for short-hand renditions:** Even under the traditional view, W may give an "opinion" that is really a ***"short-hand rendition."*** That is, if W has perceived a number of small facts that cannot each be easily stated, he may summarize the collective facts with a "shorthand" formulation.

      Example: W may testify that D was "mentally disturbed," even though this has a conclusory aspect.

2. **Modern/federal approach:** But the modern/federal view is that lay opinions will be ***allowed*** if they have ***value*** to the fact-finder. See FRE 701, allowing non-expert opinions or inferences that are "(a) rationally based on the witness's perception; (b) helpful to clearly understanding the witness's testimony or to determining a fact in issue; and (c) not based on scientific, technical, or other specialized knowledge within the scope of Rule 702 [dealing with expert testimony]."

C. **Opinion on "ultimate issue":** Of those courts that allow lay opinions, a few bar opinions on "***ultimate*** issues." But most today allow even opinions on ultimate issues. Thus FRE 704(a) allows opinions on ultimate issues except where the mental state of a criminal defendant is concerned.

1. **Exceptions:** But even the liberal federal approach excludes a few types of opinions on ultimate issues. For instance, a witness will not be permitted to express his opinion on a ***question of law*** (except foreign law), or an opinion on how the case should be decided.

II. EXPERT WITNESSES

A. **Requirements for allowing:** FRE 702 imposes ***five requirements*** that expert testimony must meet in order to be admissible:

[1] It must be the case that "scientific, technical, or other ***specialized knowledge***" will "***help the trier of fact to understand*** the evidence or to determine a fact in issue";

[2] The witness must be ***"qualified"*** as an expert by "knowledge, skill, experience, training, or education";

[3] The testimony must be based on ***"sufficient facts or data"***;

[4] The testimony must be the product of ***"reliable principles and methods"***; and

[5] The witness must have "***reliably applied***" these principles and methods "to the ***facts of the case***."

Let's quickly review each of these five requirements.

1. **Specialized knowledge will be helpful:** It must be the case that "scientific, technical, or other ***specialized knowledge***" will "***help the trier of fact to understand*** the evidence or to determine a fact in issue."

   a. **Ordinary evidence:** Therefore expert testimony will be most appropriate whether it involves the interpretation of facts of a sort that ***lay persons are not usually called upon to evaluate.*** So testimony about whether two bullets were fired from the same gun, or two DNA samples are from the same person, would be suitable for expert testimony, since lay persons usually don't have to make such determinations in ordinary life. By contrast, since juries and ordinary people are often called upon to evaluate the reliability of an eyewitness identification, expert testimony purporting to tell the jury why such I.D.s are often unreliable will often be rejected as not satisfying this requirement of "helpfulness."

2. **Qualifications:** Next, the expert must be ***"qualified."*** That is, he must have knowledge or skill in a particular area that distinguishes him from an ordinary person.

   a. **Source of expertise:** This expertise may come from either ***education*** or ***experience.***

   b. **Need for sub-specialist:** Generally, a specialist in a particular field will be treated as an expert even though he is not specialist in the particular ***sub-field*** or branch of that field.

   Example: If a medical condition involves kidney failure, a general practitioner would probably be found a qualified expert, even though she is not a sub-specialist in nephrology.

3. **Based on "sufficient facts or data":** The third requirement is that the testimony be ***"based on sufficient facts or data."*** This requirement, plus the two that follow, reflect an attempt by the Rule drafters to ***keep out unreliable testimony***, sometimes called "junk science." We explore this factor more in Paragraph B, "Basis for expert's opinion," *infra*.

4. **Product of "reliable principles and methods":** The fourth requirement in FRE 702 is that the testimony must be the ***"product of reliable principles and methods."*** In the case of "scientific" testimony, this requirement is essentially a requirement that the testimony be based on "good science."

   Example: Testimony based on astrology would probably be rejected, because the court would probably not be satisfied that it was based on "reliable principles and methods."

   a. **Applies to non-scientific testimony:** This requirement of reliable principles and methods applies not just to scientific testimony but to ***other types of expert testimony based on technical knowledge.***

5. **Reliable application to the facts of case:** Finally, FRE 702 requires that the principles and methods referred to above be ***"reliably applied ... to the facts of the case."*** This is just common sense: the most reliable of "principles" and "methods"

won't lead to useful testimony unless the witness shows that she is applying those principles and methods to the actual facts of the case.

Example: Suppose that W, a prosecution DNA expert, offers to testify that under the principles of DNA comparison, a sample of blood purportedly found on the body of a murder victim, V, matched the blood of the defendant, D. If W (and other witnesses put on by the prosecution) cannot demonstrate that the sample tested by W in fact was found on V's body, W's testimony will be meaningless, and will be excluded.

B. Basis for expert's opinion: The expert's opinion may be based upon any of several sources of information, including: (1) the expert's ***first-hand knowledge***; (2) the expert's ***observation*** of prior witnesses and other evidence at the trial itself; and (3) a ***hypothetical question*** asked by counsel to the expert.

1. **Inadmissible evidence:** Today, the expert's opinion may be based on evidence that would otherwise be ***inadmissible***. Under FRE 703, even inadmissible evidence may form the basis for the expert's opinion if "experts in the particular field would ***reasonably rely on those kinds of facts or data*** in forming an opinion on the subject[.]"

   Example: Driver tells an accident investigator that the accident occurred when his brakes failed. The investigator writes a report, which is read by Expert, an accident analysis specialist. Even though Driver's statements are probably otherwise-inadmissible hearsay, if experts in the field of accident analysis would rely on such hearsay statements, Expert's opinion may be based upon this statement.

2. **Disclosure of basis to jury:** Some courts require the expert to ***state the facts or assumptions*** that he has based his opinion on, as part of his direct testimony. But most courts, and the Federal Rules, do not require this.

   a. **Inadmissible underlying facts:** Indeed, where the underlying facts or data are otherwise ***inadmissible*** (e.g., a report by another expert that is itself based on inadmissible hearsay), FRE 703 says that the expert (and the proponent of the expert's testimony) ***shall not disclose*** those facts or data unless the court affirmatively finds that their probative value outweighs their prejudicial effect.

   b. **Cross-examination:** However, the ***cross-examiner*** may require the expert to state the underlying facts or data on which he or she has relied. See FRE 705.

3. **Hypothetical questions:** If the expert's underlying facts and assumptions come from a ***hypothetical question***, courts today are easy-to-satisfy about the source of these underlying facts and assumptions. Thus:

   [1] the underlying assumptions need not be supported by ***evidence in the record*** at the time of the question, or even by admissible evidence at all; and

   [2] the assumptions may be based upon ***opinions by others***, if an expert in that situation would rely on such an opinion.

   But there must be ***some basis*** for the assumptions in the hypothetical — if the assumptions are so far-fetched that no jury could possibly find them to be true, the hypothetical question will be stricken.

C. Some procedural aspects:

1. **Cross-examination by use of learned treatise:** All courts allow an expert to be cross-examined by use of a learned treatise that contains a differing view.

   Example: The cross-examiner asks, "Isn't it true, Doctor, that according to Smith's Handbook of Pathology, lung cancer is sometimes caused by asbestos exposure or other factors, not always smoking as you have asserted?" The question is valid, even if Doctor does not agree with the Handbook's statement (as long as there is some proof that the Handbook is accepted as authoritative).

   a. **Use for impeachment where no reliance made:** Most courts today allow the use of the treatise as impeaching evidence even if the expert ***did not rely upon it*** in forming his opinion, so long as the expert concedes that the treatise is authoritative.

   b. **Substantive use under the FRE:** The Federal Rules even allow the treatise to be used ***substantively***, not just for impeachment, as long as the statement in the treatise is read to an expert witness who concedes that the treatise is authoritative.

      Example: In the above example, the statement in Smith's Handbook that lung cancer is sometimes caused by asbestos exposure would become substantive evidence of that fact, even if neither Doctor nor any other expert ever testified that the fact was true.

2. **Court-appointed expert:** The Federal Rules allow the appointment of an expert ***by the court***, in which case each party may cross-examine the expert.

III. SPECIALIZED EVIDENCE — THE *DAUBERT* / FRE 702 STANDARD

A. The requirement of reliability: As we've just seen, in federal courts, when expert testimony based on "scientific, technical or other specialized knowledge" is to be introduced, the proponent must show that the test or principle is the ***"product of reliable principles and methods"*** that are "reliably applied ... to the facts of the case." (FRE 702). This language is essentially a codification of a major Supreme Court case, *Daubert v. Merrell Dow.*

1. **Factors:** Under *Daubert* and FRE 702, the federal court should normallyconsider the following factors, among others, in deciding whether the test or principle is "the product of reliable principles and methods." (A "yes" answer makes the test/ principle more likely to be scientifically valid).[1]

---

1. These factors are not mentioned in FRE 702. But it's clear that the drafters of 702 intended that the factors mentioned in *Daubert* (and in later cases interpreting *Daubert*) be considered by courts in determining whether particular testimony meets the "reliable principles and methods" standard of 702.

- ❑ whether it can be ***reliably tested***;
- ❑ whether it's been ***subjected to peer review*** and/or ***publication***;
- ❑ whether it's got a reasonably low ***error rate***;
- ❑ whether there are ***professional standards*** controlling its operations;
- ❑ whether it's ***"generally accepted"*** in the field. (This used to be an absolute requirement for science in the federal courts, but *Daubert* makes it merely one factor.)
- ❑ whether it was developed for ***purposes other than merely to produce evidence*** for the present litigation.

2. **Non-scientific expert testimony:** *Daubert* itself (where the above factors were listed) dealt only with "scientific" testimony. But a post-*Daubert* Supreme Court case, *Kumho Tire*, says that the same principles apply to non-scientific testimony that relates to "technical" or other "specialized" knowledge. So *all expert testimony* must now satisfy these "reliability" factors.

3. **State response:** State courts (even ones adopting the FRE) don't have to follow *Daubert* if they don't want to. Some already have. Others have rejected *Daubert* and continue to apply the older "generally accepted" standard.

IV. PARTICULAR TYPES OF SCIENTIFIC EVIDENCE AND EXPERTISE

A. Probabilities: Courts increasingly accept ***probability*** evidence where it supplies a scientifically reliable way of estimating the probability that a disputed event occurred.

Example: In a paternity case, most courts will now accept the results of analysis of genetic markers, whereby an expert testifies that not only are D's genetic markers consistent with those of the child, but only, say, one adult American male out of 3,000 would have markers consistent with those of the child. Similarly, some courts would allow evidence in a rape case that only one in 10,000 males would have semen containing genetic markers consistent with the markers found in the semen in the victim, and that D's semen has such markers.

B. Speed detection: The results of ***radar*** and VASCAR are commonly admissible to prove the speed at which D's vehicle was traveling. But most courts require the prosecution to prove that the particular speed detection equipment in question was properly calibrated and properly used.

C. Voice prints: Courts are almost evenly split as to the admissibility of ***"voice print"*** analysis, whereby the voice of an unidentified suspect on a taped telephone call is compared with a sample given by D after his arrest.

D. Neutron activation analysis: Neutron activation analysis (NAA) is generally admitted as a method of identifying a small sample of material (e.g., whether a hair found near a crime scene belongs to D).

E. Psychiatry and psychology:

1. **Mental condition of criminal defendant:** Courts generally allow a psychiatrist or psychologist to testify as an expert on the ***mental condition*** of a criminal defendant. However, courts try hard to keep the expert from crossing over into areas that are properly the province of law rather than medicine (e.g., whether the defendant knew right from wrong).

   a. **FRE provision:** Thus, FRE 704(b) provides that "[i]n a criminal case, an expert witness ***must not state an opinion*** about whether the defendant ***did or did not have a mental state or condition*** that constitutes an ***element of the crime charged or of a defense***. Those matters are for the trier of fact alone."

   Example: In a federal case in which D claims insanity, the defense psychiatrist would be permitted to say that D is a schizophrenic, but will probably not be permitted to say that this condition prevented D from appreciating the wrongfulness of his conduct, now the substantive federal insanity standard.

2. **Reliability of evidence:** Courts hesitate to allow expert psychiatric or psychological testimony concerning the reliability of other witnesses' testimony. Thus evidence that a particular eyewitness identification is likely to be unreliable for psychological reasons, or that a particular alleged victim is probably telling the truth because she shows the signs of Rape Trauma Syndrome, will be rejected by many courts.

CHAPTER 10

BURDENS OF PROOF, PRESUMPTIONS, AND OTHER PROCEDURAL ISSUES

I. BURDENS OF PROOF

A. Two burdens: There are two distinct burdens of proof, the burden of ***production*** and the burden of ***persuasion.***

1. **Burden of production:** If P bears the burden of ***production*** with respect to issue A, P has the obligation to come forward with some evidence that A exists. This burden is sometimes also called the burden of "going forward."

   a. **Consequence of failure to carry:** If a party does not satisfy this burden of production, the court will decide the issue against him as a matter of law, and will not permit the jury to decide it.

2. **Burden of persuasion:** If P has the burden of ***persuasion*** on issue A, this means that if at the close of the evidence the jury cannot decide whether A has been established with the relevant level of certainty (usually "preponderance of the evidence" in a civil case), the jury must find against P on issue A. This burden is also often called the ***"risk of non-persuasion"*** — if neither P nor D have persuaded the jury about whether A exists, to say that P bears the burden of persuasion or the risk of non-persuasion means that he is the one who will lose when the jury decides this issue.

3. **One shifts, other does not:** The burden of ***production*** as to issue A can, and often does, ***shift*** throughout the trial.

   Example: Suppose P has the burden of showing that D received notice of a fact. If P comes up with evidence that D received notice — e.g., P's own testimony that he told the fact to D — the burden will shift to D to come up with evidence that he did not receive notice.

   a. **Burden of persuasion:** The burden of ***persuasion***, by contrast, always ***remains*** on the party on whom it first rests.

B. Allocating the burdens in civil cases:

1. **Factors:** In most issues in civil cases, both the burden of production and the burden of persuasion are on the ***plaintiff.***

   Example: In a negligence case, the plaintiff bears the burdens of production and persuasion with respect to showing D's negligence, P's harm, and the causal link between the two. But D bears both burdens with respect to contributory negligence, in most jurisdictions.

   a. **Factors:** Courts consider a number of factors in determining where to place the burdens, including: (1) which party is trying to change the *status quo* (he is more likely to bear the burdens); (2) who is contending that the more unusual event has occurred (he is more likely to bear the burdens); and (3) which way do policy considerations cut (the court may allocate the burdens in a way that promotes some extra-judicial social policy).

2. **"Prima facie" case:** The collection of issues on which a civil plaintiff has the burden of ***production*** is sometimes called his ***"prima facie case."***

   Example: P has established a *prima facie* case for negligence if he has produced enough evidence of D's negligence, P's own harm, and a causal link between the two, to permit the case to go to the jury.

C. Allocation in criminal cases: In criminal cases, the Due Process Clause of the U.S. Constitution places limits on the extent to which the burdens of proof may be placed on the defendant:

1. **Element distinguished from affirmative defense:** The state is more limited in allocating the burdens as to an ***"element"*** of the offense than it is on allocating the burdens as to an ***"affirmative defense."*** An element of the crime is an aspect that is part of the basic definition of the crime; an affirmative defense is an aspect that is not part of the basic definition, but which the defendant is allowed to show as a mitigating or exculpating factor.

   Examples: "Intent to kill" is an element of the crime of murder, but "self defense" is generally an affirmative defense.

2. **General rules of allocation:**

   a. **Elements:** The ***state*** is constitutionally required to bear ***both*** the burdens of production and persuasion with respect to ***all elements*** of the crime.

b. **Affirmative defense:** The ***defendant*** may constitutionally be required to bear both burdens with respect to affirmative defenses.

c. **Overlap:** If the state defines an affirmative defense in a way that causes that defense to overlap almost completely with some element of the crime, the state must bear both burdens.

Example: Suppose the state makes "malice aforethought" an element of murder, and defines malice aforethought to include "any deliberate act committed by one person against another." If the state makes "heat of passion" an affirmative defense, the state, not D might have to bear the burden of proof and persuasion, because a court might hold that proof that D acted in the heat of passion is tantamount to proof that he did not act with malice aforethought.

d. **Allowable affirmative defenses:** At least the following may be established as affirmative defenses on which D bears both burdens: ***insanity, self-defense,*** and ***extreme emotional disturbance.***

D. Satisfying the burden of production:

1. **Civil case:** In civil cases, on most issues (those as to which the persuasion burden follows the "preponderance of the evidence" standard), the party bearing the production burden must come forward with enough evidence ***so that a reasonable jury could conclude, by a preponderance of the evidence, that the fact exists.***

a. **Judge decides:** It is the judge, not the jury, who decides whether the party bearing the production burden has satisfied that burden.

Example: At the close of P's case, the judge decides whether P has come up with enough evidence of negligence that a reasonable jury could find that D was negligent by a preponderance of the evidence. The judge may find that P has done this even though the judge himself believes that it is less likely than not that D was negligent.

b. **Cross-examination of adversary:** If the burden of proof on issue A in a civil case is borne by P (as is usually the case), P will have to come up with a witness or real evidence tending to prove that A exists. It will not be enough that P conducts a withering cross-examination of a defense witness's denial of A. (But if it is D who bears the burden of proving A, his cross-examination of P and P's witnesses may be enough for him to avoid a directed verdict against him.)

2. **Criminal case:** In a criminal case, the prosecution, to satisfy its burden of production on all elements of the case, must come forward with enough evidence on each element that a reasonable jury could find that the element was ***proved beyond a reasonable doubt.*** (In other words, the persuasion burden affects the production burden.)

E. Satisfying the burden of persuasion:

1. **Civil cases:** On most civil issues, the burden of persuasion must be satisfied by a showing that A exists ***"by a preponderance of the evidence."*** That is, the party bearing the burden must show that the existence of A is "more probable than not."

a. **Sheer statistics:** Most courts refuse to find that this burden has been met by evidence that is ***purely statistical***. (*Example:* If P testifies that he was hit by a blue bus, and shows that 60% of all the blue buses in the town are owned by D, this will not be enough to meet P's persuasion burden.) Instead, the party bearing the persuasion burden must come up with some evidence that will lead the jury to have an ***"actual belief"*** (rather than a mere statistical estimate) in the truth of the fact in question.

2. **Criminal cases:** In criminal cases, the prosecution's burden of persuasion on all elements of the crime means that these elements must be proved ***"beyond a reasonable doubt."*** This is required by the Due Process Clause. *In Re Winship*. (But issues other than elements of the crime may be decided according to a lesser standard. For instance, a confession usually only has to be shown to be voluntary by a preponderance of the evidence.)

II. PRESUMPTIONS

A. Generally: The term "presumption" refers to a relationship between a "basic" fact (B) and a "presumed" fact (P). When we say that fact P can be presumed from fact B, we mean that once B is established, P is established or at least rendered more likely.

B. Effect of presumptions in civil cases: In civil cases, most courts hold that a presumption has one of two types of effects: (1) a ***"bursting bubble"*** effect; or (2) a so-called ***"Morgan"*** effect.

1. **"Bursting bubble":** Most courts believe that a presumption should be given the following effect: if B is shown to exist, the burden of production (but not the burden of persuasion) should be shifted to the opponent of the presumption. This is called the ***"bursting bubble"*** approach, because once the opponent discharges his production burden by coming up with some evidence that the presumed fact does not exist, the presumption ***disappears from the case***, and the jury decides the issue as if the presumption had never existed.

   Example: A presumption is established that where a letter has been properly addressed and mailed — the basic fact — the letter will be presumed to have been received by the addressee — the presumed fact. Suppose that P is the beneficiary of this presumption, and that P starts out bearing the burden of proving that D received the letter. If P shows that the letter was properly addressed and mailed, under the bursting bubble view D will have to come up with some evidence that he never received the letter, but once he does so, the presumption will not be mentioned to the jury, which will be told that P has the burden of persuading the jury that D received the letter.

2. **Morgan (minority) view:** A ***minority*** of courts follow the so-called ***"Morgan"*** view, that the presumption should not only shift the burden of production, but ***also the burden of persuasion***, to the presumption's opponent.

   Example: On the above letter scenario, once P showed that he properly addressed and mailed the letter, it would become up to D to not only come forward with evidence that he never received the letter, but also to persuade the jury by a preponderance of the evidence that he never received it.

3. **Federal Rules:** The Federal Rules adopt the ***majority, "bursting bubble"*** view. Under FRE 301, "In a civil case ... the party against whom a presumption is directed has the burden of producing evidence to rebut the presumption. But this rule ***does not shift the burden of persuasion,*** which ***remains on the party who had it originally.***"

   a. **Instructions to jury:** Under the majority/federal "bursting bubble" approach, the judge normally will ***not mention*** that the presumption exists (e.g., he will not say, "The law presumes that a properly addressed and mailed envelope was received by the addressee unless there is evidence to the contrary"). But the judge has discretion to tell the jury that it ***may*** presume P if B is shown.

4. **Conflicting presumptions:** If a case presents two ***conflicting presumptions***, and neither is rebutted by the opponent, the court will generally apply the presumption that reflects the weightier social policy. If neither presumption reflects a social policy (both merely reflect an estimate of probabilities, or concerns for trial convenience), both presumptions will generally be held to have ***dropped*** from the case.

5. **Constitutional questions:** A civil presumption that is given either the "bursting bubble" or "Morgan" effect presents no significant constitutional issues. But a so-called ***"irrebuttable presumption"*** (which is really a substantive rule) must meet the same constitutional standard as any other substantive rule of law — the legislature must have had a ***rational reason*** for linking the basic fact to the presumed fact.

C. **Effect in criminal cases:** The constitutionality of a presumption in a ***criminal case*** depends on precisely the effect given to the presumption:

1. **Permissive presumptions:** A so-called ***"permissive"*** presumption (one in which the judge merely instructs the jury that it "may" infer the presumed fact if it finds the basic fact) will almost always be constitutional, so long as the fact finder could "rationally" have inferred the presumed fact from the basic fact, the presumption will be upheld.

   Example: The jury is told that where a weapon is found in a car, the jury may infer that each person in the car possessed that weapon. Since the presumption was rational on these circumstances, it was constitutional even though it relieved the prosecution from showing that each D actually knew of or possessed a gun.

2. **Mandatory:** But a ***"mandatory"*** presumption is subjected to much more stringent constitutional scrutiny:

   a. **Shift of persuasion burden:** If the presumption ***shifts the burden of persuasion*** to D, and the presumed fact is an ***element of the crime***, the presumption will normally be ***unconstitutional.*** Such a presumption runs afoul of the rule that the prosecution must prove each element of the crime beyond a reasonable doubt.

   Example: D, a dealer in second-hand goods, is charged with knowingly receiving stolen goods. The judge tells the jury that a dealer who buys goods that are in fact stolen, and who does not make reasonable inquiries about the seller's title to the goods, shall be presumed to have known they were stolen unless he shows that he didn't know this. Since this presumption has the effect of shifting to D the burden of showing that he did not know the goods were stolen — an element of the crime — it is unconstitutional.

b. **Possibly constitutional:** But even a presumption that shifts the burden of persuasion on an element of the crime will be constitutional if the presumed fact flows from the basic fact beyond a reasonable doubt, and the basic fact is shown beyond a reasonable doubt. However, few if any presumptions can satisfy this stringent pair of requirements.

D. Choice of law: In federal diversity cases, the court must apply the presumptions law of the state whose substantive law applies. FRE 302.

Example: P sues D for negligence in a diversity suit in New Jersey federal court. If New Jersey law controls on the issue of negligence, then New Jersey law on the effect to be given to a presumption that one whose blood alcohol is more than .1% is legally drunk, must be applied by the federal court. Therefore, if New Jersey would apply a "Morgan" rather than "bursting bubble" approach to presumptions, the federal court must do the same.

III. JUDGE-JURY ALLOCATION

A. Issues of law: Issues of ***law*** are always to be decided by the judge, not the jury. Therefore, when the admission of a particular piece of evidence turns on an issue of law, it is up to the judge to decide whether the item should be admitted.

Example: W refuses to disclose a statement she made to L, asserting the attorney-client privilege; L is a law school graduate but is not admitted to practice. It is the judge, not the jury, who will decide the legal issue of whether the privilege applies on these facts.

B. Issues of fact: If admissibility of evidence turns on an issue of ***fact,*** the division of labor between judge and jury depends on the nature of the objection:

1. **Technical exclusionary rule:** If an objection to admissibility is based on a ***technical exclusionary rule*** (e.g., hearsay), any factual question needed to decide that objection belongs solely to the judge. Thus for factual issues in connection with a hearsay objection, an objection based on privilege, or most issues regarding the Best Evidence Rule, the judge decides.

   a. **Rules of evidence not binding:** Under FRE 104(a), when the judge makes such a finding he is ***not bound by the rules of evidence*** except those regarding privileges.

   Example: In deciding whether V's out-of-court statement, "X shot me," qualifies as a "dying declaration" exception to the hearsay rule, the judge may consider other, inadmissible, hearsay declarations by V at about the same time that shed light on whether V knew he was dying.

   The judge will normally decide such a factual issue by a ***preponderance of the evidence*** standard.

2. **Relevance:** If the objection is that the evidence is ***irrelevant***, the judge's role may be more limited:

   a. **Ordinary relevance problem:** Ordinarily, a relevance objection may be decided without any finding of fact — the judge merely has to decide whether, ***assuming*** the proffered fact is true, it makes some material fact more or less likely; this is purely a legal conclusion, so the judge handles it himself.

   b. **Conditional relevance:** In some cases, the proffered evidence is logically relevant only if some other fact exists. If fact B is relevant only if fact A exists, B is ***"conditionally relevant."*** It is the jury that will decide whether fact A exists, but the judge decides ***whether a reasonable jury could find that fact A (the preliminary fact) exists***.

   Example: P is injured when his tire blows out; D claims that he warned P of the problem. The preliminary fact is whether P heard the warning; the conditionally relevant fact is the warning's contents. The judge will decide whether a reasonable jury could find that P heard the warning; if he decides that the answer to this question is "yes," he will let the jury hear the warning's alleged contents, and it will be up to the jury to decide whether P really heard that warning and its contents.

      i. **Allowed subject to "connecting up":** The judge may allow the conditionally relevant fact into evidence ***prior*** to his showing of the preliminary fact; the conditionally relevant evidence is said to be admitted ***"subject to connecting up."***

      Example: In the tire blow-out example, D might be allowed to say what the warning's contents were, subject to subsequent proof by some other witness that P really heard the warning. If D does not come up with that later evidence, his testimony about the contents of the warning will be stricken.

C. **Limiting instructions:** If evidence is admitted that should properly be considered only on some issues, the judge will on request give a ***limiting instruction***, which tells the jury for what issues the evidence can and cannot be considered.

D. **Non-jury trials:**

1. **Same rules:** In general, ***all rules of evidence applicable to jury trials also apply to bench trials***. Thus if an item of evidence would be inadmissible in a jury trial, it is inadmissible in a bench trial.

2. **Practical relaxation:** On the other hand, appellate courts are generally less strict in reviewing evidentiary rulings made in a bench trial than in a jury trial.

   a. **"Sufficient competent evidence" rule:** Thus even if the trial judge in a bench trial admits inadmissible evidence over objection, the appellate court will not reverse if there was also admissible evidence in the case ***supporting*** the findings. The trial judge is presumed to have disregarded the inadmissible and relied on the admissible evidence. (But if the trial judge in the bench trial erroneously ***excludes*** evidence, the appellate court will be strict, and will reverse if that exclusion is likely to have damaged the losing party. Therefore, judges in bench trials err on the side of admitting too much rather than too little.)

IV. APPEALS AND "HARMLESS ERROR"

A. "Harmless error": Appellate courts will only reverse if the error may have made a ***difference to the outcome***. An error that is unlikely to have made a difference to the outcome is called ***"harmless,"*** and will not be grounds for reversal. See FRE 103(a) (error must affect a "substantial right" of a party).

1. **Standards for determining:** The test for determining whether an error is "harmless" varies depending on the context:

   a. **Constitutional criminal issue:** In a criminal case in which evidence is admitted in violation of the defendant's ***constitutional*** rights, the appellate court will find the error non-harmless unless it is convinced "beyond a reasonable doubt" that the error was harmless.

      Example: A co-defendant's confession implicating D, given to the police while in custody, and admitted against D in violation of his Confrontation Clause rights, will almost never be found to be harmless beyond a reasonable doubt, and will thus generally be grounds for reversal.

   b. **Other errors:** But in civil cases, and in criminal cases involving non-constitutional errors, the error will be ignored as harmless unless the appellate court believes it ***"more probable than not"*** that the error affected the outcome.

B. Sufficiency of evidence: If the appellate court needs to decide whether the evidence was ***sufficient*** to support the findings of fact, the standard will depend on whether the case is civil or criminal:

1. **Civil:** In civil cases, the sufficiency test mirrors the "preponderance of the evidence" standard used at the trial.

   Example: If P wins, the appellate court will ask, "Could a reasonable jury have concluded that P proved all elements of his case by a preponderance of the evidence?"

2. **Criminal:** In a criminal case where D is appealing, the appellate court will ask, "Could a reasonable jury have found, beyond a reasonable doubt, that D committed all elements of the crime?"

CHAPTER 11

JUDICIAL NOTICE

I. JUDICIAL NOTICE GENERALLY

A. Function: Under the doctrine of judicial notice, the ***judge*** can accept a fact as true even though no evidence to prove it has been offered. In a civil jury case, if the judge takes judicial notice of a fact he will instruct the jury that it must find that fact.

B. Three types: The doctrine of judicial notice has evolved to recognize three distinct types of judicial notice: (1) ***"adjudicative"*** facts; (2) ***"legislative"*** facts; and (3) ***law***.

1. **Adjudicative facts:** Adjudicative facts are those facts which relate to the ***particular event*** under litigation.

2. **Legislative facts:** Legislative facts are more general facts that do not concern the immediate parties.

   Example: A judge considering whether to impose an implied warranty of habitability for urban apartment buildings would take notice of legislative facts concerning the low bargaining power of urban tenants.

3. **Law:** Judicial notice of ***"law"*** relieves a party from having to formally plead and prove what the law is, in certain situations.

4. **Federal Rules:** The only Federal Rule dealing with judicial notice, FRE 201, deals only with notice of adjudicative facts, not legislative facts or law.

II. ADJUDICATIVE FACTS

A. General rule: At common law, there are two different types of adjudicative facts which may be judicially noticed:

[1] those that are ***"generally known"***; and

[2] those that are ***"capable of immediate and accurate verification."***

A fact will not be found to fall into either of these categories unless the court is convinced that it is virtually ***indisputable***.

1. **"General knowledge":** An instance of ***"general knowledge"*** in the community might be that a particular portion of Mission Street in San Francisco is a business district, or that traffic going towards Long Island beaches on Friday afternoon during the summertime is frequently very heavy.

   a. **Judge's own knowledge:** The fact that the ***judge himself*** knows a fact to be so does ***not*** entitle him to take judicial notice of it if it is not truly common knowledge.

2. **Immediate verification:** Some of the kinds of facts that are capable of "***immediate verification*** by consulting sources of ***indisputable accuracy***" include: (1) facts of ***history and geography***; (2) ***scientific principles***, and the validity of certain types of scientific ***tests*** (e.g., the general reliability of radar for speed detection); and (3) a court's own record of things that have happened in the same or other suits in that court.

3. **Federal Rule:** FRE 201 treats as being an adjudicative fact any fact that is "not subject to reasonable dispute" because it is either: (1) "***generally known***" within the "trial court's territorial jurisdiction" (typically, the state or portion of a state composing the "federal judicial district" in which the district judge sits); or (2) capable of being "accurately and readily determined" by the use of "***sources whose accuracy cannot reasonably be questioned***." (This basically matches the common-law approach.)

B. Jury's right to disregard:

1. **Civil case:** In civil cases, courts usually treat judicial notice as being ***conclusive*** on the issue. Therefore, the judge instructs the jury that it ***must*** treat the fact as being so. FRE 201(f).

2. **Criminal:** But in criminal cases, courts usually hold that the notice fact is ***not conclusive*** on the jury — if it were, D's constitutional right to a jury trial might be impaired. FRE 201(f).

   a. **On appeal:** This means that if the prosecution has failed at trial to ask for judicial notice of a fact, the appeals court may not take notice of that fact.

C. When taken: Most courts hold that judicial notice of an appropriate adjudicative fact may be taken ***at any time*** during the proceeding. Thus notice may be taken before trial, or even on appeal (except in criminal cases). See FRE 201(d).

III. LEGISLATIVE FACTS

A. General rule: A court may generally take notice of a ***"legislative*** fact" (i.e., a fact that does not pertain to the particular parties, but is more general) even though the fact is ***not "indisputable."***

1. **Standard:** Most jurisdictions allow the judge to take notice of a legislative fact so long as the judge ***believes it to be true***, even though it is not indisputable.

   Examples of legislative facts: (1) A fetus does not generally become viable until 28 weeks after conception (relevant to the constitutionality of state abortion rules); (2) Urban tenants have very little bargaining power (relevant to whether there should be an implied warranty of habitability of city apartments).

2. **Federal Rules silent:** The Federal Rules, and most state evidence statutes, are ***silent*** about whether and when judicial notice of legislative facts may be taken. This is simply an implicit part of the process of deciding cases.

B. Binding on jury: A judicially-noticed legislative fact will be ***binding on the jury*** even in a ***criminal*** case.

   Example: The judge's decision that cocaine falls within the statutory ban on importing "cocoa leaves and any derivative thereof" is binding on the jury.

IV. NOTICE OF LAW

A. Generally: Judges may take judicial notice of some types of ***law.*** When they do so, the consequence is that a party need not plead the provisions of the law, and need not make a formal evidentiary showing that the law is such-and-such; also, the judge may do his own research into the law.

B. Domestic law: A judge may always take judicial notice of ***domestic*** law.

1. **State courts:** For a state court, "domestic" law is the ***law of that state***, plus federal law. A state's own law is generally held to include ***administrative regulations*** (but usually not municipal ordinances, which must therefore be proved).

2. **Federal:** In federal courts, "domestic" law is usually held to include not only federal law, but also the law of ***all states*** if relevant.

C. **Laws of sister states:** At common law, one state may ***not*** take judicial notice of a ***sister state's laws***; instead, the sister state's laws must be "proved" by submitting evidence as to what that sister state's law really is. (But most states have now adopted a uniform act that allows judicial notice of a sister state's laws.)

D. **Law of other countries:** The law of ***other countries*** may not be judicially noticed, according to most states. Therefore, a party must generally plead and prove such law.

1. **Federal Rules:** But this is not true in the federal courts: FRCP 44.1 allows the judge to conduct his own research on an issue of foreign law (though a party who intends to raise an issue concerning foreign law must nonetheless give notice of this fact in his pleadings).

EXAM TIPS

TABLE OF CONTENTS of EXAM TIPS

EXAM TIPS

Exam Tips on BASIC CONCEPTS

Of the topics covered in this chapter, ***competency*** is by far the most likely to be tested. Here's what to look for on this topic:

- **Grounds:** In modern courts (federal and state), the ***only*** grounds for finding a witness, W, incompetent are that (1) W has ***no personal knowledge*** of the matter (FRE 602); or (2) W can't or won't take and understand the ***oath*** to tell the truth (FRE 603).

- **Most frequently-tested:** The most frequently-tested area is this: W is a ***small child***, and the twin issues are: (1) does W ***understand*** what it means to promise to tell the truth?; and (2) does W have sufficient maturity to be capable of ***receiving*** and ***reporting*** correct ***sensory impressions***?

  Example: W was 4 at the time of the events and is now 5; he testifies that "People who don't tell the truth get spanked." W has probably demonstrated adequate knowledge of the need to tell the truth. Also, the judge will probably find that at 4, W was mature enough to observe and recall major events, such as the fact that D shot X with a rifle.

- **Also tested:** W suffers from a ***mental deficiency*** (e.g., retardation or insanity). Typically, the court rules that this affects only the ***weight*** to be given to W's testimony, not its admissibility.

Exam Tips on RELEVANCE

No matter what the item of evidence being presented, you must first check to see whether it's ***relevant***.

- **Makes more or less probable:** Remember that an item of evidence is relevant if it tends to "make the existence of any fact that is of consequence to the determination of the action more probable or less probable than it would be without the evidence." FRE 401.

☛ **Brick is not a wall:** In analyzing relevance, remember that ***"a brick is not a wall"*** (and feel free to quote this "rule"). In other words, if an item of evidence (call it *A*) is offered as tending to prove fact *X*, the fact that *X* is still less likely to be true than not true after proof of *A* does not block *A* from being relevant, as long as *X* is more likely to be true with *A* than without *A*.

Example: D, a black man, is charged with robbing a bank. The prosecution offers a surveillance tape of the robbery, which shows that the robber is black but which does not show enough detail to demonstrate that the robber is or is not D. The tape will be relevant, and admissible, because it tends to show that the robber was black, and this fact makes it more likely that the robber is D than would be the case if the tape was not in evidence — it doesn't matter that the tape is not by itself enough to make it more likely than not that D was the robber.

☛ **Relatively rare:** Instances of evidence that is really ***irrelevant*** are relatively ***rare***. On multiple choice questions, an answer like "The testimony is relevant, and thus admissible" is more likely to be correct than an answer like "The testimony is inadmissible because it's irrelevant."

☛ **Legal irrelevance:** The most common situation where the evidence is ***irrelevant*** involves ***legal*** irrelevance — if the item in question simply doesn't tie in with the ***legal elements*** for a claim or defense, it will be irrelevant.

Examples:

- ❑ D is in a car accident, and is convicted of the criminal offense of operating an unregistered vehicle. In a later suit, the sole issue is whether D behaved negligently during the accident. The conviction will be irrelevant, because driving an unregistered vehicle doesn't make it more likely that D drove negligently.

- ❑ P sues solely for the wrongful death of her husband, H. P offers evidence that H suffered severe pain before dying. This evidence is irrelevant, because pain is not an element of damages in a wrongful death suit (though the pain would be relevant to a survival action brought by H's estate).

☛ **Probative value outweighed:** Also frequently tested: even where evidence is relevant, it's excludible if its probative value is ***outweighed*** by its tendency to cause ***prejudice***, ***confusion*** or ***waste of time***. (FRE 403) Prejudice is the most commonly tested aspect of this rule.

☞ **Graphic material:** Most common: ***graphic***, visually shocking material.

Example: In a murder case, photos of V's body taken after autopsy, when V looked gorier than after the murder itself, might be excluded as likely to cause prejudice greater than the probative value, especially if pre-autopsy photos are available.

☞ **Judge's discretion:** Remember that the prejudice/probative value balancing is largely within the judge's ***discretion***.

Exam Tips on *CIRCUMSTANTIAL PROOF: SPECIAL PROBLEMS*

Of the topics in this chapter, the most-tested by far is character evidence; habit/custom, similar happenings, subsequent remedial measures, insurance and settlements are also tested with some frequency.

Character evidence

Here's what to focus on in connection with ***character*** evidence:

☛ **General rule:** The general rule, of course, is that a person's character is ***inadmissible*** to prove "action in accordance therewith," i.e., to prove that the person acted a certain way in accordance with his character on a particular occasion. (FRE 404(a)).

Example: P sues D civilly for negligently injuring P. P won't be allowed to show that D was a generally careless person, and D won't be allowed to show that D was a generally careful person.

☛ **Character in issue:** Remember that the general rule applies only to ***"circumstantial"*** use of character evidence, i.e., X's character is used to prove that on a particular occasion, he probably acted in conformity with that character. In other words, if a person's character is itself directly ***"in issue"*** (i.e., his character is an element of a crime, claim or defense), the general "no character evidence" rule simply doesn't apply, and the evidence is admissible. However, there aren't many true instances of "character in issue."

☞ **Defamation:** One context for testing this "character in issue" aspect is ***defamation*** — in a defamation action, P's character (or at least his reputation) will generally be in issue because it relates to damages.

Example: P, a religious leader, sues D, a newspaper, for claiming that P misused church funds. W, a former member of P's congregation, testifies that even before the article, members of the congregation rumored that P was misusing church funds. This testimony is admissible, because P's reputation is directly in issue — P's damages will be reduced or eliminated if it's shown that his reputation was damaged before the article appeared.

☞ **Knowledge of trait:** Similarly, it may occasionally be a direct issue whether someone ***knew*** that X possessed a certain character.

Example: C, a child, shoots P with an air rifle. P sues C's parents, the Ds, for negligently giving C the rifle. W, C's neighbor, testifies that C is a "vicious and malicious bully." This is admissible, as showing that the Ds should have known of C's dangerous tendencies and thus not given him the rifle.

☛ **Victim's traits:** Whenever D in a criminal case is presenting evidence about the reputation or character of the ***victim*** (call the victim "V"), or about how V behaved in the particular episode, discuss whether this is allowed.

☞ **Allowable:** The general rule is that D ***may*** offer such "victim's character" evidence. See FRE 404(a)(2) — a criminal defendant may offer "evidence of an alleged victim's pertinent trait."

☞ **Self-defense:** Most often, this is tested where D is claiming ***self-defense*** — V's reputation for unprovoked violence, or his violent character, ***may*** be used to establish that a reasonable person in D's position would have believed himself to be under attack.

☛ **No specific past acts:** *Caution* — V's character for violence (like other circumstantial evidence of character) must be proved by testimony about V's ***reputation*** or by W's ***opinion*** of V's character, ***not by specific past acts*** of violence by V. (FRE 405(a)).

Example: If D is charged with murdering V in a bar-room brawl, D's self-defense claim can be supported by W's testimony that V had a reputation for getting drunk and brawling, but not by evidence that on 3 particular occasions, V got into bar-room fights.

☞ **Sexual behavior:** The other big "victim's character" area is the sexual behavior and reputation of a ***rape*** victim. Generally this evidence is ***inadmissible***. The two main exceptions under the FRE: (i) V's past sexual history with persons other than D, if offered on the issue of whether D was the source of the injury or semen; and (ii) V's past sexual behavior with D, offered on the issue of whether V consented. (FRE 412(b)(1) and (2)).

☛ **D's belief that V consented:** Most exam questions in this area arise where D claims that V ***consented*** (or that D reasonably believed that V consented). Here, D may put on evidence about V's past sexual conduct ***with D*** (e.g., D's lawyer may ask V, "Didn't you have consensual sex with D on previous occasions?" or "Didn't you sometimes play a game with D in which you pretended to resist but really were consenting?"), but ***not*** evidence about V's past conduct with ***persons other than D*** (e.g., D's lawyer may ***not*** ask V, "Didn't you have consensual sex with three other men to whom you weren't married, in the six months before this episode?")

☛ **Other crimes or bad acts by D:** Another big area for testing is D's ***other crimes*** or his ***unconvicted bad acts.***

☞ **Generally inadmissible:** Remember that the general rule is that such evidence is ***not*** admissible to show that D's other crimes or bad acts make it more likely that he committed the particular crime with which he's now charged.

Example: If D is charged with armed robbery, the fact that D was previously convicted of embezzlement can't be used to show that "a thief's a thief," i.e., that D probably committed this theft as well.

☞ **Exceptions:** However, most questions in this "other crimes and bad acts" area involve one of the many ***exceptions*** to the general rule. So before you conclude that the evidence is inadmissible because of the general rule, look hard to see if the fact pattern falls into one of these exceptions. Here are the most commonly tested exceptions:

❑ ***Common plan and scheme.***

Example: D is arrested and charged with fraudulently using a credit card belonging to V. The prosecution wants to show that when arrested, D had in her possession 5 other credit cards in D's name, as well as 20 other credit cards and drivers licenses in the names of people other than D or V. This "unconvicted bad acts" evidence is admissible to show that the particular act charged is part of V's broader plan or scheme to fraudulently collect and use credit cards, thus making it more likely that D did the particular thing charged.

❑ ***"Signature"*** or *modus operandi.*

Example: D is charged with illegally importing heroin in the false bottom of a brass statue. D claims that he bought the statue without knowing what was in it. The prosecution may show that D was convicted of smuggling cocaine in the false bottom of a brass statue 15 years before; this tends to show that D uses a particular MO, or method of operation. To put it another way, the "drugs in the brass statue" technique is so distinctive that it bears D's "signature."

❑ ***Identity.***

Example: D is charged with raping V. D's defense is that someone else must have committed the crime. The prosecution first puts on V's testimony that after the attack (in which the rapist wore a stocking mask), V told Detective that the rapist had a distinctive brown birthmark on his wrist. The prosecution then offers testimony by Detective that Detective listened to V's description, then consulted a police file of past sex offenders, and learned that one of them, D, had a brown birthmark on his wrist. Detective's testimony would probably be admissible as tending to establish D's identity as the rapist.

☛ **Need not fit in pre-defined slot:** Also, remember that the other-crimes or bad-acts evidence *doesn't have to fit into a pre-defined slot* to be admissible; thus FRE 404(b) allows admission of other crimes or wrongs "for another purpose" and then lists (non-exhaustively) some specific exceptions like plan, identity, etc. So the real question to ask is, does the other-crime or bad-act evidence *tightly link* D to some element of the crime (in which case it's probably admissible) or does it have such a loose link to the crime charged that it merely suggests that because D has a certain character trait, he's more likely to have committed the crime charged (in which case it's probably inadmissible)?

☛ **Favorable evidence of D's character:** Remember that the ***defendant*** in a criminal case may offer evidence of a "pertinent trait" of his own character (FRE 404(a)(2)(A)) — i.e., ***favorable character evidence***.

Example: D is charged with the crime of assaulting V, and pleads self-defense. He offers testimony by W that D has a reputation in the community as a peaceable, law-abiding citizen. This is admissible.

☛ **Things to look for:** Here are some special things to look out for in connection with defendant's favorable character evidence:

☞ **Criminal case:** Confirm that the case is a ***criminal*** case. (A few courts have extended FRE 404(a)(1) to cover the situation where the evidence is offered by D in a civil case but P claims that D committed crimes.)

☞ **Pertinent to crime:** Confirm that the evidence concerns a trait ***pertinent*** to the crime.

Example: D is charged with aggravated assault. He presents evidence of his good character for truth and veracity. This evidence will not be admissible, because D's truthfulness is not pertinent to this particular charge — it might be, however, if the charge were, say, embezzlement or fraud.

☞ **Reputation/opinion vs. specific acts:** Make sure that the character evidence is in the form of ***reputation*** or ***opinion*** — proof of ***specific acts*** (i.e., D's "good" acts) is ***not*** permitted. FRE 405(a).

☞ **Rebuttal by prosecution:** Remember that once D presents proof of his good character, the ***prosecution*** is then allowed to ***rebut*** this character evidence. This rebuttal evidence may be by reputation opinion or specific acts (but extrinsic evidence of specific acts is not allowed). The rebuttal evidence may be either by questions to the defense's character witness or by rebuttal witnesses.

Example: D is charged with aggravated assault of V. He puts on W1, who testifies that D has a good reputation for non-violence. The prosecution may ask W1, "Didn't you witness a fight between D and X?" But the prosecution can't introduce extrinsic evidence of the fight, such as testimony by W2 or a document. The prosecution may also ask W1, "Didn't you tell Y that you thought D sometimes flies off the handle?" And, it may present W2 to testify that W2's opinion is that D is a violent person.

Habit; Routine Business Practice

Use of habit evidence: Remember that a person's ***habit*** can generally be used to show he acted in conformity with that habit on the particular occasion in question.

☛ **Definition:** The essence of a "habit" is that it is a ***regular response*** to a ***repeated situation***.

Example: In an auto negligence case, the issue is whether D signalled before making a particular left turn. W, who was with D in the car that day but didn't watch, testifies that D drove with her on that same route every day, and at that particular turn, he almost always signalled. Admissible as habit evidence.)

☛ **3 factors establishing habit:** Before concluding that something is a "habit," check for 3 factors that should be present. (If even one is absent, the evidence is probably not of a true "habit"):

[1] ***Specificity:*** The more specific the action, the more likely it is to be a habit rather than mere proof of a character trait. So beware of general descriptions of behavior (e.g., something that sounds like reputation evidence) — these are likely to flunk the specificity test, and be inadmissible character evidence.

Example: In an auto negligence case, P offers testimony that D had a reputation in the community for his dangerous driving, and was known as "Dare-Devil Dan." If offered to show that Dan had a habit of driving dangerously and thus probably did so on the particular occasion, it's inadmissible because it's too general.

[2] ***Regularity:*** The habit must be regular. This has two sub-aspects.

☛ **Number of instances:** First, there must be a fair ***number*** of specific instances where the person adhered to the habit proved.

Example: The fact that P permitted insurance policies to lapse three times in her life is probably not sufficient evidence of habit to prove the same thing happened in the current situation.

☛ **Uniformity of response:** Second, there must be sufficient ***"uniformity of response,"*** i.e., not very many instances where the situation arose and the habit was ***not*** followed.

Example: The fact that D breached seven contracts in 20 years in business probably won't establish a habit of breaching, if D had many dozens of contracts during that period.

[3] ***Unreflective behavior:*** Finally, the behavior is more likely to be found to be habit if it's unreflective or semi-automatic, than where it's volitional and thought-out.

Example: Where D asserts an alibi defense that he was home on a particular day, evidence that it was the Sabbath, and that D had a habit of staying home to observe the Sabbath, probably won't be admitted, because D made a conscious choice each Sabbath to stay or not stay home. By contrast, signalling — or not signalling — before making a left turn meets the "semi-automatic" standard.

☛ *Caution:* But unlike the first two factors, this one is not dispositive — if specificity and regularity are shown, the court may allow as habit evidence even action with a fair degree of volition to it (e.g., a doctor's habit of always informing his patients of the risks of a particular type of operation).

☛ **Proper form:** Make sure the proof of the habit is in the proper form. Proof of ***specific instances*** known to the witness of the person's adherence to the habit is the best.

Example: "Most times when I walked with X, he jay-walked on that particular crossing."

☞ **Opinion:** Courts sometimes — but not generally — allow the witness's ***opinion*** that a person has a particular habit. Testimony that the person has a ***reputation*** for having a certain habit is virtually ***never*** allowed.

☛ **Routine practices of organization:** Remember that evidence of the ***routine practice*** of an ***organization*** or institution is admissible to show that some event occurred.

Example: To prove that a notice of appeal was mailed on a particular day, the secretary to an attorney testifies that she, the secretary, personally enclosed the notice in a properly addressed envelope, sealed it, and placed it in the basket marked "Outgoing Mail" on that day at 2 p.m. She further testifies that, as a matter of office routine, the office mail clerk empties the basket every day at 4 p.m. and immediately takes the contents to the post office. This is sufficient to meet the requirements for proving the law firm's "routine practice," and thus to establish that the notice was probably mailed on the day in question.

☞ **Specificity and personal knowledge:** Make sure the witness describes the routine business practice with ***sufficient specificity***, and that the witness has

personal knowledge of that practice.

Example: If in the above example, the testimony were merely that "We always mail notices out the day they're prepared, and I prepared this notice on May 1, so it must have gone out that day," the lack of detail about where the notices are put, who takes them to the post office and when, etc., would cause the court to deny admissibility.

☞ **Who may give testimony:** The testimony need ***not*** be given by the ***person who carries out*** the business practice, as long as the witness has detailed personal knowledge of the practice.

Example: In the first, detailed example about mailing the notice, the fact that the secretary didn't personally empty the Outgoing box every day and take the contents to the post office didn't block admission, because she had first-hand knowledge of how this was done and who routinely did it.

☞ **Proof of non-occurrence:** Remember that a business custom can be used to prove the ***non-occurrence*** of an act.

Example: In a copyright infringement suit, a film company claims that its employees never read P's unsolicited manuscript. The company's mailroom clerk testifies that it was the invariable procedure of the company to have the mail room immediately return to the sender, unread, all unsolicited mailed scripts. This will be admissible to prove that the company never read the manuscript, whether or not it received it.

Similar Accidents or other Happenings

General rule: Evidence that similar happenings occurred in the past, to show what happened on the present occasion, will often be admissible.

☛ **Substantial similarity:** "Similar happenings" evidence is most often tested in connection with ***accidents*** — the proponent typically wants to show that these other accidents shed light on what happened on the present occasion.

☞ **Issues to which it's relevant:** Evidence that similar accidents or mishaps have happened in the past can be introduced on a number of different issues (e.g., Did the accident happen this time at all? Did D know of the risks? What caused the accident?). This evidence will generally be ***admissible*** if and only if there's a showing that the ***circumstances*** surrounding the other accidents and the present one are ***substantially similar***.

Example 1: P claims whiplash from an accident that occurred while P rode D's bus. P will be allowed to show that three other people on that bus suffered whiplash, because the others and P were obviously similarly situated.

Example 2: Same basic facts. Now, P offers evidence that on other buses operated by D in the last year, there were two other accidents, in which three people suffered whiplash. Because there's probably no way to prove that the circumstances of these other accidents (e.g., the severity of the deceleration) matched those of the present accident, this "other accidents" evidence will be inadmissible.

☞ **Negative evidence:** Most often, D wants to use ***"negative"*** past-accidents evidence, by proving that because similar accidents involving D have not happened in the past, the present one either didn't happen at all, or wasn't caused by D's negligence. Again, this negative evidence will be allowed if and only if D shows the circumstances are substantially similar.

Example: P falls in D's restaurant. P shows the floor was waxed 1/2 hour before the fall, and offers some evidence that excess wax remained on the tiles after this, making them too slippery. D offers testimony by W, its manager, that in the week before the accident, more than 10,000 people used the restaurant, and he neither saw nor heard about any other falls. This testimony is inadmissible, because there's no showing that the conditions were the same during the whole week as right before the accident (and, indeed, P's waxing evidence shows that conditions *weren't* the same.)

☛ **Proof that W would have learned of accidents:** In this "negative" accident scenario, the proponent must also show that the witness is a person who would have ***learned*** of any such accidents.

Example: On the facts of the above restaurant example, the testimony could also be knocked out if there was no evidence that all falls would have been reported to W.

☛ **Similar contracts:** Also, look for attempts to introduce evidence of similar ***contracts,*** offered to show the parties' intent in the present contract, or something else about the present contract.

☞ **Same parties:** Where the other contract involves the ***same parties***, evidence about it will typically be admissible if and only if the contract's subject matter and surrounding circumstances are substantially ***similar*** to those of the present contract.

Example: D, a video store, orders blank cassette tapes from P. D refuses to accept delivery because the tapes are in paper boxes rather than clear plastic ones. D offers evidence that it placed three prior blank-tape orders from P, and that these orders all came in plastic. P shows that the present lot was sold at a special reduced price and the prior lots weren't. This change of circumstances will lead the court to find the past-contract evidence inadmissible.

☞ **Contracts with third party:** Where the other contract is between one party to the litigation and a ***third party***, it's much ***less likely*** to be admissible than where it involves both parties to the litigation.

Example: Same basic facts as prior example. Now, P offers evidence that in the prior four months, it had shipped paper-boxed videotapes to 20 other customers without objection. Assuming D didn't know about these other transactions, they won't be relevant to D's intent in entering the contract, so they'll be excluded.

Subsequent Remedial Measures

Remedial measures generally: Evidence that the defendant has taken subsequent remedial measures is ***inadmissible*** to prove D's ***negligence***.

Example: After a truck operated by D is involved in an accident, D installs a "governor" to prevent it from going faster than 60 mph. If offered to show that the truck was driven too fast during the accident, the evidence is inadmissible.

☛ **Other purposes:** But remember that subsequent-remedial-measure evidence is ***admissible*** if offered to prove something ***other than negligence*** (e.g., to prove ownership or control, or the feasibility of precautionary measures, or to impeach a witness).

☛ **Ownership central:** Most commonly-tested: repairs offered to proved ***ownership or control*** of the instrumentality. Look for a fact pattern where responsibility for the instrumentality is in dispute, yet the defendant fixes the item.

Example: P falls on pigeon droppings in an alley next to D's hotel; D claims it doesn't control the alley. P may show that since the accident, D has told its employees to regularly clean the alley.

☞ **Owner-tenant disputes:** Ownership issues are especially likely where a ***property owner*** and the owner's ***tenant*** each claim the other was responsible.

Example: P falls in a hallway leading from a hotel to a restaurant. Evidence that the hotel owner replaced the floor covering will be admissible to show that it, not the restaurant, was responsible for maintaining the hallway.

Insurance

Insurance evidence generally: Evidence that a party has liability insurance is inadmissible to show that he acted negligently or otherwise wrongfully. (FRE 411).

Example: P can't testify that after an accident, D said, "Don't worry, I have lots of insurance."

☛ **Compared with admissibility of admissions:** When the rule applies, it overcomes the more general rule allowing admissions to be admitted despite the hearsay rule. (So in the above example, it doesn't help P that D was making an implicit admission.)

☛ **Other purposes:** But again, remember that like remedial measures, the existence of insurance can be used to show something other than negligence, such as ownership or control of the insured instrumentality.

Example: After P is injured in a car accident, P sues D, who P believes is the owner of the car. D denies ownership. P offers an insurance policy on that car, written to cover D, and also offers testimony by an employee of Insurer that the policy was purchased by D. Admissible, because offered to show ownership, not negligence.

☞ **Proof of bias:** Similarly, existence of insurance can be admitted where it's part of a showing that the witness is ***biased***.

Example: In an auto accident case, W, an investigator called to the stand by D, says that his investigation showed that P, not D, was at fault. P may show that W is likely to be biased because he was retained by D's insurance company.

Settlements and Compromises; Offers to Pay Medical Bills; Guilty Pleas

☛ **Settlements:** Evidence of an offer to ***settle a claim*** is inadmissible on the issue of the claim's validity.

☞ **Collateral admissions of fact:** Most frequently-tested: admissions ***of fact*** made in conjunction with settlement offers. Here, remember that such ***collateral admissions*** are usually admissible under the common law, but not admissible under the FRE.

Example: D says to P, "Your claim seems high, but since I may have been a little negligent, I'll offer you $1,000." Both at common law and under the FRE, the fact of the offer must be excluded. But at common law, P could testify to the "I may have been a little negligent" part of D's statement. Under the FRE, the *entire statement* — including the collateral admission of fact — is inadmissible.

☛ **Medical bills:** Similarly, offers to pay, and payments, of a person's ***medical bills*** are inadmissible to prove the payor's liability.

Example: After D's car hits P, D offers to take P to the hospital and to pay the bill. This offer is not admissible to show that D was negligent or thought he was negligent.

☞ **Collateral admissions:** But here, collateral admissions of fact are ***admissible*** (in contrast to the FRE's treatment of collateral admissions in conjunction with settlement offers.)

Example: D tells P, "I'll pay your doctor bills because if I'd been driving on the right the accident wouldn't have happened." The offer to pay won't be admissible, but the statement about driving on the right will be, both at common law and under the FRE.

- **Guilty pleas:** Similarly, a person's offer (made to a prosecutor) to ***plead guilty*** to a criminal charge is inadmissible for any purpose if the plea never occurs. Likewise a person's actual ***guilty plea,*** if later withdrawn, is not admissible for any purpose.

  Example*:* In a civil case, D takes the stand. To impeach him, P's lawyer asks, "Didn't you once plead guilty to violating Penal Law §234?" If D withdrew that guilty plea, the question is improper.

  - **Discussions must be with prosecutor:** But under the FRE, the discussions must be with the prosecutor, not with other law enforcement personnel like police.

  - **Collateral admissions:** Remember that ***collateral admissions*** ("Since I was the lookout during the robbery, I'll plead to a lesser charge") are also inadmissible if they occur during plea discussions.

Exam Tips on *EXAMINATION & IMPEACHMENT OF WITNESSES*

Of the topics in this chapter, two make up the overwhelming majority of test questions: cross-examination generally, and impeachment (with its counterpart, rehabilitation).

Direct Examination

- **Leading questions:** Where your exam question involves ***direct*** examination, there's really only one rule that gets tested with any frequency: the examiner may not ask ***leading questions***. Remember that a leading question is one that suggests to the witness the answer desired by the questioner. (One common example: any question starting with "Didn't" or "Weren't").

  - **Hostile witness:** But if the witness is "hostile," remember that leading questions are ***allowed***.

Cross-Examination

Cross-examination generally: Here's what to look for when the exam question involves cross-examination:

- **Scope:** Look out for issues involving the proper ***scope*** of cross.

  - **Scope of direct:** The majority rule (followed by FRE 611(b)) is the ***"scope of***

direct" rule, i.e., cross is limited to the scope of the matters the witness testified to on her direct exam.

Example: In a car crash case, W testifies on behalf of P that D said to W after the accident, "I was speeding." W gives no other testimony on direct. D's lawyer asks W on cross, "You didn't see the accident, did you?" Strictly speaking, this violates the majority/FRE "scope of direct" rule and would be improper. However, most states give the trial judge discretion to allow the question.

☞ **Credibility:** Questions relevant to ***credibility*** are always within the scope of cross.

☛ **Leading:** Leading questions are permissible on cross.

☛ **Self-incrimination:** Also, look out for situations in which the witness under cross invokes the Fifth Amendment privilege against ***self-incrimination***. Often-tested: when W takes the 5th, what should the trial judge do? Usual answer: strike W's direct testimony.

Example: In D's murder trial, W testifies on direct, "I saw D commit the murder." On cross, D's lawyer asks W, "Isn't it true that at the time in question, you were robbing a gas station 600 miles away?" If W takes the 5th, the trial judge should normally strike all W's direct testimony, because W's invocation of the 5th now prevents D from exercising his full 6th Amendment Confrontation Clause rights.

Present Recollection Refreshed

Present recollection refreshed, generally: Whenever a witness can't remember something, consider the possibility that the doctrine of "present recollection refreshed" may apply. Here are the aspects most often tested:

☛ **W must not be able to remember:** Remember that the doctrine applies only when the witness ***cannot remember*** the answer without the document.

Example: If W gives an answer, but the questioner thinks this is the wrong answer, the doctrine doesn't apply.

☛ **What items may be used:** ***Any item*** (a writing or thing) may be used. Most fact patterns involve a writing (e.g., a newspaper article; a letter written by or to W; company files.)

☞ **Inadmissible items allowed:** The item ***need not be admissible***. That's because the item is never being admitted into evidence, only the refreshed testimony becomes evidence.

Example: W observes an accident involving P and D. At trial, W — testifying on behalf of P — can't remember the details. P's lawyer shows W a report by a policeman, X, in which X says, "An unidentified witness says that D ran a red light." If W was that witness, W can now testify about the accident with his recollection refreshed, even though the report itself is inadmissible because of hearsay.

☞ **Check for admissibility of item:** Whether or not the witness's recollection is in fact refreshed by the item, check to see whether the item itself is admissible. Most common ways: ***past recollection recorded*** and ***business record***.

☛ **Other rules on W's testimony:** Remember that even if the doctrine applies, W's testimony must ***still meet ordinary admissibility requirements.***

Example: W, listening to a police radio, hears a report about a red car speeding down a particular street. She makes a note of what she's heard. At trial, W can't remember the report, is shown her note, and then testifies to what she remembers the report saying. Even though showing W the note was a proper application of present recollection refreshed, her testimony is still inadmissible hearsay — it's not "immunized" from admissibility problems by virtue of having come from the properly-consulted document.

☛ **Opposing counsel's rights:** Frequently-tested: Does ***opposing counsel*** have the right to ***see the item*** and ***use it for cross-examination*** of the witness?

☞ **Shown to W at trial:** If the item is shown to the witness ***at trial***, all courts (and FRE 612) give the opposing party the ***right*** to inspect the item and use it for cross.

☞ **Shown to W before trial:** But if the item is merely consulted by the witness ***before*** trial, most courts (and FRE 612) leave it up to the trial court's ***discretion*** whether to allow the opposing counsel to see the item and cross-examine W with reference to it.

Impeachment — Generally

Impeachment generally: When you conclude that a particular piece of evidence is inadmissible substantively, always check to see if it's admissible for ***impeachment***. Evidence is being used for impeachment when it's used to ***destroy a witness's credibility*** (rather than to directly establish a fact at issue in the case).

☛ **Typical evidence types:** Types of evidence or questions likely to be impeaching:

[1] attacks on W's ***character***, especially ***truthfulness***;

[2] W's ***prior inconsistent statement***;

[3] W's ***bias***;

[4] W's ***sensory or mental defect***; and

[5] ***contradiction*** of W's testimony (e.g., by testimony of a different witness).

☛ **Most commonly-tested:** May a lawyer ***impeach his own witness*** (i.e., may impeachment be done on direct)?

☞ **Answer at common law:** At common law, the answer is, generally, ***no*** (but subject to exceptions, e.g. where W is hostile or Lawyer is surprised).

☞ **FRE answer:** Under the FRE and many modern courts: the answer is ***yes***. (Thus FRE 607 completely revokes the "can't impeach your own witness" rule.)

- **Multiple-choice wrong answer:** In multiple-choice exams where the FRE apply, a common ***incorrect*** "distractor" is "Inadmissible, because Lawyer can't impeach her own witness."

Impeachment By Prior Criminal Conviction or Prior Bad Acts

Importance: Impeachment by prior criminal convictions or prior bad acts are probably the most commonly-tested types of impeachment. The rules are detailed and non-obvious, so spend some time memorizing them. Here are the main things to watch for (discussion assumes the FRE, unless otherwise noted):

- **Prior convictions:** Where the impeachment is by showing W's prior ***criminal conviction***:

☞ **Dishonesty or false statement; felony or misdemeanor:** If the crime required the prosecution to prove ***dishonesty*** or ***false statement as an element*** (i.e., the crime was a *"crimen falsi"*), the evidence is always ***admissible***. This is true both at common law and under FRE 609. And it's true even if the conviction was a ***misdemeanor***, and whether W is or is not an "accused."

Example: Lawyer asks W, "Isn't it true that two years ago, you were convicted on misdemeanor charges of perjury?" Admissible.

❑ **Examples of *crimen falsi* under the FRE (and thus admissible):** perjury, criminal fraud, embezzlement, false pretenses, forgery, tax fraud (probably).

❑ **Not a *crimen falsi* (and thus inadmissible):** most crimes of violence; drug offenses; ordinary larceny (including shoplifting, but not embezzlement or false pretences), robbery, burglary.

- **No discretion:** There's ***no discretion*** in *crimen falsi* cases — the court can't conclude that the probative value is outweighed by the danger of unfair prejudice.

☞ **Felony not involving dishonesty; W not accused:** If the crime is a ***felony for which proof of dishonesty or false statements was not an element***, and W is ***not the accused***, the evidence is automatically ***admissible***, unless the conviction's probative value is shown to be "***substantially outweighed*** by the danger of unfair prejudice."

Example: W testifies as an alibi witness for D in a criminal case. Prosecution may ask W, "Isn't it true you were convicted of aggravated assault three years ago?" as long as this crime was punishable by at least one year in prison.

☛ **Maximum punishment:** Remember that what counts is the maximum punishment ***possible*** in the state or federal system where the conviction occurred, not the punishment W actually received. (So even a sentence of probation would not make the conviction inadmissible if a 1-year sentence could have been given for the crime.)

☞ **Felony not involving dishonesty; W is accused:** If the crime is a ***felony not involving dishonesty*** as an element, and the witness ***is*** the ***accused***, the judge may admit the evidence only if she determines that the probative value of admitting "outweighs" the conviction's prejudicial effect to the accused.

Example: In a criminal trial before a jury, D takes the stand, and says he didn't commit the crime. On cross, the prosecutor asks, "Weren't you convicted of burglary 6 years ago?" The question is proper if and only if the judge finds that the probative value of the evidence will outweigh the likely prejudicial effect on D.

☛ **D must take stand:** Remember that D can only be impeached if he ***takes the stand***. The fact pattern will sometimes try to distract you from this key point.

Example: In D's murder trial, Officer testifies that he previously arrested D several times for assault, and that D was convicted each time. The prosecutor then offers authenticated court records of the convictions. Neither Officer's testimony nor the court records are admissible for impeachment unless there's some indication in the question that D took the stand — without this, there's nothing to impeach.

☞ **Non-dishonesty misdemeanor:** If the crime is a ***misdemeanor not involving dishonesty***, it's ***not admissible***, whether W is the accused or not.

☞ **Limits:** Don't forget some limits on the use of otherwise admissible prior crimes:

☛ **10-years:** Most important, the conviction is not admissible (whether it's a felony or a crimen falsi misdemeanor) if ***more than 10 years*** has elapsed since the conviction or release from confinement (whichever is later), unless the judge finds specific facts making the probative value substantially outweigh the prejudicial effect. Most often, this special showing won't be made (and the conviction will be excluded).

☛ **Rehabilitation:** Also, the conviction is not admissible if it's reversed on appeal, or, in most instances, if W was pardoned.

☞ **Procedures:** Usually, the impeachment will be by ***questioning*** of the witness ("Weren't you convicted . . . .") But it may also be by extrinsic evidence, i.e., by introducing a certified ***copy of the judgment*** of conviction.

- **Prior bad acts:** Unconvicted *bad acts* that are probative of truthfulness are admissible at the discretion of the judge. FRE 608(b). Here's what to watch for:

  ☞ **Truthfulness:** The bad act must be of a sort that ***bears on truthfulness***. (The definition is basically the same as for *crimen falsi* under FRE 609. So these don't qualify: most violent crimes; status crimes like drug-addiction; and theft crimes containing no element of false statement, like shoplifting and burglary.)

  Examples of bad acts that *do* meet the "bears on truthfulness" test:

  - ❑ lying on an insurance policy;
  - ❑ defrauding customers;
  - ❑ committing perjury.

  ☞ **Good-faith basis:** The questioner must have a ***"good-faith basis"*** for believing that the witness committed the bad act.

  ☞ **No extrinsic evidence:** The bad acts must be proved only by ***questioning the witness, not*** by introducing ***"extrinsic evidence."*** This means that:

  - A ***second witness*** can't be called to testify that the first witness committed the bad act; and

  - ***Documents*** can't be introduced to show W's bad act, even during the cross-examination of W. (But a document can be referred to, as long as it's not introduced.)

    Example: W can be asked, "Didn't you once file an insurance claim, in which you falsely said your car radio was stolen?" But the false claim form itself can't be introduced.

  - **No specific-acts extrinsic testimony:** The only way ***extrinsic evidence*** can be used to show W's character for truthfulness is by reputation or opinion testimony, not by "specific acts" testimony, which is what is being discussed here.

  ☞ **Bad act led to conviction:** If the bad act resulted in a conviction, the limits of the conviction rule probably must be adhered to even if only the bad act is inquired about.

  Example: W probably can't be asked, "Did you commit perjury 12 years ago?" if W was in fact convicted and released from prison more than 10 years ago, making the conviction itself too old to introduce.

Impeachment by Opinion and Reputation Testimony

Opinion and reputation impeachment, generally: Remember that the principal witness (W1) can be impeached by the testimony of a second, or "character" witness (W2), subject to these rules:

☛ **Reputation or opinion:** W2 must testify to W1's poor ***reputation*** for truthfulness, or testify that in W2's ***opinion***, W1 is of untruthful character. (FRE 608(a)). In other words, W2 ***can't*** testify to ***specific instances*** in which W1 was untruthful.

> **Example:** W2 can say, "I think, based on my past experience with him, that W1 often lies." But W2 can't continue on by saying, "For instance, I saw him lie about his income on a welfare application."

☛ **Rehabilitation by specific instances:** But once W2 gives the reputation or opinion testimony about W1's poor reputation for truthfulness, the party who called W1 may at the court's discretion ***rehabilitate*** W1 by asking about specific instances of W1's truthfulness.

> **Example:** To W2, "Didn't W1 tell you he'd been in jail, even though you had no other way to find this out?"

Impeachment by W's Prior Inconsistent Statement

Inconsistency, generally: Look for a witness testifying on the stand who is making a statement that is ***inconsistent*** with some ***prior statement*** made by that same witness. In general, the cross-examiner may impeach this witness by using the prior inconsistent statement.

☛ **Types of proof allowed:** Proof of the prior inconsistent statement may be by ***either intrinsic*** or ***extrinsic*** evidence.

> **Example of intrinsic proof:** D testifies that a car belongs to him. L asks on cross, "When you were arrested, didn't you tell the officers that the car wasn't yours?" Proper.
>
> **Example of extrinsic proof:** W1 is an alibi witness for D. W1 says, "On April 14, the evening of the crime, I had dinner with D." The prosecutor may put on W2, who testifies, "In May, W1 told me he hadn't seen D any time in April."

☛ **Extrinsic evidence:** Most test questions focus on the special rules for showing a prior inconsistent statement by extrinsic evidence:

> ☞ **Collateral matters rule:** Most courts don't allow extrinsic proof of prior inconsistent statement on a ***collateral issue***, i.e., one that is not directly in issue in the case and that would not be directly provable apart from the inconsistency (as bias, say, would be).
>
> **Example:** Same basic facts as prior example. In the course of his alibi testi-

mony, W1 happens to mention, "On April 14, before I had dinner with D, I bought a gallon of milk from the 7-11." Prosecution puts on W2, who says, "W1 told me he never shops at 7-11 because it's a rip-off." Inadmissible, because it's extrinsic evidence of a prior inconsistent statement, not relating to an issue in the case — whether W1 did or didn't shop at the 7-11 that day isn't a direct issue in the case.

☞ **Foundation:** Under the modern/FRE approach, the extrinsic evidence (e.g., a writing) need ***not*** be shown to the witness, or summarized, before the inconsistency is revealed. (FRE 613(a).

Example: Civil suit involving auto accident. D tells an investigator, "I don't know whether I was speeding," and the investigator makes written notes of this statement. At trial, D says, "I definitely wasn't speeding." P's lawyer, L, can ask D the vague question, "Didn't you say at some other time that you didn't know you were speeding?" L need not first show the notes to D, or first warn D about the time and place of the prior statement — L can "spring" this on D by introducing the notes after D has denied making a prior inconsistent statement.

☞ **Chance to explain or deny:** But remember that extrinsic evidence of the prior incon. stmt. is not admissible unless the witness is given a chance to ***"explain or deny"*** the statement, and the party who called that witness is given a chance to rehabilitate. (FRE 613(b)). This rule can be dispensed with if "the interests of justice otherwise require", and does not apply at all where the statement is made by a party-opponent.

☛ **Hearsay:** Don't get confused by a prior statement that seems to be ***hearsay***. It's still admissible as a prior incon. stmt. if it's being used to impeach, not to prove its truth.

Example: In D's murder trial, W testifies for the prosecution that he, W, heard three gunshots immediately after hearing D shout, "I'll kill you!" D offers testimony of Police Officer, who testifies that when Officer interviewed W after the shooting, W said he hadn't heard any gunshots. Because Officer's testimony is being used to impeach W's credibility, not to prove whether D really heard gunshots, Officer's recounting of W's interview statement is not hearsay.

☞ **Admissible both ways:** Also, examine the possibility that a prior inconsistent statement may be admissible ***both substantively and as impeachment***. Two common situations where the the statement will be admissible for both purposes:

[1] A party's ***own prior statement*** is being introduced by the other party (thus qualifying substantively as an ***admission***); and

[2] a person's prior statement was given ***under oath*** at a proceeding or deposition (thus qualifying substantively under FRE 801(d)(1)(A)'s "prior inconsistent statement" exception to the hearsay rule).

Example of [2]: If W testifies at trial, his prior inconsistent statement at a grand jury proceeding may be admitted substantively.

Impeachment by Showing Bias

Commonly-tested: Impeachment by showing W's ***bias*** is commonly-tested.

Examples:

- ❑ An expert is asked, "How much are you getting paid to testify?"
- ❑ A witness for the defense is asked, "Isn't it true that the defendant bank in this case is your employer?"
- ❑ W testifies on D's behalf in a criminal case. Prosecution asks, "Isn't it true that you were also arrested for taking part in the same crime, and you're awaiting trial, so you have an incentive to help get D acquitted?"

All of the above questions are ***admissible***, assuming that any foundation requirement imposed by the jurisdiction is satisfied (see below)

☛ **Foundation:** Where the attacking party wants to use extrinsic evidence to show bias, focus on the possible need for a ***"foundation,"*** i.e., the need to give the witness who's being attacked the chance to explain before the extrinsic evidence is introduced.

☞ **Often required:** Many jurisdictions ***require*** such a foundation.

Example: In a civil suit between P and D, W testifies on behalf of P. D's lawyer puts on X, who says, "Two months ago, W told me that when this case came to trial, W was going to 'get' D good, because D blocked W from becoming a member of D's club." In some states, this testimony won't be allowed unless D's lawyer first asked W, "Did you ever tell X that you would try to 'get' D for keeping you out of his club?"

☞ **Federal courts:** Federal courts often require a foundation before the witness's own prior statement is introduced to show his bias, but not where some other kind of extrinsic evidence is used to show bias.

Example: On the facts of the above example, federal courts might require that D's lawyer first ask W about the prior statement to X. But the lawyer could introduce membership records showing that D kept W out of D's club, without first asking W about this, because here there's no prior statement by W being introduced.

Impeachment by Showing W's Impairment

Impairment of W's abilities: Remember that W can be impeached by showing an ***impairment*** of her capacity to ***observe, recall*** or ***narrate***.

> **Example:** W says she was attacked by D in a parking lot at night. W says there were no artificial lights, but she could see D's face in the moonlight. D can call an expert witness to testify that there was no moonlight on the night of the attack; this shows impairment of W's ability to observe.

Impeachment by Contradiction

Contradiction, generally: Impeachment of W by ***contradiction*** occurs where evidence is offered that contradicts W's testimony in the case.

☛ **Collateral matter rule:** Far and away the most frequently-tested aspect of impeachment-by-contradiction is the rule against impeachment on a ***"collateral matter."*** If W1 gives testimony (whether on direct or cross), the attacking party ***can't*** call W2 to contradict the truth of what W1 said if W2's evidence relates ***only to W1's credibility***.

> **Example 1:** W1 testifies on P's behalf that a car accident was caused by D's negligence. D's lawyer, on cross, asks W1 "When you witnessed the accident, were you drunk?" W1 says, "No — in fact, I've never been drunk." D then calls W2, who testifies that 2 years before the accident, W2 saw W1 get drunk on New Year's Eve. Because this evidence bears only on W1's credibility (i.e., it doesn't bear directly on a substantive issue in the case), and because this evidence couldn't be admitted if W1 hadn't said he was never drunk (in other words, the evidence doesn't bear on some independently-provable item like W1's bias or general untruthfulness), it should be excluded as collateral.

> **Example 2:** In a car crash civil case, P claims that D was negligent in speeding and in running a stop light. W1, an eyewitness to the crash, testifies on D's behalf; as part of his testimony, W1 mentions that D was wearing a green sweater at the time of the accident. P offers testimony by W2, who says only that on that day, D's sweater was blue. Because the sweater's color is not an issue in the case, and D wouldn't try to prove its color except to impeach W1, W2's testimony should be excluded as collateral. (If W1's mistake was so glaring that it couldn't be the result of honest and trivial error — for instance, if he said that D was wearing an orange hunting vest when he was in fact wearing a blue business suit — then W's contradictory testimony would probably *not* be collateral.)

☞ **Substantive issue:** But where W2's testimony contradicting W1 *does* relate to a substantive issue in the case, or to some fact provable even if it didn't directly contradict W1 (e.g., it proves that W1 is biased, or habitually lies, or lacks capacity to observe or remember accurately), then it *won't* be excluded as collatcral.

Example: W1, after giving testimony favorable to D, is asked, "Aren't you a personal friend of D?" W1 denies this. P may put on W2 to testify that W1 and D are in fact friends — this would be admissible to prove W1's bias even if W1 hadn't denied being D's friend.

Rehabilitation

Rehab, generally: Once a witness's credibility has been attacked, it may be ***rehabilitated*** by the non-attacking party. This isn't a commonly-tested area. Just be on the lookout for two issues:

☛ **Directly-related rule:** First, the rehabilitating evidence must be sufficiently ***directly related*** to the impeaching evidence.

Example: P's expert witness, W1, is asked by D's lawyer on cross, "Doctor, how much are you being paid for testifying in this case?" W1 answers, "$500." P's lawyer then calls W2, who testifies solely that W1 has a good reputation for truth and veracity. This rehabilitating evidence is inadmissible, because it doesn't relate to W1's bias, and thus doesn't refute the impeaching evidence.

☛ **Prior consistent statements:** Second, a ***prior consistent statement*** can't be used to bolster a witness's credibility, unless the other side has first claimed that the testimony was a recent fabrication or the result of improper influence or motive.

Example (inadmissible): P sues D, a cosmetics company, for an infected leg that P testifies came from using D's hair remover product. D offers testimony by W1 that P received her injuries from falling on a pitchfork. P then offers testimony by W2, P's friend, who says that P often showed W2 her leg and said it had become infected from using the hair remover. Since D wasn't claiming that P recently fabricated her story or was improperly influenced by anyone, such as her lawyer, W2's testimony as to P's prior consistent statement is inadmissible for rehabilitation.

Example (admissible): Same facts, but now D's lawyer says to P on cross, "Isn't it true that you made up this "pitchfork" story 6 months after your injury, when you met your lawyer and decided to sue?" Now, since D has claimed that P's testimony is a recent fabrication, W2's testimony as to P's prior consistent statement is admissible to rehabilitate P's credibility, if the statement was made before D met with the lawyer.

Exam Tips on HEARSAY

Hearsay typically accounts for 30-40% of a typical Evidence exam, so you need to be on the lookout for it in every fact pattern, whether essay or multiple choice.

Memorize every word of the classic definition: *"Hearsay is a statement or assertive conduct that was made or occurred out of court, and is offered in court to prove the truth of the facts asserted."* In an essay, begin your answer by quoting this verbatim, then show how it does or doesn't apply to the facts of the question.

Here's what to look for in analyzing a hearsay question (exceptions to the hearsay rule are covered in the next chapter):

☛ **Statement:** Look for a ***statement***.

☞ **Oral vs. written:** A statement may be ***oral*** or ***written***.

☞ **Need not be testimonial:** Even things that don't sound at all "testimonial" may be statements, and thus hearsay.

Example: P tells the court that a bottle's label bore the words, "Contains sodium chloride." The label has since been destroyed. The label's contents are probably a "statement," so if P is offering those words in order to prove that that's what the bottle contained, this is probably hearsay.

☞ **Non-verbal conduct:** Where what happened out-of-court is ***non-verbal conduct***, consider whether the person who did it intended it as an ***assertion*** — if it was, it can be hearsay; if it wasn't, it can't be hearsay.

Example: D is on trial for burglarizing W and W's wife Helen. W testifies that a week after the crime, W and Helen were in a park, when Helen saw D and shouted, "You're the one who burglarized my house!" W further testifies that D immediately ran away. If D's flight is found to be the equivalent of saying "I did it and don't want to be caught," W's statement about the flight would be hearsay. Probably, however, the court will find that D's flight was not intended by D as an assertion of any factual matter; in that case, W's testimony about the flight would not be hearsay.

☛ **Animals and machines:** ***Animals*** and ***machines*** don't make statements.

Example: W, a DEA agent, testifies for the prosecution that a dog sniffed D's luggage and then started barking in a way he was trained to do if he found drugs. The barking isn't a statement, and therefore can't be hearsay. Same result if W testifies that a drug-testing machine beeped in a way that signifies "I've found drugs."

☛ **Offered to prove truth of assertion:** Check whether the statement is being offered to prove the ***truth of the matters asserted therein.*** If not, the statement isn't hearsay. Most frequently-tested aspects:

☞ **Verbal acts:** The statement may be an ***operative fact*** that gives rise to ***legal consequences.*** If so, check whether the statement is being offered because of these consequences, not to prove the truth of the matter asserted. Some examples:

❑ ***Defamation*** suits.

Example: P sues D for defamation, claiming that D said, "P is a crook," during a TV interview. P puts on W, a video engineer who taped the interview, who testifies, "I heard D say 'P is a crook' during the interview." Since D's making of the statement has legal significance aside from its truth — P can't recover unless he shows D made the statement — D's statement is a "verbal act" that's not hearsay.)

❑ ***Breach of contract*** suits.

Example: W testifies that he heard P say to D, "I'll paint your portrait for $5,000," and that he heard D respond, "OK, I'll come to your studio tomorrow." Neither of these out-of-court statements — P's and D's — is hearsay, because the statements are being offered to show their independent legal significance, as offer and acceptance, respectively, not to show the truth of any matter asserted therein.

❑ Suit where giving of a ***gift*** is at issue.

Example: The administrator of X's estate sues D, an orderly in the hospital where X died, seeking the return of a watch which the orderly allegedly took. D testifies, "X said to me, 'This watch is a gift to you.' " D's testimony is not hearsay, because X's statement, coupled with the delivery of the watch, had the independent legal effect of completing the gift of the watch.

☞ **State of mind:** Statements which are not offered for their truth, but to show the ***state of mind*** either of the ***declarant*** or of a ***listener***. Look for patterns where ***knowledge, belief*** or ***intent*** is at issue. Some contexts:

❑ To show the intent of a party to ***contract*** negotiations.

Example: P, a Japanese exporter, contracts to deliver china dishes to D, an American importer. The writing does not specify the material to be used in the dishes. D refuses the goods, on the grounds that they are plastic, and the parties intended porcelain. At trial on the suit for breach, D offers the testimony of a translator, W, who says, "I translated during the negotiations between P and D. In response to a question by D, P told me in Japanese, 'The dishes will be genuine porcelain,' and that's what I told D in English." W's testimony is not hearsay, because P's statement went to D's understanding of what the contract called for — it's not being offered for the purpose of establishing the truth of P's statement.

❑ To show the state of mind of a ***criminal defendant***.

Example 1: D, a labor union president, is charged with violating a state law making it a felony for a union official to knowingly misappropriate union funds. The charge is that D authorized a large raise for himself. D offers testimony by his predecessor as president, W, who says, "Before the raise, D asked me if he could lawfully take a raise and I told him he could if he honestly believed it was reasonable and necessary." W's testimony isn't hearsay because it's being offered to prove that D believed the union rules permitted him to act as he did, not to prove that he was in fact allowed to raise his own salary.

Example 2: D, a policeman, is accused of attempting to kill his wife by shooting her with a Sureshot 202 pistol from a distance of 1/4 mile. D maintains that the shot was an accident, and that the Sureshot is not accurate at more than 1/8 mile. The prosecution calls D's former classmate from the police academy, who testifies, "In pistol class, attended by D and myself at the academy, the instructor said the Sureshot 202 is accurate up to 1/2 a mile." Admissible, because it's offered to show that D believed the pistol would be accurate, not to prove that the pistol really *was* accurate at that range.

❑ To show a witness's ***bias***.

Example: W1 says that D drove through a red light before hitting P. D puts on W2, who says, "Before trial, W1 told me, 'D blackballed me from becoming a member of the club he belongs to.' " Admissible, because it shows bias by W1 against D, and is not being offered to show that D really blackballed W1.

☛ **Witness repeats own out-of-court statement:** Remember that there can be hearsay even where the witness is testifying to his or her ***own*** out-of-court statement. As long as the out-of-court statement is being offered for the truth of the matter asserted, the fact that the in-court witness and the out-of-court declarant are the same is irrelevant.

Example: In a civil car-crash suit, D says on the stand, "After the accident, I told the police officer who came to the scene that the light was green when I drove through the intersection." This is hearsay, if as seems probable it's being offered to show that the light really *was* green.

☛ **Two steps:** Once you've determined that a particular bit of evidence is hearsay, of course consider whether it's admissible as an exception. But ***don't skip the first step*** — the fact that something would fall within an exception even if it were hearsay should never prevent you from first carefully analyzing whether it really *is* hearsay.

Exam Tips on *EXCEPTIONS TO THE HEARSAY RULE*

Once you've concluded that something is hearsay, you'll of course need to determine whether it falls within one of the many exceptions to the hearsay rule. The substantial majority of test items that are hearsay will turn out to fall within an exception, and of those that don't, most will raise an issue about whether they fall within an exception.

THE "DECLARANT'S AVAILABILITY IRRELEVANT" EXCEPTIONS

Admissions by a Party-Opponent

Admissions generally: The "admissions" exception is probably the most frequently-tested of all hearsay exceptions. Here's what to look for:

☛ **Party:** Most obviously, remember that the exception only applies where the out-of-court statement is made by a ***party*** to the present proceeding.

☞ **Bystander witnesses or auto passengers:** *Here's a common trap:* The statement is made by a ***bystander witness*** or a non-party ***passenger*** in a car. Even if this person is ***closely linked to a party***, her statement regarding the accident is still not an admission as long as there's no principal-agent relationship between the declarant and the party against whom the statement is now sought to be used.

Example: A car driven by Driver, and in which Passenger, Driver's friend, is riding, hits Pedestrian. Shortly after, Passenger tells Officer, "We were returning from a party, at which Driver was drinking." In Pedestrian's suit against Driver, Passenger's statement to Officer is not admissible against Driver as an admission, because Passenger isn't a party, and there's no relationship (e.g., principal and agent) by which Passenger's statement could be attributed to Driver. In fact, the statement doesn't fall within any exception, and is thus inadmissible hearsay. (But if the statement had been made by Driver, not Passenger, it would be admissible against him as an admission.)

- **Declarant closely aligned to a party:** Often, the declarant will be so ***closely aligned*** in interest with a party that you might be duped into thinking the declarant is a party — but the requirement that declarant be a party is very ***tightly construed***.

  Example: The administrator of X's estate sues Orderly, an orderly in the hospital where X died, seeking the return of a watch which Orderly allegedly took. Orderly wants to testify that X told him, "Take this watch; it's a gift from me to you." This statement is not an admission, because it was made by X, and X is not a party, only his estate is.

- **Against party:** Also, make sure the statement is being offered ***against***, not for, the party who made it.

- **Unavailability not required:** Remember that for admissions, there is ***no*** requirement that the party who made the statement be ***unavailable*** to testify.

- **Combinations:** Heavily-tested area: admissions ***combined*** with statements containing facts about insurance, offers to settle, or offers to pay medical bills. (Here, you just have to memorize the rules. For instance, factual admissions made while offering to pay medical bills are admissible under the FRE, but factual admissions made in the course of settlement negotiations aren't. See Cap. Sum., Ch. 3.)

- **Representative admissions:** Look for a situation where there's an attempt to bind one party with an admission ***made by another person***.

  - **Vicarious admission:** Commonly, a party tries to use an ***employee's*** statement ***against the employer***, arguing that the employer is vicariously responsible for the statement. Two main tricks to watch out for (especially under FRE 801(d)(2)(D)):

    - **Timing:** First, make sure the statement was made at a ***time when the employment relationship existed.***

      Example: P is injured when a plane he's flying in, owned and operated by D airline, crashes. P offers the testimony of Investigator, who says, "I interviewed Walter after the crash. Walter was a mechanic for D at the time of the crash. Walter told me that before the crash, he told the president of D that the plane had cracks, but the president ignored him. Immediately after the crash, Walter was fired; he told me that this had happened as part of a cover-up by D." Walter's entire out-of-court statement is not admissible against D as a vicarious admission, because when it was made, Walter was no longer an employee of D.

    - **Scope:** Second, make sure that that statement concerns a matter ***within the scope of the employment relationship***. Commonly-tested: An employee is involved in a car accident, and statements made by him are sought to be attributed to the employer.

Example (within relationship): An accident occurs when a delivery van driver is en route making a delivery for his employer; the driver's statement about the accident to a witness is admissible against the employer.

Example (not within relationship): In a drug case against D, Officer testifies that D tried to buy drugs from Officer. W, D's girlfriend, testifies for D, "Once Officer arrested me for prostitution, and told me he'd let me off if I bribed him. I said I wouldn't, and he said he'd get me and my friends." This isn't admissible against the government as a vicarious admission, because Officer's solicitation of bribes, and threat of revenge, probably weren't within the scope of his employment relationship. [However, it would be admissible to *impeach* Officer by showing bias, subject perhaps to the need to lay a foundation by first questioning Officer about the episode. See Capsule Summary, Ch. 4.]

☞ **Proving employer-employee relation:** Note that the statement of the employee may not be used to establish the employer-employee relationship. This must be proven ***independently***.

☞ **Authority sometimes required:** Also, note that at common-law, the employee must be shown to have been ***authorized*** by the employer to ***make the statement*** (it's not enough that the statement was about a matter falling within the scope of employment). But under FRE 801(d)(2)(D), this requirement is ***dropped*** — as long as the matter is within the scope of employment, the employee ***doesn't need to have been authorized to speak about it***.

☞ **Adoptive admission:** If a party hears or sees another person's statement, and by her words or actions indicates that she "accepts" or "adopts" that statement, the statement is binding on the party as an admission.

☛ **Implied admissions:** Most frequently-tested: an ***implied*** admission. Here, *A* claims that *B*'s ***silence*** in the face of a statement made by someone other than *B* amounts to an adoption by B of the statement. The test is, would a reasonable person in B's position have denied the statement had it not been true?

Examples where silence is ***unreasonable*** (so adoption applies):

❑ *A* is accused of murder or some other heinous crime;

❑ *A* is accused of mislabelling his products;

❑ *A* is told, "You know that's your signature" while being shown a contract.

In all 3 of the above examples, the statement will be admissible against *A* as an adoptive admission.

☞ **Co-conspirator's statement:** Where an out-of-court statement is made by one conspirator implicating another, the statement can often be introduced against the latter. Check that the statement was made: (1) while the conspiracy was ***still in force***, and (2) in ***furtherance*** of that conspiracy. (FRE 801(d)(2)(E)).

☛ **In furtherance:** Most frequently-tested: the "in furtherance" requirement, when applied to ***confessions***, ***narratives of past events***, and ***finger-pointing*** by the declarant against one who ends up being the defendant. If the court applies the "in furtherance" requirement strictly, to mean "in an attempt to advance the conspiracy's objectives," all of these kinds of statements ***won't*** be admissible. (But a lot of courts don't apply the requirement very strictly).

Example: After a burglary, the police catch X in a chase. X says, "You never would have caught me if D hadn't been so slow in finishing the job." This statement would probably be found not to have been made in furtherance of the conspiracy, and would thus not be usable as an admission against D at D's criminal trial for the burglary.

☛ **Prior inconsistent statement:** Keep in mind that the same out-of-court statement may sometimes be admissible ***both*** as a ***prior inconsistent statement*** for impeachment purposes, and as an admission for substantive purposes. This is likely to be true wherever a party makes an out-of-court statement that contradicts his trial testimony.

Example: P and D have a car accident. P hires an undercover investigator, W, who engages D in what seems to be a random conversation in a bar. D tells W, "I had a six-pack before the accident, but the police never tested me." At trial, D testifies on direct that he drove carefully and in full possession of his faculties, and on cross denies having ever said otherwise in any conversation in a bar. As part of P's case, W's testimony about what D told him in the bar will be admissible both as a prior inconsistent statement to impeach D, and substantively as an admission against a party-opponent.

☛ **Distinction:** Keep straight the differences between an admission and a ***declaration against interest***: a declaration against interest must be against the declarant's interest ***at the time it was made*** (an admission doesn't have to be); applies only when the declarant is ***unavailable*** (no such rule applies to admissions); and may be offered into evidence ***by the party who made it*** (whereas the admission may be used only ***against*** the party who made it.)

☞ **Quick rule of thumb:** If used ***against*** the party who made it, always treat the statement as an admission. If used ***by*** the party who made it, or if ***made by a non-party***, the statement can't be an admission, and will have to be a declaration against interest (if anything).

☛ **Nonhearsay:** When you're writing about the FRE, note in your answer that the admission is ***nonhearsay*** (not "hearsay subject to an exception," as at common law). This makes no practical difference, but it tends to show your grasp of fine distinctions.

Statements about a Person's Physical Condition

Physical-condition statements generally: Look for a person's statement about her ***physical condition***.

☛ **Treatment or diagnosis:** If the statement is made for purposes of obtaining ***medical diagnosis or treatment***, then it's admissible if told to a physician, nurse, ambulance driver, hospital check-in clerk, etc. (FRE 803(4)).

Example: P is injured in a car crash with D, taken to the hospital, and then complains of severe pain. P dies from the injuries. The statement is admissible at trial against D to prove damages.

☞ **Past or present sensations:** Remember that in this "diagnosis or treatment" situation, the statement can be about ***either past or present*** physical sensation.

Example: P says to Doctor, "Before the accident, I had no pain, and was able to hold a full-time job doing heavy lifting." As long as this statement related to P's attempt to get treatment or diagnosis, Doctor can repeat the statement at P's trial, even though the statement, when made, related to P's past rather than present physical condition.

☞ **Anticipation of litigation:** Even if the doctor is consulted only in ***anticipation of litigation*** (e.g., to get the doctor to testify as an expert witness for the plaintiff), the person's statements can come in, as long as they're relevant to "diagnosis."

☞ **Statement about cause of condition:** Commonly-tested: the ***cause*** of the injury is included in the statement. If (and only if) it's ***pertinent to the diagnosis***, then it's admissible.

Examples:

❑ Patient tells Doctor, "When I was hit by the car, my elbow hit the ground hard and I heard a sharp crack." The statement is admissible.

❑ Hospital record reads, "Patient says ladder collapsed and Patient fell." The record is probably admissible to prove cause of accident.

❑ Patient tells Doctor, "I was on my bicycle and D ran a stop light and knocked me to the ground." The part about the stop light is inadmissible, because it's not reasonably pertinent to the diagnosis; the rest of the statement is probably admissible.

☞ **Statements made by the doctor:** Check to make sure the statement is made *to* the doctor, not *by* the doctor.

Example: Civil suit involving injuries from car crash. P is examined by MD. MD signs an affidavit saying that P is suffering from back spasms. The affidavit will not be admissible under the "statement of physical condition" exception, because it's MD's statement about what he found, not a repeating of P's statement about his physical condition.

☞ **Statement made by one assisting the patient:** The statement can be made by ***one other than the patient*** (e.g., a friend or relative assisting the patient), if it concerns the patient's physical condition and is reasonably pertinent to treatment or diagnosis.

Example: P is unconscious after car accident; H, P's husband, brings her to hospital and says to ER doctor, "She was hit from the rear while on her bike." Admissible.

☛ **Statements not in connection with treatment or diagnosis:** But where the statement about the speaker's physical condition is *not* made for the purpose of getting treatment or diagnosis, different (and more limiting) rules apply.

☞ **Present, not past, condition:** Most important (and most often tested): The statement must be about the speaker's ***present*** (not past) physical condition.

Example: P says to W, his wife (a layperson), "Honey, I fell on the ice in front of D's house yesterday and it really hurt when it happened." Not admissible, because not a statement about P's *present* physical condition.

☞ **Statement to layperson:** On the other hand, the statement can be made to a ***layperson***, i.e., one not connected with the giving of medical care or diagnosis.

Example: Same facts as prior example, but P says to wife W, "My back is still hurting from the fall yesterday." W can repeat the statement at trial.

☞ **Present sense impression:** Note that a statement about one's present physical condition may also come in as a statement of ***present sense impression***.

Example: P says over telephone, "Ouch, I just cut myself slicing bread."

☛ **Need not be unavailable:** For the two categories of "statement about physical condition" (for treatment/diagnosis or not), note that the declarant ***need not be unavailable***.

Statements about Declarant's Mental State

Present state of mind, generally: Statements about the declarant's ***present state of mind*** are sometimes admissible, sometimes not.

☛ **Function:** When a declarant expresses ***an intention or desire to do something***, the "present state of mind" exception usually applies, and the statement is admissible to prove that the declarant ***in fact did that something***.

Example 1: Declarant's statement, "I'm going to call P and tell him to go ahead with the portrait" is admissible to prove that Declarant probably later accepted P's offer to paint Declarant's portrait.

Example 2: Declarant tells W, "I'm going to use my friend Ed's cabin this weekend." Admissible to prove that Declarant went to the cabin that weekend.

☞ **Suicide:** Common scenario: Declarant's desire to commit suicide.

Example: "I have nothing to live for," admissible to prove that declarant probably committed suicide.

☞ **Action with another person:** Watch out for cases where declarant mentions that he or she plans to take an act ***in conjunction with another person***. The statement will only be admissible to prove that the ***other person*** participated in the act, if there is ***independent corroboration*** that that participation occurred (and some courts won't let it in even in that event).

Example: Bonnie tells W, "Clyde and I plan to hold up the post office tomorrow." This will clearly be admissible to show that Bonnie held up the post office, but will be admissible to show that Clyde held up the post office only if there's some independent corroborative evidence that he did. Furthermore, some courts won't allow it against Clyde even with corroboration.

☛ **Common application of this rule:** Murder victim says, "I'm going to meet with D." Not admissible to show D met with or murdered the victim, unless there's corroboration that they met.

☛ **Past state of mind:** Statements about declarant's ***past state of mind*** are generally ***inadmissible***. In other words, the declarant's statement must be about her ***then-existing state of mind***, not her state of mind at some materially earlier moment.

Example: Defamation action. D newspaper offers testimony by W that Reporter told W, "When I wrote that piece on P two days ago, I believed every word of it." Not admissible, because Reporter's statement relates to his state of mind on a prior, not the present, occasion.

☛ **Memory or belief:** Similarly, statements about declarant's ***present memory or belief about past events*** are generally ***inadmissible to show the fact remembered or believed***.

Example: Victim says, "I believe that Dr. Shepard has poisoned me." Inadmissible, because although it's a statement about declarant's present belief, that belief relates to a past event.

☞ **Will contests:** But remember that there's an exception for ***will*** contests. (FRE 803(3), last clause.)

Example: Decedent tells W, "In the will I wrote last year, I left $10,000 to my son Mark." Admissible to show that at the time the will was written, Decedent intended to leave Mark the money.

Excited Utterances

Excited utterances, generally: Whenever the declarant ***blurts something out*** at the ***scene of an accident or crime***, the statement is probably admissible as an ***"excited utterance."***

☛ **FRE test:** Memorize the FRE test (803(2)): the exception applies to "a statement relating to a ***startling event or condition,*** made while the declarant was under the ***stress of excitement that it caused***." Check for both elements: (1) ***startling event*** or condition; and (2) stress ***caused by*** the event or condition.

☛ **Amount of time:** Most frequently-tested: Make sure that the ***amount of time*** that has passed since the event is ***short enough*** that the declarant is ***still under the stress***. Be skeptical of anything more than 1/2 hour or so, unless declarant was in shock, unconscious, or otherwise unable to reflect about the matter.

Example: A statement made by an accident victim the day after the accident, where the victim never went into shock or lost consciousness, will clearly not qualify.

☞ **Contemporaneity not required:** But *some* time may pass between event and utterance — it's the *present sense impression* exception (see below), *not* the excited utterance exception, that requires true contemporaneity between event and statement.

☛ **Identity of declarant unknown:** Frequently-tested: Even if the ***identity of the declarant is unknown***, the statement is still ***admissible***.

Example: P falls on steps. At the civil trial, W testifies for defense, "Just after P fell, I heard someone in the crowd say, 'She was taking the steps three at a time and tripped.' " Admissible even if the declarant's identity is not shown.

Present Sense Impression

Present-sense generally: If you have a declarant ***describing or explaining an event that's occurring at that very moment***, or that has ***just*** occurred, think of the ***"present***

sense impression" (PSI) exception. A present sense impression must be ***contemporaneous*** with, or ***immediately*** following, the observation.

☛ **Compared with excited utterance:** Distinguish present sense impression from excited utterance:

☞ **Stress or surprise not required:** PSI is narrower, in the sense that very little time must elapse between event and statement. But it's broader, in the sense that PSI may relate to a ***non-startling*** and ***non-stressful event***. So look for PSI especially where the event appears routine and non-startling at the time.

Example: A witness to a car accident reports to a police officer, "A few minutes ago I saw. . . ." Not a PSI, because not contemporaneous. (Might be excited utterance, depending on how "shook up" the witness still was.)

Example: Witness watches a car accident, and within 5 seconds after impact, says, "The red car didn't have its headlights on." PSI (and probably also excited utterance).

☛ **Current physical condition:** Where declarant is making a statement about his ***current physical condition***, especially about ***pain*** he's feeling, note that this is likely to be ***both*** PSI and "statement of physical condition."

Past Recollection Recorded

Past recollection, generally: If a witness on the stand ***cannot remember***, and there exists a writing written by the witness regarding the subject matter of the questioning, consider whether the ***past recollection recorded*** exception applies.

☛ **Requirements:** Check for the following requirements:

[1] the writer (or the source of the information) ***had personal knowledge*** of what he was writing;

[2] the writing was made ***shortly after the event***, so that it was fresh in the writer's or source's memory;

[3] the writer or source can testify as to the ***accuracy*** of the writing; and

[4] the writer/witness's recollection is ***presently impaired***.

☛ **First-hand knowledge:** Most-often tested: Did the writer have the required ***first-hand knowledge*** of the subject matter of the writing? If the writer is recording another person's declaration, the required knowledge will usually be missing if only the writer testifies.

☞ **Common scenario:** A police officer writes an accident report at the scene of an accident, and includes in it a statement by W, a witness. At trial, the officer cannot by himself read W's statement from his report, because the officer has no first-hand knowledge of the matters recited in the W's statement. (But the statement *can* be introduced if W testifies to having made it when his own memory was fresh, *and* the officer also testifies to writing it down accurately.)

Business Records

Business records, generally: Whenever there's an attempt to admit a ***writing*** into evidence to prove that an event mentioned in the writing occurred, consider whether the document may be admitted as a ***business record***.

☛ **Test for business record:** A writing is admissible as a business record if: (1) the writing was made ***at or near the time*** of an event, (2) by, or from information supplied by, a ***person with knowledge***; (3) the writing was ***kept in the course of a regularly conducted business activity***; and (4) it was the business' ***regular practice to make the record*** (i.e., the record was ***"regularly kept"***), (5) all as shown by the testimony of a ***qualified witness***. FRE 803(6).

Examples of business records:

- ❑ An answering service's telephone message log;
- ❑ a patient's chart in a hospital;
- ❑ a business' invoice showing that a shipment was made.

☞ **Two types of records:** Many times the same document may be considered both a business and a public record. Don't forget to mention both options.

Example: A police report made at the scene of an accident, in a jurisdiction that defines "business" broadly to include "institutions" and non-profit organizations, as the FRE do.

☛ **Document must be offered in evidence:** Do a threshold check to see if the business records exception is even plausible to apply in the circumstances. The fact that the substance of a witness's trial testimony has previously been recorded in a business record is irrelevant — unless the ***file or record itself*** is being ***admitted into evidence***, the business records exception doesn't apply.

Example: Supervisor testifies at trial to details about a construction job, including the number of workers used and the number of hours spent. The facts indicate that Supervisor had previously recorded these facts in a notebook, as part of his office routine. The notebook is not sought to be introduced. Because the notebook isn't coming in, the fact that the matters on which Supervisor is testifying were recorded in a business record is irrelevant — Supervisor's testimony is admissible as his first-hand non-hearsay knowledge, without reference to the business records exception.

☛ **Regular course of business:** Look for a record that was made in the ***regular course of business*** and in conjunction with the company's primary business.

☞ **Accident or investigative report:** Commonly tested: ***Accident or investigative reports*** made by a business in anticipation of litigation. If the report is not related to a business activity of the entity, then it is not a business record, even though it is done routinely. In other words, if the sole purpose of the accident report is to ***prepare for litigation***, it's probably not a business record; but if it's done for "regular" business reasons (e.g., to prevent similar occurrences by changing the way the business operates), it may be a business record.

Example: After an on-campus rape, Prexy, President of the College, interviews the victim in order to help the police arrest the rapist. Prexy takes notes of the victim's statements, and puts the notes in a file. This is probably not a business record, because it's probably not sufficiently related to the college's regular business.

☛ **Personal knowledge:** Confirm that the source of the material had ***personal knowledge*** of the items reported. By "source of the material," we don't necessarily mean the person who wrote the entries. *A* may recite matters to *B*, who enters them in the record; in that case, all that's required is that *A*, not *B*, have personal knowledge.

Example: *A* and *B* both work for Company. *A* inspects the contents of each shipment, and orally says to *B*, "The computer-generated invoice for this shipment is correct." *B* then writes on the invoice, "Shipment of these items confirmed." If *B* testifies at trial that the invoices were routinely marked this way based on oral statements by a person with knowledge, then a particular such invoice is admissible to show that the goods noted on it were in fact shipped; no testimony by *A* is needed.

☛ **Foundation:** Check to see that there was a ***foundation*** laid for each business record. However, this foundation can be laid by anyone with personal knowledge of ***the routine*** (i.e., that the records were routinely kept in the ordinary course of the business, based on input from someone with personal knowledge, etc.), ***not necessarily someone with personal knowledge of how the routine was applied in this particular instance.***

Example: In the above example, even *C* — let's say, an office manager who did not personally make the entries — could lay the foundation by saying in essence "It was our company practice to have each shipment checked by someone, and then the checker or someone working with the checker noted the confirmation on the invoice." In fact, it wouldn't matter that *C* didn't know the identity of the person who had the knowledge, or the person who made the notation, in this particular invoice — it's enough that *C* has knowledge of how the routine *generally* worked.

☞ **Certification:** Also, keep in mind that this foundation need ***not*** be laid by ***live testimony*** — it can instead be laid by a ***certification*** (a document) from a person with relevant knowledge, who says in the certification that the record satisfies the business-records exception. Cite to FRE 902(11) (certified records of regularly conducted activity) on this point.

- **Business duty:** Check that the ***source*** of the knowledge had a ***business duty*** to make the report. If not, many (though not all) courts will keep the evidence out, perhaps on grounds of untrustworthiness.

  - *Typical application: **Accident report**,* in which declarant is a ***witness who does not work for the business*** that is preparing the report.

    Example: P slips and falls in Store. W, another shopper, says to Manager, "P was running when she fell." Manager quotes this statement in an "accident report" routinely kept by Store. Most courts won't allow this report to come in as a business record, because W was not an employee of the business, and thus had no business duty to supply the information; the fact that W is not under the business' control also may make it less likely that W's information is trustworthy.

  - **Some other hearsay exception:** However, even if the source did not have a business duty to make the report, the source's statement as recorded in the business record will be admissible if it independently falls within ***some other hearsay exception***.

    Example: Same facts as above, but it's *P*, not *L*, who says to Manager, "I was running when I fell." Manager's report will be admissible against P, because the report was kept as a business record [assuming that it was kept for regular business reasons and not in anticipation of litigation], and P's own statement contained within the report is an admission when used against P.

- **Broad definition of "business":** Remember that ***"business"*** is defined very ***broadly*** in FRE 803(6) to include non-profits, "organizations," "occupations" and "callings."

- **Trustworthiness:** In any business records issue, always check (and in an essay, discuss) the additional requirement of ***trustworthiness***. Quote FRE 803(6): the exception applies only if "neither the source of information nor the method or circumstances of preparation indicate a lack of trustworthiness."

  - **Accident report:** Pay special attention to trustworthiness where an ***accident report*** is involved — if the business making the report is likely to be a defendant in litigation, the desire to avoid liability probably makes the report untrustworthy.

  - **Lack of detail:** Lack of trustworthiness can also be indicated by a lack of ***detail*** about ***where the information came from***.

    Example: On a death certificate, the cause of death reads, "Rung of ladder broke, and victim fell on head." If there's no indication on the certificate of where the information came from, the certificate is probably too untrustworthy to be admitted as a business record.

☞ **Computer printouts:** Pay special attention to trustworthiness where a ***computer printout*** is involved. Include in your answer (if essay) the special requirements that testimony include a description of: the equipment, how the computer was programmed and how errors in programming are detected and corrected, how data is entered, how errors in data are caught and corrected, and how unauthorized access to program or data files is prevented.

☛ **Non-occurrence:** Remember that ***non-occurrence of an event*** may be proven by ***lack of a record***, if it was the regular practice of the business to record all such matters.

Example: Libel suit against D newspaper, in a state which requires P to show he first asked for a retraction. D's office manager testifies that it's the routine practice of the paper to carefully keep in a single file all demands for retraction, and that he has searched the file for any demand by P, and found none. Admissible as a business record to show no retraction demand was made by P.

☛ **Multiple hearsay:** Be alert to ***multiple hearsay*** problems, which must be analyzed layer by layer. If the business record ***quotes a statement made by someone outside of the business***, and the record is offered to show the truth of that statement, the statement must itself fall within a hearsay exception.

Example: An operator of an answering service keeps a "Telephone Log" of all messages received. An entry in it reads, "May 3, Mr. D called P, said he accepted P's offer to paint D's portrait for $4,000." In P's contract suit against D, the log can be offered by P, but only after a multiple-hearsay analysis. The log comes in as a business record, to show that D's statement was made. D's statement itself comes in as an admission.

☞ **Statement by person working in the business:** But where the business record quotes a statement by one working ***in*** the business, no multiple hearsay problem exists — the business records exception covers everything.

Example: A and B both work for Company. A tells B, "The shipment on order 256 was complete; I checked." B writes on the invoice, "Shipment complete." Because A worked in the business, the invoice can come in as a business record to prove the shipment was complete, and no independent hearsay analysis of A's oral statement is needed.

Public Records

Governmental body: Whenever a document is prepared by a ***governmental body***, be alert to the possibility that the document may be admissible as a ***public record***. (FRE

803(8)).

☛ **3 contexts:** Look for the public records exception in three main contexts:

[1]Report by government about its activities: A government agency makes a report about its ***own activities***.

Example: To prove a police department tapped his phone, D could introduce an internal report prepared by the department saying, "We tapped D's phone."

[2]Observations in line of duty: A government official makes a written record of ***observations he made in the line of duty***, if his job required him to make those observations.

Example: In P's civil suit against D for a car crash, P could introduce a police report in which Officer says, "I saw the accident; D ran a red light."

☞**No criminal use:** This "observations made in the line of duty" exception does not allow the ***government*** to use the report ***against D in a criminal case***.

Example: Officer spots someone running away after a burglary, and writes in his report, "The burglar was a 6'2" hispanic male." In a criminal case against D for the burglary, this report can't be introduced against D. But it *can* be used *by* D to show that D doesn't fit the description.

[3]Investigation with factual findings: Government ***conducts an investigation***, and makes ***factual findings*** in that investigation. The factual findings can be introduced.

Example: The National Transportation Safety Board investigates the crash of an airplane, and finds pilot error. In a civil suit against the airline, this report is admissible as a public record to show airline negligence.

☞**No criminal use:** Again, this exception ***can't be used by the government against D*** in a criminal case.

Example: The FBI investigates a bank robbery, and concludes in a report, "Devon did it." This report can't be introduced against Devon at his criminal trial, though it could introduced *by* Devon as a public record, if he so desired.

☛ **Other hearsay exception:** Be alert to the possibility that the document is a non-qualifying public record yet falls within ***some other hearsay exception***. Courts are split about what to do where the document satisfies a non-public-records hearsay exception (e.g., business records, or past recollection recorded) and is also a public record that's inadmissible under the public-records provision.

☞ **Police report:** In the most common case raising this issue, a ***police report*** about a crime might be an investigative report (a type of public record) and a business record. Here, the rule preventing the public record from being introduced against a criminal defendant will prevail, preventing the business-records use.

Learned Treatises

Treatise exception, generally: Where a published reference work is sought to be admitted for the truth of matters stated in it, think of the "learned treatise" exception (FRE 803(18)). Most frequently tested issues:

- **Adjunct to testimony:** The treatise can't be "free-standing" — it must come in as an ***adjunct*** to testimony by an ***expert*** witness. (It can only come in if it's ***"called to the attention"*** of an expert witness on ***cross***, or ***relied on*** by an expert on ***direct***.)

- **Not an exhibit:** Make sure that the treatise is not entered into evidence ***as an exhibit*** — all that may happen is that the publication's ***contents*** are ***read*** into the record.

- **Shown to be reliable authority:** Make sure that the treatise is shown to be a ***reliable authority***. There are three ways to do this: by the witness herself, by another expert, or by judicial notice.

  - **No reliance required:** When the treatise is used on cross, don't be sidetracked by the fact that the ***witness didn't rely*** on the treatise — as long as some other expert says that it's a reliable authority, or the judge takes judicial notice that it is, that's enough to allow it to be read.

    Example: On direct, Expert 1 states that "Causes of Cancer" is a reliable authority. Now, Expert 2 may be cross-examined with passages from the book, even if Expert 2 says the book isn't authoritative, and/or denies having relied on it; these passages can be substantive as well as impeaching evidence.

- **Must be scholarly:** The exception applies only to scholarly works. Thus it typically doesn't apply to articles in popular magazines or in general newspapers.

Commercial Publications

- **Published compilations, generally:** "Compilations" can be used, if relied upon by the public or specialists for the type of information in question. (FRE 803(17). ***"Lists," "directories"*** and ***"market quotations"*** are examples.

  Example: D is charged with burglary. He asserts the alibi defense that he was watching a particular movie on cable tv at the time. The tv listings page from the local cable guide may be introduced to prove that the movie wasn't playing on any channel at the time in question.

Ancient Documents

☛ **20-year rule:** Under the FRE, a document in existence for ***20 years*** or more can be admitted as a hearsay exception (the "ancient documents" exception), if its authenticity is established.

Example: The issue is whether a deed issued 15 years ago was made while the grantor, Bill, was of sound mind. An affidavit by Bill's brother Dave, signed at about the same time, states that Dave thinks Bill is insane for enumerated reasons. The affidavit is not admissible as an ancient document, because it's too new; but if it were 22 years old, it could be introduced as an ancient document, to prove that at that time Bill was insane.

THE "DECLARANT UNAVAILABLE" EXCEPTIONS

The remaining exceptions require that the declarant be ***"unavailable."***

Sample fact patterns: Here are examples of fact patterns where the witness will be considered to be unavailable:

- ❑ W is ***dead***;
- ❑ W deliberately ***avoids service***;
- ❑ W does not respond to a ***subpoena***;
- ❑ W takes the stand, but ***refuses to testify***. (Most often, W takes the 5th Amendment.) It doesn't matter whether W's refusal is lawful (i.e., a privilege in fact applies) or wrongful (i.e., W can be held in contempt).
- ❑ W claims a ***lack of memory*** as to the declarant's statement.

Former Testimony

Former testimony, generally: Where there is past testimony that one party wishes to offer at the present trial, but the testifier is unavailable, consider the hearsay exception for ***former testimony***.

☛ **Hearing required:** Remember that the former testimony must have been given at a ***"hearing."*** (FRE 804(b)(1)). A "hearing" is in essence a proceeding in which the testifier testifies ***under oath***, and is subject to ***cross-examination***.

Examples that qualify:

- ❑ A ***preliminary examination*** in a criminal case.
- ❑ A ***deposition***.
- ❑ A ***previous trial*** concerning a related or similar charge.

Examples that don't qualify:

- ❑ A sworn ***affidavit***. (This is not a "hearing" and isn't subject to cross-examination).

- ❑ A signed ***transcript*** of a ***confession or interrogation*** in front of the police or the prosecutor. (Same shortcomings as affidavit.)

☛ **Opportunity and motive:** Also remember that the party against whom the former testimony is being offered must have had the ***"opportunity and similar motive"*** to "develop" the testimony (usually by ***cross-examining the witness***) at the time it was given. (FRE 804(b)(1)).

☞ **Common "distractor":** Profs. will often try to fool you by saying in the fact pattern that no cross-examination took place in the earlier proceeding. That's irrelevant — as long as the party against whom the testimony is now sought to be introduced had an ***opportunity*** and ***incentive*** to cross-examine, the fact he didn't ***take*** that opportunity doesn't block the former testimony exception from applying.

Example: Peter is injured when a Twig-model car he owns, made by Carco, explodes. Peter brings a civil suit against Carco in Alaska state court. In that suit, Peter calls Expert to testify that the Twig was defectively designed. Carco doesn't cross-examine Expert. Later, Paula sues Carco when her Twig explodes. Expert is now unavailable. Paula may put Expert's testimony at the Peter-vs-Carco trial into evidence as substantive proof that the Twig is defectively designed. Since Carco had a similar motive to cross-examine Expert in the Peter trial as it would have today if Expert were giving live testimony, it doesn't matter that Carco didn't in fact conduct any cross.

Dying Declarations

Dying declarations, generally: When the declarant is ***badly injured*** or ***very sick*** at the time of the declaration, consider whether her statement may be admitted as a dying declaration.

☛ **Cause or circumstances of impending death:** Most important element to look for: that the statement concerned the ***cause or circumstances of declarant's impending death.***

Example where this element is not satisfied: Duane is charged with murdering Victor. Duane wants to put into evidence a statement made by Edward to Walter, in which Edward said, "Now that I'm about to die of AIDS, I wanted to get something off my chest — it was me, not Duane, who killed Victor." (Edward in fact died soon thereafter.) Not admissible as a dying declaration, because the point for which the statement is sought to be admitted relates to who killed Victor, not to the cause or circumstances of Edward's death.

Example where this element is satisfied: Valerie, believing she will soon die of gunshot wounds, says, "Dexter shot me." If Valerie dies (or is otherwise unavailable at Dexter's trial), admissible against Dexter to show that Dexter shot her.

- ☛ **Death not necessary:** There is no requirement that the declarant actually die (let alone that she die from the thing she thought she would die of). But she must be unavailable.
- ☛ **Fear of imminent death:** The declarant must believe that she will die ***imminently***. Thus if declarant believes that she has successfully escaped, say, a murder attempt, the exception doesn't apply.
- ☛ **Homicide and civil:** Remember that the FRE allow for the exception in ***criminal homicide*** prosecutions (but no other kinds of criminal cases) as well as in ***civil*** cases. (FRE 804(b)(2)).

<u>**Declarations Against Interest**</u>

Declarations against interest, generally: Whenever the declarant makes a statement that, at the time made, seems ***damaging to the declarant***, consider whether it's a declaration against interest.

- ☛ **Who can use:** Look for the declarant to be either a ***non-party***, or a party who wants to ***use his own statement***. (If the declarant is the party ***against whom*** the statement is to be used, you can avoid fulfilling the requirements of a declaration against interest — unavailability, against interest when made, and personal knowledge — by treating the statement as an admission.)
- ☛ **Pecuniary or penal interest:** Make sure that the statement was against the declarant's ***pecuniary or penal interest*** when made. (But remember that at common law, only statements against pecuniary interest, *not* those exposing the declarant to criminal liability, count.)

  ☞ **Passengers'statement about driver:** Common fact pattern: A *passenger* in a car makes a statement to a police officer at the scene of a crime or accident, and the statement is incriminating to (or against the financial interest of) the *driver* but *not the passenger.* This doesn't qualify.

  Examples:

  [1] Car accident; Passenger tells police, "We should have had our lights on."

  [2] Car accident; Passenger tells bystander, "We were coming back from a wedding at which we had both been drinking."

  In each case, Passenger's statement is against the driver's pecuniary and penal interest, but not against Passenger's own interest, because a passenger isn't responsible for putting the car's lights on or not being drunk in the vehicle. Therefore, ***neither statement qualifies*** as a declaration against interest.

☞ **Declarant's knowledge:** Make sure that the declarant ***knew***, at the time of the statement, that it was against her interest. (Hindsight doesn't count.)

☛ **Declarant unavailable:** Confirm that the ***declarant is unavailable***. This is an easy one to forget, because unlike many of the other "declarant unavailable" exceptions (e.g., dying declaration), there's nothing in the core declaration-against-interest scenario to jog your mind into focusing on this requirement.

☛ **Distinction:** In an essay, mention whether it's a declaration against pecuniary interest or against penal interest (or both).

☞ **Most frequently-tested:** A statement that would subject the declarant to ***criminal liability***. (Note in your answer that at common-law, exposure to criminal liability doesn't suffice, but that under FRE 804(b)(3) it does.)

Example 1: P sues Insurance Co. for failing to pay off on insurance claim; Insurance Co. defends on grounds that it cancelled policy for non-payment, and sent P the statutorily-required notice doing so. P offers testimony by Neighbor that Mailman, who delivered all mail to P's neighborhood during the time in question (and who is now in prison in another state) told Neighbor shortly after the time of alleged cancellation, "I just threw away a lot of the mail recently instead of delivering it, because my back hurt." Admissible, because the statement could have led to Mailman's prosecution for destruction of U.S. mail.

Example 2: Suit against a ladder manufacturer for personal injuries suffered by P when P fell from a ladder. The manufacturer may present testimony by W, who says, "X [now unavailable] told me that the fall happened because he, X, kicked the ladder out from under P." Admissible, because it was against X's pecuniary interest when made (since it exposed X to a civil suit by P), as well as against X's penal interest (prosecution for battery.)

☛ **Use by defendant:** In criminal prosecutions where the ***defendant*** wants to introduce the out-of-court statement, beware the special rule that kicks in when the declarant ***inculpates himself*** by the same statement that ***exculpates the defendant*** — here, the declaration-against-interest exception applies only if there are ***"corroborating circumstances"*** that ***"clearly indicate [the statement's] trustworthiness***." (FRE 804(b)(3)(B).)

Example: Murder trial of Dexter, for killing Valerie. Dexter produces testimony of Officer, a police officer, who says, "Zeke [now dead] confessed to me that he killed Valerie." Unless there's some independent evidence indicating that Zeke in fact killed Valerie, Officer's testimony is not admissible as a declaration-against-interest.

- **Use by prosecution:** In criminal prosecutions where the ***prosecution*** wants to use the statement, check to see if the declarant had a ***self-serving motive*** that conflicted with the supposedly against-interest aspects. If so, the statement ***won't*** be admissible.

- **Confession:** *Key scenario:* Declarant ***"confesses"*** after being caught red-handed. During the course of the confession, he ***implicates D***, against whom the confession is now sought to be used. (In this fact pattern, Declarant is "unavailable" at D's trial, usually because Declarant pleads the Fifth.) If Declarant was trying to ***minimize his own culpability*** (e.g., "D was the ringleader, and I was just the errand boy"), or was trying to ***"curry favor"*** with the authorities by implicating D, you should conclude that the declaration wasn't really against Declarant's interest when made, and should therefore not be admitted under the against-interest rule.

  - **Confrontation Clause:** Also, in any question falling into this Key Scenario (Declarant gives police a confession implicating D, then is unavailable at trial), remember that the statement would almost certainly be blocked by D's ***Confrontation Clause*** rights under the federal constitution. Cite *Crawford v. Washington* and *Davis v. Washington*. As long as Declarant's confession was "testimonial" (and if he made it in response to police interrogation, it would be), it can't be used against D whom it also implicates, unless Declarant takes the stand and is available for cross by D.

  - **Collateral statements:** Finally, remember that the ***precise statement itself*** must be "against interest" — it's not enough that the statement is ***"collateral to"*** an against-interest statement. So even if parts of Declarant's confession are clearly against his interest, other parts that aren't against his interest (e.g., parts where he implicates someone else) can't come in as being collateral to the against-interest parts. Cite *Williamson v. U.S.* on this point.

- **Near death:** If the declarant is ***near death*** at the time of the declaration, question whether the statement is truly against his interests.

  Example: Same facts as earlier example [Zeke confesses to crime for which Dexter is now charged.] Now, assume that Zeke, at the time of his confession, knew he was dying of a bullet wound. He probably wasn't very worried about criminal liability, so the court may well refuse to admit the statement, on the grounds that it doesn't have the special guarantee of truthfulness that serves as the basis for the against-interest exception.

  - **Interest in preserving assets:** Where the statement is against pecuniary interest, however, consider the possibility that the declarant, though dying, had an interest in ***preserving his estate*** for inheritance by his next-of-kin. In that case, the impending death would not be enough to remove the declarant's pecuniary interest.

PRIOR STATEMENTS BY TESTIFYING WITNESSES

Prior Inconsistent Statements

General rule: Remember that under the FRE (but not at common law), a prior inconsistent statement by a trial witness is sometimes admissible as substantive evidence.

☛ **Requirements:** Remember the two requirements for a prior inconsistent statement to be substantively admissible:

[1] the declarant must ***testify*** and be available for cross; and

[2] the prior statement must have been made ***under oath*** at a ***trial, hearing, "other proceeding"*** or ***deposition***.

Example: In a multiple-car collision case, W testifies for P that D went through a red light. D may contradict W's testimony by reading into the record W's statement at a deposition taken in the case, in which W said that the light was yellow when D went through it. This statement is admissible substantively, to prove that the light was yellow (as well as admissible to impeach W).

☛ **Nonhearsay:** Note in your answer that the FRE classify admissible prior statements as ***nonhearsay***, not as hearsay admissible because of an exception.

☛ **Distinguished from former-testimony exception:** Don't confuse this exception with the ***"former testimony"*** exception. Here, the statement must be in ***conflict*** with the current testimony. On the other hand, there's ***no requirement that the prior statement have been subject to cross examination.***

Example: A prior inconsistent statement from a witness's testimony at a *grand jury hearing* is admissible against the defendant, even though that defendant had no lawyer present to cross-examine the witness. In contrast, the statement would not be admissible under the "former testimony" exception because no cross was possible.

☛ **Present testimony:** Make sure the ***declarant*** is ***presently testifying.*** If the prior inconsistent statement is offered to contradict a prior out-of-court declaration rather than the declarant's live testimony, the exception doesn't apply.

Example: Murder prosecution of D for shooting V. The prosecution puts on W1, who says, "One day before V died of his gunshot wounds, he was pretty sure he'd die, and he said to me 'D did this to me.' " [This is admitted as a dying declaration.] Now, the defense offers W2, V's friend, who says, "After the shooting, when V thought he'd recover, he said to me in his hospital room, 'X did this to me.' " W2's testimony is not admissible as a prior inconsistent statement because it's not being offered to contradict V's live at-trial testimony. (Also, it doesn't qualify because V wasn't under oath at a proceeding when he made the statement to W2.) However, W2's testimony *is* admissible to *impeach W1*.

- ☛ **Impeachment/substantive distinction:** Distinguish between use of a prior inconsistent statement for ***impeachment*** purposes and use for ***substantive*** purposes. What we're talking about here is substantive use. (But don't forget that if you determine that the statement is substantively admissible, then it's automatically also available for impeachment.)

- ☛ **Consider admission:** If the statement was not given under oath at a formal proceeding, but was made by (and is sought to be used against) a ***party***, consider whether it's admissible as an ***admission***.

Prior Consistent Statement

Not often tested: Prior consistent statements are rarely tested. When they are, remember the FRE approach: the consistent statement is admissible only to rebut an express or implied charge that the witness has been ***improperly influenced***, or has recently ***fabricated*** his story. Note that the prior consistent statement must have been made ***before*** the influence or fabrication came into existence.

Prior Identification

Identification statements, generally: Remember that prior statements of ***identification*** are fairly easy to admit. Under FRE 801(d)(1)(C), a statement that "identifies a person as someone the declarant perceived earlier" is nonhearsay if the declarant testifies at trial and is available for cross.

- ☛ **Typical scenario:** So the typical scenario involves a trial witness who testifies that ***at some earlier point in time***, she identified D as the perpetrator.

  Example: W testifies at trial, "After the rape, I picked D out at a lineup as the person who raped me." Admissible.

- ☛ **Change in appearance:** Common scenario: W is asked at trial to identify the defendant as the perpetrator of the crime charged. She says she can't, because his appearance is now different. The prosecution then asks W to repeat the previous identification that took place after the crime.

  Example: W says at trial, "I can't now ID the defendant as the man who raped me, because the defendant has a beard covering his face, and the man who raped me didn't, and I can't tell if the two are the same." The prosecution then shows that W picked a person out of a lineup conducted after the rape, and that the person picked was in fact D. Admissible.

Residual ("Catchall") Exception

Catchall generally: In any hearsay problem where you don't find any exception that applies, consider whether the ***residual ("catchall") exception*** (FRE 807) applies.

- **Most important:** The two most important things to watch for in analyzing the catchall are:

  [1] The statement must have "***circumstantial guarantees of trustworthiness***."

  [2] The statement must be ***"more probative"*** on the point for which it is offered than any other reasonably available evidence. Therefore, be most on the lookout for the catchall when the ***declarant is unavailable*** (though unavailability is not a strict requirement).

- **Grand jury testimony against D:** Most likely scenario for use of the catchall: The prosecution wants to use a person's ***grand jury testimony*** against a criminal ***defendant***. (This can't come in under the former testimony exception, because the defendant wasn't present during the grand jury testimony.) Usually this happens where the testimony is from someone who refuses to testify at trial.

  ☞ **Witness was intimidated:** If the reason the witness refuses to testify is because he was ***intimidated by D***, then the answer is easy: point out that a separate Federal Rule, 804(b)(6), makes the statement admissible because the declarant's unavailability was procured by the defendant's intentional wrongdoing. (And, by the way, note that under 804(b)(6), you ***don't*** have to consider whether the declaration has any ***guarantees of trustworthiness*** — even a completely ***untrustworthy*** declaration gets ***automatically admitted*** if the declarant is unavailable because of the defendant's intentional wrongdoing.)

  ☞ **Confrontation Clause:** Also, in any scenario where W's grand jury testimony is sought to be used by the prosecution against D in D's criminal trial, note that D's rights under the ***Confrontation Clause*** of the Sixth Amendment probably prevent this use if W is not available to be cross-examined about the statement by D at D's trial. See *Crawford v. Washington*, saying that any out-of-court "testimonial" statement by W (including grand jury testimony) can't be admitted against D in a criminal trial if W doesn't take the stand.

- **Near miss:** Also, allude to the "near miss" problem, if the facts just miss qualifying for one of the traditional hearsay exceptions. Say that most courts don't hold the "near miss" against the proponent, and allow the catchall to be used despite the near-miss if the required "circumstantial guarantees of trustworthiness," etc., are present.

Exam Tips on
CONFRONTATION AND COMPULSORY PROCESS

Whenever your question involves a criminal prosecution, and evidence is being introduced against the defendant, check for the possibility of a Confrontation Clause problem.

Most commonly, you'll have to decide whether the use of *hearsay* presents a Confrontation Clause problem. If so, do the following analysis:

- **Check for "testimonial" declarations:** First, check to see whether the out-of-court declaration is ***"testimonial."*** (The main types of "testimonial" declarations are ones made ***at preliminary hearings, grand jury hearings, prior trials,*** and above all, ones made during ***police interrogations*** and in ***forensic reports.***)

  - **Testimonial:** If the out-of-court declaration ***is testimonial***, say that the Confrontation Clause blocks it from being used against the accused unless the declarant is made available for cross by the accused either at the time the statement is made or at the accused's trial. [Cite *Crawford v. Washington* and *Davis v. Washington* on this point.]

    Example: Several hours after the fatal shooting of V by persons unknown, X is questioned by the police about the shooting. X says, "I didn't shoot V, but I did lend my gun to D knowing that D wanted to shoot V, and I then watched as D did the shooting." At D's murder trial, X pleads the Fifth. The prosecution then offers (as a declaration against interest) testimony by Ollie, the police detective who interviewed X, about what X said concerning the shooting. Because X's statement during interrogation was "testimonial" (i.e., it was made as part of a police investigation into past criminality, not, say, to deal with a present emergency), it can't come in against D unless X is made available for cross by D. Since X has pleaded the Fifth, he's not available for cross. Therefore, the Confrontation Clause blocks X's statement from being used against D.

    - **D intentionally causes unavailability:** But if the criminal defendant ***intentionally caused*** the declarant to become unavailable (e.g., by killing him), and the defendant did so for the ***purpose of preventing testimony*** by the declarant, keep in mind that it ***doesn't matter*** whether the out-of-court declaration is deemed testimonial, because the defendant will be deemed to have ***forfeited*** any Confrontation Clause rights he may otherwise have had. [Cite *Giles v. California* on this point.]

      Example: D hears that V is about to testify against D in an upcoming criminal trial in which D is accused of killing X. D kills V for the purpose of preventing him from testifying. The prosecution will be allowed to put in evidence that 2 months before V's death, V told an investigating officer, "I saw D kill X." Even though V's out-of-court declaration is testimonial, the fact that D killed V for the purpose of avoiding V's testimony means that D will be deemed to have forfeited any Confrontation Clause right to exclude V's declaration.

☞ **Non-testimonial:** If the out-of-court declaration is ***not testimonial,*** say that under *Crawford* and *Davis*, ***no Confrontation Clause scrutiny*** needs to be done ***at all.***

Example: V calls a 911 operator, and says, "Send the police — my boyfriend Bob is beating me up." V doesn't take the stand at Bob's trial for battery. The recording is admissible as an excited utterance without any Confrontation Clause analysis, because under *Davis* it's non-testimonial (i.e., it's focused on getting emergency help, not on aiding the authorities in investigating past events or in prosecuting crimes).

☞ If the focus of a ***police interrogation*** is on dealing with an ***ongoing emergency***, presume that any declaration made by a victim is ***non-testimonial***, and thus admissible without Confrontation Clause issues.

Example: Immediately after V is wounded in the stomach by D in a knife fight, O, a police officer, sees V and says, "Don't you need medical help?" V responds, "Yeah, D knifed me; for God's sake, call an ambulance." V then dies. Since the primary intent of V and O in the conversation was to deal with an ongoing emergency (getting help for V), not making a case for later prosecution, V's statement is not testimonial, and can be introduced without Confrontation Clause issues. [Cite *Mich. v. Bryant*.]

☛ **Confession implicating someone else, used during joint trial:** Special variation to watch for: *A* and *B* are tried together, and *A*'s confession implicating himself and *B* is used. If the same jury hears *A*'s confession implicating *B* (and *A* doesn't take the stand), then *B*'s Confrontation Clause rights are violated even if the prosecution only purports to be offering the confession against *A*. [Cite *Bruton v. U.S.*]

Exam Tips on PRIVILEGES

Usually, it's not hard to spot whether a fact pattern poses an issue of privilege — the pattern will probably tell you that the witness refuses to testify, and often it will tell you the asserted grounds. The problem thus is almost entirely one of determining whether the particular privilege applies.

Here's what to look for:

General

When a fact pattern contains an issue regarding a privilege:

☛ **Summary of rules:** Know the controlling rule of law. Each state, of course, sets up its own rules of privilege. In the federal courts, the ***FRE do not contain specific privilege rules***; therefore:

[1]for civil ***diversity*** cases, the federal court uses the ***state*** law on privilege; and

[2]in ***criminal*** cases, and in ***"federal question"*** civil cases, the court uses its ***own judgment***, i.e., "federal common law."

☛ **Eavesdroppers:** Watch for ***eavesdroppers***, a commonly-tested scenario. The modern rule is that the presence of an easvesdropper does ***not*** destroy the privilege of a confidential communication, if and only if the eavesdropping ***wasn't reasonably to be anticipated***.

Example: During a recess of a criminal trial, D tells his wife, "I should have known that X would spill his guts." A reporter who is sitting behind D hears the statement and testifies to it. D should probably have anticipated the possible presence of a reporter; if so, he'll lose the spousal privilege and the reporter's testimony will be allowed.

Attorney-Client

Privilege generally: When an attorney is being asked to divulge information about a party to a lawsuit, consider whether the attorney-client privilege applies.

☛ **Attorney-client relationship:** First, look for an ***attorney-client relationship***. The client must have been ***seeking professional legal advice*** when communicating with the attorney.

Example: Suit by P against D for breach of an oral contract in which P is to paint D's portrait. P produces testimony that D said to his attorney-wife W, "Since oral agreements are valid, I'm going to call P and tell him to go ahead with my portrait." Since P wasn't attempting to procure legal advice from W when he made the statement, the attorney-client privilege doesn't apply.

☞ **No payment required:** Remember that the attorney ***doesn't have to be paid or retained*** in order for the privilege to apply, as long as an attorney-client relationship (i.e., an attempt to get professional legal advice) existed at the time of the communication.

Example: P wants to bring a product liability action against D, a drug manufacturer, for liver damage he says D's pills caused. P initially consults attorney X about his claim, and tells X that his liver was malfunctioning even before he took the pills. X declines to represent P. The privilege still applies.

☛ **Confidential communication:** Make sure the evidence is a ***"confidential communication."*** Look for a disclosure by the client and an intent that the disclosure remain secret.

☞ **Lawyer's observation:** A communication may be protected even though it is nonverbal. However, a lawyer's ***observation of a client's physical appearance*** that third parties could also have made is not covered. Profs like to use this as a trick question.

Example: D is the driver of a car in which his attorney, L, is a passenger. The car crashes, injuring P, a pedestrian. In a civil suit by P against D, D is not represented by L. P calls L to testify, and asks, "Didn't D appear to be drunk just before the accident?" L's answer can't be blocked by the attorney-client privilege, because the answer doesn't involve any communication between L and D, merely L's observations of D's physical appearance.

☞ **Previously-prepared documents:** ***Previously-prepared documents*** that a client gives to an attorney are ***not*** a communication.

Example: P sues D, a car manufacturer, for defective design of the Thunderwheel. P subpoenas from D records of tests that D performed on the Thunderwheel before the accident occurred. D objects on the grounds that D has given these records to its lawyer, thereby subjecting them to attorney-client privilege. D will lose — only materials prepared for the purpose of communicating with a lawyer can be protected under the attorney-client privilege. [Nor are the documents protected by attorney work-product, since they weren't prepared in anticipation of litigation.]

☛ **Waiver:** Confirm that the privilege hasn't been ***waived.*** Look for the presence of ***third parties*** — if a third party is present whose presence wasn't reasonably necessary, the privilege will be lost.

Example: D makes the communication to L, his lawyer, in front of a cab driver who has nothing to do with the litigation or the conference. The privilege is lost.

☞ **Necessary presence:** But if the third party's presence is ***reasonably necessary*** to the conference, then the privilege isn't waived. (*Examples:* Employees of Client; guardian of Client; investigators; joint clients.)

Example: Pedestrian is injured by a truck driven by Driver and owned by Driver's boss Employer. Driver and Employer attend a conference with Lawyer, who represents Employer, and Investigator, who has been retained by Lawyer to help defend the anticipated suit. In the civil trial of Pedestrian's suit against Driver and Employer, Pedestrian attempts to compel Driver to testify about admissions Driver made at this meeting. Driver won't have to testify —

all communications at the meeting are privileged even though Employer and Investigator were present, since their presence was reasonably necessary.

☛ **Joint clients:** But if the meeting involves ***joint clients*** who later are asserting ***claims against each other***, the privilege doesn't apply to evidence about those claims.

Example: Same facts as prior example. Now, Owner makes a cross-claim against Driver as part of Pedestrian's suit. Owner can testify to admissions made by Driver in the meeting with Lawyer — this testimony will be admissible only as to the Owner-vs.-Driver claim. Same result if Owner sued Driver in a later suit separate from Pedestrian's suit.

☞ **Inadvertent disclosure:** If the privileged material is ***inadvertently disclosed*** to a third party, remember that FRE 502 says that ***no waiver*** occurs, as long as the disclosing party took ***reasonable steps*** (though unsuccessful) to avoid such disclosures beforehand, and then took reasonable steps to ***remedy*** the mistaken disclosure after it occurred.

☛ **Inapplicable instances:** Other instances where the privilege doesn't apply:

☞ **Lawyer vs. client:** A claim by the ***lawyer against the client***, or vice versa.

Example: If Client sues Lawyer for malpractice, either may put on evidence about communications between them.

☞ **Crime or fraud:** Furtherance of ***crime or fraud***.

Example: Product liability suit by P against D for making pills that damaged P's left main coronary artery. D subpoenas Lawyer, whom P originally consulted but who would not take the suit, and asks, "Didn't P tell you he had a defective left main coronary artery before he began taking our pills?" D cannot block the question, because any such admission by P would have indicated that P was hoping to persuade Lawyer to participate in a fraud, by bringing a fraudulent claim.

Physician-Patient

Privilege generally: When a doctor is being asked to divulge information about a party to a lawsuit, consider whether the ***physician-patient*** privilege applies.

☛ **Related to treatment:** Remember that the communication must be ***related to treatment*** of a condition, or to diagnosis that is expected to lead to treatment.

Example: D is on trial for drug possession. The prosecution calls W, an M.D., who testifies that he gave D a physical exam, and that during the exam D stated that he, D, was a drug addict and asked W if W would like to buy drugs. These statements by D will not be privileged, because they don't relate to the diagnosis or treatment of a condition.

☞ **Expert-testimony preparation:** If the communication is done solely to permit the M.D. to serve as an ***expert witness*** in litigation (i.e., no treatment is contemplated), most states hold that the privilege does *not* apply.

☛ **Physical condition in issue:** Also, the privilege doesn't apply where the patient has ***placed her physical condition in issue***. Common scenario: A personal injury suit.

Example: P sues D, a cosmetics company, for injuries she claims she suffered where her leg became infected as a result of using a hair remover made by D. D calls Doc, who testifies that when he examined P's leg injury, P told him she had infected it by falling on a rusty pitchfork. Not privileged, because P's suit has placed her physical condition in issue.

☛ **Not usable in criminal proceedings:** Remember that the majority rule is that the privilege ***can't be used in criminal proceedings.***

☛ **Held by patient:** Remember that the privilege is ***held*** exclusively by the ***patient***. So the doctor can't assert the privilege if the patient doesn't want to, and if the patient is a litigant the other party can't assert the privilege either.

☞ **P's doctor's testimony opposed by D:** A common scenario is that the defendant objects to testimony by the plaintiff's doctor.

Example: Personal injury suit. W, an MD, testifies for P that she examined P, and that P described pain she was feeling in her lower back. D objects on grounds of patient-physician privilege. Objection overruled: only the patient can assert the privilege. [Also, observe that there's no hearsay problem, because there's a hearsay except for statements of physical condition made to a doctor for treatment or diagnosis.]

☛ **Psychotherapist / psychologist:** Remember that the privilege also applies, in virtually every state, to confidential communications between a patient and a ***psychotherapist*** (including non-M.D. ***psychologist***).

Self-Incrimination

Self-incrimination, generally: Whenever someone refuses to answer a question, consider whether the Fifth Amendment privilege against ***self-incrimination*** may be invoked.

☛ **Must take stand:** If the witness is ***someone other than a criminal defendant***, make sure that the witness has ***taken the stand and been asked a question.*** (A criminal defendant may, in his own case, refuse to take the stand at all, but anyone else must take the stand before claiming the privilege.)

Example: Murder trial of D. The prosecution subpoenas W, who the prosecution thinks was present at the scene of the crime. W may not refuse to appear in court, or to take the stand, on Fifth Amendment grounds. She must take the stand and be asked questions; only then may she plead the Fifth.

☞ **Civil proceedings:** The privilege may be invoked at a ***civil proceeding***, if the witness reasonably believes that the answer might tend to incriminate her for purposes of some later theoretically-possible prosecution.

Example: W, a witness in a civil case involving a car crash, testifies to witnessing the crash. D's lawyer asks her, "Weren't you actually robbing a store in Carson City on the day this accident occurred?" W may plead the Fifth, even though she has never been charged with the robbery — it's enough that W's answer might possibly be used against her in a later prosecution for the robbery.

☞ **Strike from record:** If W does plead the Fifth, the trial judge has discretion to order any earlier testimony by W in the matter ***stricken from the record***, on the grounds that W's plea has deprived the party opposing W from ***meaningfully cross-examining*** W.

☛ **No comment allowed:** Also, point out in your answer that ***no comment*** may be made upon a criminal defendant's ***refusal to testify*** on his own behalf.

☛ **Testimonial and compulsory:** Make sure the evidence is ***testimonial and compulsory.*** Common traps (where the evidence does *not* violate the Fifth Amendment):

- **Admission to W:** The evidence consists of testimony of a witness regarding an ***admission*** made by the defendant. The privilege never applies to *A*'s repetition in court of an out-of-court statement made by *B*.

  Example: D's trial for murdering V. The prosecution puts on W, who testifies, "D said to me, 'I killed V.' " D cannot raise any Fifth Amendment claim against this testimony.

- **W's observations of D:** The evidence consists of testimony of a witness based on her ***observations of the defendant.***

- **Audiotape or videotape of D:** The evidence consists of an ***audiotape*** or ***videotape*** of the defendant, that was recorded without his knowledge, while he talked to a non-law-enforcement person; since the defendant isn't "compelled" to give the evidence, the Fifth Amendment doesn't apply.

  Example: The police secretly videotape D telling his friend, "Sure I did it, but they'll never catch me." There's no Fifth Amend. privilege, because D's statement wasn't compulsory.

☛ **No explanation required:** Remember that it's unnecessary for the person invoking the privilege to ***show how*** the statement might be incriminating. In a criminal case, D has the absolute right to claim the privilege without any showing at all. A witness who is not a criminal defendant may invoke the privilege unless it's virtually impossible to conceive of circumstances in which the answer called for would be incriminating.

- **Use vs. transactional:** Determine what kind of immunity, if any, has been granted. Be sure to distinguish between ***use*** immunity and ***transactional*** immunity. Typically, you'll be told which of the types has been granted, and you'll have to figure out the consequences of that grant.

  - **Consequence:** When a witness is given immunity (either type), she is ***no longer entitled to claim*** the Fifth Amendment, and must give the testimony or be held in contempt.

  - **Use immunity:** Use immunity prevents the ***use*** of a person's testimony or its fruits in a subsequent ***criminal proceeding*** against that person.

    - **Fruits disallowed:** Use immunity prevents ***even the indirect use*** of the testimony. Thus any kind of ***"fruit"*** that is ***in any way derived*** from the testimony is blocked.

      Example: Mayor, the Mayor of Gotham, is subpoenaed by a grand jury investigating municipal bribery. After being given use immunity, she testifies that Commish, Gotham's Building Commissioner, has frequently taken bribes and shared them with her. Both Mayor and Commish are indicted for taking bribes. The only evidence against Commish is Mayor's grand jury testimony. Commish pleads guilty in return for promising to testify against Mayor. This testimony will be barred by the grant of use immunity to Mayor — because Mayor's testimony was the only evidence against Commish, his plea bargain and testimony against Mayor are the indirect fruits of Mayor's immunized testimony, and therefore may not be used against Mayor.

    - **No bar to prosecution:** Remember that use immunity ***doesn't protect against prosecution***, just against use of the immunized testimony. So if the government can go forward without any direct or indirect use of that testimony, the prosecution is allowed.

      Example: Based on descriptions obtained from bank employees, D is arrested for robbing X Bank. D is subsequently picked out of a line-up by a bank employee, and is charged with armed robbery in state court. He is then subpoenaed by a federal grand jury investigating robberies of certain federal banks. After being granted use immunity, D admits his participation in robbing X Bank. D may still be tried in state court if the only evidence presented is the testimony of the bank employees who picked him out of the lineup, because that testimony did not derive in any way from

D's immunized testimony.

- **Where immunity doesn't block use:** Watch for instances where use immunity ***doesn't*** render evidence inadmissible:

  - **Use against someone other than W:** For instance, the prosecution is not barred from using the immunized testimony against ***someone other than the witness.***

    Example: Sidekick is given use immunity, then asked in a grand jury proceeding about crimes that he carried out for his employer, Boss. Sidekick implicates Boss in various crimes. Boss is now prosecuted for those crimes. The grant of use immunity to Sidekick doesn't prevent Sidekick's grand jury testimony from being used against Boss, because the grand of use immunity only protects the witness (Sidekick), not anyone else.

- **Transactional immunity:** Transactional immunity *prevents criminal prosecution* for the *entire transaction(s)* about which the person has testified, even if the prosecution doesn't make use of the immunized testimony. So it's broader (better for the witness) than use immunity.

  - **Subsequent civil suit:** A common trap involves a subsequent ***civil suit*** — the immunized testimony ***can*** be used in the civil suit (since the immunity only applies to ***criminal prosecutions***).

    Example: D, a member of a professional crime organization, is offered transactional immunity in return for testifying against other members of the organization. He so testifies, and during the course of his testimony admits having killed V. V's wife then brings an action for damages resulting from the wrongful death of V. This action may proceed, and may in fact make use of D's immunized testimony. [Same result if the immunity was use rather than transactional.]

<u>**Marital Communications / Spousal Immunity**</u>

Generally: When a spouse is asked to testify, consider whether the privilege for ***confidential marital communications*** and/or the ***adverse testimony privilege*** (spousal immunity) applies.

- **Distinction:** *Distinguish between the two privileges:*

  - ❑ The privilege for ***confidential marital communications*** only prevents disclosure of confidential ***communications*** made by one spouse to the other during the marriage.

  - ❑ The ***adverse-testimony*** privilege (or principle of "spousal immunity") gives a criminal complete protection from ***adverse testimony*** — whether it relates to a communication or not — by his or her spouse.

☞ **Both, neither or one:** Sometimes both privileges will apply, but often only one will.

Example: Suppose Wife sees Husband kill V. If the jurisdiction recognizes the adverse testimony privilege, that privilege will apply, so that Wife can't be forced by the prosecution to testify to what she saw. But the confidential communications privilege won't apply on these facts, since there's no communication, merely observation.

☛ **Confidential communications:** For the privilege for confidential marital communications:

☞ **Communication required:** Look for a ***communication***. Gestures are usually covered; a few courts also cover acts that are not intended to communicate, but that take place in private.

☞ **Spouse's physical appearance:** The spouse's physical appearance generally isn't a communication, so it can't be covered.

Example: In a rape prosecution, D's wife testifies that D returned home on the night in question with scratches on his arm. The testimony doesn't violate the confid. commun. privilege, because there was no "communication," merely an observation of something physical. [But if the testimony was that D intentionally pulled up his sleeve to *show* his wife his scratches, this gesture might be found to be communicative and thus covered.]

☞ **Confidential:** Make sure that the communication was intended to be ***confidential***. This is the most frequently-tested aspect.

☛ **Presence of third parties:** Thus, look out for the presence of third persons. If a third person's presence is known to the speaking spouse, there's no intent to keep the communication confidential, and thus no privilege. (*Example:* H makes the disclosure to W at dinner, with the butler present. No privilege.)

☞ **Who owns the privilege:** Where the defendant spouse objects, but the testifying spouse seems willing to testify (even if it's because she's being threatened with being prosecuted herself), flag the issue of, ***"Whose privilege is it?"*** Courts are split; some say it can be asserted by ***either***, but others that it can be asserted only by the spouse who ***made the communication*** (who will usually, but not always, be the defendant if it's a criminal trial.)

☞ **Made during marriage:** Remember that the communication must have been made ***during the marriage***. But the parties' ***present marital status doesn't matter.***

Example: Even if H and W are now divorced, H can prevent the prosecution from using W's testimony against H about something H said when they were married.

☞ **Civil vs. criminal:** The privilege applies to ***both criminal and civil suits*** (but not to a suit between the spouses, e.g. a divorce suit.)

☛ **Adverse testimony / spousal immunity:** In analyzing whether the adverse testimony privilege (spousal immunity) applies, look to these factors:

☞ **Civil vs. criminal:** The ***nature of the proceeding.*** Most states limit the spousal immunity to ***criminal cases.***

☞ **Who holds:** ***Who holds*** the privilege. In federal cases, the privilege belongs to the testifying spouse, not the party spouse. [*Trammel v. U.S.*]

Example: Prosecution of H. W cuts a deal to testify against H in return for not being prosecuted herself. H can't block W's testimony, because the privilege belongs to the testifying spouse, not the litigant spouse.

☞ **Marital status:** The parties' ***marital status.*** It doesn't matter whether they were married when the act or communication occurred; all that's required is that they be married now.

Example: W can refuse to testify against H as to something H told her before they were married.

☞ **Communication not required:** Remember that this privilege covers ***all testimony*** by the spouse, even testimony ***not involving any communication.***

Example: In a jurisdiction where the privilege exists, W may refuse to testify about whether she saw scratch marks on H after he allegedly raped V.

☞ **Federal vs. state recognition:** Remember that all federal courts recognize the privilege (though as noted only the testifying spouse may assert it), but only a slight majority of states recognize it.

Exam Tips on *REAL AND DEMONSTRATIVE EVIDENCE; WRITINGS*

Whenever a piece of evidence (a tangible "thing" as opposed to the testimony of a witness) is offered into evidence, here's what to look for:

Authentication

Authentication, generally: Confirm that the item has been properly ***authenticated***.

☛ **Self-authenticating items:** Look for ***self-authenticating documents*** — these don't need any sponsoring witness.

Examples of self-authenticating items:

❑ ***Trade inscriptions*** that seem to indicate origin, ownership or control.

Example: Product liability action, claiming that there was glass in a can of corn eaten by P. P offers the can, which bears the label "David Foods, Inc." P will have to show that the can is the one he ate from, but he won't have to show that the can was made by David Foods — the label is self-authenticating, to show that it was affixed by David Foods (though David Foods is allowed to rebut this showing.)

❑ ***Certified copies*** of ***public records***.

Example: In suit against insurance company, P's estate can offer a certified copy of P's death certificate to show P is dead, without having to put on a sponsoring witness who testifies, "This is a copy of P's death certificate, which I know to have been copied from the county's files."

☛ But most types of documents are ***not*** self-authenticating under the FRE.

Example: Personal or business *letterhead* is not self-authenticating, so a litigant can't simply introduce, unsponsored, a letter on letterhead for the purpose of establishing that the letter was written by the person or business whose letterhead it is.

☛ **Sponsoring witness:** If the item does not fall into one of the (comparatively few) categories of self-authenticating items, make sure there is a ***sponsoring witness***, who testifies that the item is what its proponent claims it to be. Make sure that the sponsoring witness's testimony falls into one of the two following categories:

[1] **Personal knowledge:** Either the sponsoring witness has ***personal knowledge*** that the item is what the witness claims it is (e.g., "This is the knife that D used when he stabbed me — I recognize the distinctive carved pearl handle") *or*

[2] **Chain of custody:** The sponsoring witness(es) testifies as to the ***chain of custody*** for the object.

Example: Officer testifies, "I seized the plastic bag with white stuff in it from D's pocket; I turned it over to the inventory clerk at the police evidence lab." Clerk testifies, "I marked the bag, then gave it to Lab Technician," and so forth.

☛ **Handwriting:** A common issue is the identification of ***handwriting*** on a document. Most common sub-issue: can a ***nonexpert*** make the identification? Remember the rule (FRE 901(b)(2)): nonexpert opinion on the genuineness of handwriting may be given if based on "a familiarity with it that was ***not acquired for the current litigation***."

Example: Contract suit. D denies signing the contract. P calls W, who testifies that W and D were partners for years, during which time W got to know D's signature, and that the signature on the disputed contract appears to be D's. Admissible even though W is not a handwriting expert, because W acquired familiarity with D's handwriting or signature through means other than preparing for litigation.

☞ **Acquired during litigation preparation:** Conversely, if W acquired her familiarity with the writing in preparation for the litigation (e.g., by comparing known samples of X's writing with the disputed samples), W must be a handwriting expert.

☞ **Other methods:** Also, remember two other methods of authenticating handwriting: an ***admission*** by the writing, and a ***comparison performed by the jury*** between the disputed sample and a known sample.

☛ **Wills:** Remember the special rule for ***wills***: Under FRE 903, no attesting witness needs to testify, unless local state law so requires. But some states still require at least one attesting witness to testify to the will's execution.

☛ **Photograph or film:** When the item is a ***photograph*** or ***film***:

☞ **Chain of custody:** There's no requirement that a chain of custody be proven, only that a witness testify that the photo is a fair and accurate representation of what it purports to illustrate.

☛ *Trap:* A question mentions that a photo or videotape was ***mislaid*** for a period of time, or that ***possession was transferred*** from person to person (with no clear chain of custody proven). None of this matters.

☞ **Photographer need not testify:** The ***photographer doesn't have to testify***. (*Somebody* has to testify that the photo is a fair representation of what it purports to represent, but that somebody doesn't have to be the photographer.)

☞ **Exact depiction not needed:** The photograph ***doesn't*** have to be an ***exact depiction*** of the entire scene as it was. It just has to fairly and accurately represent the thing(s) in issue.

Example: In a car-crash suit, a photo is offered to show the streets and traffic-flow where the accident took place. The fact that the landscaping on the sidewalk is different in the photo than it was at the time of the accident is irrelevant, because this isn't in issue; therefore, the photo can come in.

☛ **Drawing, chart or illustration:** A physical ***drawing, chart*** or ***illustration*** of a witness's testimony is admissible, if the witness testifies from personal knowledge that the drawing is a fair representation of what it purports to illustrate.

Example: W is asked about previous business dealings between two parties. He offers into evidence a chart he prepared after refreshing his recollection by looking at company files. He states that the chart reflects his personal knowledge. The chart will be admissible if the judge thinks it would help the jury and not be misleading. This is true even if the chart contains statements not explicitly made orally by W.

☛ **Computer print-outs:** Where what's being offered is a ***computer print-out***, the authentication must be by evidence: (1) ***"describing a process or system"*** used to produce the result, plus (2) evidence showing that the process or system "produces an ***accurate result.***"

Example: If a computer print-out of account balances is offered by P to show that D owes P money, P must first: (1) describe how customer-balance information gets entered into the system; and (2) show that the system for data entry, and the computer program that manipulates the data, are accurate.

☛ **Telephone conversation:** Where what's at issue is the ***parties to a telephone conversation***, authentication is vital and often tricky. Distinguish between outgoing and incoming calls:

☞ **Outgoing calls:** For ***outgoing calls*** (calls made ***by*** the witness), authentication usually requires a showing that: (1) W made a call to the ***number assigned by the phone company*** to a particular person, *and* (2) the ***circumstances*** show that the person who talked ***was in fact*** the person the caller was trying to reach. FRE 901(b)(6).

☛ **Circumstances:** For requirement (2), the most common "circumstances" are:

❑ ***Self-identification*** by the person on the other end.

Example: P wants to testify that he called D, and that D said something. P can do this by showing that: (1) he called the number listed in the phone book for D; and (2) when someone answered, P asked, "Who's this?" and the person answered, "It's D." ***or***

❑ ***Voice identification*** by the witness/caller.

Example: In above Example, P could say, "I dialed D's number, and I recognized D's voice from prior conversations with him."

☞ **Incoming calls:** For ***incoming calls*** (calls made ***to*** the witness), there must be a showing that the caller ***was in fact*** the one who she seemed to be. The most common ways to do this:

- ❑ W testifies that he recognized the voice of the caller from having spoken to her previously; ***or***

- ❑ The caller is shown to have had knowledge that only the caller had.

  Example: P wants to show that the person who left a message on P's answering machine was D. If P testifies that the caller said, "I accept your offer to sell your house for $225,000," and P also testifies that the only person who knew that P wanted to sell at this price was D, the required authentication is made.

Trap: To prove that the caller was X, it's ***not enough*** for W to testify that the caller said he was X — there must be ***some additional evidence*** that the caller really *was* X (e.g., that W recognized the voice, that the caller had special knowledge, etc.)

Best Evidence Rule

B.E.R. generally: The Best Evidence Rule (B.E.R.) requires that the ***original writing*** must (if available) be produced when, and only when, the contents of a ***writing*** (or other document) are being proved.

☛ **Limits of what Rule covers:** So the "best evidence" is ***not*** required when ***something other than a writing's contents*** is being proven. In other words, there's no general rule requiring that every fact be proven by the "best evidence" of that fact.

  Example: The authenticity of D's signature on a letter is at issue. P's witness, W, testifies, "I knew D's signature 10 years ago, and this letter contains D's signature." D can't object that testimony by someone who's seen D's signature more recently is the "best evidence" of that signature's validity and must be offered instead.

☛ **Legally operative effect:** Common situation: a writing has a ***legally operative effect.*** Here, the B.E.R. is very likely to apply.

  Examples:

  - ❑ Suit against insurer. D wants to show that it sent a notice of cancellation to P. D's testimony, "I sent a notice of cancellation" won't suffice; the notice must be produced if available.

  - ❑ Prosecution of movie company for obscenity. Testimony about what the film shows won't suffice; the film itself must be produced. (Under the FRE, films and photos are covered by the B.E.R.)

  - ❑ Libel suit. The allegedly libelous document must be produced; testimony about what the document said won't suffice.

☛ **What to look for:** Look for situations where W's testimony ***relies*** almost entirely on ***what a document says***. (Distinguish these situations — covered by the B.E.R. — from those in which W relies in significant part on W's own personal knowledge — not covered.)

Example 1: V's cause of death is at issue. W testifies, "I found a suicide note at the scene, in which V said, 'I have nothing more to live for.' " The note must be introduced if available, because W's testimony is addressed to the issue of what the note said.

Example 2: Whether D has a police record is at issue. W can't testify, "I consulted our records, and saw that D was arrested and convicted for shoplifting," unless the records are also introduced.

☛ **Writing happens to contain info being proven:** *Very common trap:* The B.E.R. ***isn't*** triggered merely because a writing ***happens to contain the same info*** as that being proven. If W ***independently*** has the same personal knowledge of a fact as is reflected in a document, W's testimony can be used instead of the document.

Example: The issue is what costs P sustained in performing a contract. P may testify based on his own memory of those costs — even if the memory was "refreshed" by consulting business records. The fact that the records contain the same cost figures doesn't mean that the records must be introduced, because P is testifying to his own knowledge of the costs themselves, and the fact that those same costs are recorded somewhere is coincidental.

☛ **Photos and recordings:** Remember that under the FRE, the B.E.R. applies not only to writings, but also to ***photographs*** and ***recordings (video and audio)***. FRE 1002.

☞ **X-rays:** X-rays form a common scenario involving the B.E.R. (But be careful: B.E.R. applies only where the *contents* of the X-ray are really what's being proved, not some independently-known medical condition that happens to be shown on the X-ray.

Example: Issue is whether P had a fractured arm. If W says, "I took an X-ray, and it showed a fracture," the B.E.R. applies and the X-ray must be introduced. But if W says, "Based on a physical examination and the results of my reading of an X-ray, I concluded that P had a fracture," probably the B.E.R. doesn't apply.

☛ **Collateral writings exception:** Always check whether the ***collateral writings exception*** to the B.E.R. applies: If W's testimony relates to a minor issue in the case, then even if W is testifying about what a writing said, the B.E.R. ***doesn't*** apply.

Example: W is asked how he remembers the date of a meeting. He says, "I remember it was May 3rd, because the day of the meeting the newspaper announced my daughter's engagement, and I know that story ran on May 3rd."

Even though W is testifying as to the contents of a writing (the newspaper story), the B.E.R. won't apply, because the issue is collateral: it relates only to W's credibility as to the date. Thus the article doesn't have to be introduced.

☞ **Impeaching credibility:** When the contents of a writing are being used for ***impeaching a witness's credibility***, it's usually collateral (and thus need not be produced under the B.E.R.)

Example: W testifies on behalf of D in a criminal assault case. The prosecution, to attack W's credibility, asks W, "Didn't you once file a false insurance claim?" Even though this question is an attempt to prove the contents of a document, the B.E.R. doesn't apply [and the claim form doesn't have to be produced by the prosecution] because the only issue to which the question relates is W's truthfulness, a collateral issue. [In fact, the claim form can't be introduced even if the prosecutor wants to, because of the rule barring "extrinsic evidence" on a collateral matter.]

- **Original unavailable:** Remember that the B.E.R. only applies where the original is ***available*** (or its unavailability is due to the proponent's ***bad faith***). In many exam q's, you're told that the original is lost or destroyed without fault, so you automatically avoid a B.E.R. problem (though you should mention the B.E.R. issue anyway, if it's an essay question.) Common scenario: the original is ***burned*** in a fire that's not the proponent's fault.

- **Use of "duplicate":** If the B.E.R. *does* apply, remember that it's normally satisfied by the introduction of either the original or a true ***"duplicate"*** of the writing. FRE 1003. For instance, a ***photocopy*** is admissible, unless there's a "genuine question" about the original's authenticity, or admitting the copy would be unfair.

Exam Tips on *OPINIONS, EXPERTS & SCIENTIFIC EVIDENCE*

Lay Opinions

- **Threshhold issues:** When a non-expert witness is testifying to what appears to be an opinion, examine two threshold issues before you apply the rules on opinions:

  [1] **Opinion:** First, make sure it really *is* an opinion, not some other form of evidence, such as reputation.

  Example: If the examiner asks, "Isn't it correct that your dog is generally known to be gentle?" this question is really asking for reputation evidence, not opinion evidence.

[2] **Made in court:** Second, check that the statement is being ***made in court***. The special rules on lay opinions apply only to in-court testimony, not to things said out-of-court (which may pose hearsay problems, but usually don't pose opinion problems.)

Example: P wants to introduce a letter to P by W, in which W says, "In my opinion, D was travelling excessively fast before his car hit yours." This letter poses hearsay problems, but you don't need to worry about the opinion rules.

☛ **Two requirements:** Remember that a non-expert witness may testify to an opinion if the opinion is *both*:

[1] ***rationally based on the perception*** of the witness; and

[2] ***helpful*** to a clear ***understanding*** of the witness's ***testimony*** or the ***determination*** of a ***fact*** in issue. FRE 701.

Commonly-tested:

☞ **Where W can't easily state underlying facts:** Look for W's ***sense impressions***, or W's perceptions of someone's or something's ***appearance***, stated in terms of an opinion but based on ***common everyday knowledge***. These are admissible when it ***isn't reasonably practical*** for W to state the ***detailed underlying facts*** that caused her to form her opinion.

Examples:

❑ In a case where X's mental competence is in issue, W states that X's appearance changed over time from one of neatness and alertness to one of disorder and absentmindedness. That's admissible.

❑ In a case where D is alleged to have driven at excessive speed, W states, "I saw D's car come around the bend, and in my opinion, D was driving too fast for the road and weather conditions existing at the time." Admissible.

☛ **Lack of opportunity to perceive:** Common trap: W didn't have had a ***sufficient opportunity*** to ***perceive*** the elements on which her opinion is based.

Examples:

❑ If W hears a screeching sound made by one of the cars involved in an accident, but didn't see the car, W may not give an opinion as to the speed of the car.

❑ Where V is a pedestrian hit by a car, V can't testify, "I was hit by D, who was driving like drunken lunatic," if there's no evidence that V had an opportunity to observe D's behavior closely enough to form a rational opinion about whether D was in fact drunk.

☛ **Handwriting or voice ID:** Remember that a non-expert may make a handwriting or voice identification (a form of opinion), if based on the witness's personal experience with the subject's voice or writing.

Expert Opinions

Generally: Expert testimony is allowed where "***scientific***, ***technical***, or other ***specialized knowledge***" will help the trier of fact either: (1) ***understand the evidence***; or (2) ***determine*** a ***fact*** in issue. FRE 702.

☛ **Technical issue:** Look for a fact pattern where W is talking about some ***technical issue*** about which the ordinary person wouldn't have knowledge. That's your tip-off that you have to decide whether the requirements for expert testimony are met.

☛ **Foundation:** Make sure that a ***foundation*** has been laid, demonstrating the witness's expert ***credentials***. The witness must be shown to possess some special technical expertise. This expertise may have been acquired by education, formal training, ***informal work experience*** ("on the job training"), or even amateur pursuit (a ***hobby***).

Example: A car mechanic can probably testify about what's likely to have caused a sudden brake failure, even though the mechanic has no formal training for diagnosing and fixing cars, just work experience.

☛ **Stipulation:** Even though one party concedes (by offering a ***stipulation***) that the other's expert witness is qualified, the party offering the expert testimony is still permitted to ***continue questioning*** the witness about her qualifications. (The jurors determine ***how much weight*** to give an expert's testimony based on her qualifications, so the opponent of the witness can't, by offering to stipulate, take away the calling party's right to present these qualifications to the jury in detail.)

☞ **Impeachment:** Similarly, an expert may be ***impeached*** on cross by challenging her credentials, because this calls into question how much weight the jury should give to her testimony.

Example: The court permits W, a chemist, to testify as an expert witness. On cross, opposing counsel may ask W, "Isn't it true that you flunked two chemistry courses while you were in graduate school?"

☛ **Examples** of ***appropriate*** expert testimony:

- ❑ After a home is burglarized, a half-eaten piece of cheese is found in the kitchen. D is tried. W, a dentist, testifies that based on a comparison of impressions of D's teeth and a cast of the piece of cheese, in W's opinion the bite in the cheese was made by D. Admissible.

- ❑ After P's motorcycle is destroyed, its pre-accident value is in dispute. W, a motorcycle dealer, who never saw the bike but reviewed a picture of it and was told its make, model and year, testifies that in his opinion, such a motorcycle is customarily bought and sold on the used market for between $4,000 and $5,000. Admissible.

Example of ***inappropriate*** expert testimony:

❑ W, a police officer, testifies that based on his 15 years of police experience, the skid marks made by D's car before an accident indicated that the car was travelling at 75 mph. Unless there's some evidence that W has particular expertise in interpreting skid marks (not just general expertise in police work), the testimony is inadmissible because the requisite foundation (showing of credentials) hasn't been laid.

☛ **Bases for expert opinion:** Opinion may be based on: (1) W's *personal knowledge* of the facts; (2) facts presented in the courtroom in the form of a *hypothetical*; or (3) facts told to W outside the courtroom, and *not in evidence*, as long as they are of a *type reasonably relied upon* by experts in the particular field. FRE 703.

☞ **Most frequently-tested:** An opinion based on ***material not in evidence***. Trap: The material relied on is ***inadmissible*** (usually hearsay); this ***doesn't matter***.

Example: W, an accident reconstruction specialist, testifies, on behalf of P, "Based in part on P's statement to me that she was going no more than 55 mph on a dry road when her brakes failed to work, I conclude that there must have been a manufacturing defect in the brakes." The fact that W's statement is based on inadmissible hearsay — P's out-of-court statement, in effect offered to prove that the accident happened the way P said it did — doesn't prevent W's testimony from being admissible. But P would have to show that accident reconstruction experts customarily rely on such oral accounts from accident survivors. (Also, P's lawyer would have to convince the judge that the probative value of introducing P's statement would outweigh its prejudicial value — otherwise, the statement itself could not be repeated by W to the jury, even though the opinion itself could still be admitted. See FRE 703.)

☞ **Sometimes tested:** use of a ***hypothetical***. This is allowed, as long as the facts assumed in the hypothetical either have been or will be put ***in evidence***.

Example: P claims whiplash. W, an orthopedist who has never treated or examined P, is called by P and asked, "If a person is sitting in the front seat of a stopped car that is hit from behind at 8 mph, is it possible for the person to sustain whiplash." W responds that it's possible. Admissible, if evidence that the impact occurred in this way has been or will be admitted.

☛ *Trap:* Just because a highly-trained or highly-educated witness is testifying, don't assume that she's giving an opinion or that her opinion constitutes expert testimony. If she's testifying about matters she ***personally observed***, and her testimony ***doesn't*** include opinions requiring ***specialized knowledge***, the rules on expert testimony ***don't apply***.

Example: P sues D bus company for whiplash. D claims no other passengers were injured. P calls W, an emergency-room doctor at the local hospital, who testifies that he treated 3 other passengers on that bus that day for what they said was neck pain. This isn't expert testimony, because it's a statement of W's personal knowledge of facts, and doesn't involve any opinion or inference requiring expertise.

☛ **Ultimate issue:** Look for an opinion on an ***ultimate issue of fact***. Mention that FRE 704(a) says that an otherwise-admissible opinion isn't deemed objectionable just because it embraces an ultimate issue of fact to be decided by the jury.

Example: If P claims that D exceeded the 60 mph speed limit and that negligence *per se* applies, W's testimony, "D looked like he was going over 60" is still admissible even though it covers the key factual issue in the case.

☞ **Conclusory terms not allowed:** But W's opinion ***can't*** be posed in ***conclusory legal terms***, because then W is treading on an area reserved to the judge and jury.

Examples:

❑ Obscenity prosecution. Professor of film art testifies, for the prosecution, "In my opinion this film is 'obscene'." Inadmissible, because it's a legal, not factual, opinion.

❑ Psychiatrist testifies for the defense in a criminal case that "In my opinion, D didn't have malice aforethought when he shot V." Inadmissible, because it's a legal conclusion. (W should have restricted his testimony to a description of D's state of mind in non-legal terms, e.g., "D acted on a spur-of-the-moment impulse.")

Scientific Tests and Principles

When an expert's testimony concerns a scientific test or principle, check that the applicable test for reliability is satisfied. Because of the Supreme Court's adoption of the *Daubert* standard, this topic is especially likely to be tested.

☛ **Federal cases:** For ***federal*** courts, apply the *Daubert*/FRE 702 standard, by which: (1) the testimony must ***assist the trier of fact*** to understand the evidence or determine a fact in issue; (2) the witness must be ***"qualified"*** as an expert by ***"knowledge, skill, experience, training or education"***; (3) the testimony must be based upon ***"sufficient facts or data"***; (4) the testimony must be the product of ***"reliable principles and methods"***; and (5) the witness must have "***reliably applied*** [these] principles and methods ***to the facts*** of the case."

☞ Pay special attention to factors (4) and (5) above (reliable principles/methods, applied reliably to the facts).

☞ As to factor (4), briefly cite some of the ***factors*** going to whether the testimony is the product of ***"reliable principles and methods."*** Here are the most important ones: (i) whether the test/principle can be ***reliably tested***; (ii) whether it's been subject to ***peer review*** and ***publication***; (iii) its ***error rate***; (iv) whether it's ***"generally accepted"*** in the field, etc. (Note that "general acceptance" is still *a* factor under *Daubert*, even though no longer the *sole* factor.)

Example: Burglary prosecution; prosecutor says a piece of cheese left at scene has teeth marks that were made by D. Prosecution offers testimony by W, a dentist who's an expert on dental identification. Before W can testify to his ID of D, there'll have to be some showing that bite-mark identification is the product of "reliable principles and methods." If W testifies that there have been tests of the accuracy of such ID's, that the technique has been written up in peer-reviewed forensic journals, that it has a false-positive rate of less than, say, 1%, and that it's "generally accepted" by criminalists as a method of ID, this showing will be met. W will also have to show that he's applied the techniques of bite-mark ID to this particular bite mark in a "reliable" way (e.g., that he's compared the cheese with the dental records in a sufficiently precise way that his conclusion that there is a match is reliable).

☛ **State cases:** For ***state*** courts, mention that some have adopted *Daubert* but that some still use the *Frye* "generally accepted" standard (by which the test or principle can't come in unless its generally accepted by experts in the particular field).

☛ **Judicial notice:** If a test is very well established, the court may take ***judicial notice*** of its reliability instead of requiring proof of reliability.

Example: Probably lab tests for heroine and cocaine are now so well-established that the court may dispense with a showing of scientific reliability, and instead take judicial notice of reliability.

☛ **Execution of test:** Regardless of the standard used, there'll still need to be a showing that the ***particular way*** in which the test was ***carried out*** was reliable.

Example: D is charged with drug smuggling, based in part on a showing that a trained dog sniffed D's luggage and signalled the presence of cocaine. Before this evidence is admissible to show that the luggage indeed contained cocaine, the prosecutor will have to show (in addition to the general reliability of dog-sniff drug IDs) that the particular dog was appropriately trained, that the handler was trained in how to interpret the dog's responses, and that standard procedures were followed in the particular case involving D.

☛ **Re-enactment:** Where the test is a re-enactment (to show that a certain result could or could not occur in certain conditions), the proponent of the re-enactment must show not only that the methodology is reliable but also that there was a ***substantial similarity*** between the original conditions and the test conditions.

Example: In a personal injury action against D (a motorcycle manufacturer), P claims that a fork on his motorcycle bent when he hit a bump, and that this bending caused him to lose control of the motorcycle and collide with a car. D's attorney offers into evidence a film showing a test on a motorcycle fork, showing the fork not bending while being subjected to 15,000 pounds of pressure. D will have to show identity of conditions between the original accident and the test (e.g., that the fork was the same, that the amount of pressure was the same, that the direction of the force was comparable, etc.)

Exam Tips on BURDENS OF PROOF, PRESUMPTIONS, ETC.

The material in this chapter is less-commonly tested than that in most of the other chapters.

☛ **Bursting bubble:** The single most frequently-tested issue is: what effect does a presumption have once the party not benefitting from it produces some substantial evidence of the non-existence of the presumed fact? Under FRE 301, the answer is: the presumption ***no longer has any effect;*** it's a "bubble" that has "burst" (for instance, it doesn't shift the burden of persuasion), and the jury ***can't be instructed*** about the presumption.

Example: D in a contract case claims she notified P by letter that she was withdrawing from the contract (as she was permitted to do). D testifies that she put the letter in an envelope, with proper postage, addressed to P at his place of business (a P.O. box), and that she placed it in a U.S. mailbox. (This is enough to trigger the presumption that a properly-mailed letter was received by the addressee.) P testifies that he got his mail each day from a locked post office box, and that he never received any such letter. Because P has come forward with enough evidence of non-receipt of the letter to rebut the existence of the presumed fact (i.e., to allow a reasonable jury to conclude that P didn't get the letter): (1) the jury *may not be told* that it can "presume" that P got the letter; (2) the burden of persuasion remains on D (so if the jury thinks there's a 50-50 chance that P got the letter, P wins); and (3) the jury may still "infer" (just not "presume") from the fact of D's mailing that P received the notice.

Exam Tips on JUDICIAL NOTICE

Questions on judicial notice are more common than you might expect, especially on multiple-choice exams (since the issue is very testable).

- **Requirements:** A fact may be judicially noticed — so that proof of it isn't required — if either:

  - ❑ It's ***generally known*** in the community.

    Example: D is criminally charged with transporing toxic waste across state lines, by transporting waste from Detroit to Chicago without a license. If it's generally known in the community that Detroit and Chicago are in different states, then this fact may be judicially noticed.

    or

  - ❑ It's capable of ***immediate and accurate verification*** by use of easily-available sources that are ***indisputably accurate***. Information that can be found in encyclopedias, almanacs, atlases, and the like typically qualify.

    Example: W says that a certain event happened "on Father's Day of 2010." If a calendar would show that in 2010, Father's Day fell on June 17, the judge may take judicial notice of this fact.

- **Procedural issues:** Pay attention to the ***procedural issues*** surrounding judicial notice. In particular, watch for how the ***jury is instructed***:

  - **Civil:** In ***civil*** cases, the jury should be instructed that they ***must accept as conclusive*** any fact of which the judge has taken judicial notice. FRE 201(g)

  - **Criminal:** But in ***criminal*** cases, the judge must instruct the jury that it ***may*** — but is ***not required to*** — accept as conclusive any fact judicially noticed.

- **Requirement:** Also, keep in mind that the judge ***must*** take judicial notice of any fact that meets the requirements, if requested by a party and supplied with the required information. (Also, the judge ***may*** take judicial notice on her ***own***, without a request from a litigant.) FRE 201(c) & (d).

SHORT-ANSWER QUESTIONS

Note: These questions are taken from the "Quiz Yourself" questions in *Emanuel Law Outlines: Evidence*, which were in turn extracted and adapted from *Law in a Flash: Evidence* flashcards.

CHAPTER 2
RELEVANCE

1. A police detective finds a bloody brown left-hand glove, size 11 Isotoner, at a murder scene. A similar glove, but for a right hand, is later found at the residence of the victim's ex-husband, OJ. (No left glove is found at OJ's residence.) OJ is charged with the murder. The glove is offered as evidence that OJ is the murderer. Is the glove direct or circumstantial evidence? _______________

2. To impeach Walt Dipsey's primary witness, the Evil Stepmother, Snow White plans to introduce testimony of seven diminutive witnesses in the neighborhood who will testify that the Evil Stepmother has a reputation for untruthfulness. On what basis can Dipsey exclude some of the witnesses? _______________

CHAPTER 3
CIRCUMSTANTIAL EVIDENCE

3. Phil Zbiblenik, a carriage driver in Metropolis' Central Park, is sued for negligence when he falls asleep at the reins and his horse tramples the wedding reception of Mr. and Mrs. Amin Love. At the trial, the Loves seek to introduce evidence that on a previous occasion Phil had fallen asleep while working, disrupting a celebrity tennis tournament. The evidence is offered to show that it's likely Phil fell asleep again in the present situation. Is the evidence admissible, under the FRE? _______________

4. Frank N. Stein is seeking sole custody of his son, Bier, from his former wife, Albertyne. Albertyne seeks to introduce character evidence showing that Frank conducts chemical experiments which would create an unhealthy atmosphere in which to raise a child. Stein's lawyer objects, saying that since Stein hasn't put his character at issue, the evidence shouldn't be admissible. How do you rule? _______________

5. Sam Sleezeball is charged with selling obscene material. At trial, the prosecutor seeks to open his case by introducing testimony from Sam's neighbors that Sam is a trench-coat pervert who is frequently involved in shady enterprises. Sam objects. How do you rule? _______________

6. Bouncer was charged with passing a bad check when he purchased an assault rifle while wearing a Bill Clinton mask. Bouncer claims he was out-of-state when the crime occurred. At trial, the prosecution attempts to introduce evidence that Bouncer had purchased two other assault rifles with bad checks while wearing a Bill Clinton mask. (Bouncer was never convicted for these other purchases.) Is this evidence admissible under the FRE? If so, for what purpose(s)? ______________

7. Bart Egg, defendant in a criminal trial, wants to offer the testimony of Amy Ubble as to Bart's good reputation, to prove he didn't commit the crime in question. Bart's lawyer first shows that Amy is familiar with Bart's reputation. Then, when the lawyer asks what that reputation is, Amy hesitates, then says: "Well, I haven't heard anything bad about him." Is this "negative" reputation testimony admissible, under the FRE? ______________

8. Killer Smith offers testimony at his murder trial that he has never started a fight in his whole life. The prosecutor then introduces testimony by Killer's lifelong friend that in the friend's opinion, Killer has always been hot-tempered and violent. Can Killer successfully object to the testimony? ______________

9. David is on trial for the murder of Goliath. He claims self-defense and that Goliath was the first aggressor. May David introduce evidence of Goliath's violent nature to prove that Goliath was the aggressor? ______________

10. Otto Dingle is charged with raping Mata Hari. Dingle claims "consent" as a defense, and offers reputation evidence of Mata's renowned unchastity. The prosecutor objects, claiming that the victim's past behavior is inadmissible in rape cases. Under the FRE, how do you rule? ______________

11. Psycho Bates, proprietor of the Bates Motel, is on trial for the murder of Wo Begonia, who had merely stopped at the motel to ask for directions. Betsy Boddie appears as a reputation witness for Bates, claiming his reputation in the community is "very good." On cross-examination, the prosecutor asks Betsy: "Have you heard about Mr. Bates stabbing Marion Crane to death in the shower in 1962?" Defense counsel objects to the question. How do you rule? ______________

12. Jack T. Ripper is on trial for murdering Divine Brown, a prostitute. Ripper offers testimony by Hugh, who says that Ripper is known in the community as a non-violent, peaceful person. The prosecutor puts on a rebuttal witness, Elizabeth, who attempts to testify that if Ripper has a good reputation, the reputation is ill-deserved, because Ripper was previously convicted of mayhem. Ripper objects. How do you rule, under the FRE? ______________

13. Duke is on trial for raping Gilda. The prosecution seeks to introduce testimony by Magdalena that 14 years ago, Duke raped her, an act for which he was never charged. Magdalena would testify that the rape took place when Duke, a stranger to her, attacked her in a parking lot. The rape of Gilda is alleged to have occurred following a date between the two. There are no meaningful similarities between the two crimes other than the fact was Duke was the alleged rapist. The prosecution's theory in seeking introduction of the Magdalena rape is that because Duke raped before, he's likely to have raped on the present occasion. Duke has not taken the stand as a witness. Is Magdalena's testimony admissible, under the FRE? ______________

14. Fast Freddie, proprietor of the Lots O' Lemons Car Lot, sells Sydney Suquer a used car. The car makes it two miles before the wheels fall off and the engine disappears in a cloud of black smoke. In a suit based on breach of warranty, Freddie denies giving warranties as a part of his sales. To prove that Freddie routinely gives warranties, Sydney seeks to introduce evidence of a prior customer who got a guarantee. Any objection? ________________

15. Captain Hook loses his hand when it is sucked into the blade of his Mayhemart Food Processor, as he is feeding carrot sticks into the work-bowl as per the manufacturer's instructions. Hook sues Mayhemart for defective design. Mayhemart argues that there is nothing wrong with the design, and that Hook's accident was a bizarre aberration. In support of this argument, Mayhemart offers proof that 250,000 of the same model food processor were sold in the last two years, and the company has never received a complaint like Hook's. Under what circumstances, if any, will the evidence be admissible? ________________

16. Captain Hook cuts off his hand on the drill with which he works. Hook brings a negligence action against his employer, Croc-O-Dial Metalworks. (There's no workers' compensation statute on the island where this happens.) Hook offers, as evidence of negligence, testimony that the day after the accident, Croc-O-Dial placed safety devices on the machines. Croc-O-Dial objects. How do you rule? ________________

17. Batman finds that, every time he hits a pothole in the road, the ejector seat flips his passenger, the Boy Wonder, out of the Batmobile. Batman sues the manufacturer in strict liability for defective design of the seat. The manufacturer claims that the design was safe because the seat could not be made safer. Batman seeks to introduce evidence that, in the next model year, the manufacturer modified the ejector seat so it would only eject passengers when a secret button is pushed. Will this evidence be admissible to show the feasibility of safeguards? ________________

18. Buddy Goode drives a truck for the Ashe Hauling Company. Buddy's vehicle sideswipes Molly Motorist, who suffers severe injuries. At Motorist's trial against Ashe, Ashe's President claims that Buddy is an independent contractor, and not an employee or agent of the company. Motorist's attorney then asks whether Buddy is covered by Ashe's liability insurance policy. Is there a basis to permit admission of the testimony over objection? ________________

19. While Huey, Dewey and Louie are pheasant shooting from a boat in a lake, Donald carelessly drives his "Ski-doo" personal watercraft into them, injuring all three. All three sue Donald, but Huey and Dewey settle with him for a payment of a portion of the damages they were seeking. As part of the settlement, Huey and Dewey agree to testify against Louie in Louie's suit against Donald. When they so testify, can Louie introduce into evidence the fact that Donald settled with Huey and Dewey? ________________

20. Stolitz Naya, engineer for the St. Petersburg Local, dozes off at the controls. He doesn't realize Anna Karenina has fallen in front of the train, and he runs her over, severing her legs. Anna lives — changing the course of Russian literature — and shortly after the accident, Naya calls her and says, "Gee, I'm sorry. I fell asleep at the wheel. It was all my fault. I'll pay your medical bills." Under the FRE, can (1) this statement (or any part) or

(2) Naya's payment of Anna's medical bills, be admitted as evidence of liability at a subsequent trial? ____________

CHAPTER 4

EXAMINATION AND IMPEACHMENT OF WITNESSES

21. Macbeth is on trial for the murder of Duncan. Banquo is called as a witness for the prosecution, and testifies that he saw Macbeth leaving the castle shortly after midnight. It has already been established that the murder occurred at midnight, in the castle. Prosecutor asks, "Did you see anything else suspicious?" Banquo responds, "No, that's all I know." Prosecutor continues, "You're sure you didn't see anything else to suggest something strange had happened?" Banquo answers, "No." Prosecutor asks, "You didn't notice anything on Macbeth's hands?" In fact, Macbeth's hands were covered in blood, and Banquo had said so in his previous deposition. (a) What objection should the defense raise? ____________ (b) Will that objection succeed? ____________

22. George Washington, believing Benedict Arnold will be his best witness, calls Arnold to the stand. To Washington's surprise, Arnold testifies in a light highly unfavorable to Washington. Can Washington seek to minimize the damage to his case by impeaching Arnold's credibility? Answer with respect to both the FRE and the common law. ____________

23. Yolanda Layr is a witness for the defendant in a civil case. The plaintiff seeks to impeach Yolanda by offering proof of her prior conviction for taking property by false pretenses, a misdemeanor. The defendant objects. What result? ____________

24. Zoom Crashbang is a witness in a civil case. To impeach him, the adverse party offers evidence that Zoom has been convicted of vehicular homicide, a felony. Under the FRE, will this evidence be admitted to impeach Zoom? ____________

25. Butch Cassidy gives up his life of crime and, after he's paid his debt to society, becomes an accountant. Twenty years after his last felony conviction, for larceny, and fifteen years after he was released from prison, he is called as an eyewitness in a civil automobile-collision case. Under the FRE, may he be impeached with evidence of the larceny conviction? ____________

26. Lucius Lucullus appears as a witness for the defense in a negligence suit. On cross-examination, plaintiff, in order to impeach Lucullus, asks him: "You falsified your tax return two years ago, didn't you?" Defense objects, on the grounds that Lucullus was never charged with tax evasion. How do you rule? ____________

27. Cock Robin is on trial for shooting Mr. Sparrow with his little bow and arrow. Big Bad Wolf is a witness for the prosecution. On cross-examination, defense counsel seeks to impeach him by asking: "Mr. Wolf, isn't it true that you terrorized the Three Little Pigs, threatened them, and obtained title to their brick house through lies and trickery?" Wolf denies it. He has never been convicted of a crime involving these acts. Later, during the defense case, Cock Robin's lawyer offers the testimony of Nice Lamb to the effect that he personally witnessed Wolf obtain title to the Pigs' house through threats and extortion. Under the FRE, is this evidence admissible to prove that Wolf's denial on cross was a lie? ________________

28. McCoy is a witness in a case. To impeach him, Hatfield is called to the stand, and testifies: "I've known him for years, and I think he's a two-faced, lying swine who wouldn't know the truth if it hit him in the face." The opposition objects to this form of impeachment. Under the FRE, how do you rule? ________________

29. The Three Bears sue Goldilocks for trespass. The Bears' lawyer calls Ranger Rick to the stand, and asks him if he saw Goldilocks at the Bears' house on the night in question. Ranger Rick answers: "I was there, and through the window I saw the defendant sleeping in the Mama Bear's bed." Goldilocks' lawyer can't shake Rick's statement during cross, and makes no reference to any previous statement made by Rick. Rick is dismissed from the stand, and moves out of the jurisdiction without leaving a forwarding address. Later, Goldilocks' lawyer attempts to enter into evidence Rick's sworn statement, taken at the time of the incident, saying he hadn't seen Goldilocks or anyone else at the house. The Bears' counsel objects, claiming a proper foundation for admitting Rick's prior statement is lacking. How do you rule? ________________

30. Dr. Jekyll witnesses a hit-and-run car accident one evening. When the perpetrator is sued for negligence, Dr. Jekyll is called as a witness by the victim. On cross-examination, he's asked, "Isn't it true that you have frequent blackouts in the evening, after which you can't remember anything?" Jekyll denies it. Counsel then seeks to offer a newspaper story about Dr. Jekyll's periodic transformation into Mr. Hyde. Opposing counsel objects, claiming extrinsic evidence is impermissible here, because Jekyll's blackouts are a "collateral matter." How do you rule? ________________

31. Hamlet is on trial for the murder of Yorick. The prosecutor claims Hamlet had long been jealous of Yorick. Hamlet denies knowing Yorick at all. The prosecutor calls Horatio as a witness, who offers to testify: "Hamlet told me, 'Alas, poor Yorick — I knew him, Horatio.' " Admissible? ________________

32. One of the King's Men is on trial for murdering Humpty Dumpty by pushing him off a wall. Wanda Wye testifies for the prosecution: "I saw the whole thing on my way to a Girl Scout Jamboree." The defense calls another witness, Wilfreda, who testifies that Wanda was *really* on her way to an assignation with her boyfriend. Upon objection, the defense claims the question is permissible because it reflects on Wanda's veracity. How do you rule? ________________

33. Cy Witness sees Guy Fawkes set fire to the Houses of Parliament. In Fawkes' arson trial, the prosecution calls Cy as a witness, and he testifies as to what he saw. The defense does not cross-examine Cy. The prosecution then offers the testimony of Biggle Scoop, a newspaperman to whom Cy told the story at the time of the fire, to show Cy hasn't changed his story since the incident. Is Biggle's testimony admissible? ________________

34. Uzi Submachine-Gun Kelly, mobster, is on trial for a gangland-style murder. Whitey Knuckles appears as a prosecution witness, testifying that he saw Kelly commit the murder. On cross-examination, Kelly's counsel asks Whitey, "Didn't you tell the police at the time of the murder that you didn't see Kelly anywhere near the scene of the crime?" Whitey admits that he did. On redirect, can Whitey explain that he made the earlier statement out of fear and that it was a lie? ______________

35. Stepdad is charged with having sexually assaulted his 15-year-old step-daughter, Pamela, in May, 2012. Pamela testifies against Stepdad. On cross, Stepdad's lawyer asks Pamela, "Isn't it true that you hate Stepdad because you saw him hit your mother in April of 2012, and that you made up this whole story about rape and incest to get back at him?" Pamela denies this. The prosecutor, saying that he wants to rehabilitate Pamela's credibility, calls Psycho, the psychologist at Pamela's school. Psycho says that in June, 2012, Pamela told Psycho that Stepdad had sexually assaulted her the prior month. The defense objects. Result? ______________

CHAPTER 5

HEARSAY

36. Evan Keel, a passenger on the last flight of the Hindenberg, is tried for negligence in lighting a cigarette that ignited the blimp. Keel's defense is that the "No Smoking/Fasten Seat Belts" sign was off when he lit up. The prosecution offers testimony by Walter Resc, a rescue worker, who will testify that when the fiery blimp touched down, Joe Surv (who survived the accident but later died of an unrelated illness) said to Resc, "The No Smoking light was on when Keel lit up." Hearsay? ______________

37. The Indians who own Manhattan Island renege on their offer to sell the island to Peter Minuit. Minuit sues, claiming they had an oral contract for the sale. To prove they had a contract, Peter offers the testimony of Clyde Tory: "I heard Chief Broken Arrow tell Minuit, 'It's decided, then. Manhattan is yours for $24 and a baseball stadium in Cleveland.' " The Indians' lawyer objects on hearsay grounds. Assuming that oral contracts for the sale of land are valid, is the statement hearsay? ______________

38. Charles Foster Kane is arrested for possession of cocaine, which the prosecution asserts was contained in a "snowy" paperweight on Kane's desk. The prosecutor offers as evidence a lab report stating, "The 'snow' in the subject paperweight is 95% pure cocaine hydrochloride." Is the report hearsay? ______________

39. Rasputin, the Mad Monk, enters Czar Nicholas' study and tells him, "I am having an affair with your wife." The Czar pulls a pearl-handled pistol from his desk and shoots the Mad Monk. At the Czar's trial for murder, Rasputin's statement is offered by the Czar to prove that the killing was provoked. Is it hearsay? ______________

40. Bob Caulfield dies. In his will, he leaves his entire estate to one of his sons, D.B., and nothing to his other son, Holden. Holden contests the will, claiming undue influence by D.B. D.B. wants to rebut by proving that he had always been his father's favorite, long before the alleged undue influence. He offers the testimony of his father's lifelong friend, Spike, who will testify: "Bob told me fifteen years ago that 'D.B. is the finest child in my family.' " Is the statement hearsay? ______________

41. Elmer Fudd is on trial for the attempted murder of Daffy Duck. Fudd pleads insanity.

Bugs Bunny, a prosecution witness, testifies that Elmer is perfectly normal. To impeach Bugs, Elmer has Sylvester the Cat testify that, the day after the incident, Bugs told Sylvester: "That Elmer Fudd is a real looney tune." Is Sylvester's testimony hearsay? ________________

42. Gerhardt Werbezirk, world expert on fire protection, designs the sprinkler and fire protection system at the Koko-nut Grove nightclub. Later, he takes his family to the club. A week later, a horrible fire occurs at the nightclub, killing Paul. Paul's estate sues the club's owner. The owner attempts to introduce the Werbezirk's family outing as evidence that: (1) Werbezirk must have believed the system he designed was safe (or he wouldn't have taken his family there); and (2) if he believed it was safe, it probably *was* safe. Under the FRE, will Werbezirk's conduct be considered hearsay? ________________

43. The Gingerbread Boy runs away and the Fox eats him. At Fox's murder trial, Mugwump, a witness, testifies: "When they were searching for Gingerbread Boy, Aardvark told me Fox said he'd eaten the Gingerbread Boy." The statement is offered by the prosecution to prove that Fox ate the Gingerbread Boy. Is Mugwump's testimony admissible under the rule making admissions by a party-opponent non-hearsay? ________________

44. Sniffo is a bloodhound who searches out drugs for the FBI. His "beat" is the airport. While patrolling luggage, Sniffo indicates to his handler, Kay Nyne, that there are drugs in a suitcase. When the suitcase's owner, Maryjane Paraphernalia, is tried on drug charges, Kay testifies for the prosecution: "Sniffo indicated there were drugs in the suitcase." Hearsay? ________________

CHAPTER 6

EXCEPTIONS TO THE HEARSAY RULE

45. Claudius stops for a cigarette while hiking on Mount Vesuvius. He flicks his ash into the crater, which ignites, the volcano explodes, and the city of Pompeii is history. Claudius is arrested on criminal negligence charges and pleads guilty. Subsequently, survivors of the disaster file civil negligence suits against him. Can they introduce the prior guilty plea as an admission by a party-opponent? ________________

46. Wimp sues Atlas for battery, claiming that Atlas kicked sand in his face, permanently damaging his eyesight. At trial, Atlas offers into evidence Wimp's application for Bungling Brothers Clown College, submitted two weeks after the incident, to which Wimp attached a certificate from his optometrist, Dr. Convex Kincaid. The certificate states that Wimp's eyesight is perfect (a requirement for Clown College). Does the certificate satisfy an exception to the hearsay rule? ________________

47. Des Pirado is a passenger on an Acme Airways flight that crashes in the Andes, injuring Des. In his suit against the company, Des offers as evidence the exclamation of the pilot, I.M. Dian, just before the plane crashed: "Holy Cow! I knew they shouldn't have glued the tail on! We should have taken another plane!" Des claims this statement is an admission by a party-opponent. Acme objects, claiming that the making of such a statement is outside the scope of the pilot's duties, so that the statement is inadmissible. Under the FRE, how do you rule? _______________

48. Oink, Grunt and Slop — the Three Little Pigs — are going home from a wild party. (They're friends but have no other relationship.) Oink is driving when the car hits and injures B. B. Wolf, a pedestrian crossing the street at a crosswalk. Murray the Cop arrives five minutes later. Wolf subsequently sues Oink for negligence, claiming Oink was driving while intoxicated. Wolf offers the testimony of Murray the Cop: "At the scene, while everyone else was out of earshot, Grunt told me: 'We were on our way home from a party, where we were all drinking like there was no tomorrow.' " Oink objects. Will Murray's testimony be admissible? _______________

49. Three months after Moe, Larry and Curly rob the Bucks Bank, Curly is stopped on the highway and ticketed for speeding. When the patrolman approaches the car, Curly blurts out, "The Bucks Bank job was Moe and Larry's idea." At Moe and Larry's trial, the state seeks to introduce the patrolman's testimony as to Curly's statement. Under the FRE, is the statement admissible as an admission by a party-opponent? _______________

50. Little Bobo decides to play a trick on Isaac Newton. Bobo climbs a tree and, when Newton sits down in its shade, Bobo drops an apple on his head. Newton comments, "Ouch! I think my skull is fractured!" At Bobo's trial on battery charges, Newton's comment is offered to prove Newton was in pain. Bobo objects, on hearsay grounds. How do you rule, under the FRE? _______________

51. Mary arrives in an ambulance at the hospital's emergency room, and is brought in in a wheel chair. The ER physician, Dr. Welby, asks her what happened. She says, "I was riding the escalator at Macy's, when I caught my heel in a hole in the metal, and fell. I think my ankle's broken." (The ankle indeed turns out to be broken.) At Mary's negligence trial against Macy's for improperly maintaining the escalator, Macy's claims that Mary must have fallen outside the store. Mary offers Dr. Welby to repeat what she told him about what caused her injury, to prove that she really did fall on the escalator at Macy's. Is his testimony admissible under the "medical treatment or diagnosis" exception of the FRE? _______________

52. As proof that MacArthur returned to Corregidor in the Philippines, his statement "I shall return" is offered as evidence. Assuming MacArthur is still alive, what hearsay exception, if any, will the statement fit under the FRE? _______________

53. Mutt and Jeff work for a shipping line. One day Mutt comments, "Look, Jeff, I think that crate is leaking a sweet-smelling oil." He then suggests they pry it open to see what's inside. The crate explodes. In a subsequent lawsuit, Mutt's statement is offered under the "present state of mind" exception to the hearsay rule to prove that the crate was leaking. Is the statement admissible, under the FRE? _______________

54. Joe Phlebitz tells Mrs. O'Leary, "I'm planning to give you my cow next week." The Great Chicago Fire takes place two weeks later, and the cow caused it. In a lawsuit for negligence, Mrs. O'Leary denies ownership of the errant cow. The "udder" party offers Phlebitz' statement as proof that Phlebitz probably indeed gave Mrs. O'Leary the cow. O'Leary objects, claiming the statement is inadmissible hearsay. Will the statement be admissible under the "present state of mind" exception to the hearsay rule under the FRE? _______________

55. Dr. Bovary is charged with the murder of his wife, Emma. At his murder trial, the Bovarys' maid, Felicity, offers to testify that on the day of her death, Emma told Felicity: "I'm frightened, because Dr. Bovary has threatened to kill me." This statement is offered as evidence that Dr. Bovary killed Emma. Is Felicity's testimony admissible, over objection, under the "present state of mind" hearsay exception? ________________

56. At trial, Fred testifies, "Romulus told me that he and Remus were about to set out to found Rome." This testimony is offered to prove that Remus subsequently took off to found Rome. (There's no other evidence about whether Romulus ever left, or about whether Remus joined him.) Is Fred's testimony admissible under the "then existing state of mind" exception to the hearsay rule, under the FRE? ________________

57. Tom-Tom the Piper's Son is on trial for larceny, for stealing a pig. Tom-Tom defends on grounds that he didn't realize the pig wasn't his. His friend, Fred-Fred, testifies: "He told me the day afterwards, 'You know, I took the wrong pig. I thought it was mine.' " The prosecution objects. Under the FRE, will the statement be admissible under the "state of mind" hearsay exception? ________________

58. During Cinderella's magic night on the town, the Fairy Godmother turns a pumpkin into a coach. The pumpkin's owner, Frank, files suit against Fairy Godmother. As proof that the event took place, Frank offers the testimony of Furd, a bystander, who testifies: "I heard someone shout 'Holy Cow! She's turning that pumpkin into a coach!' " Furd admits that he never knew who made the statement. The defense objects on hearsay grounds to the admission of the statement. Under what hearsay exception, if any, is the statement admissible? ________________

59. Francis Bacon is in court claiming he wrote the plays ascribed to Shakespeare. (He asserts that before he could publish them, Shakespeare stole the manuscripts and published them under his own name.) Bacon offers the testimony of Shakespeare's friend, Fred, that, while Fred and Shakespeare were at a tavern, a glass fell on Shakespeare's head and shattered. Dazed and excited, Shakespeare shouted: "Bacon wrote the plays!" Shakespeare objects. Bacon claims the statement is admissible under the excited utterance exception to the hearsay rule. Is he right? ________________

60. Frasier and Niles are chatting on their front porch one day, when they see Sam Malone zoom by in his Corvette, through a red light, and into the side of another car. Frasier looks on calmly, and comments, "There goes Sam Malone, watching the women instead of the road again." At a subsequent trial concerning the accident, Frasier's statement is offered into evidence to prove Sam wasn't paying attention to the road. Is the statement admissible under the FRE, notwithstanding that Frasier was unexcited when he made it? ________________

61. Bush, an avid quail hunter, is out hunting one day. Unfortunately, one of his shots hits Clinton, playing golf on a neighboring course with his friend Al. Clinton sues Bush for battery. By the time the case gets to trial, Clinton's witness, Al, can't remember what happened. While Al is on the witness stand, he is handed some notes he took at the time of the incident. However, he still can't remember anything. If Al testifies that the notes were correct when made, under what hearsay exception, if any, can they now be read into the record? ________________

62. Peter Pan gives John, Wendy and Michael fairy dust to help them fly. He is arrested on narcotics charges. Wendy is called as a witness at trial. She can't remember exactly what happened, but, when she is shown some notes she made at the time of the incident, she is able to remember the events perfectly without further reference to the notes. Are the notes admissible under the "recorded recollection" exception to the hearsay rule? ________________

63. Sisko, captain of the tugboat U.S.S. Defiant, is injured when a large cruise ship under the command of Captain Picard rams him in Subic Bay. Sisko sues Picard for negligence. The incident is alleged to have happened on May 1. Picard's defense is that he wasn't even in Subic Bay at the time. At trial, Sisko seeks to introduce a sworn affidavit by Captain Janeway, another captain who happens to be currently lost at sea. In the affidavit, Janeway states that to her knowledge, Picard takes his ship to Subic Bay every May 1, and has done so for 50 years. Is the affidavit admissible over a hearsay objection? ________________

64. Jed works for the Quo Vadis Railroad Company. One of his duties is to prepare a report on any accident in which a Q.V. train is involved. (These reports are mainly used by the railroad to defend against claims by shippers whose merchandise is damaged.) When the Venus de Milo is first sculpted, it is crated and transported on the Quo Vadis, where it suffers damage. The incident is described in Jed's accident report: "Statue was improperly packaged by owner. Fell out of box, onto tracks, and wham! Next car of train sheared its arms clean off." Venus' owner sues Q.V. for negligence. The railroad seeks to introduce Jed's report into evidence, in support of the railroad's defense that the accident was caused by the owner's negligence in packing the statue. (a) What hearsay exception is the railroad's best chance for getting the report into evidence? ________________ (b) What's the likely outcome of the railroad's attempt in (a)? ________________

65. Jessie Hahn sues the No-Tell Motel for injuries she claims she incurred lying on a faulty mattress. Jessie offers as evidence the emergency room records of the hospital that treated her at the time. The records are regularly and scrupulously kept by personnel who attend to the patients and who must maintain such records. The records include Jessie' statement: "The mattress at the No-Tell was faulty." Is the statement admissible to show that the mattress was in fact faulty? ________________

66. OK Simpleton is charged with murdering his wife. A police incident report prepared during the investigation the day the body was found contains the following statement: "Footprints that appear to be from two different pair of shoes seem to be leading away from body; these prints look like they were left after the murder." The signature on the report is illegible, and the prosecution and police department say they don't know who prepared it. Since Simpleton is charged with having committed the murder alone, he seeks to introduce the report to establish that there must have been two murderers. (a) Under what hearsay exception, if any, is the report most likely to be admitted? ________________ (b) If your answer to (a) names an exception, will the report in fact be admitted under the exception you cite? ________________

67. Unem Ployd brings a civil suit against Ma Belle Corp., alleging that Ma Belle refused to hire Ployd and that the refusal was based on illegal racial discrimination. In its defense, Ma Belle seeks to introduce a report by the state Equal Employment Opportunity Commission, which recently conducted a review of Ma Belle's hiring practices, and concluded that Ma Belle did not practice racial discrimination in hiring. Are the report and this conclusion admissible under the FRE's "public records and reports" exception, to prove that Ma Belle generally doesn't discriminate? ________________

68. The Black Knight keeps a fire-breathing dragon as a pet. One night it gets loose, sneezes, and starts the Great Fire of London. The Lord Mayor of London, while sitting at his desk working on official business, looks out the window and is a witness to the whole incident. Although it's not his job to worry about reporting or recording the causes of natural disasters, he takes notes on what he sees. At a subsequent trial, the Lord Mayor's notes are offered under the FRE's "official records and reports" exception to the hearsay rule. Admissible? ________________

69. George Washington is on trial for having chopped down a cherry tree. The prosecution seeks to admit against George a police "incident" report prepared by Officer Madison of the Mt. Vernon police force. The report says, in part, "At 2200 hours, I observed a person who looked like Geo. Washington — had ill-fitting teeth and a white wig — chop down a cherry tree. Suspect ran away before I could apprehend him." Madison is not available to testify at the trial (he moved away and can't be found), which is why the prosecution wants to use the report instead. The report bears Madison's signature, and the legend "Mt. Vernon Police Department - Incident Report" at the top. Each officer on the Mt. Vernon force is required to write up reports of any criminal activity observed by the officer while on duty. Can the report be admitted against George as a "public record or report," under the FRE? ________________

70. A civil suit involves the issue of whether defendant, a cigarette company, knew that cigarettes could cause cancer in 1954. Plaintiff offers a letter found under the following circumstances: Nicco Tine, the president of defendant, died in 1962. In his safe deposit box was found a carbon copy of a letter purporting to have been written by Tine to his son in 1953, in which he says, "Tommy, the scientists at the company have just finished experiments showing that smoking probably can cause lung cancer." The box was not discovered and opened until 2012. No other evidence has been offered proving that Tine actually wrote this letter. What hearsay exception, if any, allows the introduction of the letter into evidence for the purpose of proving that the scientists did the experiments referred to in the letter? ________________

71. J. Needlepoint Morgan fraudulently convinces Commodore Peterbilt to sell all of his shares in International Bubble Makers to Morgan for 10¢ a share, a small fraction of their value. At trial, Peterbilt seeks to introduce a copy of the *Wall Street Journal* as evidence of the market price of the stock on the date of the sale. Can Morgan successfully object on the grounds that the newspaper's republication of the stock prices is hearsay? ________________

72. Ralph dies, covered by an insurance policy that pays double in the event of an accidental death. The insurance company refuses to make the double payment, contending that Ralph died of natural causes. Ralph's widow, Alice, sues the insurer. At trial, the insurer attempts to introduce Ralph's death certificate, which was filled out and signed by Ralph's doctor, in which the cause of death is listed as "brain tumor." The certificate is offered to prove that Ralph indeed died of a brain tumor. Under the FRE, is the certificate admissible? ________________

73. Burke is arrested on murder charges. Burke and his attorney, Nick Rofelia, attend a preliminary examination in the murder case. At that examination, Hare, who's the defendant in a separate prosecution for concealing the bodies of Burke's victims, is a prosecution witness. At Burke's trial Hare refuses to testify (fearing the effect his testimony would have on his concealment case), even when ordered to do so by the trial judge. The prosecutor now offers a transcript of Hare's preliminary examination testimony as substantive evidence. Under what FRE hearsay exception, if any, is the transcript admissible, and why? ________________

74. Clouseau sues Kato for battery. Previously, Kato was tried and convicted on criminal battery charges arising from the same incident (Clouseau was the complainant). At the criminal trial, Dreyfus, a witness, had testified that he saw Kato attack Clouseau without provocation. Kato cross-examined Dreyfus at the criminal trial. Under the FRE, in the current civil trial, will Dreyfus' testimony be admissible, over Kato's objection? ________________

75. Goldilocks is arrested for breaking and entering the Three Bears' house. Mama Bear suffers a complete nervous breakdown after the crime, and can't testify. Instead, a sworn affidavit as to her recollection of the facts, given to the police immediately after the break-in, is offered under the "former testimony" exception to the hearsay rule. Might it qualify, under the FRE? ________________

76. Sleeping Beauty appears as a witness at a trial on behalf of plaintiff. Defense counsel doesn't cross-examine her, although given the chance to do so. She subsequently pricks her finger with a needle and falls asleep for 100 years, making her unavailable to testify in a subsequent trial where the parties and issues are substantially identical. When her recorded testimony is offered under the "former testimony" exception to the hearsay rule, defense counsel objects on the grounds that Sleeping Beauty wasn't cross-examined at the first trial. How do you rule? ________________

77. The French Maid rushes into the Master's study, only to find him on the carpet, bleeding profusely, with a sharpened umbrella through his chest. She rushes to him, props him up, and he mumbles feebly: "The butler did it." He slumps over and dies. At the butler's murder trial, the prosecutor offers the French Maid's testimony as to the Master's statement, to prove the butler did it. Butler objects on hearsay grounds: "Everyone always says I did it." How do you rule, under the FRE? ________________

78. Brutus and friends attack Julius Caesar on the steps of the Capital. As Brutus stabs him, Caesar, believing himself mortally wounded, looks up, and exclaims, "Et tu, Brute?" Caesar unexpectedly survives, changing the course of history. At Brutus' attempted murder trial, Caesar is one of the spectators. A bystander at the stabbing, Innocente Witnius, is testifying, and says: "I heard Caesar say, 'Et tu, Brute?' " On objection, is the statement admissible as a "dying declaration" under the FRE? ________________

79. Rosebud Rosenbluhm suffers smoke inhalation when she is watching a play at the Iroquois Theatre and the theatre catches fire. Firefighters carry Rosebud outside, where she sees Iva Match, who set the fire. With her last ounce of energy, Rosebud points at Iva, and screams, "That's her! I saw her pour gasoline on the curtain and set it afire! She killed me!" Rosebud then wilts and dies. The prosecutor charges Iva with arson, but not with the homicide of Rosebud. Under the FRE, can Rosebud's statement be used as a "dying declaration" against Iva at trial, over Iva's hearsay objection? ________________

80. King Khufu, owner of the greatest of the Pyramids, dies. In his will, he leaves the Pyramid, "Man's greatest architectural achievement, mine and mine alone, to my son, Bhufu." Khufu's second wife, Joanne, contests the will, claiming that the Pyramid was always community property and therefore now passes to her, not Bhufu. She offers as evidence the testimony of a neighbor, Cal: "Before Khufu died, he told me he realized the pyramid was community property." Under what hearsay exception, if any, will Khufu's statement to Cal be admissible? ________________

81. Scrooge McDukk, a fabulously wealthy man, is prosecuted for income tax evasion. McDukk is elderly and has had several heart operations. At trial, the defense offers the testimony of Launchpad McQuakk, who will testify: "McDukk's cousin, Donald Dukk, told me that he himself prepared Scrooge's tax return, that he, Donald, knew he had put some questionable deductions into the return, and that the old man knew nothing about any wrongdoing." The defense offers nothing further about the circumstances surrounding Dukk's statement. The prosecutor objects. Is the statement admissible as a "declaration against interest" under the FRE? ________________

82. Bert Littlefish is stopped by police for a traffic violation, and turns out to have 19 kilos of cocaine in his car. While interrogated by Otto, one of the arresting officers, Bert gives a 10-minute account of his involvement with the drugs, in which he claims, basically, that he was just a courier for the drugs, and that the real mastermind was Ernie Kingfish. Bert says Ernie arranged for the drugs to be smuggled in and delivered to Bert, and would have picked them up from Bert and re-sold them if Bert had not been arrested. At Ernie's federal smuggling trial, Bert refuses to repeat this story, even though given immunity. The prosecution seeks to have Otto recount all of Bert's statement to Otto, including those parts that implicate Ernie while not specifically implicating Bert (e.g., "Ernie was the mastermind, who arranged for the drugs to be smuggled in.") Can Otto so testify, under the FRE? ________________

83. Homer Simpson's will provides that, if his son Bart reaches age 30 while Homer is still alive, Homer's estate is to go to his daughter Lisa and, if Bart doesn't reach 30 before Homer's death, then the estate is to go to Homer's other daughter, Maggie. When Homer dies, Bart has been dead for three years, but his birth certificate can't be found so it's hard to prove how old he was at his death. In the lawsuit that ensues to determine who is entitled to Homer's estate, Lisa offers the testimony of Molly Burns-Simpson, Bart's widow. She would testify that she lived with Bart during the last year of his life, during which he told her he was 33. Maggie Simpson objects on hearsay grounds. Under what hearsay exception, if any, is Molly's statement admissible? ________________

84. Spartacus sues the Cisalpine Gaul Tavern under a Dramshop Act, for injuries he received when Crassus ran over him while he was crossing the street. (Spartacus claims the Cisalpine Gaul let Crassus drink too much.) The tavern calls Crassus as a witness, and expects him to testify that he was sober when he left the Tavern. In fact, on direct testimony, Crassus says he may have had a few too many at the tavern, after all. Can the tavern now introduce a statement from Crassus' pre-trial deposition, in which he claimed he left the bar sober, as substantive evidence that he was in fact sober? ______________

85. The Joker successfully pulls off a bank job by super-gluing the bank manager's hands to a wall so the police can't be alerted. At Joker's trial, in order to prove that Joker committed the heist, the manager testifies that he picked Joker out from a valid line-up as the super-gluer. Is the manager's testimony hearsay under the FRE? ______________

86. Charlotte Corday stabs Jean Paul Marat to death in his bathtub. Marat's maid, Fifi, sees Corday enter and leave the bathroom. The police ask Fifi to draw a picture of the woman she saw, and she does so. The picture bears a striking resemblance to Corday. Fifi dies of a heart attack the next day, and Corday is arrested the following week. At Corday's murder trial, Fifi's drawing is offered as evidence against her. On objection, the prosecution claims the picture is non-hearsay because it's a prior identification. Under the FRE, how do you rule? ______________

87. Snow White is found dead in the forest, and the medical examiner concludes that she suffered head injuries when she hit her head on a rock after falling or being pushed. A grand jury is duly convened to investigate the death. Grumpy is called as a witness. (There is evidence that Grumpy desperately loved Snow White, and there's no evidence he had anything to do with her death.) Grumpy testifies, under oath, "I saw Sneezy kill Snow White — he sneezed right in her face, and she fell down and hit her head on a big rock. It looked to me like he did it on purpose." The prosecutor questions Grumpy briefly about his statement, and Grumpy supplies details in a convincing way. Sneezy is then put on trial for manslaughter. Grumpy refuses to testify at Sneezy's trial even after being granted immunity and threatened with contempt. (There's some evidence he's afraid of what Sneezy will do to him if he testifies.) There is no other evidence pointing unequivocally to Sneezy as the culprit. Putting aside any constitutional issues, under what hearsay exception, if any, can the transcript of Grumpy's grand jury testimony be introduced against Sneezy? ______________

CHAPTER 7

CONFRONTATION AND COMPULSORY PROCESS

88. The state calls Harry Houdini as a key witness at a criminal trial. Just as the prosecutor finishes his questioning, Houdini's appendix bursts and he dies. What should the trial judge do with respect to Houdini's direct testimony, and why? ______________

89. Pretty Boy is on trial for conspiracy to distribute cocaine. The prosecution has a recording of a telephone conversation between Scarface and a person who is (unbeknownst to Scarface or Pretty Boy) a government informant. In the phone conversation, Scarface tells the informant how Pretty Boy plans to distribute cocaine to the informant. (At the time, Scarface is assisting the distribution scheme.) Scarface refuses to testify on Fifth Amendment grounds. The prosecution offers the tape under the hearsay exception for a co-conspirator's statement. Pretty Boy objects, claiming his rights under the Confrontation Clause would be violated by allowing the tape into evidence. How do you rule? ______________

90. Bart is arrested for drunk driving. Because the arresting officer's breathalyzer is broken, Bart is taken to police headquarters. He consents to having a blood sample taken from him, which is sent to a police lab. A technician, Ted, uses a gas chromatograph to analyze the sample's blood alcohol content (BAC). The machine reports that the BAC of the sample is .12%, which is above the minimum for DUI. Ted then fills out a form in which he states, "The sample labelled 'Bart' was shown by the chromatograph to have a BAC = .12%" Ted then signs a certification at the bottom of the form, saying that it "is true to the best of my knowledge and belief." Bart is charged with DUI. In court, the prosecution presents testimony by Tilda, another technician in the lab, who is familiar with how the lab uses gas chromatographs, describes the process for the jury, and offers the report in evidence. Under cross-examination by Bart's counsel, Tilda acknowledges that she did not personally watch Ted do the test on the sample, or otherwise review his work. However, she testifies that "I have worked alongside Ted for years, and know that he performs every gas chromatograph test carefully and accurately." Bart's lawyer objects to the introduction of the report into evidence on Confrontation Clause grounds. How should the court rule?

____

91. While Bugs Bunny is under surveillance near the Statue of Liberty, he is stopped on suspicion of planning to blow up the Statue, based on an informant's tip that Bugs and friends are planning an explosion for two months hence, on the anniversary of 9/11. He is taken to a New York City police station, and questioned about his plans. After polite questioning (no torture) by Officer Krupke, Bugs says, "Well, I was just casing the Statue to give advice to my friend Donald Duck about how to blow it up; Donald was going to arrange the explosion." Donald is later arrested in Queens, New York, and brought to trial for conspiring with Bugs to blow up the Statue. (Bugs is not put on trial.) At Donald's trial, the prosecution puts Bugs on the stand to ask him about the conspiracy, but Bugs pleads the Fifth. The prosecution then puts on Officer Krupke, who offers to describe how Bugs gave the statement implicating Donald. The prosecution asserts that the statement is admissible under the declaration-against-interest hearsay exception. Donald asserts that it's barred by the Confrontation Clause. Who wins? ________________

92. Butthead is arrested and kept in custody on armed robbery charges. While in custody, he gives a confession implicating both himself and his friend Beavis. Now, Beavis and Butthead are both defendants in a joint trial on the armed robbery charges. Butthead declines to take the stand. The prosecution offers Butthead's confession, and agrees that the judge should issue a limiting instruction to the jury that the confession is admissible only against Butthead, not against Beavis. Should the judge admit the confession on this basis? ________________

CHAPTER 8
PRIVILEGES

93. Charles Kiting visits Attorney Myles Crooked and says, "I'm planning on bilking millions of innocent people out of their life savings in a fraudulent real estate investment scheme and I need your help in setting it up." Crooked agrees, and they set to work. When Kiting is subsequently tried for fraud, Crooked is called as a witness by the state. Kiting objects to his testimony, claiming attorney/client privilege. How do you rule? _______________

94. Pinnocchio drives a truck for the Geppetto Wood Chipper Company, owned by Gino Geppeto. He hits a car driven by Jim N.E. Cricket. Cricket sues Geppetto. Geppetto and Pinnocchio meet with a lawyer, John E. Corkran, to discuss their case. Corkran calls in his paralegal to take notes on the case. At trial, Cricket calls Pinnocchio to testify to admissions Geppetto may have made during the conference with Corkran and his paralegal. Geppetto objects, citing attorney/client privilege. How do you rule? _______________

95. Lizzie Borden runs in to the legal offices of Dewey, Cheatham and Howe, brandishing an axe dripping blood. When one of the women in the waiting room screams, Attorney Dewey runs out, and Borden tells him (in front of the screaming woman): "I've just murdered my parents! Will you defend me?" Dewey does so. At her trial, prosecutor calls the woman from the waiting room to testify to Borden's statement. Borden objects, claiming attorney/client privilege. How do you rule? _______________

96. Popeye sues Bluto for battery. Bluto calls Dr. Seahag as a witness. The defense asks Seahag about comments made to her by Olive Oyl, concerning Olive Oyl's obtaining medical treatment from Dr. Seahag. Can Popeye's attorney object on the grounds of doctor/patient privilege? _______________

97. Peter Pan is knocked unconscious in a barroom brawl. He is rushed to the Emergency Room, where he is examined and treated by Dr. Feelgood. As Feelgood is examining Peter, a packet of angel dust falls from Peter's pocket. At Peter's trial for possession of a controlled substance, the prosecutor calls Feelgood to testify as to what he saw in the emergency room. Peter objects, claiming doctor/patient privilege. How do you rule? _______________

98. Beethoven is called as a witness by the plaintiff in a civil suit for battery. When Beethoven is asked whether he was at the scene of the incident, he refuses to answer, invoking his Fifth Amendment privilege against self-incrimination. Plaintiff moves that Beethoven be ordered to answer. The judge believes that there is no chance that the answer itself will incriminate Beethoven, and only a relatively small chance (perhaps 5-10%) that if Beethoven is forced to answer, the answer will lead prosecutors to other material incriminating him. How should the judge rule on Beethoven's Fifth? _______________

99. Bonnie and Clyde successfully rob a series of banks. After accumulating an adequate amount of cash, they settle down and marry. At Clyde's subsequent federal trial for one of the bank robberies, the prosecution seeks to introduce Bonnie's testimony as to conversations she and Clyde had at the time of the robbery. Bonnie is willing to testify, because she's been told it will help her get a lighter sentence when she is tried later. Clyde objects. Which, if either, of the marital privileges applies? _______________

100. Mickey is on trial in federal court for conspiring with Donald to defraud Goofy. At Mickey's trial, the prosecutor calls Mickey's wife Minnie to the stand to testify as to a conversation between Mickey and Donald that she heard while married to Mickey. Mickey objects, citing the spousal testimony privilege. Can Minnie testify anyway, if she wants to? _______________

101. Rebby Hensable is charged with beating his eight-year-old daughter. The prosecution offers testimony by Hensable's wife's that Hensable did, in fact, hit his daughter. Hensable objects, on the grounds of the spousal testimony privilege. Can Mrs. Hensable testify over her husband's objections? ________________

CHAPTER 9

REAL AND DEMONSTRATIVE EVIDENCE, INCLUDING WRITINGS

102. Patrolman Pete testifies he stopped defendant, Shernott Home, and found a package of white powder on his person. He testifies that he turned the package over to the police lab. The prosecutor then seeks to introduce a package of cocaine into evidence, saying it's the package that was found on Home's person. The defense objects on the grounds that the package hasn't been authenticated. How should the judge rule? ________________

103. In David's murder trial for the killing of Goliath, the prosecution seeks to enter the murder weapon, David's slingshot, into evidence. The prosecutor calls David's best friend, Sparky, to the stand, and asks if he recognizes the slingshot. Sparky responds, "Yup, that's David's, all right. It's got notches in the handle for every giant he's killed. I'd know it anywhere." Must the court now admit the slingshot into evidence? ________________

104. Shortly after the *Titanic* sinks, surviving passengers sue its owners, the White Star line, for negligence. They seek to admit into evidence a letter bearing the signature of the ship's captain, Smith, which he appears to have written to his wife during the fateful trip. It reads: "Double my insurance, honey. If this baby's unsinkable, my name's Jones." The letter is written on paper bearing a "*Titanic*" letterhead and Smith's imprinted monogram. Will the letterhead and monogram alone authenticate the letter? ________________

105. Howard Huge, eccentric billionaire, dies. In a will contest, Huge's maid testifies that she knows Huge's signature because she had often seen that signature on her weekly paychecks. She further testifies that the signature on the will in question is Huge's. Under the FRE, has the will been properly authenticated so as to permit its admission into evidence? ________________

106. Jacques Coustodian, janitor for a Las Vegas restaurant, is cleaning the men's room one night when he finds, scrawled on the wall of one stall: "I, Howard Hughes, being of sound mind and body. . . ." followed by a disposition of Hughes' property, and a signature purporting to be Hughes'. At a trial determining the bathroom will's authenticity, Coustodian is called to the stand. He is given a paper containing a signature known to be Hughes' and asked if it matches the one he saw. He says it does. Assuming a non-witnessed will can be valid, has the bathroom will been authenticated? ________________

107. A typewritten letter purportedly written by Michelangelo to Leonardo da Vinci is offered into evidence. The letter includes the sentence, "By the way, in answer to the question in your February 25 letter, I don't think La Giaconda would look good with a mustache. The mysterious smile is plenty. Can't wait to see the finished product." Leonardo was working on the painting in secret, and Michelangelo was one of the few to know about it. Could a jury determine the authenticity of the letter — i.e., that it was written by Michelangelo — on this statement alone? ______________

108. Nosmo King once underwent hypnosis therapy in order to give up smoking. As a result, whenever he hears the word "cigarette," he barks like a dog. In a trial, Percy seeks to introduce into evidence his recollections of what he says was a telephone conversation between himself and Nosmo, in which Nosmo called him. The conversation allegedly included this snippet:

Percy: Excuse me while I light a cigarette.

Caller: Grr — Arf! Arf! Arf! Arf! Arf!

Percy says that the caller identified himself as Nosmo, but Percy also admits that he, Percy, had never before (or since) spoken to Nosmo, so he doesn't know for sure that the caller really *was* Nosmo. Can Percy's recollection and description of the caller's speech patterns be enough to authenticate the conversation as one involving Nosmo? ______________

109. Georgy Porgy kisses the girls and makes them cry. At his subsequent trial on battery charges, Georgy's friend, Orgy, testifies that right before the incident, Georgy had sent him a letter (which Orgy says he still has), in which Georgy seemed intent to go on a kissing rampage. The letter itself is not introduced, even though it's available. Is Orgy's testimony admissible? ______________

110. Pied Piper sues Mayor Hamelin for breach of contract. Piper claims he was never paid for his services in ridding Hamelin's property of rats. Hamelin testifies, "I paid the Piper $1,000 on April 1." On cross of Hamelin, Piper shows that before testifying, Hamelin consulted his check register to see whether it contained a record of such a payment (though Hamelin did not mention the register in his direct testimony). Must the register be produced, under the Best Evidence Rule? ______________

111. The Pied Piper sues the Mayor of Hamelin for breach of contract. To prove the contract's terms, the Piper offers a photocopy of the contract into evidence, without explaining the whereabouts of the original. The Mayor objects, claiming the Best Evidence Rule requires that Piper produce the original contract. How do you rule, under the FRE? ______________

112. The contents of a letter from Mata Hari to Banda are relevant in a trial in which Mata Hari is a party. Banda is not in the jurisdiction and has had no fixed address for a year, although the letter is believed by the litigants still to be in Banda's possession. Under the FRE, will oral testimony about the contents of the letter be admissible, notwithstanding the Best Evidence Rule? ______________

113. Mike Angelo takes his statue of David to the Renny Sanz Art Gallery to be polished. The statue is destroyed through the Gallery's negligence. When Mike sues the Gallery, he calls an expert witness to determine the value of the statue. The witness, Vermi Celli, is a licensed art appraiser, and says so during his testimony. Will the Best Evidence Rule require that Vermi produce his license to prove his status? ______________

114. Ophelia Butts has her appendix removed by Dr. Goren Guts. The next time she has an X-ray, she finds out that Dr. Guts accidentally left a pocket radio in her abdomen. In her malpractice suit, Butts doesn't produce the incriminating X-ray, but testifies that she saw the X-ray and that it had a clear outline of a pocket radio where her appendix used to be. Will her testimony be sufficient, or must she produce the X-ray? ________________

115. In a close encounter of the third kind, a Martian lands in Tim O'Hara's back yard, destroying his vegetable patch. When Tim sues the Martian for damages, Tim offers a photograph taken after the landing, to show the extent of the damages. In order for the photograph to be admissible, must the photographer testify to the circumstances under which the photograph was taken? ________________

116. In the trial for the murder of Jay Gatsby, the jury requests a view of the scene of the crime — Gatsby's swimming pool at his mansion in West Egg, Long Island. Must the judge grant the request? ________________

117. Smog Monster is on trial for destroying downtown Tokyo. Godzilla is testifying for the prosecution. To aid his testimony, Godzilla uses a small, plaster model of the city, and squashes with his fist the replicas of the buildings Smog Monster destroyed in real life. Smog Monster's lawyer objects, claiming that the model requires authentication by the person who built it. Is he correct? (Assume that monsters from Japanese horror movies are competent to testify in the jurisdiction, and that American law applies). ________________

CHAPTER 10

OPINIONS, EXPERTS, AND SCIENTIFIC EVIDENCE

118. Bart Luck is found dead in his study by his maid, Hazel. Cardinell Syn is arrested and tried for murdering Bart by filtering sodium cyanide into the study. Hazel testifies for the prosecution: "When I found him, there was a faint smell of almonds in the room." (The distinctive smell of sodium cyanide is often likened to the smell of almonds.) Defense counsel objects, claiming that Hazel isn't competent to offer her opinion on the presence of sodium cyanide and that expert testimony is needed. How do you rule? ________________

119. Bluto's pit bull, Mittens, has bitten several children in the neighborhood, although no one has ever brought suit or notified the police. One day, Mittens bites Olive Oyl. Olive sues Bluto. Olive calls Wimpy, a neighbor, who testifies as to Mittens' past conduct and to the way in which Bluto supervised Mittens. During Wimpy's testimony, he says, "I sure wouldn't have let Mittens run around loose like Bluto did." Under the FRE, is this testimony admissible, if objected to? ________________

120. At a trial, expert testimony concerning hieroglyphics is required. One party offers the testimony of Jean-Claude Champollion, who speaks several ancient languages and was the first to "crack" the Stone. However, Champollion, age 17, is completely lacking in academic credentials and has not published anything. Can he still qualify as an "expert"? ________________

121. Claire Voyant is a recognized expert on ghosts. She is called to testify as an expert witness in a trial where an issue is whether the house of Mrs. Whatsit is haunted. Must Claire have personally examined the house in order to be able to testify as an expert? ________________

122. Napoleon Bonaparte's nephew, Joseph, challenges Napoleon's will on the grounds of lack of testamentary capacity. A psychiatrist, Able Elba, is called as a witness. He has been shown Napoleon's psychiatric reports for the last five years of his life (the will was written two years before Napoleon died), and he has interviewed Napoleon's relatives and doctors. Napoleon's executor asks him: "Did Napoleon have the capacity to make a will?" Joseph objects. Assuming Elba is basing his opinion on a proper source, is the question permissible, under the FRE? ________________

123. Mrs. Sprat is on trial for killing the local grocer. Mrs. Sprat pleads "not guilty," and relies to a large extent on the fact that the person who committed the crime weighed around 400 lbs. and Mrs. Sprat weighs only 125 lbs. at the time of trial, two months after the crime. Mrs. Sprat calls an expert witness, Dr. Sal Ulite, who testifies that it is medically impossible to lose 275 lbs. in two months. On cross-examination, the prosecutor asks: "Are you familiar with Dr. Di Uretic's treatise 'How to Lose Weight and Influence People'?" Dr. Ulite admits she is not, offhand, familiar with the text. Prosecutor continues: "How do you reconcile your opinion on weight loss with Dr. Uretic's opinion that 'Under careful supervision patients can safely lose 150 lbs. a month'?" Under the FRE, can the statement from Uretic's book be admitted as substantive evidence? ________________

124. Same facts as prior question. Now, assume for purposes of this question that the judge holds that the quoted portion of Dr. Uretic's treatise was properly read to the jury as substantive evidence. May this portion of the treatise be admitted as an exhibit? ________________

125. Evelyn Copralight is an expert in the exotic and bizarre field of fecology; that is, the science of determining a person's mental competence by examining his stool sample. At trial, the defense seeks to have Copralight testify as an expert to prove that defendant is mentally unbalanced judging from his stool sample. What's the best argument for not allowing Copralight's expert testimony? ________________

126. Rodney Coaker is detained at Miami Airport on suspicion of drug smuggling. Agents don't find major quantifies of drugs in his luggage. However, they pass his clothing through a newly-designed "cocaine spectrometer," which supposedly can detect minuscule amounts of cocaine. The spectrometer reports that there are trace quantities of cocaine in Coaker's underwear. He is tried on federal cocaine-smuggling charges. At trial, the designer of the spectrometer testifies that the device is reliable, and that the results reported for Coaker's underwear indicate that cocaine must have come in contact with the underwear shortly before the test. The design of the cocaine spectrometer has never been made public or subjected to peer review; nor has the device so far become generally accepted as a method of drug testing. Do these facts mean that the court should bar the use of the spectrometer evidence? ________________

CHAPTER 11

BURDENS OF PROOF, PRESUMPTIONS, ETC.

127. In a contract dispute between Lincoln and Davis, Davis denies that he ever received a document Lincoln mailed to him. Lincoln produces evidence that the letter was properly addressed and mailed. Davis does not produce any evidence that he didn't receive the letter. The jurisdiction imposes a presumption that a properly addressed and mailed letter was received by the addressee. If the jury *believes* the letter was properly addressed and mailed, *must* it find that Davis received the letter? ________________

128. Whether or not Judge Crater is still alive is at issue in a civil case. The jurisdiction applies a presumption that one who has not been seen or heard from for 7 years is dead. The party who seeks to prove his death shows that Crater hasn't been seen in seven years and that he hasn't contacted anyone in his family or any of his associates. The opponent offers no rebuttal. Will the judge now be "presumed" dead, under the FRE? ________________

129. Jefferson sues Washington, claiming that Washington entered into a written contract with Jefferson under which Jefferson would ghost-write Washington's autobiography, "Father of My Country." The case is tried before a jury, operating under the FRE. Jefferson offers in evidence a document that purports to be signed by Washington, embodying the ghost-writing arrangement. Washington's lawyer attacks the document as a forgery. The trial judge believes that the document probably is a forgery, but he's not sure. Must the judge let the document into evidence? ________________

130. Ayn Puty's leg is mangled and severed in an industrial accident. In a suit against her employer, Acme Iron Works, Ayn's lawyer seeks to admit the severed leg into evidence. Acme's lawyer doesn't object. Acme loses the case and appeals, objecting to admission of the leg. Under the FRE, since Acme didn't make a timely objection, is its right to appeal waived? ________________

CHAPTER 12

JUDICIAL NOTICE

131. Juliet files a paternity suit against Romeo. Is the fact that the normal human gestation period is approximately 280 days a fact suitable for judicial notice? ________________

132. Blair Wolf is on trial for a battery which allegedly took place after dark on April 1. Is the time at which the sun set on April 1 a fact suitable for judicial notice, assuming it's relevant? ________________

133. Custer and Sitting Bull are involved in an automobile collision on April 1 at a bend on Little Big Horn Street. Custer sues Sitting Bull for negligence in crossing the double yellow line. Sitting Bull claims he was swerving to avoid a large tree which had fallen across his lane, which he couldn't see in time to stop. Sitting Bull asks the judge to take judicial notice of the fallen tree. In fact, the judge knows about the fallen tree because he lives on Little Big Horn Street. May the judge properly take judicial notice of the fallen tree? ______________

134. Jeffrey Dahmhim is on trial for depriving a black man of his civil rights by eating him. Dahmhim takes the stand, and says, "I may be a member of the Ku Klux Klan, but I'm no racist." The prosecutor asks the judge to take judicial notice of the fact that the KKK is a white supremacist organization. The judge does so. (Assume that this is proper, as it probably would be.) Under the FRE, when the judge is giving the jury its instructions, may he tell it to accept as proven that the KKK is a white supremacist organization? ______________

ANSWERS TO SHORT-ANSWER QUESTIONS

1. It is *circumstantial* evidence, because it is ***indirect,*** and requires one or more ***inferences*** to establish the existence of a material fact — that OJ committed the crime. The inferences go like this: Where a glove is found at a crime scene, the person who dropped the glove is probably the criminal. If a glove found at a crime scene is an unusual one that is similar or identical to one known to have been possessed by X, then it's likely that X is the one who dropped it. Therefore, X is probably the criminal.

2. Dipsey can object on the grounds that the testimony is *cumulative* and will cause ***undue delay and waste time.*** Note, of course, that all the testimony is relevant, but its probative value is outweighed by the waste of time caused by its cumulative nature. See FRE 403.

Note that FRE 403 allows, in addition to exclusion for waste of time / needless cumulation, exclusion where the probative value is substantially outweighed by the danger of unfair prejudice, confusion of issues, or misleading the jury.

3. No. Here, Phil's negligence in disrupting the tennis tournament is offered as circumstantial evidence that he likely did the same thing again. The evidence won't be admissible, because it's circumstantial character evidence — a specific prior act offered to show Phil's general character for carelessness, to prove that Phil probably acted in conformity with that character on the present occasion. It is thus inadmissible under FRE 404(b) ("Evidence of a crime, wrong, or other act is not admissible to prove a person's character in order to show that on a particular occasion the person acted in accordance with the character.")

This evidence might be admissible to prove a common plan, motive, or lack of mistake, etc. FRE 404(b), 2nd sent. But none of these "other purposes" seems applicable here.

Note that the evidence here could not prove habit (admissible to show action in accordance therewith, under FRE 406), since habit is a regular response to a repeated situation, and a single instance can't show this.

4. Objection overruled. The general rule that character can't be proved to show action in accordance therewith doesn't apply where character is directly ***in issue*** in the case, in the sense that character is an ***element of a charge, claim or defense***. Stein's character is automatically "in issue" here, because it's an essential element of Stein's claim for sole custody – Stein's character goes to which parent will be a better guardian for the child. Consequently, under FRE 405(a) and (b), all three types of character evidence are admissible: reputation, opinion, and specific acts. (In common law jurisdictions, the modern trend is also to allow all three.)

5. Objection sustained. The testimony is inadmissible character evidence, because every indication is that it's being introduced solely to suggest that because Sam is a pervert, he's more likely to be guilty of the present offense than he would be if he weren't a pervert (i.e., that he's got the character trait of perversion, offered to show he probably acted in accordance with that trait on the present occasion). The prosecutor can only introduce character evidence to rebut character evidence introduced by Sam, or to impeach Sam's testimony. FRE

404(a)(2)(A) and (a)(3). Neither of these exceptions applies here: Sam hasn't introduced favorable evidence of his own character (we know this because the prosecution's just getting started), and Sam hasn't taken the stand so there's no testimony by him to impeach.

6. The evidence would be admissible for the limited purpose of showing "identity," but not to show Bouncer's criminal predisposition. FRE 404(b)(1) says that "Evidence of a crime, wrong, or other act is not admissible to prove a person's character in order to show that on a particular occasion the person acted in accordance with the character." So the prior purchases can't be used to show, in essence, that if Bouncer illegally bought guns in the past, he probably did so on the present occasion as well.

But 404(b)(2) goes on to say that other crimes or wrongs may be introduced for other limited purposes, one of which is to show ***"identity."*** Because Bouncer has put the identity of the purchaser in issue (rather than, for instance, admitting he made the purchase but claiming he didn't have the mental state for the crime), the prosecution will be allowed to show that the prior and present acts are so similar and so idiosyncratic that they bear Bouncer's unique "signature," thus establishing that he is the perpetrator.

NOTE: Under 404(b), other crimes or wrongs may be introduced for other limited purposes in addition to identity, including proof of motive, opportunity, preparation, plan, knowledge, or absence of mistake or accident.

7. Yes. Amy's testimony that she hasn't heard anything bad about Bart is admissible as favorable evidence of his reputation under the "Mercy Rule."

More precisely: FRE 404(a)(2)(A) applies the Mercy Rule, by which a criminal defendant can submit evidence of his good character, as circumstantial evidence that he probably didn't commit the crime. 405(a) allows character evidence, when admissible at all, to be in the form of reputation evidence. Courts construing this provision allow negative reputation evidence.

Note, however, that the prosecutor will then be free to ***rebut*** Amy's testimony with evidence of Bart's ***bad*** character. The prosecutor will also be able to question Amy about her knowledge of specific instances of bad conduct in Bart's past. FRE 405(a), last sent.

8. No. The prosecutor can introduce character evidence to rebut character evidence introduced by the accused. Under the FRE, this rebuttal evidence can be in the form of either reputation or opinion evidence. (At common law, only reputation, not opinion, evidence would be allowed.) FRE 404(a)(2)(A) and 405(a). Killer "opened the door" by introducing evidence that he never started a fight, so the prosecution can rebut by showing that Killer had a reputation for violence, or that in the witness's opinion Killer was violent.

9. Yes. FRE 404(a)(2)(B) says that "a defendant may offer evidence of an alleged victim's pertinent trait[.]" So by application of this rule, the accused may introduce pertinent character evidence of the victim's violent propensity, to prove that the victim was the aggressor. (The *quid pro quo* is that once the defendant does so, the prosecution may put on evidence that the victim was peaceful. FRE 404(a)(2)(B)(i).)

10. Objection sustained. Under FRE 412 (the federal "rape shield" statute), evidence offered to prove a victim's sexual predisposition is generally inadmissible in criminal cases. An exception exists for "evidence of specific instances of a victim's sexual behavior with respect to the person accused of the sexual misconduct, if offered by the defendant to prove consent[.]" 412(b)(1)(B). However, this exception doesn't apply here, for two reasons: (1) Otto's proposed evidence does not relate to Mata's conduct with *him*; and (2) Otto's evidence is reputation evidence rather than specific-acts evidence. No other exception in FRE 412 applies, so the evidence is inadmissible.

11. Objection overruled. Under FRE 405(a), a reputation witness may be cross-examined about specific instances of conduct bearing on the reputation. (Theoretically, the rationale for this is that if the witness doesn't know about the specific instances – assuming they were commonly known – the witness's knowledge of the defendant's reputation is suspect. In reality, the questioner is trying to slip in the specific instance for its truth.)

Note that the question about specific instances must be asked in ***good faith***. That is, the questioner must have a reasonable belief that the episode really occurred, and that a witness who knew the details of the defendant's reputation would have heard of it. Note, also, that a trial court could decide that the "specific acts" evidence here is substantially more prejudicial than it is probative; in that case, the judge could exclude it under FRE 403. However, courts will normally give the jury a limiting instruction on the evidence, and allow the question.

COMMON LAW RULE: At common law, the wording of such a question was crucial to its admissibility. It had to be in the format given: "Have you heard? . . ." not "Did you know? . . ." But the FRE don't recognize this distinction.

12. Objection sustained. Under the "Mercy Rule," the defendant in a criminal trial can offer pertinent character evidence, in the form of reputation or opinion testimony, to prove his innocence. After he does so, the prosecution can cross-examine the character witness, and in so doing can inquire into "relevant specific instances of the [target witness's] conduct" (FRE 405(a)). Thus the prosecutor could have asked Hugh on cross, "Didn't you hear that Ripper was once convicted of mayhem?"

Alternatively, once the accused uses the Mercy rule, the prosecution may put on substantive – i.e., direct rather than cross – rebuttal evidence. 404(a)(2)(A). But FRE 405(a) says that this evidence may be by ***reputation*** or ***opinion*** testimony; by negative implication, the rebuttal may ***not*** be by ***specific instances*** of conduct. (405(b) allows proof of specific instances of conduct on the issue of character, but only where character is an "essential element" of a charge, claim or defense, which is not the case here.) So it was improper for the prosecution to ask Elizabeth about specific instances of the accused's bad character, and Ripper's conviction for mayhem clearly falls into this category.

13. Yes, probably. If the matter had to be determined solely by reference to FRE 404(b)(1), the Magdalena rape would be inadmissible, because that provision says that "Evidence of a crime ... is not admissible to prove a person's character in order to show that on a particular occasion the person acted in accordance with the character."

However, Congress has made it dramatically ***easier*** for the prosecution to introduce evidence of the defendant's ***prior sex crimes*** for the purpose of showing that the defendant probably committed the sex crime for which he is now charged. FRE 413, in subsection (a), says that "In a criminal case in which a defendant is accused of a sexual assault, the court ***may admit evidence that the defendant committed any other sexual assault.*** The evidence may be considered for its bearing on ***any matter to which it is relevant.***" So the fact that Duke previously raped Magdalena is admissible to show, in essence, "If he did it before, he probably did it again." However, the trial judge still has discretion to exclude the evidence under FRE 403, if she believes that the evidence's ***probative value is substantially outweighed*** by the possibility of ***unfair prejudice to the defendant***. Such a finding could be based on the fact that the circumstances surrounding the two crimes (stranger rape vs. date rape) are quite different, and the fact that the prior crime took place a long time ago. But unless the judge makes this "substantially outweighed" finding (which she probably won't, given Congress' intent in enacting 413 to cover a broad range of prior sexual assault crimes), the evidence will be admissible.

14. Yes. The only way the experience of prior customers would be relevant is to show Freddie had a "habit" of giving warranties. Evidence of a single prior guarantee is insufficient to demonstrate a person's habit or an organization's routine practice; to establish habit or routine practice, the behavior must be proven to be a ***regular response to a repeated situation***. (If this *had* been enough to establish a habit, it would have been admissible. Under FRE 406, evidence of habit is admissible to prove that a person acted in accordance with that habit on a particular occasion. This is true regardless of whether there are eyewitnesses to the actual act, and whether or not there's corroboration of the existence of the habit.)

15. There is no blanket rule excluding this sort of "no prior accidents" evidence (which is the reverse of "similar happenings" evidence, also admissible subject to limits). However, the general requirement of relevance means that such "safety history" evidence will only be admissible if Mayhemart establishes that (1) the material circumstances of other customers' use were ***substantially similar*** and (2) Mayhemart probably ***would have gotten complaints*** if similar accidents had happened.

16. Objection sustained. Under FRE 407, evidence of subsequent remedial measures is inadmissible to prove negligence or culpable conduct. That's exactly what Hook is trying to do here. This rule is designed to encourage people to make things safer by not using this information against them to show negligence. (However, subsequent remedial measures are admissible for non-culpability purposes, such as proving ownership or control, or to rebut a claim of impossibility of precautions, etc. FRE 407.)

17. Yes. If the ***feasibility*** of safeguards is ***disputed***, the fact that the safeguards whose feasibility was denied by the defendant were later implemented by him may be proved, notwithstanding the "no proof of subsequent remedial measures" rule. FRE 407. (The "yes" answers assumes that the technology used in the later model year was available at the time the seat in question was designed. If it wasn't, then the redesign doesn't bear on the feasibility of safeguards, and would be excluded.)

RELATED ISSUE: Suppose the manufacturer here hadn't argued that a safer design was impractical (merely that the design used was not unreasonably dangerous, the standard for strict product liability). Could Batman nonetheless have introduced the subsequent redesign to show that a safer seat was feasible, and thus by inference that the old design wasn't reasonably safe? Courts are split on this issue of whether the ban on subsequent remedial measures evidence applies to a showing of later design improvements when offered in a strict product liability case. Some hold that a strict liability case isn't about negligence or culpability, so the ban on subsequent remedial measures should not apply. Other courts (especially a lot of federal courts) hold that there is inevitably some element of culpability in an unsafe-design product liability case, and that the same policy reasons for barring remedial measures in negligence cases (don't discourage the taking of such measures by making them admissible) apply in strict liability cases.

18. Yes. Though evidence of liability insurance is inadmissible to prove Buddy's negligence, such evidence can be admitted to prove agency, ownership, control, or witness bias. FRE 411. Here, the fact that Buddy is covered by Ashe's liability policy tends to establish that Ashe controlled Buddy, and is therefore liable for Buddy's acts under respondeat superior.

19. Yes, but ***only*** for the purpose of demonstrating ***bias*** on the part of Huey and Dewey — ***not*** to prove Donald's ***liability*** for the accident. FRE 408. Remember that settlement offers, and completed settlements, are inadmissible to show the payor's liability. The reason is that settlements and settlement offers are of low probative value, since a litigant (here, Donald) may only be attempting to "buy peace" by settling.

20. (1) **Yes** and (2) **no**. Under FRE 409, the actual payment of medical bills, or an offer to pay, is not admissible to prove liability, due to the possibility that such payment may be prompted only by humanitarian motives. However, ***admissions of fact*** accompanying offers to pay medical bills are admissible. Thus, "Gee, I'm sorry. I fell asleep at the wheel. It was my fault," is admissible; "I'll pay your medical bills" (and the fact that the bills were in fact paid) are not.

RELATED ISSUE: Assume that this had been a negotiation situation: "Gee, I'm sorry, I fell asleep at the wheel. It was all my fault. I'll pay you $5,000 to settle." Here, unlike the medical bills situation, the admission accompanying the settlement offer is ***not*** admissible under FRE 408; nor is the offer to settle or the settlement itself.

21. (a) **That the prosecutor is leading the witness**, i.e., suggesting the answer desired by the questioner.

(b) **No, probably.** It is true, as a general rule, that ***leading questions are impermissible on direct examination***. However, there are exceptions. The facts here fit one of them: leading questions are permissible on direct examination when they serve to ***jog the witness's memory about something he once knew***, rather than to supply the answer to him. This is especially true where, as here, the question merely clues the witness in to a particular ***area*** or ***issue***, rather than supplying the specific substance of the answer – the Prosecutor may be suggesting that something was on Macbeth's hands, but isn't suggesting exactly what that something was. Also, the fact that Banquo is already on record as having remembered the answer in his deposition supplies an extra safeguard against the possibility that it's the Prosecutor, rather than Banquo, who is truly the one supplying the answer. (But if the prosecutor asked, "Did you see *blood* on Macbeth's hands?" this *would* be impermissible leading, because it would suggest the precise answer desired by the questioner, not merely the area to which the answer relates.)

22. FRE: **Yes**. Under FRE 607, a party can impeach the credibility of a witness even if the witness was called by that party. COMMON LAW: **Yes**. Under the common-law rule, impeachment of one's own witness is generally not allowed; however, there are several exceptions, including where, as here, the party is honestly ***surprised*** by harmful testimony from his own witness.

23. Objection overruled, both under the FRE and under the majority common-law approach. Under FRE 609(a)(2), if a witness has been convicted of a crime for which ***dishonesty or a false statement*** was an element (***"crimen falsi"***), that conviction is admissible for impeachment purposes even if the offense was only a ***misdemeanor.*** The crime of taking property by false pretenses is defined in such a way as to require the prosecution to prove a false statement, so that the crime is a *crimen falsi*, and thus usable for impeachment.

Observe that Rule 609(a) makes an important distinction between *crimen falsi* and other crimes. Where the crime is not a *crimen falsi* (and thus admissible only if it's a felony, not a misdemeanor), 609(a)(1) makes admissibility "subject to Rule 403," so that the judge has discretion to exclude the conviction if she finds that the "***probative value*** is ***substantially outweighed*** by the danger of ... ***unfair prejudice***[.]" But 609(a)(2), dealing with *crimen falsi*, makes no reference to 403, and simply says that the evidence of the conviction "must" be admitted – so where, as here, false statement was an element of the crime (whether the crime was a misdemeanor or a felony), the judge ***must*** admit it for impeachment no matter how little its probative value or how great its prejudicial effect on the opponent.

Also, observe that misdemeanors that do *not* reflect on the witness's veracity are generally *inadmissible* to impeach.

24. Yes, probably, even though the material doesn't reflect on Zoom's truthfulness or honesty. FRE 609(a) distinguishes between felonies in which dishonesty/false statement was not necessarily an element (dealt with in subsection 1) and all crimes (felonies or misdemeanors) in which dishonesty/false statement was an element (dealt with in subsection 2). Vehicular homicide clearly falls in the first category. Subsection 1 says that such convictions "must be admitted, subject to Rule 403" if the witness is (as here) not the accused in a criminal case. So the judge *must* admit the conviction unless she in the exercise of her discretion finds that the test of Rule 403 (allowing exclusion of relevant evidence whose "probative value is substantially outweighed by the danger of unfair prejudice[.]") is satisfied.

Courts usually find that even a violent crime not defined so as to require proof of dishonesty or false statement nonetheless has some bearing on the perpetrator's credibility. The court here therefore probably won't find that the tough test of Rule 403 (i.e., the requirement that probative value be "substantially" outweighed by prejudice, etc.) is satisfied. (The court can probably take into account the facts of the ***particular crime*** on which Crashbag was convicted, not just the nature of vehicular homicide in general; so if Crashbag, for instance, left the scene of the accident, this additional element of dishonesty would make it less likely that the judge would find that the "substantially outweighed" test of Rule 403 was satisfied.)

25. No, probably. Under FRE 609(b), evidence of a conviction is normally inadmissible if a period of more than ten years has elapsed since the date of the conviction or of the witness's release from confinement due to the conviction, whichever occurred later. However, an ***exception*** to this general rule exists if ***both*** of the following conditions are satisfied:

1. The court decides that, "in the interests of justice . . . the ***probative value*** of the conviction supported by specific facts and circumstances ***substantially outweighs*** its ***prejudicial effect.***" (609(b), 1st sent.); ***and***

2. The party trying to use the old conviction gives the adverse party "sufficient ***advance written notice*** of intent to use such evidence to provide the adverse party with a fair opportunity to contest the use of such evidence." (609(b)(1) and (2))

Even if the second requirement was satisfied here (we're not told), it's very unlikely that the court will find the first one to have been, since the conviction is much more than 10 years old, and there don't seem to be any "specific facts and circumstances" here giving it special probative value.

26. Objection overruled. The question is proper, because a witness can be impeached by inquiring, on cross-examination, about specific unconvicted bad acts, if these are "probative of the character for truthfulness or untruthfulness of: (1) the witness[.]" FRE 608(b)(1). Filing a false tax return is generally accepted as probative of truthfulness. (Note that under 608(b), the court "may" (not "must") allow such questions about unconvicted bad acts; so the court has discretion as to whether to allow the question.)

IMPORTANT: Under the collateral issue rule, if the witness denies the unconvicted bad acts, they can't be proven via ***extrinsic*** impeachment (e.g., testimony by some other witness; introduction of an arrest warrant). FRE 608(b), 1st sent. The examiner must ***"take the answer of the witness."***

27. No. Under FRE 608(b), ***specific instances*** of the conduct of a witness to attack or support credibility ***may not be proven by extrinsic evidence***. Thus, unconvicted bad acts, when used to impeach the witness's general character for truthfulness, can be proven only by intrinsic evidence — that is, through the testimony (given under cross-examination) of the witness who purportedly committed the bad acts (here, Wolf). Once the witness denies the bad acts, the examiner must "take the answer of the witness."

28. Objection overruled. Under FRE 608(a), the credibility of a witness may be attacked by evidence in the form of ***opinion*** or ***reputation***, so long as the evidence refers only to the witness's character for ***truthfulness*** or ***untruthfulness***. The evidence here qualifies as opinion evidence. (Under the common law, the credibility of a witness can only be attacked by reputation evidence, not [as here] opinion evidence.)

Observe that Hatfield wouldn't be allowed to testify to ***particular acts*** of untruthfulness by McCoy; these would violate the rule against showing specific bad acts by extrinsic evidence. See FRE 608(b), 1st sent. Also, note that evidence of the witness's *truthfulness* (not, as here, *un*truthfulness) cannot be introduced by the proponent of the witness until the witness's character has been attacked.

29. Objection sustained. Under both the common law and FRE 613(b), when prior inconsistent statements are offered to impeach a witness, the witness must be given a chance to ***explain or deny*** the prior inconsistency. This provides the foundation for the introduction of the inconsistent statement. Since Rick is now unavailable to explain or deny the prior statement, the statement should be excluded.

Note that, under the common law, the rule of *Queen Caroline's Case* required that the witness be given a chance to explain or deny the prior statement ***before*** being questioned. However, the FRE and most modern courts do not require this – it's enough that the witness is given the chance to explain afterwards.

The party attacking Rick's credibility (Goldilocks) wasn't required to actually call Rick back to the stand to explain or deny; Goldilocks was entitled to thrust onto the party who wants to explain the inconsistent statement (the Bears) this burden of calling Rick back. However, the attacking party does bear the risk that the witness will have become unavailable by the time the other party learns of the inconsistent statement and wants to explain it. Goldilocks' lawyer should have used the inconsistent statement during the original cross-examination of Rick; having waited, the lawyer loses the right to admit the statement now that Rick is unavailable to explain or deny.

Observe that by 613(b), the court can dispense with the right to explain or deny if "justice so requires." However, in view of Goldilocks' lawyer's unused chance to bring out the prior statement during the original cross, the court is very unlikely to use this power here.

30. Objection overruled. The use of extrinsic evidence to impeach is always permissible when a witness's ***perception***, ***memory***, or ***mental capacity*** is questioned. Since a witness's ability to perceive and remember are always deemed material, the "collateral matters" rule doesn't apply. (The "collateral issue" rule forbids impeachment with extrinsic evidence only if the evidence is *solely* relevant for impeachment.)

31. Yes, to impeach Hamlet. Horatio's statement, of course, contradicts Hamlet's testimony. Impeachment by contradiction is allowed, as a general rule, only where the contradiction relates to a ***material issue***. (If the contradiction doesn't relate to a material issue, it is inadmissible under the "collateral issue" rule.) This requirement is satisfied here, because the contradiction relates to Hamlet's acquaintance with Yorick, and that acquaintance is a material issue in the case (the prosecution's claim of jealousy couldn't be true if Hamlet didn't even know Yorick). Note that no foundation is necessary prior to introducing such contradiction evidence.

32. Objection sustained. Under the ***"collateral issue"*** rule, extrinsic evidence can only be introduced to impeach a witness if it also bears on a ***substantive*** issue in the case (or if it proves something deemed important, like bias). Here, if the "boyfriend" testimony is true, it only proves Wanda is lying — it doesn't make any substantive fact at issue in the case either more or less probable. So the collateral issue rule applies, and the evidence is inadmissible.

COMPARE: Suppose the defense called Wilfreda to impeach Wanda as follows: "Everyone in town knows Wanda is a bald-faced liar!" Here, the testimony will be admissible, because witnesses may be impeached via extrinsic evidence in the form of poor ***reputation*** for honesty, under both FRE 608(a) and the common law. (In fact, under the FRE – but not the common law – extrinsic ***"opinion"*** evidence, e.g., Wilfreda's opinion that Wanda is generally dishonest, may be used as well.)

33. No. A witness's testimony can't be ***"bolstered"*** unless and until he's been impeached. (There are exceptions, such as a showing that the victim in a rape case made a timely complaint. But no exception applies here.) Since the defendant didn't cross-examine Cy at all, it certainly couldn't have impeached him.

34. Yes. On redirect, a witness may be ***"rehabilitated,"*** by being given the chance to explain facts brought out in cross-examination.

35. Objection sustained. It's true that when a witness has been impeached by a claim that she has been improperly influenced or motivated, or by a claim that her story is a recent fabrication, the witness may be rehabilitated by showing that she previously made a statement that is consistent with her present testimony. See FRE 801(d)(1)(B). But both at common law and under this provision of the FRE (as interpreted by the Supreme Court in *Tome v. U.S.*), the prior consistent statement must have been made ***before*** the improper motive, influence or fabrication came into existence. Since the alleged improper motive arose in April 2006 (when Stepdad supposedly hit Pamela's mother), and since the prior consistent statement was not made until after that episode, the statement doesn't qualify. Therefore, it can't be used for rehabilitation (and it's inadmissible hearsay).

36. Yes. ***Hearsay is an out-of-court statement offered to prove the truth of the matter asserted.*** FRE 801(c). The statement here is Surv's: "The light was on." It was made outside of court, and it's being offered to prove the truth of its assertion, namely, that the "No Smoking/Fasten Seat Belts" light was lit. Thus, it's hearsay. (Note that if the statement were offered for some other reason than to prove the truth of the matter asserted, for instance, to prove Surv's ***belief*** that the light was on, not to prove that in fact the light was on, then the statement would be admissible as non-hearsay.) Remember that just because the statement is hearsay, this doesn't necessarily mean it's inadmissible; it may be admissible under an *exception* to the hearsay rule. However, there's no exception that seems to apply here.

37. No, because the words aren't being offered to show the factual truth of any matter asserted in them. (Indeed, there really *is* no matter here whose truth is being asserted.) Tory's testimony is being offered to show that an oral contract was in fact formed, and to show the terms of that contract. The words of an oral contract are ***legally operative facts*** (or ***"verbal acts"***), since they have a legal significance independent of their substantive content. Where legally operative facts are offered for their legal significance, they're not hearsay.

38. Yes. Since the lab report is an out-of-court statement being offered to prove that the snow is cocaine, it's hearsay. A statement need not be spoken to be hearsay; a ***document*** offered to prove the truth of an assertion in its contents can also be hearsay. The "statement" here is the lab report's sentence, "The 'snow' in the . . . paperweight is . . . cocaine." Since the statement is being offered to show that the snow *is* cocaine, it's hearsay. Of course, even though a statement is hearsay, it isn't necessarily inadmissible — the one here, for instance, might be (though probably isn't) admissible under the "public records" exception, FRE 803(8).

39. No. Hearsay is an out-of-court statement offered to prove the truth of the matter asserted. FRE 801(c). The assertion here is Rasputin's: "I am having an affair with your wife." However, it's not hearsay because it is not being offered for the truth of its assertion (that the Czarina and Rasputin were in fact having an affair), but only to show the statement's ***effect on the listener***, the Czar (that the statement so enraged him that he shot Rasputin).

40. No. It's being offered as ***circumstantial evidence of the declarant's (Bob's) state of mind***, not to prove that D.B. is in fact the finest child in the family. It's therefore not hearsay.

41. No. Hearsay is an out-of-court statement offered to prove the truth of the matter asserted. FRE 801(c). The out-of-court statement by Bugs, "That Elmer Fudd is a real looney tune," is being offered to ***impeach*** Bugs's current testimony, not to establish the truth of its assertion—namely, that Elmer was insane. Prior inconsistent statements, when used for impeachment purposes, are by universal understanding excluded from the definition of hearsay. (The same is true of prior consistent statements used to rehabilitate the witness.)

42. *No, because the conduct was non-assertive.* Under FRE 801(c), non-assertive conduct — that is, conduct not intended as communication — is not considered hearsay (because it's not a "statement," under 801(a), and only statements can be hearsay). The rationale is that non-assertive conduct is less subject to fabrication than assertive conduct and is therefore more reliable than assertive conduct. Here, for instance, Werbezirk is unlikely to have made the club visit to fool someone into thinking that the club was safe.

NOTE: Non-assertive conduct does not mean nonverbal conduct, since nonverbal conduct can be intended to communicate, e.g., a nod of the head. FRE 801(a).

COMMON LAW RULE: At common law, non-assertive conduct *was* considered hearsay if offered as an implied assertion of the actor's beliefs and of the consequent truth of those beliefs.

43. No. The statement is ***"multiple hearsay,"*** or "hearsay on hearsay," i.e., an out-of-court declaration which quotes or paraphrases another out-of-court declaration. Under FRE 805, hearsay included within hearsay is not excluded under the hearsay rule provided that ***each part*** of the combined statement satisfies an exception to the hearsay rule.

The principal out-of-court declarant here is Aardvark, whose statement is "Fox said he'd eaten the Gingerbread Boy." That statement is offered to prove that Fox ate the Gingerbread boy (so it's hearsay), and it doesn't fit an exception. The fact that Aardvark's statement subsumes an additional statement (Fox's statement that he did the eating), and the fact that that additional statement is non-hearsay because it's an admission, doesn't save the overall package from inadmissibility.

44. No. "Statements" from non-human sources, such as ***animals*** and ***machines***, aren't considered hearsay. (See, e.g., FRE 801(c), giving hearsay status only to "statements," and 801(a), defining "statement" to include nonverbal conduct only if the conduct is by "a person.")

45. Yes. A guilty plea is admissible as an admission, because a plea is considered a "statement" by a party. Note, however, that the plea is not necessarily conclusive — Claudius can explain the circumstances of the guilty plea, and thus affect the weight the jury places on it.

46. Yes, as an *adoptive admission* by Wimp. Wimp adopted the statement in the certificate when he attached it to his application. Adoptive admissions are admissible (against the party who did the adopting) on the same basis as regular admissions. FRE 801(d)(2)(B).

47. Objection overruled. The statement is admissible against Acme, since Dian is an employee, and an agent, of Acme Airways, and the statement was made in the scope of the agency (his duties as a pilot). Under the FRE, any statement an agent makes ***during the existence of the agency***, on a ***subject*** that's ***within the scope of the agency***, is admissible against the principal as an admission. FRE 801(d)(2)(D). There's ***no*** requirement that the principal have ***authorized*** the statement. (Note that the agency must be established by independent evidence; the out-of-court statements can't be the sole basis for the authority.)

48. No. The statement is hearsay, and no exception applies. Hearsay is an out-of-court statement offered to prove the truth of the matter asserted. FRE 801(c). Here, the out-of-court statement by Grunt is being offered for the truth of its assertion, namely, that Oink had been drinking prior to driving home. The statement can't be admitted as an admission under FRE 801(d)(2), because Grunt ***wasn't authorized to speak for Oink***, nor was he Oink's agent, partner, or coconspirator, nor did Oink adopt Grunt's statement. Nor does the hearsay exception for *declarations against interest* (FRE 804(b)(3)) apply: the statement wasn't against *Grunt's* interest when made (even though it was against Oink's); also, there's no indication Grunt is unavailable as a witness.

49. No. FRE 801(d)(2)(E) treats as non-hearsay, when used against a party, a statement by a ***co-conspirator*** of that party, but only if the statement "was made by the party's coconspirator ***during and in furtherance of the conspiracy."*** The statement here, though made by a co-conspirator of the defendants, was made three months after the robbery and had nothing to do with completing or furthering the robbery. Therefore, it doesn't qualify under 801(d)(2)(E), and is thus inadmissible hearsay.

50. Objection overruled. The statement is admissible under the "statement of then-existing ***mental, emotional, or physical condition***" hearsay exception of FRE 803(3). In fact, 803(3) specifically says, parenthetically, that a statement about the declarant's then-existing "pain or bodily health" is covered. So the statement, "Ouch! I think my skull is fractured!" can be offered to prove that Newton was in pain due to what he believed to be a skull fracture. (However, 803(3) *won't* support using the statement to prove that Newton's skull actually *was* fractured, because 803(3) doesn't allow a statement of "belief" to be used to prove the truth of the fact believed. But the exceptions for present-sense-impression [803(1)] and excited utterance [803(2)] *would* be usable to introduce the statement to show an actual fracture.)

51. Yes, probably. FRE 803(4) gives a hearsay exception for statements "made for — and ***reasonably pertinent to — medical diagnosis or treatment***," and extends the exception to cover statements about the "inception or ... general cause" of "past or present symptoms[.]" Mary's statement about the cause — that her foot got caught in a hole in the step of an escalator — was probably "reasonably pertinent" to Dr. Welby's attempts to diagnose and treat her. However, it's possible that a court might take a narrow view of "reasonably pertinent," and hold that her identification of the particular place (Macy's) was not reasonably pertinent. At the very least, her statement that the accident occurred on an escalator would seem to be pertinent (and thus admissible) even if the part about Macy's isn't.

52. The "statement of present state of mind" exception. FRE 803(3) allows evidence of "the declarant's then-existing state of mind (such as ... intent or plan)." The rule doesn't expressly say whether the statement of intent can be admitted to show that the declarant ***carried out*** his intent. But courts interpreting the provision have generally held that a statement about what the declarant plans to do is admissible not only to prove that the declarant had that intent, but also to prove that he probably followed through on that intent.

53. No, because it can't be offered to prove the crate was leaking. It's hearsay, because it's an out-of-court statement offered to prove the truth of its assertion. FRE 801(c). The declarant is Mutt: "Look, Jeff, I think. . . ." It's being offered to prove the truth of its assertion, that the crate was leaking.

The most likely hearsay exception it could fit is the "present state of mind" exception, FRE 803(3). However, that exception specifically ***excludes*** "a statement of . . . ***belief*** to ***prove the fact . . . believed***" (except in connection with wills). Since the statement is being offered to prove the fact believed (that the crate was leaking), the exclusion applies. Therefore, the statement can't come in for the purpose for which it's being offered.

54. Yes. Under FRE 803(3), the statement is admissible as a declaration of the speaker's "then-existing state of mind." Courts interpreting 803(3) allow statements of intent to show not only that the intent existed, but also to show that the speaker probably ***acted in accordance***

with the intent. The out-of-court statement: "I'm planning to give you my cow" is being offered to show that Phlebitz followed through with his intention, so the statement falls within the "present state of mind" exception.

55. No. The main problem is that the statement describes not only the speaker's present state of mind (fear of Dr. Bovary), but also what a ***person other than the speaker*** (Dr. Bovary) ***did to induce that state of mind*** (threaten to kill). Courts generally do not allow the "present state of mind" exception to be used for the purpose of proving what someone other than the speaker did to induce the declarant's state of mind. The main reason for this is that there is an extreme risk of prejudice, substantially outweighing any probative value the statement might have.

Observe that the facts here are a variation on the famous case of *Shepard v. U.S.* ("Dr. Shepard has poisoned me," offered to show that the Dr. in fact poisoned her.) There, the Supreme Court disallowed the use of the "state of mind" exception to prove the fact believed. Here, we're dealing not with proof of the fact believed, but proof of what another did to induce the declarant's state of mind; however, similar issues — risk of prejudice, and desire not to let the "state of mind" exception swallow up the entire hearsay rule — apply to both situations.

Note, also, that this is a "***multiple hearsay***" problem: Felicity is repeating in-court what Emma said about what Dr. Bovary said ("I'll kill you.") Multiple hearsay isn't admissible unless ***each level is independently admissible***. FRE 805. Here, Dr. Bovary's statement is probably admissible as a statement of his intent, offered to show that the speaker later acted in accord with that intent (so that if Emma had survived, she'd be allowed to testify at trial to Dr. Bovary's threat). But, for the reasons given above, the second level — Emma's out-of-court repetition of Dr. Bovary's threat — doesn't fall within the "present state of mind" (or any other) exception, so the entire "package" must be excluded.

56. Unclear, but probably not. It's true that the FRE contain an exception (803(3)) for statements of present state of mind, and that a statement of intent may be introduced to prove that the *declarant* followed through on his own expressed intent. But courts interpreting 803(3) are split as to whether and when *A*'s statement of intent to do something together with *B* can be used to prove that <u>*B*</u> did the thing. Most courts seem to hold that, at most, this use can only be made if there is some ***corroborating evidence*** that *B* joined with *A*. Since there's no corroboration here that Remus ever joined, most courts would probably hold 803(3) inapplicable.

57. No. The "state of mind" exception (FRE 803(3)) is, more precisely, an exception for statements about the declarant's "***then-existing***" state of mind. Here, the problem is that Tom-Tom's statement describes his state of mind at an ***earlier time*** (when he took the pig), not his state of mind at the time he was speaking. So the exception simply doesn't apply.

A different way of looking at the problem would be to argue that Tom-Tom's statement was a statement about his present memory (equivalent to "I now remember that at the time I took the pig, I thought it was mine.") But this view, too, runs into difficulties: FRE 803(3) specifically says that ***a statement of memory or belief is not admissible to prove the fact remembered or believed*** (except in connection with wills). Since Tom-Tom's statement, on this view, is an attempt to prove the fact remembered (not the fact that the pig really was Tom-Tom's, but the fact that at the moment of taking, Tom-Tom's mental state was "intent-to-take-his-own-property"), it falls within this bar.

RELATED ISSUE: Suppose Fred instead testified: "Just before he took the pig, Tom-Tom told me, 'I'm taking this pig because it's mine.' " The statement *would* fit the "then-existing state of mind" exception of FRE 803(3), and would be admissible to show Tom's lack of intent to deprive another of his property.

58. The "excited utterance" exception: the statement was made under the stress of excitement, due to a startling event, and it concerns the event. See FRE 803(2). The declarant of an excited utterance can be a ***bystander*** (rather than a person actually involved in the event), and ***needn't be identified*** by the person giving the in-court testimony about what the declarant said.

59. No. The statement isn't an excited utterance, since an excited utterance must ***relate to the startling event that prompted it*** in order to be admissible. Shakespeare's statement didn't have anything to do with the glass's falling on his head; therefore, it can't be an excited utterance. FRE 803(2).

RELATED ISSUE: Note that the statement *is* admissible as an ***admission*** against a party-opponent (non-hearsay under FRE 801(d)(2), and an exception to the hearsay rule under the common law).

60. Yes. Although the statement is hearsay — it's an out-of-court statement offered to prove its truth, namely, that Sam wasn't watching the road — it's admissible as a ***present sense impression*** under FRE 803(1). Unlike the excited utterance exception, the present sense impression exception ***doesn't require that the declarant be under the stress of excitement*** when he makes the statement. Note that, as with all exceptions under FRE 803, Frasier's ***availability*** to testify is ***immaterial***.

RELATED ISSUE: If Frasier's statement had been made while he was stressed or excited ("Oh, my God, he's not watching where he's going! He's going to hit that parked car!"), it would be admissible as an "excited utterance" under FRE 803(2). (It would probably also satisfy the present-sense-impression requirements of 803(1).)

61. The "recorded recollection" exception (colloquially, ***"past recollection recorded"***), under FRE 803(5). The notes satisfy all the prerequisites for admissibility under FRE 803(5): (1) they were made by Al at the time of the accident, when the shooting was still fresh in his mind; (2) Al had first-hand knowledge of the shooting, since he was there; (3) Al's memory of the event is impaired, and can't be refreshed; and (4) Al has verified that the notes were true when made. Therefore, as long as they're properly authenticated, the notes are admissible into evidence.

RELATED ISSUE: If ***someone other than Al*** had made the notes, and right after the accident Al read them and stated (or, probably, even thought), "Yes, that's what happened," then the notes would still be admissible; under the FRE, as long as Al ***adopted*** the written notes when made, they are just as admissible as if he had made them himself.

62. No. Under FRE 803(5), if a witness's present recollection is ***revived*** by her reference to the notes and the notes are no longer needed, they are not admissible under the "recorded recollection" exception to the hearsay rule. One of the prerequisites for admissibility under the past recollection recorded exception is that the witness's present recollection continues to be at least partially impaired; if the witness's present recollection has been revived, then that recollection is no longer impaired, and the notes are therefore inadmissible under the exception.

63. No. The affidavit is hearsay, since it's an out-of-court statement being offered for the truth of the matter asserted, namely, that Picard has a habit of taking his ship to Subic Bay every May 1. Affidavits, unlike deposition transcripts (see FRE 804(b)(1)), are not admissible ***even if the affiant is unavailable***. Since neither the affidavit nor the statement in it falls within any hearsay exception, the affidavit is inadmissible.

Observe that although hearsay problems usually arise in the form of live trial testimony by a witness about what someone said out-of-court, a hearsay problem can also be presented where, as here, someone tries to introduce a *document* that contains a statement offered for the truth of the statement.

RELATED ISSUE: If Janeway were *testifying at trial*, she'd be allowed to testify about what Picard did every May 1, because evidence that someone had a particular habit is admissible to show that he acted in accord with that habit on the occasion in question. See FRE 406.

64. (a) **The business records exception**, FRE 803(6).

(b) **Probably not**. First, to qualify under the b.r. exception the report must be kept as part of the "regular practice" of a business activity. Some courts (though probably not a majority) read "regular practice" to mean "routine" or "related to the main function of the business"; these courts conclude that accident reports (especially ones made in anticipation of litigation) don't qualify. That is, to these courts Q.V.'s main function is transporting goods, and accident reports don't relate closely to that function.

An even bigger problem is that 803(6) expressly requires that "(E) neither the source of information nor the method or circumstances of preparation indicate a ***lack of trustworthiness***." Since Jed knows that the main use of his reports is to help Q.V. defend against claims, he's got a strong interest to write up the reports so as to blame the customer rather than the railroad. So a court would probably conclude that the circumstances here make the report self-serving and untrustworthy.

65. No, probably. This is a case of "hearsay on hearsay," where there's a hearsay statement (Jessie's statement) inside another hearsay statement (the emergency room records). Thus, ***both*** hearsay statements must be admissible under exceptions to the hearsay rule, or neither will be admitted. FRE 805.

The emergency room records are probably admissible as a business record under the FRE 803(6). However, Jessie's statement is probably *inadmissible hearsay*. It's being offered for the truth of the matter asserted (that the mattress was faulty); however, it's probably not admissible as a statement for purposes of medical diagnosis or treatment under the FRE 803(4) exception, since it probably wasn't reasonably pertinent to her treatment. Nor does it fall within any other exception. Therefore, the entire hearsay on hearsay is *inadmissible*.

66. (a) **FRE 803(8)'s "public records" exception**.

(b) **Yes**. The report can come in either under 803(8)(A)(ii) (for "a matter observed while under a legal duty to report") or 803(8)(A)(iii) (for "factual findings from a legally authorized investigation"). It's true that (A)(ii) contains the words "but not including, in a criminal case, a matter observed by law enforcement personnel." But this language has widely been interpreted to ban only use *against* criminal defendants, not *by* them.

Nor does it matter that it's unknown who wrote the report. Nothing in the public records exception (or, for that matter, in many of the other exceptions, such as the "excited utterance" exception) requires that the identity of the declarant be known. If the report is a public record — and that's clear from the facts here — details of precisely how it was made are immaterial, as long as the circumstances don't affect the report's trustworthiness (which they don't seem to do here).

67. Yes. The report and its conclusion are admissible under FRE 803(8)(A)(iii), which gives a hearsay exception "in a civil case or against the government in a criminal case," for "factual findings from a legally authorized ***investigation***." The report here is certainly an "investigation." An interesting aspect of this provision is that it has been interpreted by the U.S. Supreme Court (*Beech Aircraft v. Rainey*, 1988) to allow introduction of ***interpretations*** and ***conclusions*** in reports, not just narrow factual findings. So the broad conclusion here — no racial discrimination — is admissible.

RELATED ISSUE 1: The text of FRE 803(8) doesn't say whether the report has to be based on the government author's ***first-hand knowledge***. The general Adv. Comm. Notes to 803 say that "neither this rule nor Rule 804 dispenses with the requirement of firsthand knowledge." But most courts interpreting 803(8) in particular have concluded that as long as the report seems trustworthy, the fact that the report is based in part on statements by third parties rather than entirely on the first-hand knowledge of the government author is ***irrelevant***.

RELATED ISSUE 2: Suppose the report ***quoted statements by individuals*** (e.g., "Joe Smith, who works for Ma Belle, told the investigator, 'I've never seen racial discrimination at the company.' ") Such statements by non-government third-parties are ***not*** admissible under 803(8)(A)(iii) to prove what the statements assert; only findings and conclusions *by* the government workers who prepared the report, not statements made *to* the preparers, fall within the exception.

68. No, because the notes weren't made by an official who was ***under a duty to report*** the event. The relevant Rule (FRE 803(8)(A)(ii)) allows admission of "a matter observed while under a legal duty to report[.]" The facts tell us that it's ***not*** the mayor's job to report on, or record, events like this, so the "legal duty to report" condition isn't satisfied.

RELATED ISSUE: If necessary, the notes could be used by the Lord Mayor to *refresh* his memory while on the stand. If that didn't work, they might then be admissible as a "recorded recollection" under FRE 803(5), if it was shown that the notes were made when the events were fresh in his memory.

69. No. The report would have to come in, if at all, under FRE 803(8)(A)(ii), covering reports of "a matter observed while under a legal duty to report[.]" But the problem is that (A)(ii) contains a special (and very important) exclusion: it ***excludes*** "in a ***criminal case*** a matter observed by ***law enforcement personnel***." It was precisely to prevent police reports from being used against criminal defendants that the exclusion was adopted.

RELATED ISSUE: Suppose the prosecution tried to get the report in as a ***"business record"*** under FRE 803(6) (and suppose the report met all the requirements for business records, e.g., made by a person with knowledge, kept in the course of a regularly conducted business activity, etc.). Does the fact that the report is specifically excluded under 803(8) mean that it can't come in under 803(6) either? Most courts have concluded that the answer is "*yes*" — that Congress, in prohibiting use of law enforcement reports against criminal defendants in 803(8)(A)(ii), meant to keep them out for purposes of all other hearsay exclusions (such as the business records and "catchall" exceptions). See, e.g., *U.S. v. Oates* (2d Cir. 1977). (But a court might allow the report to be used as *past recollection recorded* if Madison took the stand but couldn't remember the incident.)

70. The "ancient documents" exception. FRE 803(16) provides a hearsay exception for "A statement in a document that is at least 20 years old and whose authenticity is established." So the letter qualifies as long as its authenticity is established. FRE 901(b)(8) specifies that an ancient document can be authenticated by "evidence that it: (A) is in a condition that creates no suspicion about its authenticity; (B) was in a place where, if authentic, it would likely be; and (C) is at least 20 years old when offered."

Here, there's nothing to create suspicion that the document may be invalid; a safe deposit box is a logical place for a person's important correspondence to be; and the date on the letter (plus the length of time since the last opening of the box) indicates that the document is at least 20 years old. So the letter's authenticity will probably be found to be established even without testimony that Tine wrote it, and the 803(16) hearsay exception will apply so that statements in the letter can come in.

71. No. It's true that normally, newspaper articles, if introduced to prove the truth of statements contained in them, are hearsay (and usually not within any exception). But a newspaper's stock-price listings fall within FRE 803(17)'s exception for "market quotations, lists, directories, or other compilations that are generally relied on by the public or by persons in particular occupations."

72. Yes, it's admissible under FRE 803(9), the *"public records of vital statistics"* provision. That provision grants a hearsay exception for "A record of a ***birth, death,*** or ***marriage***, if reported to a public office in accordance with a legal duty." Since doctors are everywhere required to fill out a death certificate giving a cause of death for one who dies while under the doctor's care, the certificate here was "reported to a public office in accordance with a legal duty." The fact that the doctor was ***not himself a public official*** (thus preventing the certificate from being a "record of a public office" as required by the basic public-records exception, FRE 803(8)) is ***irrelevant***. (Indeed, it's precisely to reach records of vital statistics reported by non-public persons that FRE 803(9) exists.)

73. It's admissible under the *"former testimony"* exception given in FRE 804(b)(1). All four requirements for this exception are satisfied, because: (1) Hare is ***"unavailable"*** (see below for why), (2) his former testimony was made at a "hearing" (since a preliminary hearing is a form of hearing); (3) Burke had an ***opportunity*** to ***cross-examine*** Hare at the preliminary exam (every defendant has such a right), and (4) Burke had a ***"similar motive"*** to cross-examine Hare at the preliminary exam as at the trial (since the same facts and issues were involved). Note that the witness's ***refusal to testify*** at the present trial (after being ordered to do so) is sufficient to make him "unavailable"; see FRE 804(a)(2). (At common law, simple refusal *wouldn't* suffice.)

74. Not unless Dreyfus is *unavailable* to testify (something the facts do not suggest to be so). Under FRE 804(b)(1), former testimony cannot be introduced unless the declarant is unavailable to testify. If Dreyfus *were* unavailable, the testimony would qualify because: there is a substantial identity of parties and issues, the former testimony was at a "hearing," and the party against whom the testimony is now sought to be used (Kato) had an opportunity and similar incentive to cross-examine the witness.

75. No. Under FRE 804(b)(1), to qualify for the former testimony exception, the testimony must have been given in a ***"hearing,"*** trial or legal deposition, and the party against whom the evidence is now offered must have had a chance to examine (usually cross-examine) the witness. Here, Mama was not testifying at a "hearing," trial or deposition, and Goldilocks had no opportunity to cross-examine her. (So affidavits will *never* qualify; nor will testimony at coroner's inquests, nor *grand jury* testimony offered against a criminal defendant.)

76. Objection overruled. Under the former testimony exception to the hearsay rule, it doesn't matter whether the witness was ***actually*** cross-examined at the first trial, as long as the party against whom the evidence is now sought to be used had an ***opportunity and similar incentive to do so***. All the other requirements of the exception are apparently fulfilled — it is former testimony, at a "hearing," and the declarant is unavailable — so the testimony will be admissible.

77. Objection overruled. Master's statement is an out-of-court statement that is being offered to prove the truth of the matter asserted — that the butler "did it." So it's hearsay. However, the statement qualifies as a ***dying declaration***. FRE 804(b)(2) gives an exception for: "In a prosecution for ***homicide*** or in a ***civil*** case, a statement that the declarant, ***while believing the declarant's death to be imminent***, made ***about its cause or circumstances."***

Here, we have: (1) a homicide prosecution; (2) a statement made at a time when the declarant (Master) believed he was about to die; (3) explaining the cause of the impending death (action by the butler); and (4) declarant now unavailable (required for all FRE 804 exceptions), so all requirements are met.

78. No. Under the FRE (and the common law, as well), the statement doesn't fit the dying declaration exception, because ***Caesar is available to testify***. The out-of-court statement here, "Et tu, Brute?" is being offered to prove the truth of its assertion — that Brutus did it. The statement doesn't fit the "dying declaration" exception of FRE 804(b)(2), because that exception requires that the declarant be unavailable to testify at trial. (Normally, of course, the declarant will be dead, and thus indisputably unavailable; but a declarant who recovers and is unavailable for some other reason can nonetheless qualify, under the FRE.) (Recall that at common law, the declarant must ***actually have died*** in order for the statement to fit the dying declaration exception.)

79. No. Dying declarations are only admissible, under FRE 804(b)(2), "in a prosecution for ***homicide*** or in a civil case." (But if Iva were being prosecuted for *killing* Rosebud, Rosebud's statement *would* qualify as a dying declaration under FRE 804(b)(2), because Rosebud is unavailable, she believed she was about to die, and the statement concerned her personal knowledge as to the circumstances of her death.)

NOTE: Under the traditional common law rule, the dying declaration exception could *only* be utilized in homicide cases; the FRE allow the exception in civil cases as well.

80. As a "statement against interest" (also colloquially called a "declaration against interest") (FRE 804(b)(3)). The statement qualifies, because it was *against the declarant's proprietary interest when made* (Khufu was admitting the Pyramid wasn't solely his), *made knowingly and willingly* and with *no motive to lie,* and Khufu is now *unavailable* as a witness. Therefore, it's admissible, even though it's hearsay.

81. No, probably. Although the FRE allow declarations against penal interest within the hearsay exception, there's a proviso: if, as here, the statement is offered in a criminal case and tends to expose the declarant to criminal liability, it's not admissible unless it's ***"supported by corroborating circumstances that clearly indicate its trustworthiness***[.]" FRE 804(b)(3)(B). This requirement is especially focused on situations in which the statement exculpates an accused. Its rationale is that declarants who are friends or relatives of an accused are likely to have an incentive to try to shield the accused from liability, and thus may not be trustworthy; therefore, we need extra guarantees of reliability in this situation. There do not seem to be any such corroborating circumstances present here.

82. No, for two distinct reasons. The first issue, of course, is whether these statements implicating Ernie can come in as declarations against interest. The particular statements that the prosecution seeks to introduce were not themselves specifically against Bert's interest (since they shifted blame to Ernie, and didn't further implicate Bert beyond the extent to which he was already implicated by virtue of having gotten caught red-handed with the 19 kilos). These statements were, however, ***"collateral"*** to the explicitly self-inculpatory ones; that is, they were part of the same overall narrative, and concerned the same overall events. The Supreme Court has held that, in federal courts interpreting FRE 804(b)(3), a non-self-inculpatory statement ***cannot be admitted as a declaration against interest*** merely by virtue of the fact that the statement is "collateral to" (i.e., related to) a declaration that is self-inculpatory; only if the ***particular declaration in question*** is against the declarant's interest can it come in. See *Williamson v. U.S.* (U.S. 1994), a case whose facts are similar to those of this question. So only those individual declarations by Bert that specifically inculpate him can be admitted against Ernie under 804(b)(3). (*State* courts construing provisions similar to 804(b)(3) are not bound by the *Williamson* decision, which affects only the FRE *per se*.)

A second problem with allowing Otto to recount Bert's statement is that this would violate Ernie's rights under the ***Confrontation Clause*** of the Sixth Amendment to the federal constitution. According to *Crawford v. Washington* (U.S. 2004), any out-of-court ***"testimonial"*** statement can be admitted against an accused only if the maker of the statement is available for cross-examination either at the time the statement was made or at the accused's trial. *Crawford* makes it clear that statements given in response to a police interrogation that's not focused on an ongoing emergency are "testimonial" for this purpose, so Bert's statements while under interrogation by Otto are testimonial. The facts tell us that Bert has refused to repeat his story inculpating Ernie at Ernie's trial, so Bert is not "available for cross-examination" about the story. Consequently, Bert's entire story — even the parts that *do* specifically implicate Bert — may not be admitted against Ernie on account of the Confrontation Clause.

83. It's admissible under the FRE's "reputation/family history" hearsay exception. Under FRE 804(b)(4)(A), an unavailable declarant's statement about his *own* birth or similar fact of personal or family history is admissible, "even though the declarant had no way of acquiring personal knowledge about that fact[.]" Since Bart is dead, and thus unavailable, his statement about his age falls under the exception. (804(b)(4)(*B*), which applies to statements about a person made by a relative or intimate associate, would similarly apply, if Molly testified, "Bart's mother, Marge, told me just before Bart's death that Bart was 33." Marge would, however, have to be unavailable.)

RELATED ISSUE: Suppose Molly's testimony was, "I lived with Bart, and although he never told me his age, at his death he was ***reputed*** by his family to have been 33." This, too, would be admissible; FRE 803(19) gives a hearsay exception for "a reputation among a person's family ... or among a person's associates or in the community ... concerning the person's birth, adoption, legitimacy, ancestry, marriage, divorce, death, relationship by blood, adoption, or marriage, or similar facts of personal or family history." (Note that for this "reputation" exception, *neither* the person whom the reputation concerns, nor any person whose statements were the source of the witness's knowledge of the reputation, need be unavailable.)

84. Yes. The tavern can use the deposition as substantive evidence under FRE 801(d)(1)(A), which defines as non-hearsay a ***prior inconsistent statement*** given ***under penalty of perjury*** (i.e., under oath) at a ***trial***, ***hearing*** or other proceeding, or in a ***deposition***, if the declarant is ***available to testify*** and be ***cross-examined***. Since the deposition testimony isn't hearsay, it's substantively admissible (to prove the truth of the matter asserted in it). (Note that the tavern could also use the deposition testimony to *impeach* Crassus; when a prior inconsistent statement is used to impeach a witness, the statement is never considered hearsay, because it's offered to prove that the witness is not credible because he's changed his story, not offered to prove the truth of the matter asserted in the prior inconsistent statement.)

85. No, since it's a *prior identification*. Under FRE 801(d)(1)(C), ***an out-of-court statement identifying a person, made after the declarant has perceived him or her and where the declarant is presently testifying and available for cross-examination, is specifically excluded as non-hearsay.*** (The same rule applies at common law.)

86. Objection sustained. The picture is not admissible as a prior identification, since Fifi ***isn't presently testifying*** and ***isn't available for cross-examination***; under FRE 801(d)(1)(C), these two requirements are *prerequisites* for a prior identification's admissibility. Without them, the prior identification is hearsay. (That is, it's the equivalent of Fifi's saying out of court, "The person who stabbed Marat looked like this. . . .") (Note that although the picture's hearsay, it may still be admissible under the *present sense impression* exception to the hearsay rule, assuming the picture was drawn immediately after Fifi saw Corday entering and leaving the bathroom.)

Anyway, there's probably a second difficulty with admitting the picture. According to *Crawford v. Washington* (U.S. 2004), the Sixth Amendment's ***Confrontation Clause*** means that any out-of-court ***"testimonial"*** statement can be admitted against an accused only if the maker of the statement is ***available for cross-examination*** either at the time the statement was made or at the accused's trial. Responses to a police interrogation whose purpose is to build a case for prosecutors are considered testimonial. Therefore, the drawing is probably "testimonial," since the picture is the equivalent of Fifi's telling the police, under interrogation, "The stabber looked like this." Since Fifi was never subjected to cross-examination by Corday (and obviously won't be now at Corday's trial, since Fifi's dead), *Crawford* should block the use of the picture on Confrontation Clause grounds).

87. The "residual" or "catchall" exception of FRE 807. The testimony can't come in under the former-testimony exception of 804(b)(1), because the party against whom it's now offered (Sneezy) didn't have an opportunity to cross-examine Grumpy (one witness never has an opportunity to cross-examine another at a grand jury).

Under the residual exception of 807, hearsay can come in even though it doesn't meet a specific exception, if: (1) the statement has ***"circumstantial guarantees of trustworthiness"*** that are "equivalent" to those inherent in the specific exceptions; (2) the statement is offered as evidence of a ***"material fact"***; (3) the statement is "***more probative*** on the point for which it is offered than ***any other evidence*** that the proponent can obtain through reasonable efforts"; (4) use of the evidence is consistent with "the interests of justice"; and (5) the proponent gives ***advance notice*** of his intention to offer the statement.

Here, (2) through (4) seem satisfied, given the absence of any other evidence and the centrality of the issue to which the testimony relates. (5) can be satisfied as long as the prosecutor gives Sneezy advance notice (enough in advance to give Sneezy a "fair opportunity to meet the evidence"). The real issues are: (a) does the statement have the requisite "circumstantial guarantees of trustworthiness"?; and (b) can the residual or catchall exception be applied to situations that "just miss" qualifying for a specific exception?

As to issue (a), probably the requisite circumstantial guarantees of trustworthiness are satisfied. Grumpy had no apparent motive to lie (for instance, he was not himself a suspect). Also, he was testifying about matters that he claimed to have himself witnessed (not merely repeating something someone else told him, for instance). Additionally, he was testifying under oath. (Lastly, the fact that Grumpy's unavailability seems to be due to intimidation by Sneezy would also weigh in favor of admitting the transcript.) As to issue (b), most courts are willing to apply the residual exception even where the facts "just miss" qualifying for a specific exception (here, the exception for former testimony). A few courts, however, might hold that Congress carefully considered the grand jury situation when it codified the former-testimony exception, and made a clear policy decision — which a court considering the residual exception shouldn't overturn — that former testimony shouldn't be usable against one who had no opportunity to cross-examine the witness at the time the testimony was given.

Notice that the question tells you to ignore any constitutional issues. That's because *Crawford v. Washington* would probably make Grumpy's grand jury testimony inadmissible as a violation of Sneezy's Sixth Amendment ***Confrontation Clause*** rights. *Crawford* says that any out-of-court ***"testimonial"*** statement can be admitted against an accused only if the maker of the statement is available for cross-examination either at the time the statement was made or at the accused's trial. It's perfectly clear that statements made to a grand jury are "testimonial" for this purpose, and also clear that (1) Grumpy wasn't available for cross-examination by Sneezy at the grand jury; and (2) Grumpy's refusal to testify at Sneezy's trial means that Grumpy is "unavailable for cross-examination" at trial, as *Crawford* uses that term. Therefore, even if the requirements of the catchall are satisfied, the statement can't come in because of *Crawford*.

88. Strike the testimony, because the defense was deprived of its right to ***cross-examine*** Houdini. The defendant in a criminal trial has a right under the Sixth Amendment to ***confront*** witnesses against him. This right consists mainly of the right to cross-examine. Even where (as here) the unavailability of the witness for cross was not due to the fault of the calling party, the confrontation clause dictates that the direct evidence not be used against the defendant. The same result would occur if Houdini pleaded the Fifth Amendment instead of answering questions on cross. (In fact, if the court believes that the direct testimony was so critical and influential that an instruction to strike will not be sufficient to undo its effect, the court should order a mistrial.)

89. Objection overruled. Before we get to the Confrontation Clause argument, let's review how the case would be analyzed under the common law and the FRE. A ***co-conspirator's statement*** (if made *during* and in *furtherance* of the conspiracy) is an exception to the hearsay rule at common law and an exclusion from the hearsay rule under FRE 801(d)(2).

Crawford v. Washington (U.S. 2004) and *Davis v. Washington* (U.S. 2006) hold that "non-testimonial" out-of-court statements don't have to undergo Confrontation Clause analysis at all. (This was a change from the holding in the earlier case of *Ohio v. Roberts.*) Scarface's statement was clearly "non-testimonial" — since he did not even know he was speaking to an informant, he was not making a statement that he thought would be used in conjunction with some sort of law enforcement proceeding. Therefore, under *Crawford* and *Davis*, Scarface's out-of-court declaration cannot be a Confrontation Clause violation.

90. Objection sustained. The facts here are on all fours with *Bullcoming v. New Mexico* (U.S. 2011). By a 5-4 vote there, the Supreme Court held that the testimony by the tester's colleague — even one who was familiar with the particular type of forensic test in question — was not sufficient to satisfy the Confrontation Clause's requirement that a "testimonial" out-of-court statement in a forensic report, if offered for its truth, must be supported by the testimony of someone who was personally involved in the preparation of the report. For instance, because Ted wasn't present for cross, Bart's counsel had no chance to quiz him about whether he might have made a mistake on the test in question, whether the sample might have been mislabeled, whether Ted had a history of making mistakes in such tests, etc. Therefore, under the logic of the majority in *Bullcoming*, the presence of Tilda as an alternative witness was not sufficient to give Bart a fair opportunity to use the tools of cross-examination to show that the report might have been erroneous, and introduction of the report would violate Bart's Confrontation Clause rights.

91. Donald. Under *Crawford v. Washington* (U.S. 2004), declarations against interest that are ***"testimonial,"*** when used against an accused, violate the accused's Sixth Amendment Confrontation Clause rights, unless the declarant is subject to cross-examination on behalf of the accused either at the time of the declaration or at the accused's later trial. *Crawford* indicates that where police conduct an interrogation whose focus is on crime-detection rather than dealing with an ongoing emergency, the responses of the person being interrogated will almost always be found to be "testimonial." Therefore, the prosecution can't use Bugs' statement implicating Donald against Donald unless Bugs was made available for cross by Donald either at the time the statement was made (which he wasn't) or at Donald's trial. Since Bugs has pleaded the Fifth, he's not deemed subject to cross by Donald. Therefore, it would violate Donald's Confrontation Clause rights for the statement to be admitted against him.

92. No (and it's reversible error as to Beavis if she does). Even with a limiting instruction, the jury is likely to consider the confession as substantive evidence against Beavis, not just against Butthead. Therefore, before D1's confession may be introduced against D2, D1 must take the stand and be meaningfully available for cross-examination. Since Butthead refuses to take the stand (a refusal that's within his rights because of the Fifth Amendment, even if Beavis tries to require him to testify), the confession can't come in at all, on account of Beavis' Sixth Amendment right to confront witnesses against him. *Bruton v. U.S.*

The post-*Bruton* case of *Crawford v. Washington* reinforces this conclusion — *Crawford* says that one defendant's testimonial statement implicating himself and another can't be admitted against the latter, if the confessor doesn't take the stand. Here, Butthead's confession under interrogation is "testimonial" (virtually all statements made in response to non-emergency police interrogation are, *Crawford* says), so under *Crawford* using this confession against Beavis would violate Beavis' Confrontation Clause rights, unless Butthead is made available to be cross-examined by Beavis' lawyer.

Therefore, the typical solution in situations like this is to have ***separate trials*** (or at least ***separate juries***); then, only the jury hearing the case against Butthead would hear Butthead's confession.

93. Objection overruled. Where legal services are sought in connection with ***planning or committing a future crime or fraud*** (as opposed to defending against prosecution for an already-committed crime or fraud), there is no attorney/client privilege.

94. Objection sustained, even though others were present. It's true that the attorney-client privilege does not apply if the communication isn't "confidential," and that the presence of persons other than the attorney and the client will usually prevent confidentiality from existing. However, where the "others" are people ***reasonably necessary to the professional consultation*** — e.g., a business associate, joint client, parent, or spouse — the communication will still be considered confidential.

RELATED ISSUE: Say Geppetto lost the case, and cross-claimed against Pinnocchio for indemnity to cover amounts recovered by Cricket. If Pinnocchio called the paralegal to testify as to Geppetto's admissions in the conference, the testimony *would* be admissible — because the attorney/client privilege isn't applicable to joint consultations with an attorney if the later suit is between those who conferred. (Note, however, that the communication would still be privileged as to a *third party* — it's just not applicable as between those conferring.)

95. Objection overruled. To be privileged a communication must be ***confidential.*** Thus, the presence of a third party (the screaming woman) destroyed the privilege here. (Note that although there was no formal attorney/client relationship established before the statement was made, preliminary discussions are covered by the privilege. Thus if Lizzie and Dewey had been alone when they had this preliminary discussion, the privilege would have applied.)

96. No. A third party isn't entitled to assert the privilege, because the privilege exists solely for the *patient's* benefit. Since Olive Oyl (the patient) isn't a party to the case, she's not present to assert it herself; however, *Seahag* could assert it on her behalf, which is what usually happens.

97. Objection overruled. Where the information the doctor receives covers something non-medical, or the facts are those a layperson could observe, they will be considered outside the scope of the privilege.

98. [Yes, we concocted this whole question just to make that pun. Sorry.] **The judge should allow Beethoven to remain silent**. First, a person may assert the Fifth even where the response would not by itself support a conviction — it's enough that the response could "furnish a ***link in the chain of evidence*** needed to prosecute." *Hoffman v. U.S.* Second, the witness need not prove that the answer might furnish such a link; rather, the burden goes the other way: only if the court finds it "***perfectly clear*** . . . that the answer ***cannot possibly have such tendency***" to incriminate, may the court disallow the Fifth Amendment plea. *Id.* So where, as here, the court concludes that there is a real (but small) chance of incrimination, the plea must be honored.

99. Neither. Bonnie and Clyde weren't married at the time of the conversations, so the ***marital confidences*** privilege doesn't apply. As to the ***spousal testimony*** privilege, in federal courts this privilege is vested solely in the testifying spouse (cf. *Trammel v. U.S.*). Therefore, since Bonnie's willing to testify, Clyde can't assert the privilege; this is true even though Bonnie may have been in a sense "coerced" to testify by the threat of heavier punishment if she didn't.

RELATED ISSUE: Suppose Bonnie and Clyde had been married when the robberies and the communications took place, but are now divorced. The marital confidences privilege would apply because the communications took place during the marriage; divorce doesn't destroy the privilege. But the spousal testimony privilege couldn't be invoked (even if Bonnie wanted to invoke it), because it is only applicable if the witness and the defendant are married at the time of the testimony.

100. Yes — the choice is entirely hers. In federal criminal trials (as well as in some state courts), a spouse *may* testify against the other spouse *regardless* of whether the other spouse consents, since the privilege to testify belongs to the *witness-spouse* only. *Trammel v. U.S.* (Note that if Minnie wished to testify as to *things Mickey told her in confidence* while they were married, she would probably be prevented from doing so if *Mickey* objected, since all courts who recognize the marital confidence privilege agree that the spouse who made the communication can assert the privilege.)

101. Yes. The spousal testimony privilege doesn't apply where one spouse is charged with a ***crime against the other spouse or their children.*** (The marital confidences privilege doesn't apply either, in this situation.)

102. Objection sustained. Absent evidence about who possessed the package (and what they did to or with it) from the time it was turned over to the lab until its production at trial — what's called a ***"chain of custody"*** — the package hasn't been authenticated and isn't admissible. FRE 901(a). The reason is that without a chain of custody, we don't know that the package is the *same one* that was originally seized by Pete.

103. Yes. Once an item of physical evidence has been "authenticated," it's admissible if relevant. The requirement that each item of evidence be authenticated is satisfied by "evidence sufficient to support a finding that the item is what the proponent claims it is." FRE 901(a). Sparky's testimony here is certainly sufficient to support a finding that the item is indeed David's slingshot.

104. No. The rule accepted by most courts is that letterheads, monograms, and other self-identifying statements are ***not*** by themselves generally enough to establish that the person or business with whom they are associated is the author or owner of the object. This is generally true under both the common law and the FRE. FRE 902 does have specific exceptions for other kinds of self-authenticating documents, such as official publications, including pamphlets issued by a public authority and certified copies of public records (FRE 902(4)), newspaper and periodicals (902(6)), trade inscriptions and the like (e.g., tags or labels) (FRE 902(7)), and commercial paper (902(9)). (But affidavits are not self-authenticating.)

However, the circumstantial evidence surrounding the letter (e.g., that it was found in Smith's wife's papers, if it was), when added to the letterhead and monogram, probably *would* be enough to constitute authentication. See FRE 901(b)(4), giving as an example of authentication "The appearance, contents, substance, internal patterns, or other ***distinctive characteristics*** of the item, taken together with all the circumstances."

105. Yes. A non-expert can testify to the authenticity of handwriting as long as familiarity with the handwriting was not acquired for the purposes of the litigation. FRE 901(b)(2).

RELATED ISSUE: The maid's ***interest*** in the outcome of the will would not affect her competency as a witness, under the FRE. (See FRE 601, making everyone competent to be a witness unless the Rules otherwise specify; no rule disqualifies a witness on account of interest.) However, in a federal case in which state law supplied the "rule of decision" (i.e., a diversity case), state law of competency would have to be followed. 601. In any event, the maid's interest in the outcome would obviously have quite an effect on the *weight* and *credibility* of her testimony.

106. No, because Jacques has no personal knowledge of Hughes' signature. Only an expert, or the jury itself, can determine the authenticity of a signature by comparing writing samples. FRE 901(b)(3).

RELATED ISSUE: Had Jacques actually seen a document known to contain Hughes' signature somewhere prior to the litigation, he would have been competent to testify as to the bathroom signature's authenticity. FRE 901(b)(2).

107. Yes. Under the ***"Reply doctrine,"*** a letter's authorship can be authenticated on the grounds that it contains information that is ***special knowledge known to the author and few others.*** So here, it's highly unlikely that the letter was by one other than Michelangelo, because no one else (or almost no one else) would have known enough to make the reference to the subject's smile.

108. Yes. It's true that when a witness testifies to a call that he received, the caller's self-identification is not sufficient authentication, because of the dangers of impersonation by the caller and fabrication by the witness.

However, under FRE 901(b)(4), ***a person may be identified by any distinctive characteristics that provide a clue to identity*** — be it a manner of speech, a distinctive expression, unique information, or the like. Here, the caller's barking, together with his self-identification as Nosmo, would be sufficient to constitute authentication.

109. No. Orgy's testimony attempts to reveal the contents of the letter. (He's not just testifying that he received a letter from Georgy, he's testifying about what the letter said.) Therefore, ***the Best Evidence Rule applies***, so that the letter itself, rather than merely Orgy's testimony about what it says, must be introduced. FRE 1002.

RATIONALE: Orgy's testimony is a recollection/interpretation of Georgy's actual words. Therefore, it's likely to be a less accurate source than the letter itself would be.

110. Yes, if Hamelin is testifying essentially ***on the basis of what he learned from the regis-***

ter. In that event, the writing will have to be produced, because Hamelin is only reciting what the writing says. Thus the register, and not Hamelin, is the basis of the evidence and the jury is entitled to it. This is true even though Hamelin didn't explicitly mention the register in his direct testimony.

RELATED ISSUE: Suppose Hamelin was testifying as to his ***direct recollection*** of the transaction (done without consulting any writing prior to testifying), but it also happened that the transaction was originally recorded in the check register. Now, Hamelin's testimony would ***not*** violate the Best Evidence Rule, because he would be testifying from first-hand knowledge, not from what he learned from a document. (Of course, there can be close questions, as where the witness is testifying from his own memory, but he confirmed that memory by checking the written document before testifying. In that situation, the B.E.R. ***doesn't*** apply — it applies only where the witness is essentially ***reciting what the document says***.)

NOTE: Where the B.E.R. applies on the issue of whether a check was written, the Rule probably does not require that the ***canceled check*** be offered into evidence — the check register probably suffices. However, if the check register is introduced instead of the canceled check, the register may be viewed with distrust by the jury.

111. Objection overruled. Under FRE 1001(e), a photocopy of a document is called a ***"duplicate"*** of that document. Under FRE 1003, the ***duplicate is admissible to the same extent as the original***, unless there's a "genuine question" about the authenticity of the original or it would be "unfair" to admit the duplicate. Since what's being offered here is a photocopy, and there's no question (so far as the facts tell us) about the authenticity of the original contract, and there's no reason to believe use of the photocopy would be "unfair," the copy should be admitted notwithstanding the B.E.R.

By the way, only ***highly-accurate mechanical/electronic reproductions*** of the original can be "duplicates," under 1001(e). In addition to photocopies, examples would include carbon copies, microfilm, copies of sound recordings, and other techniques not involving human interpretation. Inexact types of copies (e.g., handwritten transcriptions) are ***not*** "duplicates," and thus are not admissible unless it is shown that the original is unavailable and its unavailability is not due to serious misconduct of the proponent.

112. Yes. Because the original ***can't be subpoenaed***, it's deemed to be "unavailable." FRE 1004(b). Thus, secondary evidence, like notes, copies, and oral testimony, will be admissible to determine the letter's contents.

RELATED ISSUE: The same rule applies if the original is lost or destroyed (through no bad faith of the proponent), or it's in the possession of an opponent who refuses to produce it in court, or the fact sought to be proved by the writing isn't material. FRE 1004(a), (c) and (d).

RELATED ISSUE: The same rule applies if the writing is in the possession of a person in the jurisdiction who has a legal right to withhold it (e.g., because it's ***privileged***).

113. No. Because Verni's license relates only to a ***collateral matter***, the Best Evidence Rule does not apply. Under FRE 1004(d), an original is not required where a writing, recording, or photograph is not closely related to a "controlling issue." McC §234.

114. Since Ophelia is testifying from knowledge she gleaned from the X-ray and the X-

ray is available, it will have to be produced. X-rays are treated the same as writings and photographs for purposes of the Best Evidence Rule. FRE 1002.

115. No — this is not necessary, according to the majority rule. As long as *some* witness testifies, based on personal knowledge, that the photograph accurately and correctly represents the facts contained therein, the photograph will be admissible. Testimony by the *photographer* is not necessary; nor is testimony about the circumstances under which the photograph was taken.

116. No. The court has broad discretion in granting jury views. Views will be allowed only where counsel and all parties can be present, with strict safeguards so that the jury is not exposed to too much extraneous information. Also, the court will generally try to ensure that the conditions (e.g., time of day) are as nearly as possible identical to those that obtained when the crime was committed.

117. No. A witness may use models, photos, and maps to illustrate his testimony as long as he testifies from personal knowledge that the exhibit ***fairly represents what it is designed to represent***. Thus, there's no need for separate testimony from the photographer, model-builder, etc. NOTE: The judge has discretion to *exclude* demonstrative evidence if he believes it will likely be misleading or useless.

118. Objection overruled. Lay opinion testimony is admissible for "sense impressions" within the everyday experience of ordinary people. Hazel's testimony to the "almond" smell is thus admissible. (But if she were to testify that she smelled the "smell of sodium cyanide," this statement probably wouldn't be admissible, unless she were shown to have a special knowledge or expertise in identifying the smell of that chemical.)

119. No, probably. Under FRE 701, non-expert testimony is limited to opinions or inferences that are (1) rationally based on the perception of the witness; (2) helpful to a ***clear understanding*** of the witness's testimony or to the determination of a ***fact in issue***; and (3) not based on scientific, technical or specialized knowledge. Wimpy's statement about what Wimpy would have done – which is tantamount to a statement that in Wimpy's opinion Bluto was negligent – certainly doesn't seem to satisfy either branch of condition (2): it doesn't help the fact-finder understand the substance of Wimpy's testimony (exactly how Bluto kept Mittens), and it's hard to see what material fact it helps establish. Also, a court is less likely to allow lay opinion on an issue that is very closely identified with one of the "ultimate" issues in the case; whether Bluto was negligent is such an issue here.

120. Yes. Under FRE 702, although education or training certainly help to qualify an expert, his knowledge, skill, and experience alone can suffice. Thus, a convicted burglar could give expert testimony as to the use of crowbars, wires, etc. in burglary, or a marijuana user could give expert testimony that a particular sample of marijuana hails from Hawaii.

121. No. An expert may testify based on three types of information:

1. ***Personal observation***; FRE 703;

2. Facts ***presented to the expert at trial*** (e.g., a hypothetical question); FRE 705; OR

3. Facts of which the expert "has been made aware," typically ***outside the courtroom***; FRE 703. (This category is the one that applies here).

In fact, the second-hand data relied upon need not even be ***admissible***, if it's of a ***type upon which experts in the field reasonably rely***. So if Claire has been given, prior to the trial, facts about the house (e.g., photos; sound recordings; depositions by people living in the house), and these items are ones that experts in the field of ghost-analysis customarily rely upon, that would be sufficient to allow her to testify.

122. No. Elba's expert opinion won't be helpful to the trier of fact, as required under FRE 702. The question of Napoleon's "testamentary capacity" would require a ***legal*** opinion, not a psychiatric opinion. Had the question been "Did Napoleon have the mental capacity to understand the nature and extent of his property, to know the natural objects of his bounty, and to formulate a rational scheme of distribution?" it would probably be permissible, because it would call for opinions that are (more or less) in the domain of psychiatry.

123. Yes, but only if the prosecution establishes that Uretic's book is a reliable authority. FRE 803(18). If it does so, the statement will be substantively admissible. This can be done through testimony of the witness being cross-examined, through direct testimony by another expert, or by the court's taking judicial notice of the fact. *Id.*

NOTE: There's an additional requirement (satisfied here) before a treatise can be used substantively: it must have either been "***called to the attention*** of [the] expert witness on cross-examination" (which happened here), or "relied on by the expert on direct examination[.]" FRE 803(18). So if the prosecution had not mentioned the treatise while doing the cross of Dr. Ulite, it wouldn't have been entitled to put the treatise into evidence thereafter unless it came up with its own expert who relied on (not just confirmed the authoritativeness of) the treatise in forming her own opinion. So, for instance, the prosecution couldn't have simply read the treatise to the jury after dismissing Ulite from the stand.

COMMON LAW RULE: At common law, virtually all courts would have rejected the treatise as substantive evidence. Furthermore, many courts would have regarded the question as improper even if used just for impeachment, on the grounds that only treatises that the witness relied upon could be used to impeach him.

124. No. Even under the liberal FRE approach to treatise evidence, the treatise can't be admitted as an exhibit; it may only be read orally to the jury. FRE 803(18), last sent. The purpose of this limitation is mainly to prevent the treatise from being taken into the jury room (because it might have too much influence if it was).

125. That fecology does not consist of "reliable principles and methods." FRE 702 allows expert testimony on scientific or other "specialized knowledge," but only if, among other things, the testimony is "the product of reliable principles and methods," which are "reliably applied to the facts of the case." (These requirements are based upon the Supreme Court's opinion in *Daubert v. Merrell Dow Pharmaceuticals*, requiring that the proponent of scientific evidence establish the evidence's "scientific validity.") Unless the defense can show that fecology consists of "reliable principles and methods" (which would be shown by factors such as error rate, peer review, etc.), the evidence must be excluded.

126. Not necessarily, though they would certainly be ***factors*** that would ***tend*** to induce the court to exclude the evidence. Under *Daubert v. Merrell Dow Pharmaceuticals*, federal courts may not admit evidence derived from use of a scientific technique unless that technique is shown to be "scientifically reliable," as well as applicable to an issue in the case. These principles are now reflected in FRE 702's requirement that expert testimony be "the product of reliable principles and methods," which are "reliably applied ... to the facts of the case." The fact that the technique has not yet been subjected to peer review, and the fact that it has not yet become generally accepted, are factors tending towards a finding of non-reliability, but these factors are not dispositive. If the sponsoring expert is extremely well-credentialed, if he testifies that he and others have extensively tested the machine, and if he reports a low error rate for the machine, these positive factors might be enough to overcome the two negative factors.

127. Yes. Once the "basic fact" (here, proper mailing) is proven , the burden of producing evidence disproving the "presumed fact" (here, receipt of the letter) is shifted to the party against whom the presumption operates (here, Davis). Therefore, since Davis didn't come up with any evidence that he didn't receive the letter, the jury must find that he received it.

RELATED ISSUE: However, this presumption, like most, is ***rebuttable***. Thus if Davis can produce substantial rebuttal evidence to prove the letter did ***not*** arrive, the presumption will be destroyed. (The jury *could* still conclude that the letter was received, based on Lincoln's proof of proper mailing, but the jury wouldn't be *required* to so conclude.) Occasionally, the rebuttal evidence can be so compelling that it shifts the burden of production as to the presumed fact all the way back to the other party. (But there's probably no evidence Davis could come up with in this mailing situation that would cause this to happen, so the jury would probably remain free to find that Davis received the letter.)

128. Yes. Under FRE 301, the party against whom a presumption is directed has the ***burden of going forward*** with evidence to rebut the presumption. If he doesn't, the court will instruct the jury that if it believes the basic facts, it must presume the existence of the presumed fact. Here, since the basic facts necessary to establish the presumption (that Crater has unexpectedly been absent for seven years, and that no one who should have heard from him [e.g., his family and friends] has done so) were proven, the presumed fact, that Crater is dead, will be treated as established (in the absence of rebuttal).

129. Yes. The document is relevant if and only if it really was signed by Washington. Therefore, it falls under FRE 104(b), which states that "When the relevance of evidence depends on whether a fact exists, proof must be introduced ***sufficient to support a finding*** that the fact does exist. The court may admit the proposed evidence on the condition that the proof be introduced later." The fact that the judge isn't sure whether the document is genuine or not indicates that there's enough evidence to "support a finding" that it was signed by Washington. (In other words, there's enough evidence that a reasonable jury could find, by a preponderance of the evidence, that Washington signed it.) Consequently, under 104(b) the judge should admit the document, and leave it to the jury to decide whether Washington signed it. This question illustrates the general principle that questions of authenticity are left to the jury (as long as there is enough evidence of authenticity for a reasonable jury to decide either way).

130. No, probably. Under FRE 103(a), a party may claim error in a ruling to admit evidence "only if the error affects a substantial right of the party and: (1) [that] party, on the record: (A) timely objects or moves to strike; and (B) states the specific ground, unless it was apparent from the context[.]" However, 103(e) says that "[a] court may take notice of a ***plain error*** affecting a substantial right, even if the claim of error was not properly preserved." There's a good chance that the appellate court will rule that admitting a severed leg is so inherently prejudicial, and such an egregious mistake, that it amounted to "plain error." If so, Acme's appeal will be heard even though Acme did not make a timely objection.

131. Yes. This is a ***"notorious fact"*** — one subject to common knowledge in the community. Thus, if either party asks the judge to take judicial notice of the fact, the judge *must* do so, under FRE 201(c)(2). In fact, the judge *may* take judicial notice of the gestation period even in the absence of such a request, under FRE 201(c)(1).

132. Yes. Although such a fact is not generally known, it's a ***"manifest fact,"*** i.e., one capable of verification through a readily accessible, undoubtedly accurate source — an almanac. Thus, it's suitable for judicial notice under FRE 201.

133. No. The judge's personal knowledge is irrelevant to judicial notice. The only facts that can be judicially noticed are ***notorious facts*** (subject to common knowledge in the community) and ***manifest facts*** (capable of verification through readily accessible, undoubtedly accurate sources). The condition of a roadway at a particular time *wouldn't* qualify, so its condition will have to be proven.

134. No. Under FRE 201(f) (2nd sent.), the judge in a ***criminal*** case must instruct the jury that it ***may***, but ***isn't required to***, accept as conclusive any fact judicially noticed. (The same rule applies at common law.) (Contrast this with ***civil*** cases, where the judge must instruct the jury to accept as ***conclusive*** any fact judicially noticed. FRE 201(f), 1st sent.)

MULTIPLE-CHOICE QUESTIONS

Here are 30 multiple-choice questions, in a Multistate-Bar-Exam style. These questions are taken from *"The Finz Multistate Method,"* a compendium of 1100 questions in the Multistate subjects (*Contracts*, *Torts*, *Property*, *Evidence*, *Criminal Law* and *Constitutional Law*) written by the late Professor Steven Finz and published by Wolters Kluwer Law & Business. To learn more about this book and other study aids, go to **www.aspenlaw.com**.

1. Finney operated a chain of fast food restaurants which specialized in fried fish. Finney entered into a valid written contract with C-Foods, for the purchase of "six thousand pounds of frozen pinktail fish filets of frying quality," to be delivered by C-Foods over a period of six months. One week after C-Foods made its first delivery pursuant to the contract, however, Finney notified C-Foods that the product delivered was unacceptable because the filets delivered weighed only eight ounces each, and that they were cut from Grade B pinktail fish. Finney offered to return the unused portion of the delivery, and refused to make payment.

   C-Foods subsequently brought an action against Finney for breach of contract. At the trial of that action C-Foods offered the testimony of Cooke. Cooke testified that he was the head chef at a leading hotel, and that he had been employed as a chef in fine restaurants for more than thirty years. He testified further that in that time he had purchased large quantities of fish on numerous occasions, and was familiar with the terminology used in the wholesale fish industry. Cooke stated that when the phrase "pinktail fish filets of frying quality" is used in the wholesale fish business, it means boneless pieces from six to nine ounces in weight and cut from Grade A or B pinktail fish. Upon proper objection by Finney's attorney, Cooke's testimony as to the meaning of the phrase should be

   (A) admitted as evidence of trade terminology.
   (B) admitted only if Cooke qualifies as an expert on the preparation of fried fish in fast food restaurants.
   (C) excluded since it is an opinion.
   (D) excluded unless the parties specifically agreed to be bound by the terminology of the wholesale fish industry.

Questions 2-3 are based on the following fact situation.

Dr. Withey was hired by the defense to examine the plaintiff in a tort case. At trial, Dr. Withey stated that during the course of the examination the plaintiff said, "My arm hurts so much, I don't see how I'll ever be able to go back to work."

2. Which of the following would be the defendant's strongest argument in support of a motion to strike the testimony?

   (A) The plaintiff's statement was made in contemplation of litigation.
   (B) The doctor was not examining the plaintiff for the purpose of treatment.
   (C) The plaintiff's statement was self-serving.
   (D) Evidence of the plaintiff's statement is more prejudicial than probative.

3. Dr. Withey then stated that during the course of the examination the plaintiff also said, "When I was struck by the car my right elbow struck the ground so hard that I heard a sound like a gunshot." If the defendant objects to this testimony, the court should

   (A) sustain the objection, since the statement is hearsay.
   (B) sustain the objection, since the examination was not performed for the purpose of diagnosis or treatment.
   (C) overrule the objection, since the statement was part of a pertinent medical history.
   (D) overrule the objection, since the statement described a former sense impression.

4. Fritz, a house painter, was charged with stealing three valuable figurines from the home of Valens while painting the interior of that home. At Fritz's trial, Valens testified that he first noticed that the figurines were missing about an hour after Fritz left his home. He stated that he looked Fritz's number up in the telephone book and properly dialed the number listed therein. Over objection by Fritz's attorney, Valens stated that a man answered the phone by saying, "Fritz speaking." Valens stated that he then said, "Fritz, where are the figurines?" and that the person at the other end of the line said, "I'm sorry. I took them." The objection by Fritz's attorney should be

   (A) sustained, unless independent evidence establishes that Fritz was the person to whom Valens was speaking.
   (B) sustained, since Valens did not actually see the person to whom he was speaking.
   (C) sustained, since the statement is hearsay.
   (D) overruled.

5. After his vehicle collided with Pringle's on March 1, Dicton retained Addie, an attorney, to represent him in any possible litigation which might develop. Addie hired Vesto, a private investigator, to interview Pringle regarding the facts of the accident. On March 5, Vesto followed Pringle into a bar, sat next to him, and engaged him in conversation. During the conversation, Pringle described the accident which he had with Dicton, and said, "Just between you and me, I drank a six-pack of beer just before

the accident happened. It's a good thing nobody smelled my breath." Eventually Pringle commenced a personal injury action against Dicton. At the trial of the action, Pringle testified on direct examination that he had been driving at a slow rate of speed when Dicton's vehicle suddenly pulled out a driveway into his path.

On cross-examination, Dicton's attorney asked Pringle whether he had drunk alcohol during the hour prior to the accident. Pringle answered that he had not. Dicton's attorney then asked, "Didn't you tell an investigator from my office that you had consumed an entire six-pack of beer just before the accident?" If Pringle's attorney objects to the question, the court should

(A) sustain the objection, since Pringle's prior statement was not made under oath.
(B) sustain the objection, since it was unethical for Dicton's attorney to make contract with Pringle through an investigator.
(C) sustain the objection, since the statement is hearsay not within any exception to the hearsay rule.
(D) overrule the objection.

6. Postum was crossing the street on foot when she was struck by a Daxco delivery van driven by Currier, a Daxco employee in the process of making a delivery for Daxco. Following the accident, Currier was charged with reckless driving and pleaded not guilty. At the trial on the charge of reckless driving, Currier testified in his own defense. He stated that at the time of the accident, he had taken his eyes off the road to look for the address of the place to which he was supposed to make his delivery, and that as a result he never saw Postum before striking her.

   Postum subsequently brought an action against Daxco for personal injuries resulting from Currier's negligence under the theory of respondeat superior. At the trial of *Postum v. Daxco,* Postum proved that Currier remained in Daxco's employ until Currier died from causes not related to the accident. Postum then offered a transcript of Currier's testimony at the reckless driving trial. Upon objection by Daxco's attorney, the transcript should be

   (A) admitted under the prior testimony exception to the hearsay rule.
   (B) admitted under the past recollection recorded exception to the hearsay rule.
   (C) admitted as a vicarious admission under the official written statement exception to the hearsay rule.
   (D) excluded as hearsay not within any exception to the hearsay rule.

7. Vason was found dead in his garage, hanging by the neck from a rope tied to a roof beam. His widow Alma brought an action against Vason's psychiatrist Si under the state's wrongful death statute. In her complaint, Alma alleged that Si was negligent in his treatment of Vason, whom he knew or should have known to be suicidal. In his answer, Si denied that he knew Vason to be suicidal, denied that he had treated him negligently, and denied that Vason's death was a suicide. At the trial of the wrongful death action, Nina, a nurse employed by Si, testified that the day before Vason's death,

she heard Vason say to Si, "I think suicide is the only way out." Upon objection by Si's counsel, which of the following statements is most correct?

I. The statement should be admitted for the purpose of establishing that Vason's death was a suicide.

II. The statement should be admitted for the purpose of establishing that Si knew or should have known that Vason was suicidal.

(A) I only.
(B) II only.
(C) Both I and II.
(D) Neither I nor II.

8. Angel was insured by Innco Insurance Company under a policy which required Innco to pay the total value of any damage to Angel's motorcycle resulting from collision. After Angel's motorcycle was totally destroyed in a highway accident, Angel submitted a claim to Innco as required by the terms of her policy. Innco offered only two thousand dollars, although Angel claimed that the motorcycle was worth twice that amount. Angel subsequently instituted an action against Innco for benefits under the policy. At the trial of Angel's action against Innco, which of the following is LEAST likely to be admitted as evidence of the motorcycle's value?

(A) Angel's testimony that it was worth four thousand dollars.
(B) Angel's testimony that two days before the accident she had received an offer of four thousand dollars from someone who wanted to purchase the motorcycle.
(C) The testimony of a used motorcycle dealer who had never seen Angel's motorcycle, but who, after examining a photograph of it, stated that motorcycles like it were regularly bought and sold for prices ranging from three thousand five hundred to four thousand two hundred dollars.
(D) the testimony of an amateur motorcycle collector, who had bought and sold many motorcycles like Angel's, that two days before the accident he had looked at Angel's motorcycle because he was interested in buying it, and that in his opinion the motorcycle had been worth four thousand dollars.

Questions 9-10 are based on the following fact situation:

Lanham was the owner of a three-story professional building. The entire second floor of Lanham's building was rented to Dr. View, an optometrist. Persons visiting the office of Dr. View either rode in an elevator located inside the building or climbed a stairway which was fastened to the outside of the building and which led from the street level to the second floor only. Priller was a patient of Dr. View's. One day upon leaving Dr. View's office and descending the stairway on the outside of the building, Priller fell, sustaining serious injuries. She commenced an action against Lanham, alleging that the stairway was dangerous in that it was too steep, it lacked a handrail, and the stair treads were too narrow. Lanham denied that the stairway was dangerous. In addition, as an affirmative defense, he denied control over the stairway, asserting that it had been leased to Dr. View as part of the second-floor office.

9. At the trial, Priller called Walker, who had been employed by Lanham as building manager at the time of the accident, but who was presently unemployed. Walker testified that two days after the accident Lanham instructed him to install a handrail on the stairway, and to post a sign which read, "CAUTION: Steep and narrow stairway!" Lanham's attorney objected to the testimony and moved that it be stricken. Which of the following would be Priller's most effective argument in response to the objection and in opposition to the motion to strike?

   (A) Walker is no longer in Lanham's employ.
   (B) The testimony is relevant to establish that the stairway was dangerous.
   (C) The testimony is relevant to establish that Lanham was aware that the stairway was dangerous.
   (D) The testimony is relevant to establish that Lanham was in control of the stairway.

10. On cross-examination by Lanham's attorney, Walker testified that he had been employed by Lanham as building manager for a period of three years prior to the accident. He stated that the condition of the stairway was substantially the same during that period as it was on the day of Priller's accident, and that although many people used the stairway every day, Walker had never before heard of anyone falling while using it. Priller's attorney objected to this testimony. Should the court sustain Priller's objection?

    (A) Yes, since evidence that no accident had occurred in the past is not relevant to the issues on trial.
    (B) Yes, unless there is evidence that Walker would have heard of such accidents had they occurred.
    (C) No, if Lanham raised a defense of contributory negligence.
    (D) No, since Walker was called as Priller's witness.

11. In an action by Pillow Products against Daphne, Pillow alleged that it had entered into a written contract with Daphne for the purchase of satin material which Pillow intended to use in manufacturing its products, and that Daphne failed to deliver the material as promised. At the trial, Legg testified that he worked in the Pillow Products legal department, and that he had negotiated the contract in question. He stated further that, although the original and all copies of the contract had been destroyed in an office fire, he knew the substance of its contents. When Pillow's attorney began to question Legg about the contents of the contract, Daphne objected. The trial court should

    (A) sustain the objection, since Legg's testimony would violate the parol evidence rule.
    (B) sustain the objection, since Legg's testimony would violate the best evidence rule.

(C) overrule the objection, since the absence of the original document has been explained.

(D) overrule the objection, since the Statute of Frauds is satisfied by the fact that a written memorandum of agreement was made.

12. Rider, an investigative reporter for the *Daily Globe,* wrote a series of articles exposing corruption in city government. In the articles, he said that "a building permit can be obtained for just about anything in this town if bribes are given to the right city officials." As a result of the series, a grand jury began investigating the allegations of corruption. When Rider was called to testify, however, he refused to divulge the sources of his information, claiming reportorial privilege. Rider was charged with contempt. While his prosecution on that charge was pending, the grand jury continued with its investigation by causing the city's mayor, Mayo, to be served with a subpoena. When asked whether she knew of any city official accepting bribes for the issuance of building permits Mayo refused to answer, invoking her Fifth Amendment privilege against self-incrimination. After being granted use immunity, however, she testified that Cooms, the city's building commissioner, regularly accepted bribes for the issuance of permits, and that Cooms regularly shared the bribe money with Mayo.

After Mayo's testimony, both Mayo and Cooms were indicted by the grand jury on charges of bribery. Because there was no other evidence against Mayo, prior to the trial, the prosecutor agreed to accept a plea to a lesser offense from Cooms if he would testify against Mayo. At Mayo's trial, if Mayo objects to the testimony of Cooms, the objection should be

(A) sustained, if the prosecutor had no evidence against Cooms other than Mayo's testimony.

(B) sustained, since a prosecutor may not bargain away the rights of one co-defendant in a deal with another.

(C) overruled, because the proceeding was instituted as a result of the statements made in the articles by Rider, not as a result of the testimony of Mayo at the grand jury hearing.

(D) overruled, if the testimony of Cooms was voluntary and not the result of coercion.

13. Pelton sued Transport Inc. for damage which resulted from a collision between Pelton's motorcycle and one of Transport's trucks. After receiving the summons, Thomas, the president and sole stockholder of Transport Inc., notified Lottie, the company attorney. Lottie said that she wanted to meet with Thomas and the driver of the truck. At Lottie's request, Thomas went to Lottie's office with Darla, who had been driving the truck at the time of the accident. While discussing the case with Lottie in the presence of Darla, Thomas said that on the day before the accident he was aware that the truck's brakes were not working properly, but that because of a heavy work load he postponed making the necessary repairs.

At the trial of Pelton's suit against Transport, Pelton attempted to have Darla testify to the statement which Thomas made to Lottie about the brakes. Transport's attorney objected on the ground of the attorney-client privilege. Should Darla be permitted to testify to Thomas's statement?

(A) Yes, because the attorney-client privilege does not apply to testimony by one who does not stand in a confidential relationship with the person against whom the evidence is offered.
(B) Yes, because it is presumed that a communication made in the presence of third persons is not confidential.
(C) Yes, because communications made by or on behalf of corporations are not privileged.
(D) No.

14. At the trial of an automobile accident case, for the purpose of showing the relationship and directions of the streets involved, the plaintiff offered into evidence a photograph of the intersection where the accident occurred. The plaintiff testified that on the day of the accident the intersection looked exactly as depicted in the photograph, except that on the day of the accident some of the trees on the street had small Christmas ornaments on them. Upon objection, should the photograph be admitted in evidence?

(A) Yes, if the absence of Christmas tree ornaments did not prevent the photograph from being a fair representation of the intersection at the time of the accident.
(B) Yes, but only if the photograph was taken within a reasonable time following the accident.
(C) No, unless the photographer who made the photograph testifies to its authenticity.
(D) No, not under any circumstances.

15. Peterson was sitting in his car at a dead stop waiting for a traffic light to change color, when his vehicle was struck in the rear by a car operated by Dodge, rendering Peterson unconscious. Police were called to the accident scene and as a result of their investigation Dodge was charged with "operating an unregistered vehicle," a misdemeanor. The following day, Dodge pleaded guilty to the charge and was sentenced to five days in jail.

Peterson subsequently asserted a claim for damages resulting from Dodge's negligence. Because of admissions which were made in the pleadings, a hearing was held on the sole questions of whether Dodge was negligent. At the hearing, a transcript of Dodge's conviction for operating an unregistered vehicle should be

(A) admitted.
(B) excluded, because it is not relevant to the question of negligence.
(C) excluded, because it was not the result of a trial.
(D) excluded, because it is hearsay, not within any exception.

16. A state statute provides that the owner of any motor vehicle operated on the public roads of the state is liable for damage resulting from the negligence of any person driving the vehicle with the owner's permission. Pavlov was injured when a vehicle operated by Dawson struck her while she was walking across the street. At the scene of the accident, Dawson apologized to Pavlov, saying, "I'm sorry. It isn't my car. I didn't know that the brakes were bad." Pavlov subsequently instituted an action against Oster for her damages, asserting that Oster owned the vehicle. She alleged that Oster was negligent in permitting the vehicle to be driven while he knew that the brakes were in need of repair, and that he was vicariously liable under the statute for the negligence of Dawson. Oster denied ownership of the vehicle. At the trial, Pavlov offered testimony by Mecco, a mechanic, that on the day after the accident Oster hired him to completely overhaul the brakes. Upon objection by Oster, the evidence is

    (A) admissible, to show that Oster was the owner of the vehicle.
    (B) admissible, to show that the brakes were in need of repair on the day of the accident.
    (C) inadmissible, because the condition of the vehicle on any day other than that of the accident is irrelevant to show its condition at the time the accident occurred.
    (D) inadmissible, under a policy which encourages safety precautions.

17. Keller had been a member of a professional crime organization for twenty years, and had participated in many crimes during that period of time. Because Keller's testimony was crucial to the district attorney's attempt to break the crime organization, he was offered immunity if he would testify against other members of the organization. He did so, and his testimony resulted in several convictions. Keller subsequently wrote and published a book entitled *Contract Killer,* in which he described in detail many of the crimes which he committed, including the shotgun murder of Vicuna. Following the publication of *Contract Killer,* Vicuna's wife commenced an action against Keller for damages resulting from the wrongful death of her husband. At the trial, a police officer who had been called to the scene of Vicuna's shooting testified that just before Vicuna died he heard him say, "I saw Keller pull the trigger on me." If Keller moves to strike the police officer's testimony, his motion should be

    (A) granted, since a dying declaration is admissible only in a trial for criminal homicide.
    (B) granted, if Keller received transactional immunity.
    (C) denied, if Vicuna believed himself to be dying when he made the statement.
    (D) denied, if the jurisdiction has a "dead man's statute."

Questions 18-19 are based on the following fact situation.

After the crash of Wing Airlines Flight 123, an action for wrongful death was brought by the husband of a passenger killed in the crash. During the trial, the plaintiff called Weston, an employee of the State Aviation Agency which investigated the circumstances surrounding the crash.

18. Weston testified that during the course of his investigation he questioned a mechanic named Marshall on the day of the crash. He said that Marshall stated that he and a mechanic named Stevens had been assigned by the Wing Airlines airport supervisor to inspect Flight 123 before take-off, but that they did not inspect the plane as directed. If Weston's testimony is objected to, the judge should rule it admissible

    (A) if Weston testifies that Marshall claimed to be an employee of Wing.
    (B) only if independent evidence indicates that Marshall was employed by Wing at the time the statement was made.
    (C) only if independent evidence indicates that at the time the statement was made, Marshall was authorized to speak for Wing.
    (D) if Marshall is unavailable to testify.

19. Weston also read aloud from an investigation report which quoted an unidentified witness to the crash as stating that she heard an explosion several seconds before she saw the plane burst into flames. He testified that the report from which he was reading was one kept in the regular course of business by the State Aviation Agency, that the entry from which he was reading had been made by another investigator who worked for the Agency, that the investigator who made the entry was sworn to investigate airplane crashes and to keep honest and accurate records of the results of those investigations, and that the investigator who made the entry was now dead. Upon appropriate objection, the evidence should be ruled

    (A) admissible as a business record.
    (B) admissible as an official written statement.
    (C) admissible as past recollection recorded.
    (D) inadmissible as hearsay not within any exception.

Questions 20-21 are based on the following fact situation.

Kane's dog frequently dug holes in the lawn of Kane's neighbor Nixon, who had telephoned Kane to complain in a loud voice on several occasions. One day, after the dog dug up Nixon's prize rosebush, Nixon ran to Kane's house and banged on Kane's front door. When Kane opened the door, Nixon shouted, "You dirty son of a bitch." Kane struck him in the face with his fist, and closed the door. Nixon later sued Kane for battery, and Kane asserted the privilege of self-defense. At the trial Kane offered the testimony of a local shopkeeper who stated that he knew Nixon's reputation in the neighborhood, and that Nixon was known as "a bad actor who will fight at the drop of a hat." He also offered the testimony of the local parish priest who stated that he had known Kane for years, and that everyone in the community thought of him as a peaceable man who would never resort to violence except in self-protection.

20. If Nixon's attorney objects to the testimony of the shopkeeper, the objection should be

    (A) sustained, since evidence of Nixon's character is not relevant to his action for battery.
    (B) sustained, since Nixon is not the defendant.
    (C) overruled, since the testimony is relevant to Kane's assertion of the privilege of self-defense.
    (D) overruled, since Nixon placed his character in issue by bringing the lawsuit.

21. If Nixon's attorney objects to the testimony of the parish priest, the testimony should be

    (A) excluded, if it is offered as circumstantial evidence to prove that Kane did not strike Nixon without justification.
    (B) excluded, unless the priest testified that his own opinion of Kane coincided with what the community thought about him.
    (C) admitted, because Kane is the defendant.
    (D) admitted, for the limited purpose of establishing Kane's state of mind at the time of the occurrence.

22. After receiving a tip, police officers stopped a car being driven by Davidson, and forced him to open the trunk. In it, the officers discovered a canvas bag containing seven pounds of cocaine. They seized the car and the cocaine as evidence, and placed Davidson under arrest. Without advising him of his rights to remain silent and to consult with an attorney, they questioned him about the cocaine. During the questioning, Davidson said, "I don't know anything about it. It isn't even my car."

    Davidson was charged with illegal possession of a controlled substance. Subsequently, Davidson's motion to suppress the use of the cocaine as evidence was granted, and the charges against him were dismissed. Davidson thereupon commenced an appropriate proceeding against the police department for recovery of his automobile. On presentation of his direct case, Davidson testified that he owned the seized automobile, but had registered it to a friend for purposes of convenience. On cross-examination, the attorney representing the police department asked, "After your arrest, did you tell the arresting officers that it wasn't your car?"

    If Davidson's attorney objects to this question, the objection should be

    (A) sustained, because Davidson's interrogation was in violation of his *Miranda* rights.
    (B) sustained, because Davidson's motion to suppress was granted.
    (C) overruled, because the automobile in which the cocaine was transported is "fruit of the poisonous tree."
    (D) overruled, because his denial that he owned the car was a prior inconsistent statement.

23. In the trial of a tort action in a United States District Court, if the substantive law of the state is being applied, which of the following statements is correct regarding confidential communications between psychotherapist and patient?

    I. The United States District Court MUST recognize the psychotherapist-patient privilege if it is recognized by the law of the state.

    II. The United States District Court MAY recognize the psychotherapist-patient privilege even if it is not recognized by the law of the state.

    (A) I only.
    (B) II only.
    (C) I and II.
    (D) Neither I nor II.

24. Derringer was charged with violating a federal law which prohibits the unlicensed transportation of specified toxic wastes across a state line. At his trial in a federal district court, the prosecution proved that Derringer had transported certain toxic wastes from Detroit, Michigan to Chicago, Illinois. The prosecuting attorney then moved that the court take judicial notice that it is impossible to travel between those two cities without crossing a state line. Upon proper objection by Derringer's attorney, the prosecution's motion should be

    (A) granted, if it is generally known within the territorial jurisdiction of the court that it is impossible to travel from Detroit to Chicago without crossing a state line.
    (B) granted, but only if the prosecution presents the court with a reputable map or other reference work indicating that a state line lies between the cities of Detroit and Chicago.
    (C) denied, but only if Derringer's attorney demands an offer of proof for the record.
    (D) denied, if the fact that Derringer traveled across a state line concerns an ultimate issue of fact.

25. Draper was charged with the second degree murder of Valle under a statute which defined that crime as "the unlawful killing of a human being with malice aforethought, but without premeditation." Draper's attorney asserted a defense of insanity, and called Draper as a witness in his own behalf. After Draper testified on direct and cross-examination, his attorney called Dr. Wendell to the witness stand. Dr. Wendell stated that he was a psychiatrist, had practiced for thirty years, had treated thousands of patients with illnesses like Draper's, and had testified as an expert in hundreds of criminal homicide trials. He testified, "After listening to Draper's testimony, I am of the opinion that Draper did not have malice aforethought as our law defines it on the day of Valle's death." On cross-examination, Dr. Wendell admitted that he had never spoken to or seen Draper before, and that his opinion was based entirely on his observations of Draper's testimony.

Which of the following would be the prosecuting attorney's most effective argument in support of a motion to exclude Dr. Wendell's statement?

(A) Dr. Wendell's testimony embraces the ultimate issue.
(B) Dr. Wendell's opinions were based entirely upon courtroom observations.
(C) Dr. Wendell had insufficient opportunity to examine Draper.
(D) Whether Draper had "malice aforethought" is a question to be decided by the jury.

26. Dempsey was charged in a state court with third degree arson on the allegation that he set fire to his own house for the purpose of collecting benefits under a fire insurance policy. At his trial, Dempsey called Wrangler as a witness in his favor. On direct examination by Dempsey's attorney, Wrangler testified that at the time of the fire he and Dempsey were together at a baseball game fifty miles away from Dempsey's home.

On rebuttal the prosecuting attorney offered evidence that two years earlier Wrangler was released from custody after serving a five year sentence in a federal prison following his conviction for perjury. If Dempsey's attorney objects to the introduction of this evidence, the objection should be

(A) overruled, but only if Wrangler is given a subsequent opportunity to explain the conviction.
(B) overruled, because perjury is a crime involving dishonesty.
(C) sustained, because the conviction was not more than ten years old.
(D) sustained, unless the prosecuting attorney asked Wrangler on cross-examination whether he had ever been convicted of a crime.

27. At the trial of a personal injury action, Dr. Watson testified that she examined the plaintiff on the day of trial, and that at that time the plaintiff told her that she felt pain in her knee. On cross-examination, the defendant's attorney asked Dr. Watson whether she had ever met the plaintiff before the day of trial. Dr. Watson responded that she had not, and that her sole purpose in examining the plaintiff was to prepare for testifying at the trial. The defendant's attorney then moved to strike that portion of Dr. Watson's testimony which referred to the plaintiff's complaint of pain. In a jurisdiction which applies the common-law rule regarding confidential communications between patient and physician, should the defendant's motion be granted?

(A) Yes, because the examination was solely for the purpose of litigation.
(B) Yes, because the probative value of the statement is outweighed by the possibility of prejudice.
(C) Yes, because statements made to a physician are privileged.
(D) No, because the statement described what the plaintiff was feeling at the time.

28. During the presentation of plaintiff's direct case in a personal injury action, the plaintiff's attorney called Dr. Wallace to the stand for the purpose of establishing that the plaintiff had sustained an injury to her epiglammis gland.

When the plaintiff's attorney began to question Dr. Wallace about her qualifications, the defendant's attorney conceded on the record and in the presence of the jury that Dr. Wallace was an expert on injuries of the epiglammis gland and objected to any further questions regarding the qualifications of Dr. Wallace. Should the plaintiff's attorney be permitted to continue questioning Dr. Wallace regarding her qualifications?

(A) No, because the qualifications of Dr. Wallace are no longer in issue.
(B) No, if the court is satisfied that Dr. Wallace qualifies as an expert on diseases and injuries of the epiglammis gland.
(C) Yes, because the court must determine for itself whether a witness qualifies as an expert, and cannot allow the matter to be determined by stipulation of the parties.
(D) Yes, because the jury may consider an expert's qualifications in determining her credibility.

Questions 29-30 are based on the following fact situation.

Handel, a federal officer, had been informed that a person arriving from Europe on a particular airline flight would be carrying cocaine in his baggage. Handel went to the airport and stood at the arrival gate with Findo, a dog which had been specially trained to recognize the scent of cocaine. When Dodd walked by carrying his bag, Findo began barking and scratching the floor in front of him with his right paw. Handel stopped Dodd and searched his bag. In it, he found a small brass statue with a false bottom. Upon removing the false bottom, Handel found one ounce of cocaine. Dodd, who was arrested and charged with the illegal importation of a controlled substance, claimed he had purchased the statue as a souvenir and was unaware that there was cocaine hidden it its base.

29. Assume for the purpose of this question only that Dodd's attorney moved for an order excluding the use of the cocaine as evidence at Dodd's trial. At a hearing on that motion, Handel testified that he was an expert dog trainer and handler, that he had personally trained Findo to signal by barking and scratching the floor in front of him with his right paw whenever he sniffed cocaine, that Findo had successfully found and signaled the presence of cocaine on several previous occasions, and that Findo had given the signal when Dodd walked away. If Dodd's attorney moves to exclude Handel's testimony regarding the way Findo acted when Dodd walked by, that testimony should be

(A) excluded, because the sounds and movements made by Findo are hearsay and not within any exception.
(B) excluded, unless Findo is dead or otherwise unavailable.
(C) admitted, but only if Findo's effectiveness is established by an in-court demonstration.
(D) admitted, because a proper foundation has been laid.

30. Assume for the purpose of this question only that at Dodd's trial the prosecution offers to prove that Dodd had been convicted fifteen years earlier of illegally importing cocaine by hiding it in the base of a brass statue. If Dodd's attorney objects, the court should rule that proof of Dodd's prior conviction is

(A) admissible, as evidence of habit.

(B) admissible, because it is evidence of a distinctive method of operation.

(C) inadmissible, because evidence of previous conduct by a defendant may not be used against him.

(D) inadmissible, because the prior conviction occurred more than ten years before the trial.

ANSWERS TO MULTIPLE-CHOICE QUESTIONS

1. **A** Under both common law and the UCC, evidence of trade terminology is admissible for the purpose of establishing the meaning of a particular term in a contract between parties in the trade. Since the contract calls for the sale of fish at wholesale, evidence of trade terminology used in the wholesale fish industry is relevant to establish the meaning of the term in question.

   Ordinarily, a witness is not permitted to testify to her opinion. A witness who qualifies as an expert in a particular field, however, may be permitted to testify to an opinion regarding her field of expertise. Since Cooke is not offering an opinion regarding the preparation of fried fish in fast food restaurants, he need not qualify as an expert in that particular field. **B** is, therefore, incorrect. **C** is incorrect because an expert may offer an opinion regarding her field of expertise. **D** is incorrect because even if parties have not specifically agreed to be bound by the terminology of a particular industry, that terminology may be relevant in determining the meaning of unexplained terms in a contract so long as both parties are likely to have been aware of the meaning of the trade terminology.

2. **D** Hearsay is an out of court assertion offered for the purpose of proving the truth of the matter asserted. Thus, if the plaintiff's statement to Dr. Withey is being offered to prove that the plaintiff was experiencing pain in his arm, the statement would be hearsay. An exception to the hearsay rule, however, permits the admission of statements made as part of a medical history given in connection with a medical examination made for the purpose of treatment or diagnosis. Since Dr. Withey's examination was being made for the purpose of diagnosis, the patient's statement should be admissible. Under the FRE, the circumstances surrounding the medical examination in which a patient's statement was made go to the weight rather than to the admissibility of that statement. Thus the fact that the examination was not made for the purpose of treatment or that it was made in contemplation of litigation is not, alone, sufficient to prevent admission unless the prejudicial effect of the statement is likely to outweigh its probative value. While a court might not come to that conclusion, the argument in **D** is the only one listed which could possibly support the motion to strike.

   A and **B** are incorrect because, unless the probative value is likely to be outweighed by the prejudicial effect, the fact that the examination was not being made for the purpose of treatment or that it was being made in contemplation of litigation would not be sufficient to result in its exclusion. **C** is incorrect because there is no rule which prevents the admission of self-serving statements.

3. **C** Under FRE 803(4), statements purporting to describe the way in which a physical condition came about are admissible as part of a medical history if made for the purpose of diagnosis, and if pertinent to diagnosis. "Diagnosis" refers to the nature and origin of an injury. Even though Dr. Withey's examination was performed to enable her to testify, she was attempting to form a diagnosis. Since the sound made by the plaintiff's elbow striking the pavement might be pertinent to a determination of the nature and origin of plaintiff's injury, (i.e., diagnosis) the statement is admissible.

A is incorrect. A statement made as part of a medical history is admissible as an exception to the hearsay rule. **B** is incorrect because even though the examination was performed in contemplation of Dr. Withey's testimony, one of its purposes was to allow Dr. Withey to diagnose (i.e., determine the nature of) the plaintiff's injury. Although a witness might be permitted to testify to his own former sense impression, there is no exception to the hearsay rule for a witness's repetition of a declarant's former sense impression. **D** is, therefore, incorrect.

4. **D** Under the FRE, voice identification can be made by a witness who testifies that he properly dialed a number listed in the telephone book, and that circumstances including self-identification show that the person listed was the one who answered.

A and **B** are, therefore, incorrect. Since Fritz's statement is contrary to his interests, it is an admission, which is not hearsay under the FRE and is admissible as an exception to the hearsay rule under common law. **C** is, therefore, incorrect.

5. **D** Since a person who makes statements which contradict each other might not be worthy of belief, a witness may be impeached on cross-examination by inquiry regarding prior inconsistent statements. See FRE 613.

A is, therefore, incorrect. Although it may be unethical for an attorney to make contact directly with an adversary known to be represented by counsel, information obtained by such a contact is not necessarily inadmissible. In any event, **B** is incorrect because there is no reason to believe that Pringle was represented by counsel at the time of his conversation with Vesto, or, if he was, that Addie knew him to be. A statement of a party offered against that party is admissible as an admission. Under the FRE, an admission is not hearsay. (Under the common law, an admission is an exception to the hearsay rule.) **C** is, therefore, incorrect.

6. **C** Since an employer is vicariously liable for the negligence of an employee committed within the scope of employment, statements tending to establish that the accident resulted from Currier's negligence are relevant in Postum's action against Daxco. The evidence should, thus, be admitted unless excluded under the hearsay rule. Hearsay is an out of court statement offered to prove the truth

of the matter asserted. These facts raise what is sometimes called a multiple level hearsay problem (i.e., a problem involving an out of court statement which contains another out of court statement). This is so because Currier's testimony at the reckless driving trial was not made during the negligence trial and so is an "out of court" statement, and because the evidence of his statement is contained in a transcript which was also not made as part of the negligence trial and so is an "out of court" statement. In order for multiple level hearsay (i.e., the transcript containing Currier's statement) to be admissible each level must be separately admissible. The first level of hearsay is the testimony by Currier at the reckless driving trial. Under the common law, statements by an employee are admissible against the employer only if the employee had the authority to make them. But FRE 801(d)(2)(D) requires only that the employee's statement concerned a matter within the scope of his employment, and was made while the employment relationship existed. Currier's statement is therefore a vicarious admission which is an exception to the hearsay rule at common law, and is not hearsay at all under the FRE. The second level of hearsay is the transcript. Since it was made by a public official (the reporter), regarding matters in his own knowledge (that Currier made the admission), in the course of his public duties and at the time the matter recorded (Currier's statement) occurred, the transcript qualifies as an official written statement. **C** is, therefore, correct.

Under FRE 804(b)(1)(B), prior testimony is admissible as an exception to the hearsay rule only if the party against whom it is offered had an incentive and an opportunity to cross-examine when the testimony was first given. Since Doxco was not a party to the proceeding at which Currier's testimony was given, the testimony does not qualify for admission under this exception. **A** is, therefore, incorrect. The past recollection recorded exception requires that the record was made from the recorder's own knowledge and requires the recorder to authenticate the record in court. **B** is incorrect because Currier's statement was not authenticated or recorded by Currier. **D** is incorrect for the reasons stated above.

7. **C** Under FRE 803(3), statements of a declarant's then-existing state of mind are admissible as an exception to the hearsay rule. Since it is likely that a suicidal state of mind such as that indicated by Vason's statement to Si would continue until the following day, and since it is likely that a person with that state of mind would commit suicide, the fact that Vason was of a suicidal state of mind on the day before his death is relevant to the question of whether his death was a suicide. **I** is, therefore a correct statement. Hearsay is an out-of-court statement offered to prove the truth of the matter asserted in that statement. If Vason's statement to Si is offered for the purpose of establishing that Si knew or should have known that Vason was suicidal, it is not hearsay, since it is not offered to prove the truth of the matter asserted (i.e., that suicide is the only way out). **II** is, therefore, a correct statement.

8. **B** Since a statement as to the value of a chattel is a statement of opinion, and since lay opinions are not usually admissible, some qualification is necessary to demonstrate the competence of a person stating an opinion regarding the value of a chattel. Since an unaccepted offer to purchase a chattel suggests the offeror's opinion as to its value, an unaccepted offer to purchase is not usually admissible to establish the value of the subject chattel because the offeror is not necessarily an expert in the value of such chattels, and because even if the expert were an expert, his out of court statement as to its value would be hearsay. For this reason, evidence of an offer to purchase the motorcycle is probably inadmissible, and **B** is the correct answer.

In the belief that the owner of a chattel has some special knowledge about his property, courts usually allow a chattel's owner to give an opinion regarding its value. **A** is, therefore, likely to be admitted. In **C**, the motorcycle dealer would probably qualify as an expert on the value of motorcycles. An expert may testify to an opinion in response to a hypothetical question, even though he has no personal knowledge of the facts in a particular case. Thus, if the photograph can be shown to be a fair and accurate representation of the motorcycle immediately prior to the accident, the motorcycle dealer's opinion of its value may be admissible. **D** would be admissible since an expert's qualifications may be based on experience with the matter in issue, and the amateur motorcycle collector's previous purchases and sales might qualify him as such.

9. **D** Although evidence of subsequent repairs is inadmissible to establish that a condition was dangerous or that the defendant was negligent, it may be admitted if relevant to some other issue. Since it is not likely that Lanham would have taken the action indicated if he were not in control of the stairway, the evidence may be admitted for the purpose of establishing control.

A is incorrect because it suggests that some rule of privilege prevents testimony by the defendant's employee, when no such rule exists. The admissibility of Walker's testimony does not, therefore, depend on his employment status. **B** and **C** are incorrect because of the rule of policy which prohibits evidence of subsequent repairs to establish fault.

10. **B** Testimony that a witness never heard of similar accidents in the past may be admitted as circumstantial evidence that the condition was not dangerous if a proper foundation is laid. This requires showing that the condition was substantially the same on the day of plaintiff's accident as it was during the period described by defendant, that there was sufficient traffic over the condition and sufficient time to provide an opportunity for such accidents to have occurred, and that the witness was likely to have heard of such accidents had they occurred. Since Walker testified that the stairs were in substantially the same condition throughout the period described, that many people used them every day for three years, and that he never heard of such an accident, the only element

of the necessary foundation which is lacking is evidence that he probably would have heard of such an accident if it had occurred. His testimony is thus admissible if this can be shown, but is not admissible otherwise. **B** is, therefore, correct.

A is incorrect because the fact would tend to establish that the condition was not a dangerous one. Evidence of the non-occurrence of similar accidents in the past might tend to prove that the plaintiff did not use the care exercised by ordinary persons in encountering the situation. **C** is incorrect, however, because without evidence that Walker would have heard of such accidents had they occurred, the assertion of contributory negligence is not, alone, sufficient to make Walker's statement probative. **D** is incorrect because there is no rule which prevents a party from objecting to improper testimony elicited by cross-examination of its own witness.

11. **C** Under the best evidence rule, where the terms of a writing are in issue, the writing itself must be offered into evidence unless the writing is shown to be unavailable. FRE 1002. However, this rule does not apply if "all the originals are lost or destroyed, and not by the proponent acting in bad faith." FRE 1004(a). Since the original and all copies of the contract were destroyed in a fire, oral testimony as to its contents is admissible.

The parol evidence rule prohibits oral testimony of prior or contemporaneous agreements to alter the terms of a contract intended to be a complete integration of the parties, but does not prevent oral testimony regarding the contents of a written agreement. **A** is, therefore, incorrect. **B** is incorrect because the writing has been shown to be unavailable. The Statute of Frauds provides that certain contracts are unenforceable unless in writing, but does not relate to the evidence used to establish the existence of a contract. **D** is, therefore, incorrect.

12. **A** Although use immunity does not prevent prosecution relating to the transaction which was the subject of the testimony for which the immunity was granted, it does prevent the subsequent use of that testimony *or its fruits. The "fruits" include all evidence gained as a direct or indirect result of the testimony.* If the prosecutor had no evidence against Cooms other than Mayo's testimony, then Cooms' testimony was one of the "fruits" of Mayo's, and should be excluded.

B is incorrect because it is based on a distorted view of the facts. By making a deal for the testimony of Cooms, the prosecutor has not bargained away any "rights" of Mayo. **C** is incorrect because the articles by Rider did not identify Cooms. Cooms's evidence must, therefore, be seen as one of the fruits of Mayo's testimony. **D** is incorrect because the use immunity granted Mayo makes Cooms' testimony inadmissible. The fact that it was given voluntarily and without coercion is not, alone, enough to make it admissible.

13. **D** A client is privileged to prevent another from disclosing the contents of a confidential communication with his attorney. Although the presence of third persons usually results in a finding that the communication was not intended to be confidential, this is not so if the presence of those persons was essential to the communications with the attorney. Darla's presence does not have that effect, since, as the driver of the truck, she was essential to the conference between Thomas and Lottie.

A is incorrect since, if the communication was confidential, the client's privilege applies to any attempt to disclose it. **B** is incorrect because Darla's presence was essential to the purpose of the conference. **C** is incorrect because corporations are entitled to the privilege, which clearly applies to communications between lawyers and high-ranking officers of the corporation.

14. **A** If relevant, a photograph or pictorial representation is admissible if a witness identifies it as a fair and accurate representation of what it purports to be. Since the directions and relationship of the streets which were the scene of an accident are relevant to the way in which the accident occurred, a photograph which fairly and accurately depicts them is admissible. Thus, even though the absence of Christmas tree ornaments in the photograph prevents it from showing all aspects of the accident scene exactly as they appeared on the day of the accident, it is admissible if it fairly and accurately represents the directions and relationship of the streets. Since the plaintiff testified that it does, the photograph should be admitted.

B is incorrect because a photograph which fairly and accurately represents what it purports to represent is admissible without regard to when it was taken. **C** is incorrect because the authentication of a photograph may be made by any competent witness who is familiar with what the photograph purports to represent, and need not be made by the photographer herself. **D** is incorrect for the reasons stated above.

15. **B** Evidence is relevant if it tends to prove or disprove a fact of consequence. Since the hearing is being held on the sole question of whether Dodge was driving negligently, the only facts of consequence relate to that question. Dodge was driving negligently if he was driving in a way in which the reasonable person would not. Since the fact that the vehicle was unregistered is not related to how it was being driven, the conviction for operating an unregistered vehicle is not relevant to the question of negligence.

A is, therefore, incorrect. An admission is a statement made by a party and offered against that party. **C** is incorrect because, if it is relevant, a guilty plea may be admissible as an admission. At common law, admissions fall under an exception to the hearsay rule. Under FRE 801(d)(2), an admission is not hearsay. Either way, **D** is incorrect.

16. **A** The law seeks to encourage safety precautions by prohibiting evidence of subsequent remedial measures from being used for the purpose of showing fault. See FRE 407. Such evidence may be admissible for other purposes, however. Here, Oster had denied ownership of the vehicle. Since it is unlikely that anyone other than the owner would arrange to have the brakes overhauled, the testimony of Mecco is relevant to establish Oster's ownership and should, therefore, be admitted.

    B is incorrect because of the above stated rule of policy. **C** is incorrect because the evidence is being used to establish that Oster was the owner of the vehicle, not to establish the condition of the brakes. **D** is incorrect since the evidence is admissible to establish ownership.

17. **C** Under FRE 804(b)(2), a statement is admissible as a dying declaration in a civil or homicide case if it was made by a person now unavailable, about the cause of his death, upon personal knowledge, and under a sense of immediately impending death. Since Vicuna is presently unavailable and said that he saw Keller shoot him, his statement is admissible if he made it with a sense of impending death.

    Although the common law made such statements admissible in cases of criminal homicide only, **A** is incorrect because FRE 804(b)(2) extends the exception to civil litigation as well. Transactional immunity prevents criminal prosecution, but does not prevent civil litigation. **B** is, therefore, incorrect. Where it exists, the effect of the "dead man's statute" is to exclude certain evidence, not to make it admissible. **D** is, therefore, incorrect.

18. **B** Hearsay is an out of court statement offered to prove the truth of the matter asserted in that statement. An admission is an out of court statement made by a party which is offered against that party. Under the common law, admissions are admissible as exceptions to the hearsay rule. Under FRE 801(d)(2), admissions are admissible because they are not hearsay. If an employee of a party makes a statement which is offered against the employer, the statement may be admissible as a vicarious admission of the employer if it was made while the employment relationship existed and concerned a matter within the scope of the declarant's employment. If Marshall was employed by Wing as a mechanic, his statement that he failed to inspect Flight 123 does concern a matter within the scope of his employment. It would not be admissible as a vicarious admission of Wing, however, unless it can be established that Marshall was so employed. If Marshall made an out of court statement that he was so employed, it would be hearsay if offered to prove his employment by Wing. For this reason, independent evidence of the employment relationship is required.

A is, therefore, incorrect. Although the common law requires that the declarant be one authorized to speak for the party, **C** is incorrect because the FRE has abolished that requirement. **D** is incorrect because the unavailability of a declarant is not, alone, sufficient to make his out-of-court assertion admissible.

19. **D** Hearsay is defined as an out-of-court assertion offered for the purpose of proving the truth of the matter asserted in the statement. FRE 801(c). Since there appears to be no reason for offering the statement of the unidentified witness except to prove the truth of the matter which asserts, it is hearsay. A business record may be admitted under an exception to the hearsay rule only if it was made by one who had personal knowledge of the information recorded or received it from an inherently reliable source. Since the investigator did not have personal knowledge and there is no indication that the witness interviewed by the deceased investigator was an inherently reliable source, **A** is incorrect. An official written statement may be admitted as an exception to the hearsay rule only as to information which the public official who recorded it knew of his own knowledge. Since the quote from the unidentified witness concerns information which the investigator did not know of his own knowledge, **B** is incorrect. Past recollection recorded is also admissible only if the record was made from the recorder's own knowledge and if the recorder is present in court to authenticate it. **C** is incorrect for these reasons, and because even if it were admissible, past recollection recorded can be read to the jury but not physically introduced into evidence.

20. **C** Evidence is relevant if it tends to prove or disprove a fact of consequence. Relevant evidence is ordinarily admissible. Self-defense is a privilege to use force which the reasonable person in Kane's shoes would have considered necessary to prevent an attack upon himself. Evidence of Nixon's reputation for unprovoked violence is relevant because it tends to establish whether the reasonable person in Kane's shoes would have believed himself to be under attack.

A and **B** are incorrect because the evidence is relevant to the reasonableness of Kane's fear. **D** is incorrect because the plaintiff's character is not related to the essential elements of a battery action.

21. **A** Character evidence is not ordinarily admissible for the purpose of proving a person's conduct on a particular occasion. Thus, if evidence of Kane's character is offered to prove anything about his conduct on the occasion of the incident in question, it is not admissible.

B is incorrect because a witness who testifies to a person's reputation is not required to know that person or to have any personal opinion about him. The "mercy" rule which permits a defendant to offer evidence of his own character as circumstantial evidence of his innocence applies only to criminal prosecutions. **C** is, therefore, incorrect. If the evidence were allowed for the purpose stated in **D** , it would be to prove that Kane did not strike Nixon without justification. **D** is, therefore, incorrect for the same reasons that make **A** correct.

22. **D** The fact that a witness made prior statements which were inconsistent with his testimony indicates that he is not a credible witness, or at least that his testimony is not worthy of belief. Thus, for the purpose of impeachment, a witness may be cross-examined about prior inconsistent statements. Since Davidson's statement to the arresting officers was inconsistent with his statement on the witness stand, he may be cross-examined about it.

The purpose of the exclusionary rule which prohibits the use of illegally obtained evidence or confessions is to remove police incentive for violating the constitutional rights of suspects. For this reason, statements obtained in violation of a prisoner's *Miranda* rights cannot be used against him in a criminal prosecution. Because use of such statements for impeachment in a civil proceeding is not ordinarily contemplated by the police, prohibiting such use is not likely to affect police conduct. For this reason, it has been held that statements obtained in violation of a prisoner's *Miranda* rights may be used for purposes of impeachment in civil proceedings. **A** is, therefore, incorrect. **B** is incorrect for two reasons: first, Davidson's motion was to suppress the use of the physical evidence, rather than the use of statements made during the interrogation; and, second, even an order suppressing the use of his statements in the criminal prosecution would not prevent their use in this civil proceeding. If statements are obtained from a prisoner in violation of his constitutional rights, the same policy which prohibits their use as evidence prohibits also the use of leads obtained as a result of those statements. This is the "fruit of the poisonous tree" doctrine. Although this doctrine may result in the exclusion of evidence, it never is used to justify the admission of evidence. **C** is, therefore, incorrect.

23. **A** FRE 501 provides that in the trial of a civil proceeding in which state law provides the rule of decision, the rules of privilege shall be determined in accordance with state law. Thus, if a civil action is being tried in a federal court under the substantive law of a state, the federal court must apply the state law of privilege. If the state law recognizes a psychotherapist-patient privilege, the federal court must recognize it as well. **I** is, therefore, correct. If the state law does not recognize a psychotherapist-patient privilege, the federal law may not. **II** is, therefore, incorrect.

24. **A** To save time and expense in proving facts which cannot reasonably be disputed, and to avoid the embarrassment which might result from a judicial finding which is contrary to well-known fact, a court may take judicial notice of certain facts without requiring evidence to establish them. Courts will take judicial notice of facts which are either generally known within the territorial jurisdiction of the trial court or capable of accurate and ready determination by resort to

sources whose accuracy cannot reasonably be questioned. FRE 201(b). Thus, if it is generally known within the territorial jurisdiction of the court that it is impossible to travel from Detroit to Chicago without crossing a state line, the court may judicially notice that fact, making proof of it unnecessary.

Although the presentation of a map or other reputable reference would permit the court to take judicial notice, **B** is incorrect because this is not the only way; in the case of facts which are generally known, such references are not required. If the fact in question is one which qualifies for judicial notice, the objection of a party or the fact that it bears on an ultimate issue in the case will not prevent the court from judicially noticing it. **C** and **D** are, therefore, incorrect.

25. **D** It is the jury's job to determine whether the evidence proves facts sufficient to satisfy the requirements of law as charged by the court. Expert opinion may be admitted to *assist* the trier of fact to understand the evidence or to determine a fact in issue, but it may not be stated in a way which would deprive the jury of its power to determine facts. Since the jury must decide whether Draper had malice aforethought, expert testimony regarding Draper's mental capacity would be admissible. Dr. Wendell's statement, however, did not express an opinion regarding Draper's mental condition, but rather his opinion whether Draper had malice aforethought.

Although the common law once prohibited expert testimony which "embraced the ultimate issue," **A** is incorrect because FRE 704(a) (and many states) have eliminated this restriction. The opinions of an expert may be based solely on courtroom observations (or may even be based on assumed facts contained in a hypothetical question). The fact that a testifying psychiatrist has never spoken to the subject or even seen him outside a courtroom may reflect on the weight (i.e., persuasive value) of his testimony, but not on its admissibility. **B** and **C** are, therefore, incorrect.

26. **B** Under FRE 609(a), conviction for a crime punishable by imprisonment for one year or more or by death is admissible for the purpose of impeaching a witness. If either the conviction or the termination of incarceration occurred within the past ten years, the trial judge has discretion to exclude such a conviction only if it was not for a crime involving dishonesty. Since Wrangler's perjury was punished by five years in prison, since his period of incarceration terminated within the past ten years, and since perjury is obviously a crime involving dishonesty, the trial judge is without discretion to exclude evidence of Wrangler's conviction.

Although the common law requires confrontation prior to the use of certain evidence offered for the purpose of impeachment, **A** is incorrect because the FRE completely dispense with that requirement. FRE 609(b) provides that if more than ten years have elapsed since the conviction or termination of incarceration (whichever is *later*), the conviction is inadmissible unless the trial court finds that its probative value substantially outweighs its prejudicial effect. **C** is incorrect because if, as here, fewer than ten years elapsed, the conviction is admissible. Under the FRE, extrinsic evidence of prior inconsistent statements by a witness is admissible for the purpose of impeachment, but only if the witness is given a subsequent opportunity to explain the inconsistency. **D** is incorrect, however, because no such requirement exists regarding the use of convictions.

27. **D** Under FRE 803(3), an assertion of the declarant's then-existing physical sensation is admissible as an exception to the hearsay rule. The common law makes a distinction which prohibits the admission of such statements if they were made in contemplation of litigation. The FRE does not make such a distinction, however, allowing the circumstances under which the statement was made to go to the weight rather than the admissibility of the evidence.

A and **B** are, therefore, incorrect. Where it is recognized, the physician-patient privilege may prevent the admission of testimony by a doctor regarding confidential communications with the patient over objection by the *patient*. *C* is incorrect because an objection based on the privilege would not be available to anyone but the patient.

28. **D** Although the court decides whether evidence is admissible and whether a witness is competent to testify, it is for the jury to decide what weight to give testimony which the court has admitted. In doing so, the jury must determine how credible it finds a particular witness to be. If that witness is an expert testifying to her opinions, it would be impossible for the jury to make that determination without knowing the witness's qualifications. The concession by the defendant's attorney is not sufficient, since it is very likely that the jury will hear contrary opinions given by other experts. To decide which of the experts it believes, the jury must be able to compare their qualifications. For this reason, the details of Dr. Wallace's qualifications remain an issue even though the defendant's attorney concedes that she is sufficiently qualified to testify to her opinions.

A and **B** are, therefore, incorrect. If all parties agree to a fact, a court may accept it as true without requiring further proof. Thus, if all parties agree that a particular witness qualifies as an expert, the court may, on the basis of that stipulation, dispense with the *requirement* of further proof (though it may not prevent the party offering the testimony of that witness from questioning her about her qualifications). **C** is, therefore, incorrect.

29. **D** Ordinarily, evidence of the behavior of a trained dog is admissible if a foundation is laid similar to the foundation required for any other kind of scientific evidence. This means that it must be shown that the dog was competent to do the job which it was doing and that its handler was competent to interpret the result. Since Handel was an expert dog trainer and handler, and since Findo successfully detected cocaine on several prior occasions, the proper foundation has been laid, and the evidence is admissible.

Hearsay is an out of court statement offered for the purpose of proving the truth of the matter asserted in that statement. Although our society tends to personify dogs, dogs are not persons and are not capable of making statements. For this reason, the behavior of a dog cannot be hearsay (Since a primary reason for the hearsay rule is that out of court declarants are not subject to cross examination and since a dog could not be cross examined in any event, it would not be logical to apply the hearsay rule to a dog's behavior.) **A** is therefore, incorrect. **B** is incorrect because, since the dog could not testify, its availability is irrelevant to the admissibility of its behavior. Although a court might permit demonstration of a scientific method, there is no requirement that it do so. **C** is, therefore, incorrect.

30. **B** In general, evidence of a person's past "crime [or] wrong" is "not admissible to prove a person's character in order to show that on a particular occasion the person acted in accordance with the character." FRE 404(b). Evidence of a crime or bad act is, however, admissible for "another purpose, such as proving ... *absence of mistake, or lack of accident*." Here, evidence that Dodd previously smuggled cocaine using a brass statue with a false bottom tends to show that this time, it was as part of a standard "M.O.," not by "mistake" or "accident" (as he claims) that he arrived at customs with a brass statue with a false bottom containing cocaine. So **B** is correct.

FRE 406 permits evidence of habit to be used as circumstantial evidence that on a particular occasion the defendant's conduct was consistent with his habit. **A** is incorrect, however, because habit evidence requires a showing that the actor in question consistently acts in a particular way, and one prior experience is not sufficient to establish a habit. Although evidence of a defendant's previous conduct is inadmissible if offered against him for some purposes, it may be admissible if offered against him for others. **C** is thus incorrect because it is overinclusive. Evidence of a prior conviction is not usually admissible for the purpose of impeaching a witness if the conviction occurred more than ten years prior to the trial at which it is offered. **D** is incorrect, however, because Dodd's prior conviction is not being offered to impeach his credibility, but rather to establish that his claim of ignorance is not true.

TABLE OF REFERENCES TO THE FEDERAL RULES OF EVIDENCE

SUBJECT MATTER INDEX

This index includes references to the Capsule Summary and to the Exam Tips, but not to Q&A or Flow Charts